C000128471

SHIPS
AND
SOLDIERS

The final panel from the recently completed Alderney 'Bayeux Tapestry finale' showing William, 7th Duke of Normandy, being crowned King of England in Westminster Abbey on Christmas Day 1066. The final three panels, three metres long, are a representation of what might have been the ending to the original tapestry, after the Battle of Hastings panel, if it was ever completed and subsequently lost, as some think. More than 400 people, including Prince Charles and the Duchess of Cornwall have added stitches to the panel to complete the design, which was conceived and carried out mainly by Alderney residents. The linen canvas was specially woven to the same texture and colour as the original, and the same colour dyes and stitching techniques were used for the embroidery threads. It was unveiled on 5 April 2013 and was opened to the public by Jean François Le Grand, President of Le Conseil de la Manche, in the presence of a number of Normandy, Bayeux and local dignitaries, including Mme. Lemagnen, Curator of the Bayeux Tapestry Museum. It will be on permanent display in the Alderney Library, where special arrangements have been made to display it in a controlled environment as suggested by the V & A Museum in London.

SHIPS AND AND SOLDIERS

A MILITARY AND MARITIME HISTORY OF THE ISLAND OF ALDERNEY

BRIAN BONNARD

FONTHILL

Fonthill Media Limited
www.fonthillmedia.com
office@fonthillmedia.com

First published in 2013

British Library Cataloguing in Publication Data:
A catalogue record for this book is available from the British Library

Copyright © Brian Bonnard 2013

ISBN 978-1-78155-008-3

The right of Brian Bonnard to be identified as the author of this work has been asserted by him
in accordance with the Copyright, Designs and Patents Act 1988.

All rights reserved. No part of this publication may be reproduced, stored in a retrieval system
or transmitted in any form or by any means, electronic, mechanical, photocopying, recording or
otherwise, without prior permission in writing from Fonthill Media Limited

Typeset in 10/13 pt Celeste OT
Printed and bound in England

Contents

HRH The Princess Elizabeth making the speech quoted opposite.

ALDERNEY

'...From fruitful Aurney near ye ancient Celtic Shore...'

Michael Drayton, 1563-1631

'...the lone soft island of the fair-limbed kine...'

A. C. Swinburne, 'Les Casquettes', 1885

'...this small but precious jewel in my father's crown...'

The Princess Elizabeth addressing the people of Alderney, 21 June 1949

Introduction

The Preface to E. A. W. Martin's *Manuscript History of Alderney* written and dedicated in 1810, to Alderney's last Hereditary Governor, John Le Mesurier, provides, a very apposite opening to this volume for an author who is primarily a botanist;

> The Author who for a Series of years has no other occupation than that of gathering the flowers of others thoughts for the History of some certain facts, may undoubtedly surpass the summary commentaries of one whose life has been devoted to Military pursuits.
>
> In beginning this research I confess I feel somewhat like a Traveller, who, being but little acquainted with his path, is, at every turning, obliged to explore his way, and consequently frequently impeded on his journey.
>
> I acknowledge my inability fully to discuss the subjects which form a part of this Volume, but the foundation being laid, a useful structure may be erected upon it, and as it has frequently happened that the most trivial circumstances have produced events of the greatest importance, may I not hope that some little benefit may result from these pages, even if it be no more than the conveyance of an outline of the History and Situation of this Island, a subject hitherto unattempted.

The present author, who is not a professional historian, being a botanist by training, has had since childhood, an interest in studying the history of his surroundings, and, whilst living in Guernsey for some years, prior to moving to Alderney in 1986, had formed a collection of many of the books and articles written about the Bailiwick since the early 1800s.

In studying these from the viewpoint of a new homeland he became aware of the paucity of information about Alderney, included in these books.

Since the first Histories of and Guide Books to, the Channel Islands were written, around 1750, only four books, (and a small number of booklets), have been written specifically about Alderney's History. A niece of the last hereditary governor of Alderney, Louisa Lane Clarke's, *The Island of Alderney; Its Early History, Antiquities, Present State, Scenery, Customs, and Trade; Being a Companion and Guide for the Traveller*, published in 1851. This is a charming book of 120 tiny 5 x 3-inch pages scarcely larger than its title, with some fine steel engravings from the author's sketches, and was largely based on E. A. W. Martin's manuscript quoted above. The second is Victor Coysh's *Alderney*, first published in 1974, revised with some assistance from my wife and myself in 1989 and recently revised and reprinted again. The others are my own; *Alderney in Old Photographs*, reproductions of about 250 photographs and drawings made in the island between 1856 and 1956, published in 1991 and reprinted at last in 2009 after being 'out of print' for 16 years, with a *Second Series* of about 285 photographs published in 1993, yet to be reprinted, which both have brief historical notes with each of the photographs. There are also a number of books about Alderney during the Second World War, including my own works *Alderney at War* and *The Island of Dread in the Channel*, the latter a compilation of the letters I exchanged with one of the Russian wartime slave-workers and about his subsequent visit as a guest of The States, who helped to build the German fortifications in Alderney, also reprinted as paperbacks in 2009.

Most of the remaining published history of the island is to be found in a small section in each of the many books written about the Bailiwick of Guernsey, or the Channel Islands collectively, local newspapers, or in papers contributed to the Journals of various learned Societies, mostly within the several islands.

This book, the result of some 25 years research, is extracted from the more than 1,400 pages of closely typed MS, distilled from the very considerable amount of contemporary written material found in the National Archives, various other record offices and libraries, from charters, deeds and documents, newspapers and periodicals, and books; from Roman times, when reference to the various islands of the British Sea is contained in the *Antonine Itinerary*, to the present day.

Alderney is the only true 'Channel' Island, the remainder of the group being situated in the Bay of St Malo, and is also the nearest to both Britain and France. The Duke of Wellington, in encouraging the British Government to decide to build the *Harbours of Refuge* in the Channel Islands in the 1840s, described Alderney as *The Key to the Channel*. In this he echoed his arch enemy Napoleon Buonaparte who had made a similar statement some 30 years earlier, and it will be seen that its geographical position has had a considerable effect on its history over the centuries, especially in Naval, Military and Political spheres.

Although they were never fully completed, largely ill-conceived, and the one planned for Guernsey never even started, the harbours of refuge were a thinly disguised euphemism for *Naval Bases*. They were intended as an answer to the potential threat of the huge naval bases being constructed by the French at Cherbourg and St Malo.

St Catherine's Breakwater in Jersey, which has been described as 'The Harbour that Failed', began to silt up before it was completed, was abandoned with only the present arm finished, and never used for its intended purpose. Alderney's harbour scheme also was never completed, and the Breakwater suffered so badly from storm damage, both during its construction, and after completion, that within a few years it was almost halved in length. The maintenance of the remainder has cost millions over the past 145 years.

Despite this, the project has had a profound effect on Alderney. The presence of the harbour created a need to defend it, and the chain of forts built to accomplish this, were garrisoned for almost a century, both circumstances producing a drastic, and permanent change in the way of life of this small island. At the same time it created a quarrying industry that lasted until the Second World War, and was still giving employment to about half the male working population in 1940, when the island was evacuated.

Small islands inevitably have a close connection with the sea, and the Channel Islands were joined to and separated from the mainland of Europe several times in the various Ice Ages stretching back over 100,000 years. More recently Guernsey was finally separated about 15,000 years ago and Alderney about 7,000 years ago. After this occurred, there are several legends of the Channel Islands being considered as *Holy Isles* or *Blessed Isles*, by ancient peoples, and they all have a legacy of Mesolithic and Neolithic remains quite disproportionate to their size and probable resident populations during those eras.

At the same time they are greatly affected by events involving both their larger neighbours; and the nearest 'mainland', be it France or England. In historic times the Romans and later the Vikings, Normans, Spaniards, French and Germans have, over the centuries, caused frequent alarms over Alderney's safety and defence, and an almost regular fluctuation in the construction and dismantling of defence works, the garrisoning of the forts and batteries and the volume of shipping involved in supply, transport, and protection, for all this activity.

From historic times since at least the eleventh century, the adult male Channel Islanders have been expected to serve in local 'Militias' to protect themselves, aided in times of war by troops from Britain. Alderney still had, until about 2009, a small Junior Militia corps of resident young people and Jersey a Territorial Army contingent .These things have had a much greater effect in Alderney, which never had a population large enough to provide all the necessary labour, soldiers, and ships, than in the larger islands. At the same time they have also, more recently, caused the complete loss, since the Second World War, of the Alderney 'parler', or Norman-French language in the island.

From its position in the approaches to the Channel, Alderney has had a greater strategic significance than the other islands on events in both Britain and Europe.

Alderney is unique in its almost total lack, within the island, of original records of its own past prior to 1945. This factor renders any form of historical research more difficult. Almost the whole population was evacuated, at a few hour's notice, and with only two suitcases each, on 23 June 1940, ahead of the advancing German armies in Europe. This inevitably meant that little in the way of records was taken with them, and most of what was left behind was missing, or had been destroyed, when the island was freed some five years later.

The only original records to survive were the 10 Parish Registers from 1662 with some earlier marriage entries from about 1620, apparently taken to the Diocesan Archives in Winchester by the Vicar in 1940, forgotten, but found in a cellar there in 1956 and returned to the island; one book of Alderney Court records; and the property deeds taken with them by the islanders when they left.

The establishment in 1966 of *The Alderney Society Museum* in addition to displaying artefacts associated with the island's history, and in particular at that time, with the German Occupation, created a focus for the small amount of written material still available locally, and copies of documents found elsewhere have been acquired since, including Impey's ledger with details of each evacuee in UK. My late wife, an Educationalist, Naturalist and Doctor of Homeopathy, acted as Honorary Curator of the Alderney Museum in 1988 and 1989, and, in helping to catalogue these documents, many of which had not been examined in detail previously, after finding an eight-page sheepskin parchment written in Latin, probably in the early seventeenth century, amongst a pile of old newspapers in the museum shed, (being a copy of the grant of the fief of Alderney by Queen Elizabeth I to George Chamberlain in 1560) which had never been entered in the museum registers, I felt there was a need to record the details of the island's history thus revealed, in a form readily available to the public. It then remained to expand it with contemporary material from other sources, much of which was also unpublished. This volume is an attempt to present the history of Alderney's people, in relationship to the three factors which have had the greatest influence on them over the centuries:

the need for the defence of their island and homes;

their relationships with both Britain and France;

and the sea;

which, from the last time the island became detached from Europe about 7,000 years ago, until the first aeroplane service was started in 1935, was their only link with other places, and the source of much of the island's past wealth.

Opposite: Map by Robert Morden dated 1691 showing the relationship of Alderney and Burhou to the French coast.

Acknowledgements

Most of the material in this present book has been culled over about 25 years from contemporary documents; in the two Public Records Offices in England; the British Library and the libraries in Alderney, Guernsey and Jersey; Trinity House; Lloyd's Register of Shipping; the Imperial War Museum and the National Maritime Museum; as well as various local newspapers and magazines and the annual publications of the learned societies in the three principal Channel Islands.

I would like to express my appreciation to the librarians and staff of all these establishments and many local people for their help in finding material.

Finally, and most particularly, to my late wife Jean, for encouragement and comment, draft reading and criticism, and for coping over several years with papers, document copies, photographs and notes, scattered about the house.

This book is therefore dedicated with gratitude to all of them.

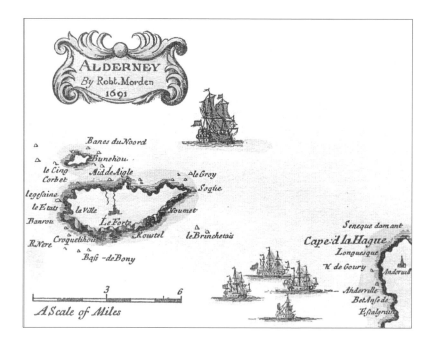

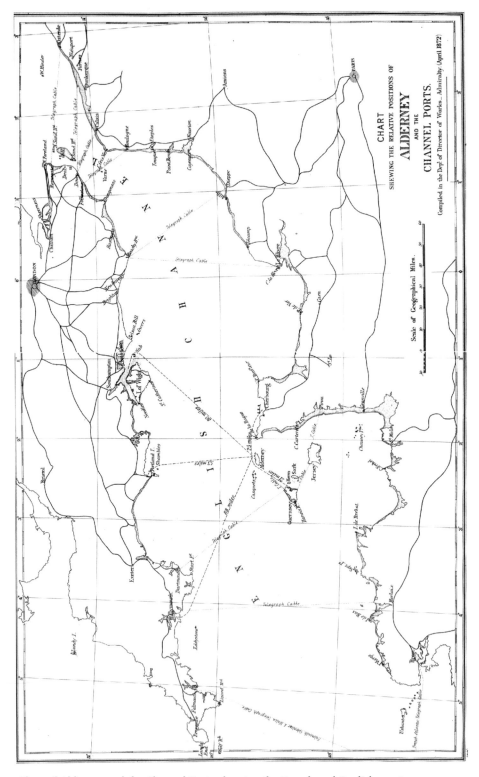

Chart of Alderney and the Channel Ports, showing the French and English coasts.

1

The Normans and the English

When William I conquered England in 1066, he was already the 7th Duke of Normandy and the Channel Islands have continued as part of the personal possessions of the English Sovereign since that time.

For the next 150 years the islands were still administered as a *comté* of Normandy, with visiting justiciers from Rouen coming to the islands regularly to try criminal cases and collect the tithes. The two knights, sitting with two knights or a *baillivus* (bailiff) and another important person from the islands, constituting the Royal Court.

In the eleventh and twelfth centuries, most men were required to be proficient in archery, to enable them to form a defensive force in time of need. Their obligation was to their immediate seigneur, who was himself required to furnish a certain number of men to his overlord. In the islands, this was the King or his Warden. The calls to service were usually of short duration, and were confined to service within the islands themselves, except to rescue the King if he should be captured by an enemy. This often involved no more than manning the watchtowers, beacons and guardposts, to guard against raiders and pirates. The service in Alderney was often performed by the women, whilst their men were working in nearby fields. Since the islands were at this time part of the larger Duchy, there was little fear of attack from the French mainland.

John granted the islands to Pierre de Préaux as a *fief* on 14 January 1200, and a charter dated 12 November 1201, is addressed to him, and to John's 'ballivi' of 'Les Iles de Jersey, Guernesey, et Auregny...' the plural suggesting that he may have appointed a bailiff in each of the islands. On 13 August 1203, he further instructed Préaux:

> to pay over to the King one-fifth of the revenues of both the Church and other tithes in the islands ... to provision the knights and esquires who defend the islands against strangers.

King John, the 13th Duke, lost the continental part of the Duchy to conquest by the French in 1204, but retained the islands. After this he appointed a Warden or Governor of the Islands as his representative. In 1206, Richard de Graye was made Governor of the Islands in return for a fee of 400 marks, and instructed to; 'maintain, defend and keep peaceful the islands of Guernsey, Alderney and Jersey, these being our domains, and not to cause, or allow to be caused, any harm or injury to our people'.

The defences of, and justice in, Alderney became the responsibility of the Warden, and although assizes were held in Alderney at various times over the next several centuries, criminal cases were dealt with, at other times, in Guernsey, despite the expense and danger of transporting the accused and any witnesses there.

It was shortly after this that King John granted the islands a written constitution, setting out the rights of the crown and the people in 18 clauses. This Constitution was recorded in a document of his son Henry III, in which he granted additional trade concessions to Philippe d'Aubigny, whom he appointed as 'Guardien (Warden) of the Isles'. Of specific application to Alderney was a relaxation of the tax of four sous tournois, for each voyage of a fishing boat, the tax of one silver mark for each foreign vessel putting into port in the islands, and the tax on the drying of conger eels (éperquérie) between the feast of St Michael, and Easter.

Henry III did not continue to use the title of Duke of Normandy, and actually surrendered the title in 1259, under a treaty which acknowledged that, under French law, they still remained a parcel of the Kingdom of France. Despite this, the Kings of England continued to style themselves *King of France* for several centuries, and thus automatically included the whole Duchy of Normandy in their claimed jurisdiction. This abandonment of the use of the title however did not mean that the islands were incorporated into the Realm of England, and they remained and still technically remain, the separate personal territories of the monarch.

In June 1225 Henry ordered d'Aubigny to pay Geoffery de Lucy the Military Commander, £200 for the pay of the Sergeants and soldiers in Jersey, Guernsey and the other islands.

A document of this period of unique reference to Alderney is known as the *Status Insulae de Aurineo*, and sets out the respective rights, in 1236, of the Crown and the Bishop of Coutances, who then held the island, and its revenues, in roughly equal halves. There were two Courts then; the King's Court and the Chapter Court. Each had its own *prévôt* or provost, but the six *jurés* or Jurats were the same for both courts, and were expected to judge impartially for either King or Bishop. They were empowered to receive the yearly rents and tithes for both parties, and to receive homage and complaints. This seems to be the origin in Alderney of the *Court of Pleas*. The document also specified that the priest was to be paid; 'with a pound of copper'.

Drogo de Barentin was appointed Warden or Guardien on 11 September 1248, and at the same time, instructed to carry out an enquiry into the customs and dues of service of the people of the islands. Henry's later grant of the islands in 1254, to his son (later Edward I), to hold

> ...in such a manner that the said lands ... may never be separated from the Crown, and that no one, by reason of this grant made to the said Edward may have any claim to the said lands ... but that they should remain to the Kings of England in their entirety for ever.

This effectively annexed the islands to the personal estates of the Crown of England in perpetuity.

Edward separated the jurisdictions of Jersey and Guernsey in 1279, and granted separate seals for the two Royal Courts on 22 November.

In an *Extente* of 1274, in the second year of his reign, the King's dues in the Islands are set out, with Alderney being worth 60 livres 9s 2d., Sark producing 61 livres 11s 9d and Guernsey worth 725 livres 0s 0d. At this time 100 livres trs. (tournois) was worth £7 2s 10d sterling.

Further Royal assizes were held in the islands in 1304; and in 1309 and 1320 during the reign of Edward II. The inhabitants had the right to refuse to attend if they lasted more than three weeks, and could not be required to go out of their own island to attend the sessions. The 1309 Assize Roll for Alderney, records the names of the two prévôts, the six jurés, and a jury of: *the twelve men of the islet of Alderney.* Eight of these 20 names could still be found in the 1989 Alderney telephone directory, and five more still exist in Guernsey. Most of these surnames also recur through the following centuries in the twentieth century.

Edward I awarded compensation to the people of Alderney in 1295, for damage caused in the defence of the island against the French in one of their periodic raids, but in 1305 raised a tax on the people to pay for the repairs to the jetty which the French had destroyed. This was almost certainly at Longis Bay.

Otto de Grandison's statue in Guernsey.

The defences of the islands were still occupying the crown when Edward III came to the throne in 1327. At this time Otto de Grandison, who had been made Guardien for life in 1308 but had not lived in the islands, had failed to keep the defences in good order. He was replaced the following year by John de Roches, who did good work in putting the defences of Guernsey into repair, but does not seem to have done much to 'the Castle' in Alderney as it is referred to in the Assize Rolls of 1309. [Today known as 'The Nunnery', a name given to the old fort of *Les murs en bas,* which has Roman origins, by the Victorian garrisons.].

The Crown representative in Alderney frequently changed over the next several centuries, between a direct appointment, in gift, or in fee-farm, from the Crown, to a person appointed as his deputy, by the Guardien or Governor of the Islands or later of the Bailiwick of Guernsey.

In 1336, Sark and Alderney were again raided by the French, although at the time England and France were bound by treaty. King Philippe of France gave assistance to King David, son of Robert the Bruce of Scotland with whom the English were at war. He loaned the Scots a fleet of ships with which they harried the Channel Islands, the South coast of England, and the Isle of Wight. These incidents in effect signalled the start of the 'Hundred Years' War', Edward having proclaimed himself to be King of France two years earlier. As a result of the raids, on 23 June 1340, an English fleet commanded by Sir Thomas Morley, intercepted the French, they reputedly sank 300 French ships in this engagement, and Edward had Admiral Bahuchet, who had been in command of the attacks on Portsmouth and Southampton, hanged from a yardarm.

In the meantime Edward had issued instructions from York on 11 May 1337, to Thomas de Ferrars, the Guardien, to muster all the men of the islands by thousands, hundreds, and twenties, and to arm them properly for the safety and defence of the islands. He was required to kill or expel all hostile forces, and he and his deputies were authorised to seize and imprison any who rebelled, or refused to obey the orders of their Duke.

Castle Cornet in Guernsey fell to the raiders in 1338, and in 1338/9, a raid took place on Alderney in which it has been stated that the Seal of Alderney was lost. (If so, this must have been the seal of the 'Lord' of the Island, because Alderney had not been granted a Royal Seal when Jersey and Guernsey received theirs, the Alderney Court being regarded as a *Manorial Court*). Another reference states that they occupied the island until they were evicted in 1340, but this could well be a confusion with the French in Castle Cornet which was then an island.

In 1340 Edward III ordered an 'arrest' of ships and sailors in Portsmouth Harbour and all other ports westward for the transport of the Warden Thomas Ferrars, with an armed force, for the relief of 'Guerneseye, Jersey and Aureny, in danger from the enemy's fleet of galleys and ships of war'. Extracts from the Calendar Rolls, in the Library of the Royal Court in Guernsey, record that on 25 March 1341, Thomas Hampton was appointed as Surveyor of the Channel Island Fortresses, an appointment which would seem to be linked to these constructions.

The Treaty of Bretigny in 1360 marked the start of a nine year pause in the Hundred Years' War. By it, Edward gave up all of Normandy that he had won, whilst retaining

THE ANCIENT DUKES OF NORMANDY

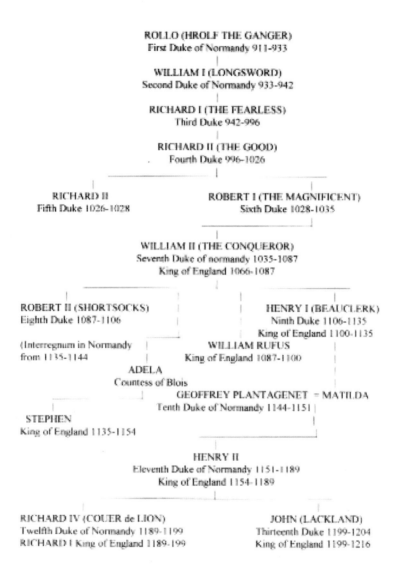

ROLLO (HROLF THE GANGER)
First Duke of Normandy 911-933

WILLIAM I (LONGSWORD)
Second Duke of Normandy 933-942

RICHARD I (THE FEARLESS)
Third Duke 942-996

RICHARD II (THE GOOD)
Fourth Duke 996-1026

RICHARD II
Fifth Duke 1026-1028

ROBERT I (THE MAGNIFICENT)
Sixth Duke 1028-1035

WILLIAM II (THE CONQUEROR)
Seventh Duke of normandy 1035-1087
King of England 1066-1087

ROBERT II (SHORTSOCKS)
Eighth Duke 1087-1106

(Interregnum in Normandy
from 1135-1144

HENRY I (BEAUCLERK)
Ninth Duke 1106-1135
King of England 1100-1135

WILLIAM RUFUS
King of England 1087-1100

ADELA
Countess of Blois

GEOFFREY PLANTAGENET = MATILDA
Tenth Duke of Normandy 1144-1151

STEPHEN
King of England 1135-1154

HENRY II
Eleventh Duke of Normandy 1151-1189
King of England 1154-1189

RICHARD IV (COUER de LION)
Twelfth Duke of Normandy 1189-1199
RICHARD I King of England 1189-199

JOHN (LACKLAND)
Thirteenth Duke 1199-1204
King of England 1199-1216

Pedigree of the Dukes of Normandy AD 911-1204.

Gascony and Calais. He instructed his Lieutenant in Alderney to restore the tithes of the church to the Chapter of Coutances, 'which had been taken into his hands because of the war between France and England'. Charles V came to the throne of France in 1369 and declared war again, Guernsey was raided by French forces in 1372. This caused Edward to appoint separate Guardiens for the two Bailiwicks of Jersey and Guernsey, a move which should have produced better defences, but failed, because the Jersey troops were not paid by the King's Receiver, Thomas de Appleby, who was based in Guernsey.

Bertrand du Guesclin raided all of the Channel Islands in 1373, and 30 years later, as Duncan notes in his *History of Guernsey*; 'Penhoet, Grand Admiral of France plundered the Channel Islands and carried away very considerable booty in 1404, but was unable to affect the castles'. It is elsewhere noted that in the summer of 1405, the Spaniard Pero Niño, working for the French, after he had burned Poole, raided Alderney with a squadron of three galleys. It was taken again for a short time in 1558, as recorded in the next Chapter.

Edward III died in 1377, and in the following year, Richard II issued a charter to the Channel Islands freeing them from certain tolls in England, and granting them *for ever* the same rights and privileges as freeborn Englishmen, whereas they had formerly been treated as his Norman subjects.

An unknown author, writing in the Alderney Parish Magazine in July 1859 stated that; 'In 1436, the English Government had erected a Blockhouse at La Baie du Châtel', a reference I have been unable to confirm, but which almost certainly refers to a refurbishment of the Nunnery, part of the walls of which seem to date from this period.

Despite Richard's charter, confirmed by subsequent monarchs, in 1443, Henry VI received a complaint from the Guernsey merchants that they were being obstructed and charged dues at Plymouth, Poole, and Southampton. Henry immediately sent orders forbidding this, 'except for those dues which all men paid', and in the same document set out a résumé of the rights and duties of the Channel Islanders.

Almost 40 years later, in 1481, giving the Papal blessing to a custom long established, in order to secure the trading links between the Islands and France in time of war, Pope Sixtus IV issued a Papal Bull of Neutrality. This declared the area round the Channel Islands 'from as far as the eye can see them' to be a neutral zone in which French, English, and others were free to come and go, and trade, without being molested in time of war. He threatened excommunication, eternal damnation, and confiscation of all their goods and chattels, and of and held of the church, for any who refused to obey, and accept its terms. This Bull was confirmed by all subsequent monarchs, and held good for two centuries until it was suspended by William of Orange in 1689, the year when James II fled to France to escape from the Protestant faction headed by William, who had married his daughter Mary. Although the suspension was only intended to be temporary, it was never repealed.

2

The Tudor Period

In 1485 Henry VII decided to try to end the anomaly of islands under the civil authority of the English Crown being subject to the Ecclesiastical authority of the French Bishop of Coutances, and on 5 November 1496 he obtained a bull from Pope Alexander VI transferring the Channel Islands to the Diocese of Salisbury. (The validity of this Bull is challenged by Lecanu in his *Histoire des Éveques de Coutances*, in which he states that the bull was a fabrication, and that the transfer to Salisbury was actually done by an ordinance of James I). In practice this arrangement turned out to be an inconvenient one, and on 20 January 1499 he obtained a second Bull from Pope Alexander which transferred the islands once again, this time to the Diocese of Winchester where they still remain. In this Bull, which is in the Public Record Office, and which set out all of the islands including the islets by name, Alderney is referred to as *Aourney*. In it the Bishop of Coutances is specifically forbidden to exercise jurisdiction over the islands or their inhabitants. Henry issued letters to the authorities in the islands informing them of this change, but once again there proved to be practical difficulties of language and distance, and the status quo remained, with the Bishop of Coutances continuing to appoint the clergy of the Church of Ste. Marie in Alderney. It was not until 1568 that the actual transfer of control to Winchester took place on the direct orders of Elizabeth I.

Whilst Henry VII was waiting for the Pope to respond to his request, the Earl of Warwick, the Guardien died, and his widow, Anne, on 13 December 1487, 'did convey to the King ... [sundry property in England] ... and the Islands of Guernesey, Gersey, Serke and Aureney, with the castles and fortresses thereon,' the islands therefore reverted to the Crown once again.

Henry VIII came to the throne of England in 1509, and his ambition to re-establish himself as King of France as well, caused the outbreak of another war between the two countries in 1512. The Channel Islands continued to benefit from the Bull of Neutrality however, and an interesting example of the application of this to Alderney, has survived in the French *Archives Nationale*, in the form of a long document of safe conduct granted on 20 April 1513 by:

Loys, Seigneur de Granville, Milly en Gastinois, le Boys Mallesherbes, conseilleur et chamberlain du roy nostre et Amiral de France, [to] ...vénérable personne, Guillaume

Fabien, prestre, natif du paix et Duché de Normandie, curé de l'eglise parroissiale en Nostre Dame de l'isle d'Aunery....

on behalf of the inhabitants of that Island, by which they were assured of freedom of travel and commerce with France until the following 1 January.

During the 1530s Henry's actions against the church in England which culminated in the Dissolution of the Monasteries, and the rejection of Papal supremacy, whilst it transformed the religion and economy of England, passed almost unnoticed in the Channel Islands, since the alien-owned church land in the islands had never been restored to those churches following Henry V's confiscation of them in 1413, mentioned above. Despite the fact that under Henry VIII's new edicts it was High Treason for the Islanders to appeal to the Pope, or to invoke the terms of a Papal Bull, it proved in the commercial interest of all parties not to disturb the existing arrangements, and Henry, and subsequent Monarchs up to the time of Charles II, continued to confirm the arrangement along with the islanders other rights, in Charters issued at the starts of their reigns, although once again in practice other events altered the situation for Alderney.

The disposal of monastic property had filled Henry's coffers, and enabled him to embark on an ambitious and extensive series of coastal defences from Tilbury to Cornwall to protect England from a possible French invasion. These were completed by about 1546. As a response to the opening by François I of France of a new naval base at Havre de Grace, to replace the silted-up port of Harfleur just East of Cherbourg, Henry decided in 1546 to include Alderney and the Scilly Isles in this defensive programme, and at the same time to strengthen the fortifications of Castle Cornet in Guernsey and Mont Orgeuil in Jersey. John Aborough was sent to the Channel Islands in that year to survey possible sites, and the logical place to establish a fort in Alderney was on the heights above its only harbour at Longis.

Henry died in 1547 but the Fort-on-the-Hill, *(Les Murs de Haut*, later known as Essex Castle), was started in about 1548, on the orders of the Duke of Somerset, protector or guardian of 10-year-old King Edward VI, as new fears of a French invasion of the islands were felt, when a small armada was being prepared at Havre de Grace. It was finally completed at an uncertain date, but probably only a few years later, about 1563, in which same period, *Les Murs en Bas* (the Nunnery) was rebuilt or strengthened, and a lookout Tower on Mont Allai overlooking Braye Bay, (which then came to be called *Mont Touraille*) was probably built.

The feared attack on Alderney came to nothing, as the French by-passed the island when they sailed on 25 July 1549, and took possession of uninhabited Sark instead. Their force consisted of 11 galleys, commanded by Leon Strozzi, Prince of Capua, and a Breton, Captain François Bruel, with about 400 men. The French also began to build similar fortifications to the Alderney fort, at Omonville and Cap de la Hague, about eight or nine miles across The Race from Alderney, in 1548.

A series of three Rolls of the reign of Edward VI, dated between 1549 and 1551, give a comprehensive account of the materials, men and ships associated with its

Sketch of 'Esssex Castle' in 1860.

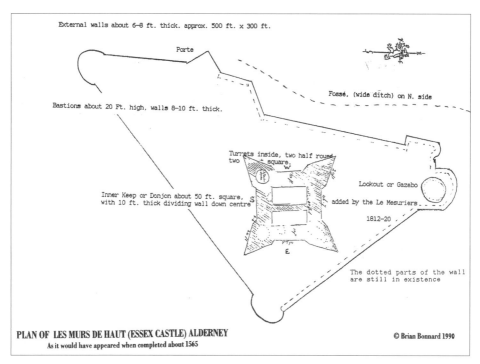

Plan of Les Murs de Haut, the 'Fortification on the Hill' (literally 'on High'). Drawn by the author.

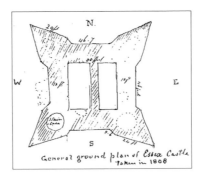

Plan of Essex castle drawn in 1808.

construction. These are written in English, but in a script which is not easy to decipher. *[Note *** below indicates an indecipherable word in the document]*.

The first, about nine feet long, appointed William Badger, a Master Carpenter, to carry out construction work under the supervision of John Aborough, and sets out the conditions for his;

> making and new building of certen Brewhouses and Bakehouses and Mills in the said Isle (of Alderney) as also take the charge of the Surveyor of the Workes of the Fort of Lunges and of the Towre Allay in the said Isle....

His commission is dated to run from 22 January 1549, to 8 January 1550, and notes all payments made, persons involved, and the items bought at Southampton; principally, wheat, malt, beer, butter cheese, bacon, flour etc. from ****, timber, lead, *** bought from ***, and payments made for their transport to Alderney in sundry vessels. The 300-ton *Valentyne* of Southampton, Master John Galley; the 300-ton *S**pstake* (?Sweepstake) Master, Thomas Gresham; the 25-ton *Michael* of Bewley, Master Bartholomew Symper; 20-ton *Marie* of Bewley; 40-ton *Marye* of Southampton, Master, Patrick Cavell; 70-ton *Trinity* of Portsmouth, Master Denys Corfe; *Marye* of Poole, Master, Thomas John Cox; *Trinity* of Newport, Master James White. These were each employed over a period of several months, and were followed in the accounts by the 20-ton *Mary* of Alderney, and about a dozen other ships from 'Hampton', Poole, Newport, and other places, including the *Julian* of Guernsey, making individual voyages. They all brought cargoes from Weymouth, Poole and Yarmouth. The value of all the payments made on this roll was £1250 8s 6½d.

After a review of the work in Alderney by Captain Richard Broke, Captain of the Royal Galleys, in October, following the fall of Protector Somerset, he urged the Council to appoint a clerk of works to supervise the payments, which Turberville and Badger were too busy to do. William Este or East was appointed to this post on 8 January 1550. The second Roll, of similar length, is the accounts of William Este from 8 January 1550 to 4 May 1551 for the materials and wages of the workmen used by William Turberville, Marshal of Alderney, (almost certainly a miscopying for *Robert*, who had been sent with a garrison of 200 men in 1548), and William Badger, Master of the Works in the construction of a Fort in Alderney. 40 masons were employed, together with other craftsmen, and payments were made to many people, including Sir Edward Pechin, Sir John Mollins, John Compton, John Aborough, William Badger and James Stoner, Merchant of Southampton.

The third roll is some 20 feet long, and is a charter, dated 4 November 1550, under the Great Seal of England, from the King and Privy Council, to Southampton merchants James Stoner, and William Hooper, 'to take in charge the provision of victuals, and other items mete and requete for the King's Majesty's Isle of Alderney aforesaid'. It gave them authority, mentioning the earlier document, as

> Through ye will written the 22nd January 1549, instructing all Justices of Peace, Mayors, Shreves, Bailiffs, Constables, Greffiers, Comptrollers and ***, and to all the King's subjects to whom it shall appertain...

to assist them, for the purchase of the supplies, which included; oxen, sheep, malt, barley, wheat, hides, tallow, offal, salt beef, pork, beer, hops, bacon, cheese, lead, sundry tools, timber, etc....

> from any and all places within our counties of Southampton, Somerset, Dorset, and Wiltshire, as well as others', and to: 'take all manner of things such as wood, coal, bond, etc. for the better furniture of the Isle of Alderney aforesaid, as well by sea as by land.

The charter was given in the presence of the Archbishop of Canterbury, the Earl of Worcester, Lord Marquis Coxsett, Anthony Wynnfold, Nicholas Wootton, Edward Worth, John Baker and Edward Montayne, and instructed all men to...

> aid and assist our friend John Stoner in the execution hereof in his name, with what Malt, Beer, Butter, Cheese, Bacon, and other necessary victuals mete and convenient for the King's men of War, workmen and labourers in Alderney, with carriage by land and water.

All the sums expended are listed, including the wages of clerks, butchers etc., a total of; '£251 in all by certificate under the hands of Anthony Buller, William Clare and William Wynlow'. This document also carries a curious entry under the moneys received:

> Eight Frenchmen, Prisoners taken in Alderney aforesaid for their Ransom upon their discharge, being of the number of 24 prisoners sent from Alderney by John Aborough to Southampton, upon the confession of this accomptante ... £13.

His entry is followed by the accounts for the sale in Alderney of the Malt, (221 quarters), Barley, (1,000 quarters), 'Brews', described as the; 'rebatement of the wheat meal, packed in casques and sent to the said island, 980 quarters at *** the quarter', and the Hides, Tallow and Offals of 800 oxen, amounting in all to £1632 4s 10d. The cost of transporting the 24 prisoners 'taken in the Isle', to Southampton, is noted elsewhere in the accounts as £24 8s 9d.

The accounts on this roll appear to have been made up to December 1551, and include an item of £19 0s 0d for the; 'passages of 380 soldiers transported from the said Isle to Southampton @ 12d a head'. Another item shows the wages of William Este, and one servant @ 4d per diem, 482 days, beginning 8 January 1549, and ending 4 May 1551, total £96 8s 0d. John Aborough had brought sundry artificers and labourers from England, and soldiers had been sent from Hurst Castle, all of whose wages amounted to £87 6s 6d.

The sum total of these accounts for this period is an impressive figure of £9,990 2s 8½d, made up as follows:

Entertainment & Wages of the Garryson	£4,577 13s 7d
Fortifications & Buildings	£4,373 14s 8½d
Empayons & Provisions	£393 2s 1d
Conduct money	£2 4s 0d
Passages	£19 0s 0d
Freight	£95 5s 4d
Rydinge charges	£46 11s 4d
Allowances & waste of Victualls	£266 2s 9d
Wages	£183 14s 6d
Transportation of Treasure	£6 13s 4d

Other sums appear within the whole account roll, which do not correlate with this summary, and appear to relate to both Este's and Badger's earlier accounts, including several sums of 'monie delivered in preste', presumably for local disbursements and pay, and additional supplies and freight charges. The Minutes of the Privy Council for 13 June 1551, give details of Turberville's appointment:

An order newlie set by the Lords of the Counscill for the Isle of Alderney videst;

Robert Turberville, Captain there @ 6/8d per diem
6 household servants for the same Captain @ 6d per piece per day
20 Gonners, whereof   One @ 12d by the day
                         4 @ 8d a piece per diem
                         15 @ 6d a piece per diem
One Clerke for the provision of victualles and keeping of a pay booke for him and his servants
    @ 2d per diem
40 Workmen, whereof Two Carpenters   @ 9d a piece per diem
3 Masons and Layers   @ 4d a piece per diem

2 Smiths	@ 9d a piece per diem
1 Couper	@ 8d per diem
25	@ 6d per diem
One overseer, being a carpenter	@ 12d per diem

One can infer from this that there was a Master-gunner, and a senior gunner for each of four separate batteries, at the time.

It is worth noting that the £4577 in Stoner's accounts for 'Entertainment and Wages of the Garryson', are made up of individual sums which show one Marshal @ 13/4d per diem, three Captains @ 4/10d, three Petty Captains @ 2/-, a surgeon, chaplain, 42 'Gonners of the Greate Ordynance', three 'typpstaves', three porters, and 270 soldiers. This suggests that with the reduction of the garrison to about 100 men, ordered the previous November, Turberville was put on half-pay.

During this period there was considerable traffic, trading and smuggling between Alderney and southern England. Local fishermen also took some of their catches to England, presumably in the hope of better market prices. The Book of Fynes, the annual accounts of the Mayors of Southampton, carries a short entry for 1553-54:

fyne for selling connger; Resseived of A man of Alderney. For that he sold Connger befor he hadd his price ... iiijs. viijd. (4/8d).

The various events of this period eventually resulted in a petition from the inhabitants to the Privy council in 1552 or early 1553. The document no longer exists, but Turberville had apparently overruled the authority of the jurats, seized much of the people's savings to help pay for the fortifications, had demanded food, building materials and forced labour and the large imported workforce had terrorised the inhabitants. Political troubles and rebellions in England over the wardship of the new young king, Edward VI meant that this complaint received little attention at the time, Edward's death on 6 July 1553, the abortive attempt to make Lady Jane Grey Queen, which had caused Sir Peter Mewtas, Governor of Guernsey, who had been involved in Northumberland's conspiracy, to be imprisoned in England and Catholic Mary, Henry VIII's daughter's accession to the throne, all conspiring to put it into the background. However, on 7 September 1553, a Flemish Corsair, recaptured Sark, which had by then been in French hands since 31 July 1549, with a force of 150 men in two ships, piloted by a Guernseyman supplied by Thomas Crompton, Lieutenant to Sir Peter Mewtas and in doing so precipitated fears of a French reprisal and a new war breaking out. This had the effect of making the Privy Council look into the complaints of the people of Alderney and on 15 September the Governor of Jersey, Sir Hugh Paulet was instructed to investigate and to dismiss Turberville if the complaints were proved.

Leonard Chamberlain who had rendered much valuable service to the new Queen Mary in securing her accession to the throne, was appointed Governor of Guernsey in a Patent dated 25 September 1553, replacing Mewtas and was knighted the day after Mary's coronation on 1 October. Crole who had been sailing under the orders of the Emperor Charles V of Spain, had claimed Sark for that monarch, but Charles was uninterested in so small a possession and advised his Ambassador in London to sell it back to the English crown. Queen Mary was not prepared to pay to recover her own island and also fearethat to receive it back from Spanish hands would irritate the French still further, they having declared their intention of retaking the island 'though it cost the lives of 4,000 men'. Crole was instructed to abandon it, after removing the armaments and demolishing the forts, so that the English could take over a deserted island and deny further access to the French. Crole removed the ordnance and sold it to Turberville in October 1553, after refusing Sir Leonard Chamberlain's offer of six florins, on the grounds that the French had offered him £1,000 for the island and the artillery. The larger cannons which he could not get on board his ships were pushed into the sea. It would thus appear that Paulet had not felt justified in dismissing Turberville and the Sark cannons became part of the Alderney defences. Meanwhile Mary had contracted a marriage with Philip, son of the Emperor Charles V and was married by proxy in March 1554. This to a large extent removed the threat of war and the fortifications in Alderney were discontinued. In October Turberville received final payment of £542 2s 2d for his expenses in connection with the fortifications, the cannons and munitions were removed to the Tower of London and the garrison disbanded.

Letters of Simon Renard (one of the four Spanish Ambassadors to the English Court), to the Emperor Charles, which were to be found in the Vienna Imperial Archives and have been calendared in English in the Spanish State Papers at the National Archives, note the difficulty of demolishing the Fort on Sark in safety because of the proximity to France and the lack of wisdom in the Spanish sending a force to occupy it now that the French had been turned out, for fear of English resistance from the other islands. He advised the Emperor that; 'they would probably make less trouble about it now that, as you say in your letters, they have treated with Crole for the artillery he found in the island'.

In another letter dated 1 November, he wrote:

Since Adrian Crole's departure and the last time I wrote to your Majesty about him, I have only heard that he has sold the munitions he found in Sark to the Lieutenant of Alderney an Englishman.

In a third letter on this subject, dated 8 November, Renard advised the Emperor:

... the Council had informed him that the French were fitting out ships and raising 1,000 men to retake Sark and to ask him to warn the Captain (presumably Crole) who seized it and command him to abandon and demolish (the fort). I told the Queen that I had received definite news last Monday, that the Captain had abandoned the island after burning and wrecking all he could and throwing the big pieces of artillery into the sea, because he had been unable to get them onto his boats and consequently their wishes had been fulfilled: but as the French were making such preparations I feared they would fortify it again.

The Council have sent me four soldiers who served the captain and whom he did not pay, in order that I might give them their wages: and they wrapped up this detail in the other negotiation in order not to seem too anxious about it.

In a further letter dated 11 December, Renard told the Emperor:

the French have certainly retaken the island of Sark and are fortifying it: and many think it will be difficult to prevent them giving trouble from Scotland by means of the heretics, the Lady Elizabeth or otherwise, for it is known that they are making great preparations.

To prevent trouble from the Protestant supporters of her half-sister Elizabeth, at the time of the arrival of her husband in England, Mary sent her to the Royal Manor of Woodstock, under the stewardship of Sir Leonard Chamberlain, whose family lived on the estate.

The Spanish Ambassador, Simon Renard and M. de Courrières, the Lieutenant of Amont, informing the Emperor of the results of the audience they had demanded of the English Chancellor, in which they had complained that the inhabitants of Guernsey and Jersey had bought the stores from Sark, 'which some subjects of your Majesty had wrested from the French some twenty days ago', received little comfort and were informed that the Queen considered that; 'the island of Sark belonged to her and had come into the King of France's possession by usurpation of her rights and if the Flemish seized it, they did so by right of might in time of war. The munitions found there belonged to them and they could dispose of them however they pleased'. A message which was also given to the French Ambassador when he threatened war because of these events. There seems to be no reliable confirmation of this reoccupation in 1554, possibly following the preparations for an expedition by the Seigneur de Glatigny, although it is recorded in the Bulletin of the Société Jersiaise (1925), that Crole was 'dislodged from Sark by the Governor of Normandy, Martin de Bellay'. If they did retake it, then their forces were certainly withdrawn after war broke out again in 1557 and the island remained uninhabited until Queen Elizabeth's grant to Helier de Carteret in 1565.

Due to a dramatic change in European politics caused by the accession of Philip to the throne of Spain and his ambitions against the Hapsburg Empire, in 1557, three years after the ordnance was removed from Alderney it was decided to refortify the island. This was never actually done and the armaments remained in London.

Turberville had evidently returned to England, where he died at his manor of Bere Regis in April 1559.

On 8 January 1558 England finally lost Calais which fell to a surprise attack by the Duc de Guise and in June 1558 Dunkirk too was lost. In the same month on the 20th, Alderney was captured by Capt. Malesarde, son of Robine de la Mer of Cherbourg and looted. He returned on 2 July with two other corsairs, the Sieur de Gouberville and the Sieur de Sèdèville, after taking his spoils back to Cherbourg where he auctioned the cattle on the quay at Tourlaville. They remained in Alderney until the 4 July, when they retired on the approach of an English fleet from Guernsey, under Sir Leonard Chamberlain.

The Sieur de Gouberville recorded in his journal that, on 3 July, they walked all over the island examining the fortifications (which had obviously not been razed to the ground as Turberville had been ordered). Back at Tourlaville, Malesarde held another auction of his spoils. At this time Sir Leonard Chamberlain was on honeymoon with his fourth wife, at Castle Cornet, where his eldest son Francis was 'Captain' and received orders to patrol the area more effectively. As a result, on 15 August 1558 the Constable of the Tower of London received a wounded 'Captain Mallyseart', taken prisoner at Alderney. The records of The Tower include an order from the Privy Council for Monsieur Malesert to be kept in safe ward with conference with no man, but a surgeon could visit him from time to time to treat his injuries. He was examined by the Council on 27 August and it was ordained that Mr Phetiplace, the man who had captured him in Alderney, should be made responsible for him. At the same time 100 French prisoners captured in Alderney were taken to Guernsey. The size of this force suggests that on his third attempt Malesarde had established a proper occupation of the island and only a sizeable force under the Governor's second son, George, had captured them.

E.A. Martin's Manuscript History of the Island of Alderney of 1810 records that, in 1560, Elizabeth I granted Alderney to George Chamberlain for the term of 1,000 years, although the later grant of 1584 to John Chamberlain makes no mention of an existing grant, nor of a particular time span. It is perhaps also significant that in her charter of 15th March 1560 in the second year of her reign, where all the customary rights and privileges of the Channel Islanders are confirmed, Alderney is included with Guernsey. It is elsewhere recorded that George, who was suspected of being involved in the plot to place Mary, Queen of Scots on the throne and he, being in England, had fled to Holland when the Duke of Norfolk was imprisoned in the Tower in September 1569.

A letter from John Chamberlain (II), the grandson of Governor Chamberlain, written to the Privy council on 3 March 1628 states that the cost of the recovery of Alderney was above £10,000 and Heylin, in his account of the islands written in 1629, states:

> the Island of Alderney, thanks to the valour of George Chamberlain, the son of Sir Leonard Chamberlain. then Governor of Guernsey, was recovered from the French, who, in Queen Mary's reign had seized upon it (in 1558, Ed.).

Alderney became a refuge for Calvinists fleeing from Europe, indeed so many Huguenot refugees reached the islands, including Ministers of the Reformed Church, that in 1564 the Governors of Jersey and Guernsey were petitioned for permission to establish the reformed churches in both St Helier and St Peter Port. This was granted and the two churches in those towns were allowed to follow the Geneva code, provided that all of the other Parishes retained the Anglican form of Service.

Alderney also became a refuge for corsairs and 40 pirates, part of them Scots and part English, were arrested here and sent to Guernsey in 1564, possibly by George Chamberlain.

Francis Chamberlain, the 'Captain' of Castle Cornet, who had been made joint Governor of Guernsey with his father in 1555, was seriously ill in January 1570 and the Captain of Hurst Castle was appointed as his deputy, he died shortly after and, Sir Leonard already being deceased, was succeeded by Thomas Leighton who first arrived in Guernsey on 14 May 1570.

far oute of good order; the ordnance cankered with rust and the local militia so ill-firnished as in my lyffe I never saw worse.

Despite the money and effort expended by Francis Chamberlain, Leighton found things in a pretty poor state. He set about improving things and making sure the Queen received all her dues and in 1572 whilst he was still diligently enquiring into all of the Queen's possessions in the Bailiwick, produced a document known as the Vieux Rental, dated 5 August 1572 and headed:

The Lands which belong to Her Majesty the Queen in the Island of Alderney, called Common Land.

A translation of the original document may be rendered as follows:

1. From an area called La Teste de Pignons on the south of the said Island, going along the ditch eastward as far as the Vallet au Fleaume and from the said boundary mark, to the boundary mark of the Canon, [probably Les Canions].
2. From the boundary mark of the Canon to the boundary mark at the foot and entrance of the Fort [now known as Essex Castle], following the Douve [ditch] to the boundary on La Ruette, then along the ditches as far as the Fort Boundary.
3. From the Fort Boundary to the boundary mark of 'Heritiers des Messieurs', from there towards the west following the ditch as far as the boundary mark below the Sergeant's field.
4. From the boundary mark of the said field, to the boundary mark at the end of the Champs des Demaines and from there to the boundary mark of the corner of St Michael, after that to the boundary mark of the Champs Reullez
5. From the boundary mark of the Champs Reullez to the boundary mark of the Huet ditch and from the said ditch to the boundary mark on La Hougue Omer, then on to the boundary mark of Cobette and thence to the boundary mark of Courtil Milliet, then to the end of the field of Richard le Cocq, to the corner of the bank, then along the Douit [stream], to the boundary stone of the Vau des Portes de Bas.
6. From the said boundary stone of the Vau des Portes de Bas one comes to the boundary mark on Les Buttes and after that to the boundary mark at the bottom of La Grande Fosse , coming from there to the mark at Champs des Millerie and then along the Courtil ès Cats to the sea at Crabby.
7. After the above mentioned Courtil ès Cats coming to the boundary mark Sausmarez and from there to the mark in the middle of Platte Saline. After leaving the middle of Platte Saline, go to the mark at the Mill Stream and from that mark, on the other side of the Stream by a ditch which forms the boundary as far as the sea.

8. From the said ditch to the West and West-south-west of the island, along the banks
   past the Cables to L'Emauve and beyond to the Plat Côtil, along the South side of
   the said Island. After coming to the Vau du Seue [Val du Sud], one comes to the Vau
   du Fray and after going past the head of La Cachalière, one follows all the banks as
   far as Les Pignons, which banks serve as boundary marks.

With very little change, these boundaries are the same as those shown on the huge
1830 map kept in the Alderney Museum, which shows the land distributed to the
inhabitants of Alderney in 1830. Twelve years later, in the ninth part of a patent signed
at Westminster on 29 May 1584, as a reward for the Chamberlain's various services in
the relief of Alderney, Elizabeth granted the island to Sir Leonard's son John for £20
down and £13 6s 8d a year. In this patent it is stated:

...as the island has for a number of years remained empty, waste and little inhabited,
nor occupied or worked by any of our subjects, we have not been given, the revenue,
income and emoluments owed to our forebears from ancient times; Furthermore, our
wealthy and faithful subjects have not had during this same time for that reason any
goods, profit or use whatever; indeed the same island by reason of its desolate and
solitary state, was, during the time of war ... and even in time of peace because of
pirates robbers and such like, abandoned by our subjects of the aforesaid islands of
Jersey and Guernsey.... From the inhabitants of the aforesaid island we have certain
tidings and we therefore, considering, weighing and pondering as well the security and
tranquility of the States and commonweals of the aforesaid islands ... are persuaded
that it is necessary to provide, do and foresee, not only that any place be not open or
available for such like enemies, but also that pirates and robbers be compelled, driven,
exterminated and ruined from the aforesaid island of Alderney or Aldreney, in so far
as may be done, so that in future our same island of Alderney or Aldreney aforesaid
may, by the English and other native subjects of ours be always occupied, cultivated
and possessed.
    KNOW THEREFORE that we, as much in consideration of the sum of £20 of good
and legal money at the treasury of our island of Guernsey ... from John Chamberlain
of Longcombe in the County of Oxon, Esquire, paid well and faithfully, whence we
give full satisfaction and acquittal for payment to the said John Chamberlain ... as well
as in consideration of the good, faithfull, praiseworthy, free and acceptable services
to us, performed by the same John Chamberlain in attacking and overcoming our
enemies, pirates and robbers and all malefactors from the aforesaid island of Alderney
or Aldreney, as well from the same island as from our said islands of Guernsey and
Jersey, hitherto disturbed, molested and greatly ruined by such devices and plots; BY
Our special grace and from certain knowledge and pure notion, we have given granted
and by these presents we give and grant for our heirs and successors to the said John
Chamberlain or by whatever other name or surname the same John Chamberlain may
be considered or known; – namely the aforesaid our island of Alderney or Aldreney,
with its laws, parts, liberties, premises and all whatsoever pertains thereto and all

and singular fortified castles, houses, buildings, structures and ruined buildings and materials and remains, lands, fields, grazing, pastures, waste fallows, deep woods, thickets, forests, mills, water banks, running waters, springs, ponds, fee service and revenue, Advowson (the right to appoint the clergy to the living), granting liberties and promulgating laws, appointing vicars of all chapels and churches whatsoever and also every manner of tithe of produce or revenue, quarrying, harbours shores, banks, sea vraic (seaweed), wrecks, farm and fee farm and knight's fee, guardianship of wards, escheat of reliefs, herriot, goods and chattels of fugitive felons and of pirates, suicides ... and whatsoever maybe ours ... from or about the maritime limits. coasts around or about the said island of Alderney or Aldreney ... or whatever was hitherto known or reputed to exist in that island ... to the aforementioned John Chamberlain, his heirs or assigns, in perpetuity ... for the twentieth part of a Knight's fee and giving thence annually to Us and our heirs and successors £13 6s 8d of lawful English money or in coin lawful and current in our said island of Guernsey...; AND LASTLY from the plenitude of our favour we have given and granted and by these presents we give and grant to the aforesaid John Chamberlain all rents and local dues of the said island of Alderney otherwise Aldreney from the Feast of St Michael the Archangel last and in addition to these the income or increase held by the said J.C. by our Gift or by Purchase or in whatsoever manner being paid, yielded or made to us or to our heirs and successors.

PROVIDED ALWAYS NEVERTHELESS that if the said island of Alderney or Aldreney henceforth and for all time shall not have been continuously inhabited, cultivated, occupied and frequented by at least 40 male subjects of ours ... then the said John Chamberlain shall forfeit to us ... the sum of £10 of English money....

The patent goes on to enumerate over several paragraphs increasing penalties for each six-month period after such a fine, that Chamberlain shall have failed to populate the island with the minimum required number of men capable of bearing arms and for the fourth occasion the penalty becomes forfeiture of the patent and the Queen becomes repossessed of everything granted. He may not sell the island without permission, but may farm the island or any part of it out for any term, by a written deed under his seal to any person in Jersey or Guernsey owing service to the crown;

...and whatever shall have been remitted or given in farm under the seal of the said John Chamberlain, his heirs or assigns shall be sufficient and of equal validity and efficaciousness as if under the seal or seals of the said our islands of Guernsey or Jersey, or any other land adjacent thereto done or granted, anything above in these presents to the contrary notwithstanding.

In witness whereof etc. E.R.

A late seventeenth or early eighteenth century parchment copy of this Latin Patent may be seen in the Alderney Museum.

It seems likely that the description of the island as laid waste and uninhabited and the requirement to maintain 40 men-at-arms, was inserted by a scribe, using the Grant of Sark to Helier de Carteret made in 1563, (which was later confirmed in letters patent issued from Greenwich on 6 August 1565), as a model, as many of these same terms appear in that document. Alderney at this time probably had a population of at least 500-600 and could have provided 80 men-at-arms if needs be. In fact the population could well have been greater, since we find that, in 1566 when he received funds from the Queen to strengthen the defences of Castle Cornet, (these funds were the result of a fine of £1,000 imposed on the Bailiff and 12 Jurats of the island who had been called to London to account for their activities in connection with the poor state of the defences of Guernsey and the recent burning of three witches), Francis Chamberlain, who had succeeded to the sole Governorship on the death of his father in 1561, asked for directions regarding Alderney, (which was according to Martin's MS. then in the fee of his brother George) and compiled a lengthy memorandum on the situation here. In this he urged that 'Alderney should be kept in good order, to retain its 700-800 inhabitants in Her Majesty's obedience' and for the sake of the valuable fishing for mackerel and conger in the local waters. He further pointed out the importance of holding Alderney, as, in enemy hands, it would be a 'scourge'. Probably encouraged by the success of Helier de Carteret's settlement of Sark, he ventured to suggest that the island could be made safe at relatively small cost, with the inhabitants providing 80 men and the crown 20 trained soldiers, to form the garrison and the expenditure of some £500 to complete the half built fort above Longis Bay.

In Sark, De Carteret later refused to acknowledge the authority of Governor Leighton over him and, having submitted a report of his recolonisation and defensive preparations to the Queen whilst on a visit to London in 1572, was rewarded by her with the declaration of Sark as an independent fief of the crown, a position it still retains. Alderney continued to be leased by the crown to a fee-farmer and has never been made a separate fief. Within little more than a year of taking up his patent, John Chamberlain was in dispute with the inhabitants of Alderney and in continual conflict with the Jurats of the island. Matters had reached such a serious impasse, that appeals were made to the Privy council, who, meeting at Greenwich on 21 June 1585, appointed the Governor of Guernsey, Sir Thomas Leighton and his deputy, his nephew Thomas Wigmore to enquire into and regulate the disputes. They travelled to Alderney to investigate and their report to the Privy Council dated 30 September 1585 was submitted (in French), 'on a parchment bearing the red wax seal of the Commissioners' and accompanied by a letter of explanation written after they left the island. On 26 May 1586. the Privy council sent letters to John Chamberlain and to the Jurats and inhabitants of Alderney urging them all to accept the 12 recommendations of the Commissioners 'for the better strengthening of the Island against forraine invasion'.

This document is generally referred to as the *Ordonnance of 1585* and sets out the respective rights of Chamberlain and the islanders. In brief summary the 12 points were:

1. Chamberlain to enjoy the whole compass of the Mountain of Fort Longis which he may enclose with the stream as a boundary (this land is now known as Essex Hill).
2. Chamberlain to enjoy the enclosure around Longis Pond.
3. The inhabitants had no rights to fold sheep or graze cattle on the Mannez Garenne

(or warren), nor on Mont Touraille (the present site of Fort Albert), except on payment of one farthing per year for each foot as was the custom.

4. Chamberlain was allowed to keep up to 300 sheep and 12 cattle on the Common Lands.
5. The inhabitants will pay champart on corn and flax, but only ordinary tithes on hemp, on certain lands detailed in a list and not on all land.
6. The inhabitants may not put animals on Burhou without a permit.
7. Each fishing boat shall only pay a tithe of 6 congers a year in future and shall not be forced to carry Chamberlain or his goods.
8. The inhabitants shall enjoy the common lands and neither Chamberlain nor the inhabitants shall enclose any.
9. The inhabitants shall provide Chamberlain with up to 60 sheep and lambs a year on payment of 2 shillings per sheep and 14 pence per lamb.
10. The jurats shall administer justice without interference.
11. Chamberlain shall not imprison anyone on any pretext, except those who fail in their military duties.
12. Chamberlain to pay one third of the cost of munitions for the artillery and both the inhabitants and Chamberlain each to provide one trained gunner.

In the next year, another Order in Council, dated 4 April 1586, directed Sir Thomas Leighton to remit

sundry fines set upon the people of Alderney by him, in respect of their wilful and lewd offence in suffering certain Frenchmen to pursue Her Majesty's subjects within her protection, without making any good endeavours to resist them ... and to convert the sum to the public defence.

It seems that this was the last payment of three annual instalments, two of which had already been paid.

The Chamberlains were known to be ardent Catholics, nevertheless George Chamberlain, (according to Miss Edith Carey, [actually John Chamberlain. Ed], in a note in the *Transactions of La Société Guernesiaise* for 1929), whilst Governor of Alderney during the French Wars, acted as Commissary General for Essex's Army and, with the connivance of Governor Leighton who had been appointed by the Queen as Essex's Guardian whilst he served in France from 1589-1592, at this time pledged Alderney to Robert, Earl of Essex for money to pay for the provisions. This statement she attributes to Revd Elie Brévint, Vicar of Sark at about this time.

Some extra support for Essex's holding the fee-farm, has recently come to light in the form of a 'copia vera' of an old charter detailed in the indenture to John Child, details of which are given in the next chapter, but the older document quoted is of a lease of Alderney dated 26 March 1590, when the Queen granted the island and all it contained to Robert, Earl of Essex for the remainder of the 1,000 years from the date of the indenture to Chamberlain and noted that the previous lease had been given to him without payment by John Chamberlain, amongst various other covenants and things.

Alderney thus was in the hands of the Earl of Essex for a short time, although it is doubtful if he ever came here, after which it once again came under the direct authority of the Governor of Guernsey for a period.

As we have seen, the Earl of Essex appears to have come into possession of Alderney to settle a debt for cash to buy provisions for his army in France about 1590, from the hands of George Chamberlain, whom Edith Carey states to have been the younger brother of Sir Leonard Chamberlain rather than his younger son, appointed Governor of Alderney in 1566, but elsewhere as has just been noted and almost certainly more accurately, we find that, on 26 March 1590, John Chamberlain had made over his rights in Alderney to Robert, Earl of Essex, without any payment. The Indenture just referred to actually records that the transfer
was made not only to Essex, but also included:

> ...the right Honble. Robert, Lord Riche, Henry Bourgechier, (Bourchier), Robert Wright and Gelley Mayrick Esquyre, their executors and assigns....

The 1770 *MS History of Alderney* suggests that this exchange might have been antedated to this date, from the time in the following year when John had abandoned his rights in Alderney to become a Military contractor and that the apparent gift was in return for the profits he expected to make as Vivandier to Essex's expedition, in which he would have provided transport and supplies for the army of about 4,000 men. His son John (II) Chamberlain had served with the English forces in Holland and later, in Essex's expedition to Ireland, where he was knighted in the field by Essex in 1599. After Essex was first arrested, in 1600, he was released and barred from Elizabeth's Court, but Chamberlain was allowed to keep the title conferred on him in Ireland.

When Essex was tried, found guilty of treason and beheaded on 25 February 1601, the lease reverted to the crown, as all his property was forfeit and the Queen's Procureur in Guernsey took possession of all the Royal revenues in the islands which were in Essex's hands. This seizure or seisin was authorised by an Act of the Royal Court in Guernsey, which still exists, dated 1 April 1601. Essex's ownership of Alderney at about this period is confirmed both in this document and in the Devereux papers at Longleat House *c.* 1595, which includes 'The Island of Alderney, valued worth /, to be sold at £1300', in a long list of the Earl's possessions to be sold in order to satisfy a debt of £29,993 4s 6d owing to Mr Peter Vasilore or Vasilove. There is however no record of the island actually being sold at this time.

Sir Thomas Leighton who had been appointed Governor in 1570, (a position he retained until his death in 1609), thus came into possession of the Guernsey revenues. Both the Civil government and the revenues of Alderney came into his hands as well and Alderney was once again included with Guernsey in Royal appointments. The living in Alderney had fallen vacant in 1591 when the incumbent, Jacques Bernard de la Fontaine, Minister since 1587, returned to France and for the next 16 years there were occasional visits of Rectors from Guernsey, or the curates had held services, but no-one was appointed to the living, despite a reminder from the Colloque of the Church in Guernsey issued to the elders in Alderney on 20 June 1592. At this period there was considerable difficulty in finding French-speaking Anglican clergy. Although I have been unable to find any definite evidence on this point, there is a paper in the Alderney Museum which, unsubstantiated by any information on the source of the statement, says that after John Chamberlain gave the lease to Essex, Essex granted a 20 year lease of the island to John's younger brother William who was guardian and agent for the young Earl of Southampton. William had leased Beaulieu House and parsonage from him in 1584 and immediately sublet it to his brother John, who was living there with his wife and son. It therefore seems possible that the Chamberlain family, who were certainly in possession of the island again in 1607 and had kept the revenues of the church for themselves, had never actually vacated it after passing it to Essex, although neither of them actually spent much time in the island.

Portrait of the 2nd Earl of Essex, *c.* 1550.

3

The Stuart Period

In the events described in this chapter, the fate of Alderney is still very much bound up with the political situation in England, and control of its affairs from Guernsey. The Papal Bull of Neutrality continued to hold good, and the various wars between Britain and France did not significantly affect trade in the islands. The defences of Alderney continued to be built and neglected by turn, and the English garrisons came and went, with the local inhabitants continuing to provide a primitive form of Militia when the need arose. The frequent changes of responsibility for Alderney between persons appointed by the Crown, and by the Warden of Guernsey, made for little continuity of policy, but the first proper appointments of a 'Captain of the Island' and a 'Commander-in-Chief' of the forces in the island are also recorded.

According to Judge J. A. le Cocq, who would have had access to the Alderney Court records, when he was writing in 1901, Sir William Essex had already been actioned by the Minister, Simon Mason, who was permitted by the Court, on 15 September 1621, to action Sir William's Procureur for his annual salary. In the same year, Lord Henry Danvers, Baron Danby was appointed Governor of Guernsey, Alderney and Sark, with Peter Osborne as his Lieutenant.

The official title of *Governor* for the King's representative in Guernsey was fixed by an Order-in-Council dated 15 June 1618, and superseded the previous varying descriptions. This title was finally abolished in 1835.

James I died in March 1625, and was succeeded by Charles I, who was his second son. Charles soon renewed hostilities against Spain. The clauses in his marriage contract to catholic Henrietta Maria, daughter of Henry IV of France had already caused considerable trouble at home with the strong puritan faction which was developing. They feared the return of 'Popery', since both King James and Prince Charles had agreed to her having her own catholic bishop and 20 priests, and this was perhaps one way of his allaying those fears.

As a result of an unsuccessful raid by the Duke of Buckingham on the Ile de Rhé in 1627, fears of French reprisals on the Channel Islands caused Charles to order the sending of the Earl of Danby to Guernsey, in 1628, with 'four good ships' to protect the Islands. As already noted, Danby had actually been appointed Governor in 1621, but had not taken up his post in the islands themselves. Financial problems in England prevented the despatch of this fleet until March 1629. An interesting point for future

Judge J. A. LeCocq in the States chamber, *c.* 1901.

historians of the Islands was that Doctor Peter Heylin accompanied him as Chaplain, and as a result of his time spent in the islands published, in 1656, his book; *A Survey of the two islands, Guernzey and Jarsey, with the isles appending, according to their politie and formes of government, both ecclesiastical and civill*, a contemporary account to which we owe much for his descriptions of the scenery, personalities and customs of the period. His account of Alderney is somewhat brief compared with the two larger islands, but records that the principal harbour was at Crabbie. He also mentions the legend of the inundation of sand (at Braye and Longis) as

> ...the just judgement of God upon the owner of those grounds, who once (but when I know not) had made booty and put to the sword some certain Spaniards there ship wracked.

Charles I confirmed the Charters of his predecessors in 1627, the islanders thus retaining all their traditional liberties and privileges, and two years later another Peace Treaty was signed with France. A further grant was made in 1627 to William Chamberlain for the defences, and arms and munitions were sent to him by the Privy Council, at which time there were said to be 160 men capable of bearing arms in the Island.

From 3 March 1639 John Colles or Collis was 'Governor' in Alderney, but he sold his rights on 27 October that year to his brother William for £200 sterling, and from then to 1642 when he died, William Colles held the grant of a lease to the island of Alderney, both of these grants appear to have come from Sir William Essex who, followed by his son Charles, was the fee-farmer. William Colles was required to go to England to assist Mr W. Wheeler at the Parliamentary Sessions of 1641 returning to Alderney on 12 May 1642. Following this Session, in 1643 the Parliamentarians had expelled all the Catholics, and Peter Le Febvre, Sieur de L'Epine was registered at the Court of Alderney on 3 November as Lt Governor of the island under Robert Russell Governor of Guernsey, Alderney and Sark.

When the English Civil War started in 1642, the Bailiwick of Jersey, and the Governor of Castle Cornet declared for the King, but strongly Calvinist Guernsey was for Parliament, and on 22 March the provisional government of Guernsey, Alderney and Sark was vested in a committee of 13 gentlemen, with Peter de Beauvoir of Les Granges as President. Their Commission required them to seize Castle Cornet and Sir Peter Osborne, kill all who resisted, and convey him before Parliament, a command they failed to manage.

The Sieur L'Epine promptly seized the property of the widow of the former leaseholder Colles in Alderney and apparently treated other islanders without due consideration. Russell wrote to him on 20 November 1643 ordering him to restore her house and property and make her an annual allowance of £300 tournois in corn or other goods, from the tithes. He was also required to treat the other inhabitants more reasonably, and to restore their rights. Russell gave the Alderney appointment to Peter De Beauvoir de Bosq on 25 March 1646. He died in 1648, and on 11 March that year Benjamin Lempriére was sworn in as Lt Governor of Alderney.

On 3 November 1647 Parliament passed a set of regulations for 'well-ordering' the affairs of Guernsey, Alderney and Sark, which noted the suffering the inhabitants had endured by their allegiance to Parliament. They appointed Edmund Ludlow, John Weaver, John Birch and John Harrington, as Commissioners to hear their grievances, with power to call in any of the commissioners previously appointed in 1642 to assist them. The records available of their meetings do not however contain any complaints from Alderney inhabitants.

At the Restoration, commissioners were once again appointed to draw up a report for 'settling the affairs of Guernsey, Alderney and the adjacent islands'.

Alderney was separated from the jurisdiction of Guernsey at that date, but the commission did recommend the renewal of an order made by James I in 1621 for the construction of the Fort in Alderney, and its garrisoning by a small unit each from Jersey and Guernsey.

It must be assumed that if this order was carried out, once again Les Murs de Haut and possibly Les Murs en Bas, were refurbished, since there are no fortifications elsewhere in the island traceable to this date.

The civil war ended in 1649, and Cromwell was established as *Lord Protector*. After his death in 1658, there was a period of dissent between the various generals and senior parliamentarians which finally resulted in the exiled King being invited to return. As might be expected in these troubled times, several changes of Governors of the islands, and also of Lt Governors of Alderney were made by the Parliamentarians, but in the period of nine years, almost up to the restoration, Col. John Bingham remained Governor of Guernsey, and appointed George Mishaw or Michau to Alderney in 1651. He was succeeded the same year by Josias Ring, but Mishaw was sworn in for a second time as Lt Governor in the Alderney Court on 23 June 1654.

Roundhead Officer Captain Nicholas Ling who had commanded the garrison in Sark from 1645-1652, became Bingham's lieutenant here, being sworn in at the Alderney Court on 19 December 1657. On his appointment he married Cecile Andros, a member of a strongly Royalist Guernsey family. In May 1658 he apparently succeeded Sir William Essex as Lt Governor. It is also recorded that on 13 July 1659 Mr William Andrews was sworn in as Lt Governor of Alderney, under Charles Waterhouse who had been appointed to the Governorship of Guernsey, Alderney and Sark in 1654. The Andrews family had become known in Guernsey as Andros by this time. Meantime the executors and descendants of Robert, Earl of Warwick, son of the 2nd Earl of Essex were attempting to recover his property. In an *Indenture* of 20 November 1658, which quoted Elizabeth's confirmation of the gift of Alderney to Essex, they conveyed the lease to John Childs, a London Merchant as 'Farmer' of Alderney for seven years at £30 per annum rent. The executors who had all been Parliamentarians and friends of Cromwell, were; Algernon, Earl of Northumberland, and Oliver, Lord St John, Lord Chief Justice of the Court of Common Pleas at Westminster, in the presence of Edward, Earl of Manchester and Mr William Pierrepoint.

Not surprisingly in the circumstances, Childs never took up his appointment, and at his Restoration 18 months later, Charles II granted the island to his own nominees.

After the Restoration of Charles II on 29 May 1660, Alderney was specifically excluded from letters patent in January 1661 appointing Sir Hugh Pollard to be Governor of Guernsey:

Excepto Tamen extra hanc concessionem nostram reservant[ur] totâ insula nostre de Aurigny alias Alderney in partibus praedictis ac omnibus Terres etc.

Translation: (From this our grant however, there are kept back the whole of our island of Aurigny alias Alderney in the aforementioned area, with all its lands etc.), Charles having already promised it, in a Sign Manual written whilst at Breda on 12 May 1660, to one of his Gentlemen Ushers, Edward de Carteret. This promise was confirmed in a patent of 29 August 1660 in which he grants:

All that island of Auregny alias Alderney, and the Islands near and adjacent unto the said Island, and all the lands, tenements and hereditaments within the said island.... to the said Edward de Carteret, James de Carteret, and Clement De Couster and their assigns, for the term of their natural lives, and the life of the longest liver of them, yielding and paying the Annual Rent of thgirteen shillings.

These three, shortly afterwards, transferred their rights to Sir George de Carteret, vice-Chamberlain to the King. Sir George de Carteret issued a commission from Whitehall on 16 August 1661 to Captain Nicholas Ling as his Lt Governor and Captain of the Militia of Alderney. It is probable that Ling had remained in the island since he was sent here in 1657.

This may well be the first reference to the Alderney Militia as a properly constituted force, despite its having been in existence for some 400 years.

Back at Whitehall soon after his return, Charles II and the Privy Council issued orders on 22 April 1661 concerning the islands:

> His Majesty having this day taken into consideration att this board the present state and condition of his Islands of Guernezey and Alderney as thought fit upon serious debates and consideration concerning the same, by advice of his privy Councill to signify and declare his royal pleasure in these particulars following, is order to the establishing of the present government thereof for his Majesties' Service and the settlements of the minds and several interests of his Subjects there, Viz.
> (The first nine Articles are related to Guernsey)
>
> (Article 10. His Majestie is graceouslie pleased that for the well being and Security of the Island and Habitants of Alderney and for the inabling them to proceed with the perfecting of the forts formerly begun there and making of a Sufficient harbour and for erecting other buildings for the advantage of the said Island, the late brief as was formerly passed for that purpose in the 18th year of King James be renewed.... And lastly his majestie is graciously pleased that untill the said Fort and Harbour att Alderney be finished, Six Soldiers and a Serjeant out of the Garrison of Jersey and the like number out of the Garrison of Guernezey be sent thither by the respective Governors of the said Islands.
> (Signed) J. Lane

On 1 September 1662, Mr George Mishaw, again acting on behalf of Sir George de Carteret offered to give £1,000 tournois towards the cost of rebuilding the harbour at Longis. To quote Judge le Cocq again:

> The States were of opinion that before they undertook the work that an engineer should be consulted. It is not known what was done, but we find the following Act of the States for the Conservation of the Harbour;
>   3 Janvier 1674. Il est ordonné que ceux qui osteront les roques petites ou grandes et demoliront la chossée de la laggue en Havre de Longis, tant forains que habitants en quelque tems que ce soit seront a 60 sous tourn d'amende à Sa Majesté'.

This harbour was under the barracks at Longy, and another source gives the date of construction of the pier as 1661, with Essex Castle being restored at the same time. The remains of a substantial pier or jetty are still to be seen on the western side of the bay, and it was this that the inhabitants could be fined for vandalising.

The revenues of the island continued to be paid to Sir George de Carteret for three years, but the Government of the island still remained in the hands of Captain Ling, until his death at the age of 80 years on 6 January 1679. Ling's grave can be found in the Old Churchyard, near the Old Vicarage wall.

Charles II, in a charter dated 11 February 1667,

...confirms and corroborates the privileges of the Island of Guernsey, also of our Isles of Auregney alias Alderney and Serke', in which he confirms all of the traditional privileges of the islanders, including that of 'Neutrality in times of War.

Sir George de Carteret died in 1679/80, and his widow, Dame Elizabeth de Carteret was appointed *Gouvernante et Dame de cette isle*, (Alderney). She appointed Edward Le Breton as the Lt Governor, and a little later about 1682 she sold the remainder of the patent to Sir Edmond Andros and his wife Dame Marie, of Guernsey for £280.

Sir Edmond Andros was the son of Amice Andros, Bailiff of Guernsey from 1661 to 1674, when Edmond himself had become Bailiff. He was Governor of New York in 1684, and was also made Governor of Guernsey from 1704 to 1706. During this time he became Lord de Sausmarez. He had two brothers John and George, and a sister Ann, and after his death in 1713, John de Sausmarez was appointed Bailiff in 1714.

In 1683 by a patent dated from Westminster on 29 August, Charles II had granted to Andros, his Wife & heirs a new 99 year patent to Alderney, in much the same wording

Remains of the original 1660s quay, photographed at half tide in 1999.

as that to de Carteret, at £13 6s 8d a year rent, payable from the dues of the island, which also recorded the particulars of the sale by Dame Elizabeth. This patent also contained the extra conditions that Andros should build a house and make other improvements, and that at any time the King or his successors could annul the patent and take over the house, making restitution to Andros or his heirs of the sums laid out. Edward le Breton continued to act as Receiver for Andros until 3 March 1684, when he resigned all his rights in favour of Thomas Le Mesurier of Guernsey, who was sworn-in as Andros' Lt Governor on 31 March. Andros bought Ling's 'house, garden, enclosed meadow and furze break' from Ling's heirs, as a residence for the new Lieutenant Governor. On 1 September 1696 Mr Charles le Marchant replaced him, but on 21 July 1703, Thomas Le Mesurier, was again sworn in as Lt Governor of Alderney.

This started the period of domination of Alderney by the Le Mesuriers, and starts another chapter in the island's history.

Les murs en bas (The Nunnery) in 1930 Longis Bay on right, Longis pond towards the top, Fort Albert above.

4

George I to 1839

The Rule of the Le Mesuriers

The period of rule of the Le Mesurier family forms a convenient start to a new chapter in the history of Alderney's Ships and Soldiers. Despite the minor legal wrangling and local disputes, things had been remarkably stable for the ordinary islanders. The price of corn, which was fixed each year at the Christmas session of Chief Pleas, was, with one exception, stable from 1670-1749, during which time it had almost doubled in England, although Sir Robert Walpole, principal Minister of the Crown from 1721 to 1742 had succeeded in keeping Britain virtually at peace.

Thomas de la Voute Le Mesurier (1648-1718) married Rachel de Sausmarez in 1680, and their portraits (*below*), were painted about this time by B. Graat of Amsterdam.

Their son Jean de la Voute Le Mesurier was born in 1682. As noted at the end of the previous chapter, Thomas became Lt Governor of Alderney in 1684. Rachel died in 1685. It is recorded in the previous chapter, from records in Guernsey, that Thomas was replaced by Charles le Marchant from 1 September 1696 to 21 July 1703, but we find an entry in the Alderney Parish Registers that Thomas Le Mesurier described as 'Lt Governor etc.' of Alderney, was godparent to Pierre Baudoin, son of Richard Baudoin, Sgnr. des Coursieres and Dem. Abigail Gauvain, on Thursday 20 January 1697. His son Jean [hereafter referred to for convenience as 'John (I)'] married Anne Andros in 1704, their first-born, Thomas died in 1710 at the age of two, and the two sisters who followed both died in infancy, the next son was Henry (1711-1779) followed by three more girls, and then John (II) (1717-1793).

The various minor international incidents between Britain and Europe had not greatly affected the island. Despite this, and although the English and French had been allies for much of the time, Dupont's *Histoire du Cotentin et ses Îles* published in 1870 records that, in a report from the Chief Engineer of the Norman Coasts to the French Naval Minister Maurepas in 1731, he stated:

> During the last War the islanders, cruising in these latitudes of their own account, have taken or destroyed more than 3,500 vessels. It is then a great mistake to regard these islands as of little importance.

He was presumably referring to The War of the Spanish Succession, a minor affair between 1718-1720, with a further skirmish over Gibraltar in 1727. This huge figure

Above left: Thomas de la Voute Le Mesurier, 1648-1718.

Above right: Rachel de Sausmarez, married to Thomas in 1680.

appears to refer to all of the Channel Islands collectively, although J. P. Warren in his 1928 paper *Alderney and Destiny* published in the *Transactions* attributes it to Alderney alone and goes on to say that the report gave details of the roadsteads, harbours and forts in Alderney. Rolleston in the 1923 *Transactions* also records that the same writer had noted that this figure was on the islander's own admission, and that

> ...in 1704 Alderney was only a rock on which some inhabitants lived like savages, having neither harbour nor roads. Things were now changed and a large number of workmen were employed on constructing jetties and a port.

Even so, it is a scarcely credible number. The later figures given there for the Le Mesuriers' activities in the late 1770s, show that what was probably the best armed vessel ever kept in the island of Alderney, *Resolution*, took 100 prizes in a year, and even that figure is open to doubt from available contemporary records.

On 28 April 1695, Charles II had granted another patent to Sir Edmond Andros. This confirmed the patent above, and goes on to state that

> ...in consideration of the said surrender as of the charges which the said Sir Edmund Andros intends to expend in building a farme and making other improvements upon the premises for our service ... for and during and unto the full end and terme of (Sic)

ninty nine years from thenceforth ensuing fully to be complete ... provided that wee
our Heires or Successors may at any tyme by writing under our or theire great or
privy Seale, make voyd this Lease and reassume the premises into our owne hands
upon payment ... of such sums of money as they have already disbursed or laid out....

When Andros died in 1713, in his will, he left Alderney to his nephew George Andros.
Both Queen Anne and George Andros died in 1714, George having previously appointed
his brother-in-law, John (I) Le Mesurier to be his Lt Governor and Commanding Officer
of the Militia, leaving the island to his two young daughters, Martha and Ann. Martha
also died shortly after, and in February 1717 King George I, acknowledged Ann Andros
as the holder of the patent. Her uncle continued to act as Lt Governor until Ann also
died in 1721, at which time his own wife (another Ann Andros) became the patent
holder, and thus he, by right of marriage, the Lt Governor and Commanding Officer.
John (I) died the following year 1722, when Ann became possessed of the grant in her
own right.

The possession of the Patent by the two young girls was opposed by Lawrence Payne,
Headmaster of Elizabeth College in Guernsey, and Thomas le Cocq, Judge in Alderney,
in a petition to the King dated 30 April 1715, asking him to grant them the Patent. On
2 February 1717 this request was rejected, but in examining Andros' patent, the Privy
Council decided that he had not fulfilled its conditions in building a house, etc. After

Sir Edmund Andros.

HM Procuror-General had made enquiries into the matter it was decreed that certain property, viz. a house, garden, field and furze break which had been built and occupied by Captain Ling, (now the *Island Hall*), and which had been bought by Andros from his heirs in 1693, should be transferred to His Majesty for the use of whoever might hold the Patent. The transfer, to the King's Procureur in Guernsey, was carried out by Ann Andros in 1721, and the property was annexed to the crown possessions in Alderney, with Ann or her heirs to continue in possession until the expiration of the 99 year lease. She continued to hold the lease until her death in 1729, meantime appointing Peter Le Mesurier as her Lieutenant on 21 January 1723, when he was sworn in at the Court, as her son was still a minor. This was almost certainly her cousin by marriage Peter (1699-1728), son of Thomas Le Mesurier's brother Pierre.

Thomas le Cocq continued his claims, and on 26 March 1726, usurped her rights, having obtained a commission from the Governor of Guernsey as his Lt in Alderney. He had himself sworn-in, in his own court on that date. Judge J. A. le Cocq's MS. states that this commission was given by the Honourable Giles Spicer, Lt Governor of Guernsey, but he is recorded as having been Lt Governor from 1711 to 1715. This same information, with a statement in French of the terms recorded, is given using the authority of what is clearly another manuscript, but whose date and author is not mentioned, loaned to W. Rolleston in 1923 by Nicholas Gaudion, a Jurat of the Alderney Court at that time, and published in the *Transactions* of La Société Guernesiaise of that year.

Ann Andros' reply to this was to have Nicholas Reserson present himself to the Alderney Court on 17 February 1728, to be sworn-in as her Lieutenant, but the court refused to administer the oath. When she died the following year, her son Henry Le Mesurier (1711-1779) by then of age, inherited the *Patent* of Andros, which was registered in the Alderney Court on 6 February 1730, but once again on 20 February 1730, Thomas le Cocq had himself sworn-in as 'Commander-in-Chief' of Alderney, having obtained a commission for this title from Lewis Dollon, Governor of Guernsey from 1726 to 1732.

Le Mesurier started an action against Thomas Le Cocq to restrain him from exercising his commission as Commander-in-Chief, and this action lasted until 21 December 1738, when the King (by then George II), by the advice of the Privy Council, issued the following sentence:

> His Majesty was pleased, with the advice of his Privy Council, to order require and command the said Thomas Le Cocq to forbear exercising any power or authority for the future as Governor or Commander-in-Chief of the said Island, and the said Le Cocq, and all others whom it may concern are to yield due obedience to his Majesty's pleasure hereby signified.

Henry Le Mesurier was thus confirmed in his patent, he married Mary Dobrée in 1740 and on 24 September 1740 presented his brother, John (II), to the Court in Alderney to be sworn as Commander-in-Chief. The Court refused to comply. Up to this time the 'Governors' of Alderney had usually not been resident, but had acted through their appointed Lt Governors and Collectors of Revenues. At this time the people of Alderney were stated to be lawless and to number smugglers and pirates amongst them. Family feuds raged to the great annoyance of their new Governor. Henry, apparently unable to cope with the situation, finally resigned the patent in favour of his more forceful brother John (II) in 1744, and took the Plaisance lands in Guernsey from John in exchange. He died there on 4 May 1779, having produced 13 children. John (II) married Mary's cousin Martha Dobrée about 1748/9, and they eventually had seven children, the eldest of whom was Peter (1750-1803).

On the 2 November 1744 John (II) Le Mesurier appointed John Le Cocq to be his Lieutenant, and Deputy Governor in the island. At that time the Court of Alderney had no official seal, since the island had come under the jurisdiction of Guernsey when the Bailiwick seals were granted in 1279. The Court therefore petitioned the King to grant them one, and a Seal of Authority was granted to the Island of Alderney on 23 May 1745, in the following terms:

> The Lords of the Privy Council of His Majesty by their Order-in-Council of this day, Authorise the Court of Alderney to possess a Seal to Certify All and Sundry Writings which may be presented to Them, and to Apply Their Seal thereto, Which Order emanates from the Act provided by the Court of the said Island of Alderney.

At this period, many Guernsey families had adopted coats of arms with the help of a Guernseyman, Matthew Perchard, who had settled in London, and set up as a goldsmith. He lived in Abchurch Street in the City, and had found, living in the White Hart in the same street, an Irishman, Patrick Wood, who specialised in the supply of coats of arms.

Wood's method was simple. Whenever a Channel Islands family asked for a design for their arms, he would consult a book on English Heraldry and pick a coat of arms having some apparent correspondence in name with theirs. When he was asked to produce a coat of arms for Alderney, he had a stroke of luck. He found that the name of a Warwickshire family 'Arderne' had, through a copying error, been spelt 'Alderne' in the late sixteenth century records of the College of Arms known as 'Garter's Ordinaries'. Their device was 'Vert, (green) a lion, crowned gules (red)', so Wood chose this noble beast for Alderney, and the seal, about 1¼ inches across, incorporating the new device surrounded by the words 'Sigillum Curiae Insulae Origny 1745' (Seal of the Court of the Island of Alderney 1745), was duly adopted by the Island Court. (See colour section plates)

Another document recorded at the National Archives in a report of a meeting of the 'Honourable the Lords of the Committee of Council for the Affairs of Guernsey and Jersey', stated that

> ...on the 16th of this instant, in the words following.- Viz;
>
> Messrs. Here the Committee Report for Allowing the Court of Justice in Alderney leave to use a Publick Seal to be inserted at length in Vide Entered Page 88
>
> Their Excellencies the Lord Justices this day took the said Report into Consideration and were pleased with the Advice of His Majesty's Privy Council to Approve thereof and accordingly to Order that the said Court be and they are hereby Authorised and

permitted to make use of a Common and Public Seal as the Seal of the said Court
under which they may pass Certify and Authenticate the Acts and proceedings of the
said Court.

This document has an impression of the 1745 seal alongside in the left margin, with the
reverse of the seal below it. This shows a depiction of the rock and three towers of the
Casquets Lighthouses surrounded by the words 'Pro Securitate Navigantium', (For the
safety of seamen). The lion does not hold anything in its right paw. (See colour section
plates).

This has not appeared on any other document I have ever seen. At an unknown
later date, the seal was apparently replaced. That in use on a document of the Alderney
Court, dated 16 March 1793, registering the appointment of Peter Le Mesurier as
Governor of Alderney, has a slightly different crown, and the sprig, (which has been
variously interpreted as a sprig of laurel, a bunch of broom [after the planta genista of
the Plantagenet Kings], or a bunch of holly), has been inserted in the lion's right paw,
(*above right*), perhaps as the Guernsey Seal contained a decoration, in the escutcheon,
to show the association with Guernsey

The Alderney seal in this form was used on all official documents for nearly 200
years, but seems to have vanished from about the time of the evacuation in 1940. A
few wax impressions still exist on old documents in the Public Record Office, and in
the Priaulx Library in Guernsey. After the war a rubber stamp was used instead. In
1989 the States had a new embossed impression type seal made, similar in pattern
to the original, and bearing the words 'Sigillum Insulae Origny', (Seal of the Island of
Alderney) round its circumference. (Again see colour section plates).

Research by the Clerk of the States and Portcullis Pursuivant, following a note in the
Heraldry Gazette, revealed that the College of Arms thought Alderney's arms to be 'of
doubtful provenance', since they were not registered at the College. Steps were taken to
remedy this.

At Government House in Guernsey, Captain David Hodgetts, the Lt Governor's ADC,
unearthed an Order-in-Council of King Edward VII of December 1906, which, at the
time Alderney was granted its own flag, confirmed the arms of the island which are
shown on the flag in the centre of the Cross of St George. By some oversight this had
not been registered at the College of Arms and had simply been filed. If a copy was
ever received in Alderney it would have vanished, with the rest of the islands archives,
during the Second World War.

The Lt Governor petitioned Her Majesty to confirm the approval given by her great
grandfather, the Queen did so, and this time the Lt Governor arranged for the arms to
be properly recorded at the College of Arms. On 20 December 1993, the arms were duly
registered and painted on vellum about 12 x 9 inches.

The Arms, painted on Vellum are now safely in the Island and are officially described
as 'Vert, a lion rampant imperially crowned Or, holding in its dexter paw a sprig of
broom proper'.

The official description at last confirms the sprig in the lion's paw as an heraldic representation of Broom, the *Planta genista* of the Plantagenet Kings. (Again see colour section plates).

What would have been an unique and important incident in Alderney's history failed to take place, owing to the weather causing the absence of the Lieutenant Governor, at the swearing-in of our new President, George Baron, on 12 January 1994. The Lt Governor's speech was read for him by Mr John Winkworth, OBE, and contained reference to the Armorial Bearings of the States of Alderney which had just been registered at the College of Arms. These were to have been presented to the States at that ceremony. Because of his absence the Armorial Bearings arrived in true Alderney fashion, later and unheralded, by post!! Despite the best efforts of the weather, Alderney has its Coat of Arms registered at long last, some 249 years after the seal was first granted. Alderney is the first of the Channel Islands States to have its own Armorial Bearings, as opposed to an Armorial Seal.

In 1747, John (II) Le Mesurier, who continued to have trouble with the inhabitants, whom he described as 'wreckers and pirates by habit and tradition', fled the island 'for fear of his life', and petitioned the Royal Court in Guernsey against Judge le Cocq. His title was confirmed by an order of the Privy Council in 1749, and by the Royal Court in Guernsey on 9 May 1751. They ordered the Court in Alderney to treat him as their Governor, to give him his seat in the Court, and they were not to hold any meeting of the States without his participation. They were further required to assist him in carrying out the laws on Quarantine, and to uphold him as their Governor in all that he had done in the interest of the king and for the good and advantage of the inhabitants.

By this time England had been at war with France since 1748, John Le Mesurier had mounted the Militia and ordered them to go to the Watch house at least twice a week, with John le Cocq his deputy, to 'go frequently if time and opportunity permit'. Despite the proximity to France there was no activity, even after Cherbourg was captured by the British on 7 August 1758. The cannons of Cherbourg and the Bells of the Abbey de Voeu were later carried through London in a triumphal procession. In Alderney, John le Cocq had been replaced as Lieutenant by John Guille on 18 April 1756.

Perhaps to consolidate his position, on 14 December 1763, John Le Mesurier surrendered his 99 year patent, which still had almost 20 years to run, to the new King George III, 'Farmer George', who had come to the throne in 1760. The King was pleased to grant him a new patent for another 99 years at the same rent of 13/- per annum.

On 3 December 1770 Peter Le Mesurier was sworn-in as deputy to his father and Lt Governor of Alderney. Peter married his cousin Mary Le Mesurier of the Plaisance estate in September 1779. The period of rule of the family was for the first time in Alderney's history, that of a permanent, resident Governor, concerned and personally involved with the people of the island, and became a time of considerable prosperity for Alderney.

The Chamberlain family had left little permanent mark on the island, there are no buildings, streets or anything else bearing their name. On the other hand, the Le Mesuriers had a great influence and effect on the life and prosperity of Alderney and have left many permanent reminders of their period as Lt Governors and later as Hereditary Governors. This lasted until 1825, a total family association of some 141 years.

The small tidal harbours at Longis, and Crabby Bay, were not suited to anything but small craft and Henry Le Mesurier revived William Chamberlain's 1608 proposal for a harbour at Braye. He was granted a portion of Common Land in 1735 to construct a Pier and Warehouses, in 1736. A claim by Judge Le Cocq's grandson, that his grandfather actually built the pier is investigated later. The jetty is shown on J.H. Bastide's Map of 1739 as the 'New Peer'. The large warehouse, which now forms the Braye Beach Hotel, is also clearly marked. Various dates up to 1756 have been attributed to the construction of the other warehouses, one of which bears this date over the door. The landward end of the jetty was defended by a battery of three, 12-pounder guns, marked as *Pohegre Petit Crabby*, with two six-pounders on Grosnez Point, and three six-pounders in a battery halfway along Braye Bay. A further battery of three 12-pounders was sited on Roselle Point on the other side of the bay, almost opposite the end of the pier.

The order on 9 May 1751 of the Royal Court in Guernsey ended the confrontation between the Judge and the Governor for a time, and after the issue of the new Charter, he devoted himself to the improvement of the conditions of the people of the island, and the cultivation of the soil.

His peaceful existence however was to be of short duration. The close proximity to France, and the frequent outbreaks of hostilities which occurred from 1748, were a cause for particular concern in Alderney.

The American War of Independence (1775-1783) caused another outbreak of war with France and Spain, who were supporting the rebels, and in 1778 John (II) gave orders to his eldest son Peter, whom he had already appointed as Colonel of the Militia, to repair the Forts and Watch Houses because of his fears of a French invasion. The island's defences were once again in poor order, and on a petition to the Crown, John received, '200 stand of arms'.

The Commandant of Cherbourg, General Dumouriez put forward proposals to his government to land 400 men on Alderney to 'carry off the inhabitants, destroy the houses, and deprive the corsairs of this recourse', because as he said, the Channel Islands exercised a 'corsairage terrible' whenever there was a war, which cost France 40 million livres and 2-3,000 sailors. This complaint appears to have been well founded, since in 1779, *Resolution, (see colour section)* belonging jointly to Henry & John, mounting 20 guns, and with a crew of 100, captured prizes worth £134,589. After his brother's death in 1779, by 1782 John had eight privateers, carrying from four to 20 guns, and in that year, prize money of £212,381. *Atalanta*, a 14 gun sloop, the plans of which can be seen in the Alderney Museum, was built in the Naval Dockyard at Sheerness for the Le Mesuriers, and launched on 12 August 1775.

Dumouriez' plan was put into action in the summer of 1780 or 1781 and according to Judge Le Cocq's 1901 MS,

...a force of three French Privateers, two brigs and a large cutter, were despatched at night under the command of Lieutenant Gauvain of the French Navy. They anchored within musket shot of the Guardhouse at Château à L'Étoc, and were attempting to land in Corblets Bay. At about 2 a.m. in bright moonlight, they were seen by the 4-

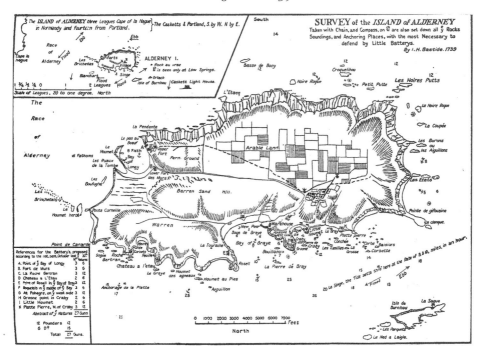

Map of Alderney by I. H. Bastide dated 1739. (North is at the bottom).

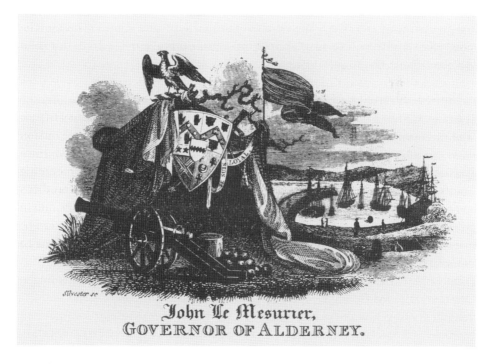

Bookplate of Governor John (II) Le Mesurier. Note that the recently built 'New Peer' is figured in Braye Bay, and the Le Mesurier coat of arms is above the cannon.

man Militia guard, John Ozard, Peter Gaudion, William Harris, and one other, who immediately opened fire on them. Their shots were so well directed as to kill or wound several of the Frenchmen on board the Privateers. There was at that time in the Alderney Roads a large English Privateer, mounting 18 guns, commanded by Capt. Chandler who, upon hearing the report of musketry, instantly beat to arms. In the stillness of the morning and the prevailing calm, the alarm was heard on board the French vessels, and, supposing that the whole Militia were under arms, as soon as daylight appeared, the privateers weighed anchor, and directed their course toward Cherbourg. In the meantime, Capt. Chandler got under sail and pursued them. Having come up with the enemy, he gave them several broadsides, probably at a respectable distance for they succeeded in reaching their port of destination, and Chandler directed his course toward Jersey. Thus by the courage of four men, the enemy was prevented from landing, and ultimately forced to retire without effecting their purpose.

Also in 1780 severe measures were taken against

> ...certain evil and ne'er-do-well men who climbed on the Forts and bulwarks and destroyed them and also threw the cannon balls which were placed there over the side. Such are to be fined 50 livres or sent to Guernsey.

Col. Peter Le Mesurier's efforts to train the Militia which he undertook personally, had been effective and produced a highly motivated force second to none in the islands, and the next year, 1781, The States required the men to provide a redcoat uniform for themselves. The States Regulation made for this purpose with regard to '*Un Habit Uniforme*', required

> ...every man capable of bearing arms to provide a suitable red coat with a collar, facings and lapels, a white waistcoat, a hat with a white band and a cockade, and a pair of long linen culottes (called in English *Trouzers*).

The Governor would provide the uniform for poor people.

Both the Governor and his son had to be absent from the island at various times, and because of these absences, Nicholas Robilliard was sworn-in as Commander of the Militia, on 30 October 1790 and again on 21 January 1793. In this year, so serious was the war situation becoming, that the States of Alderney adopted the English Mutiny Act, after a garrison of about 200 English troops had been sent to the island.

On 12 March 1793, Governor John (II) died, and his son Peter was sworn-in as Governor on 16 March. It was also agreed that the Governor should have control of the Military forces on the island except when there was a regular officer, of the rank of Brigadier-General or higher, in command of the garrison. The Militia at this time presented a loyal address to their Governor and Commander, the opening of which may be translated as follows:

Some badges of the Alderney Militia.

There are Several among us who remember the state of annihilation of the Militia before you took over the command, without uniforms, without arms, without discipline. Now, thanks to the care of our late venerable Governor and yourself, we find ourselves up to the standard of the Militia of the neighbouring islands.

We know full well the need for discipline, not to make the manner of observing it too strict, and we flatter ourselves that by your example we have happily acquired the ability of obeying and loving....

Up to that time, the defence of the island had owed a lot to the vigilance of the women of Alderney. There were beacon towers and watch-houses in various parts of the island and the women watched at these whilst the men went about their work. The beacons consisted of tar barrels on a mound, heaped with dried bracken and furze, and when an alarm was given they were to be fired-up as a signal to the other islands.

To quote Judge le Cocq again;

The dress of the Alderney women was peculiar, consisting of a scarlet cloth petticoat and jacket, a large ruff round their necks fastened under the chin by a black ribbon or a gold hook, and a round linen cap stiffened so much as to be taken-off and put-on like a man's hat. It is reported that on one occasion, when the Island was menaced by a French Man-of-war, the Governor ordered-out all the women in their scarlet dresses, and disposing them skilfully upon the heights, effectually deceived the enemy with the appearance of their forces.

The Napoleonic Period

By the end of the eighteenth century there were other batteries erected and manned at Roque Tourgis, Fort Platte Saline, the Houmet Battery, York Hill, Corblets Bay, (Stoney Hill & King's Batteries), Mannez Battery, Canard (Quesnard) Battery, the Kent, Clarence, Prince of Wales and Frying Pan batteries at Longis Bay. Essex Castle and The Nunnery also protected Longis Bay, and were strengthened in 1793, when the present covered gateway into The Nunnery was made to improve the access. The present house was built inside and the fallen eastern wall which is still lying on the beach, was probably rebuilt then. This old fort of *Les Murs en Bas*, received its present name as a nickname then, probably because the soldiers were forced to live like nuns, away from the town and the women. The *Pepperpot* on the walls of the Castle above, was added about 1810-12, presumably as a lookout post.

1794 was a potentially dangerous year for the islands. The Committee of Public Safety in France, whose members included Barère, Carnot and Robespierre, formulated a comprehensive 12-point plan to take over the Channel Islands. An army of 20,000 infantrymen, supported by 2-300 cavalry and 200 artillerymen, all under the command of General Rosignol, was assembled at St Malo, for a simultaneous attack on all of the islands to be carried out between 19 and 28 February.

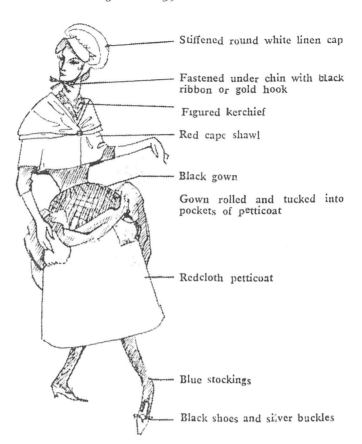

Stiffened round white linen cap

Fastened under chin with black ribbon or gold hook

Figured kerchief

Red cape shawl

Black gown

Gown rolled and tucked into pockets of petticoat

Redcloth petticoat

Blue stockings

Black shoes and silver buckles

Dress of Alderney women in the early 1800s. Sketch by Louisa Lane Clarke, 1851.

The force was to be transported in 20 ships which Admiral Cornic was ordered to assemble, and bring to St Malo for the operation. The plan was for them to all sail on the same night and attack the islands the following morning. The main force to be divided and attack Jersey and Guernsey, whilst a frigate, a gunboat and a corvette with a force of 100-150 men proceeded to Alderney to take possession of the island. On 19 February, Rosignol reported to the Minister of War that he would be ready to sail on the 22 or 23 February provided the naval section was ready to transport them, a subject on which he expressed some doubts. His doubts were apparently justified for the projected invasion never took place.

From 1792-4 there was considerable privateering and naval activity round the islands, details of which are recorded in Chapter 6. At the same time garrisons were sent, reinforced, exchanged between the islands, and withdrawn with an almost bewildering frequency. It may fairly be assumed, that following custom which was well established, two or three companies of each unit would have been stationed in Alderney, to man these batteries and the fort, whilst the main unit was in Guernsey.

The correspondence between the Le Mesuriers and the Crown, set out in this chapter and the diary of Elisha Dobrée, also referred to in Chapter 15, note most of these movements between them, and have helped in constructing the list below.

During 1794, Guernsey became a large prison camp for French prisoners-of-war, captured both in France, and from the Americas. A number of units of the Royalist French troops, and many of the emigrating aristocracy also waited for a time in Guernsey, en route for England in transports provided by the British Government.

In July 1794 John Waugh, Le Mesurier's Captain and Deputy Governor in Alderney wrote to the Secretary of War, Henry Dundas, on the 23rd, noting that the lugger *Cockchafer* had been sent to Alderney by Sir James de Sausmarez to keep in communication with the English frigates there, and report the movements of many French warships to and from Cherbourg. He recommended that the fleet should move up from Guernsey or they will miss intercepting the enemy, now numbering about 120 sail. Peter Le Mesurier, writing to Dundas from Bath at the end of August asks him to send more troops to Alderney and that barracks could easily be found for them. Waugh's assessment of the situation was that, if the French did attack it would be at Longy Harbour, Corblets, Braye or the Alarm post at La Touraille (the present site of Fort Albert). Le Mesurier returned to the island in the middle of November, recovered from his wounds, and French activity continued round the island, two squadrons totalling 62 sail passing up The Race towards Cherbourg on 4 December 1794, and on 30 and 31 January 1795 two fleets were seen to sail back again down past Sark and Jersey. He was writing to the Duke of York in June 1795 about the activities of the British squadrons, and on 7 July,

> A French boat bolted into Alderney to inform us that Sir Sidney Smith had weathered La Hague. The French fleet in the last gale went from the Road into the Harbour and 14 were lost on the coast.

In 1795 the British Government sent a further detachment-of-the-line known as *Invalids* (a term used to describe soldiers 'disabled from active service' in 1794), to act under the Governor's orders, and shortly after, the salvaged guns of the frigate *Amethyst*, 'wrecked in The Swinge on Les Grunds rocks', on 5 January 1796, were mounted as a battery. In reporting the wreck, Le Mesurier stated that he hoped to save most of the stores. By this time there was telegraph communication between Guernsey, Alderney and Jersey, via a station on Sark, established by the Prince de Bouillon. Whilst the Governor was supervising the installation of one of the Guns, it fell on him, breaking his thigh, and his leg in two places, and fracturing several ribs.[1] During this period a French Frigate came close in and the guns were fired.

By a lucky chance, its Commander was killed in the first salvo, and in the subsequent confusion, a sortie of Alderney boats was made, including the Governor's privateer, which had little difficulty in capturing the prize.

On 24 October 1797 Le Mesurier wrote to Col Brownrigg at the Horse Guards. 'The five Companies of Invalids, *[nominally 500 men]* are not enough for the defence of Alderney. Remember Jersey in 1781!'. He requested permission to raise a corps of

'Fencibles' on his own, or on the Goverment's account; 'as the Invalids are no good for repelling a sudden night attack ... the Hereditary Government of the Island of Alderney has been held by my ancestors under the Crown of England for near a century and a half and it is the dearest wish of my heart to transmit it to my descendants in the same pure and loyal state in which I have received it'.

His request for permission to raise the Fencibles was refused. A French Privateer had been captured under the guns of the Batteries by troops of the garrison, on Christmas Day 1797. There was much evidence of other French privateer activity, and in April 1798 he reported that the French at Granville were getting ready to attack Alderney and his force was still inadequate.

It was more than a year before he was recovered from this injury and in fact he never made a full and complete recovery. He eventually died in 1803, probably as a result of the injury.

Further reinforcements arrived, sufficient troops then being present to justify the presence of a Brigadier. There were troubles in 1797-8 with absentees from Militia service, which resulted in fines of £100 tournois or corporal punishment being authorised, and a long-running feud which developed between the Governor and the Brigadier-General, Charles W. Este, who was sent to the island in 1799 caused more problems.

In 1797, the British Government, still concerned about the activities of Napoleon, across the Channel, had divided the coastline of Britain into 12 districts for defence, of which Guernsey, Sark and Alderney formed one, and pushed forward the construction of defence works all round. This threat apparently subsided in 1798 when he turned his attention to Egypt and the Levant, but returned in 1801 when an invasion force was again concentrated along the Channel coasts.

On 4 December 1798, The Governor appointed his eldest son John (III), (1781?-1843) then a Major in the 89th Regiment of Foot, (later to become the Royal Irish Fusiliers) and recently returned from Egypt, as his Lt Governor, and he was duly sworn-in in the Court on the 8th.

The defence activity in the Bailiwick received a new impetus under the command of the Lt Governor of Guernsey, Sir John Doyle. The Peace of Amiens in May 1802, bought Napoleon some time in which to pursue his other ambitions and activities, but the British, once more fearing invasion, declared war on France again in May 1803.

Peter Le Mesurier died on 9 January 1803, (See picture in colour section) and John (III) Le Mesurier was sworn-in on the 21st, as what was to prove to be the last Hereditary Governor. He appointed Lt Col. James Fahy as his deputy. In October Sir John Doyle, who had already, somewhat belatedly, sent one company of Royal Engineers, to comply with orders from the Duke of York to reinforce Alderney, wrote:

Since which the appearance of some French boats near Cape La Hague has excited fresh alarms among the inhabitants, and they sent me an address of their States, praying further assistance.

I have accordingly y'day sent another complete company of the same Corps, which I could ill spare, but I consider that the loss of Alderney, however insignificant in itself, would be highly injurious to the common cause at the moment, by encouraging the enemy and depressing our own people.... The men of the 2 coys. are for the most part well instructed in the exercise of the Great Guns, which must be their principal mode of defence.

The same year on 19 November, ships under Captain Dunbar were passing Alderney and saw the Garrison at their Alarm posts. Col. Fahy sent a boat out to tell him that there was a French flotilla of 30 vessels in sight. Dunbar gave chase and, according to Fahy's report, captured three of them and drove the remainder onto the rocks where they were pounded with a continuous cannode from *Paulette*, within musket shot for three-and-a-half hours, by which time the wind was very high and increasing to a gale so there was little chance of their escaping.

At that time Doyle ordered the destruction of all roads and avenues around the island perimeter, and in particular one near *L'Atterage de Hernaine* which was the principal causeway for the islanders to gather vraic from the beach in Hannaine Bay. Fort Doyle was also built on the site of the Houmet Battery as part of this strengthening of the defences.

The large garrison of over 500 men present on Alderney at this period brought the inevitable amount of sickness and death amongst the troops. To provide a suitable place to bury them the *Stranger's Cemetery*, more properly known as *La Cimitière de Ste. Michel*, at the junction of Longis Road and Valongis, was dedicated on 7 March 1802. Judge le Cocq's MS once again furnishes the details:

After many complaints on the part of the Minister Mons. Solier to the Commandant of the Garrison C. W. Este Esq. that there were not enough spaces in the Town Cemetery to bury the Soldiers of the Garrison who died in the island, the States being assembled for that reason on 1 March 1802 authorised the Officers of the King and the Douzaine to mark out a piece of ground at St Michel, for that purpose, and when this should have been done, the said ground would be consecrated on Sunday afternoon by the said M. Solier to serve for the interment of the soldiers and strangers who die in this island.

There follows the order of service, the psalms and prayers used, and the Prayer for the Consecration of the Cemetery.

Watchtowers or Guardhouses were erected on Essex Hill, Platte Côtil, La Touraille, The Butes, and Les Rochers, where the magazines were situated. The barracks on the cliffs above Clonque, The Giffoine, Corblets and Longis had all been erected about 1782-92.

The total armaments of all these batteries, including those mentioned earlier, amounted to 72 guns and 13 carronades, (a shorter, lighter cannon), when the Peace of Amiens was signed in 1802. With the coming of peace some of the temporary batteries were dismounted.

Telegraphic communication by semaphore, between Jersey, Guernsey, Sark and Alderney had already been established by Vice Admiral Philippe d'Auvergne, the Prince de Bouillon, at some time before 5 January 1796. The station on Alderney was on the edge of the south cliffs about half a mile to the west of the Telegraph Tower, and the base of a wooden mast with the stay rings can still be seen there. These actually date from 1894 when the telegraph was re-erected following several long term failures of the submarine telegraph cable laid in 1863. This emerges from the sea a few score yards away in Telegraph Bay, and can ccasionally be seen after a storm scours the sand away. Prior to this the bay was known as Fouleur Bay.

A plot of Crown land was ceded to the Admiralty and the Tower was erected in 1810-11 with a semaphore mast designed by 'the ingenious Mr Mulgrave' to quote a contemporary paper, to improve the service. Being of course entirely dependent on the weather for visibility, the Telegraph was of somewhat limited use.

Telegraph Tower in 1990.

Peter Archer Mulgrave, (1778-1847), was appointed Inspector of Telegraphs in 1809 at a salary of 15/- a day. He established the position of the telegraph on 'Beacon Heights' on 28 August 1809 and the tower with its semaphore mast was completed in 1811. It had three floors with accommodation for the operators and one of the two arms had a cross piece. Its line of signal was to the station built on Sark and thence to either Jersey or Guernsey as needed. During its construction proceedings were taken in the Alderney Court, against a farmer who obstructed the contractor's access, by digging a ditch. The Channel Island Stations were discontinued on 11 May 1814, but resumed again on 12 April 1815. They were suspended permanently on 13 July 1815 and the Tower was let to a tenant. The date of the first lease is not known, but an inventory exists from when it was let in 1821.

A *Plan of the Fortified Coast of Alderney*, about 10ft. long, drawn by John Mackelcan and dated 11 January 1802, gives full details of the batteries existing at the time, and by its large scale shows clearly the shape of each battery and the position, size and number of its guns. As well as showing two or three small unnamed emplacements in the middle parts of the island and on Clonque and the west coast, he notes the following;

Rocque Turgy two nine-pdrs; Saline Battery dismantled by General Este; Houmet Battery (site of Fort Doyle), two 18-pdrs; York Battery 10 18-pdrs, two six-pdrs, two five-and-a-half-inch Howitzers; Braye Battery (shown as a crab-shaped emplacement roughly on the 'Crusher site'), seven nine-pdrs, two nine-pdr carronades; Rocquere Battery (middle of Braye Bay), dismantled by General Este; Rozelle Battery four 18-pdrs, one 32-pdr; Grosnez Battery (site of Château à L'Étoc), three 18-pdrs; Stoney Hill Battery (above present Corblets Quarry), two 18-pdrs, two nine-pdr carronades; a battery (which would have been on the site of the quarry), marked removed by General Este; Corblets Barracks was marked with a house for four officers and barracks for 100 men, with just in front of it King's Battery, Corblets Lines, with four 20-pdrs, two 20-pdrs, and one nine-pdr carronade; a battery on the site of Fort Corblets marked 2, 20-pdrs, 1, 18-pdr dismantled; Manez Battery two nine-pdrs, one six-pdr, and nearby, Manez Guardhouse with one six-pdr; Quesnard Battery two nine-pdrs; Longy Battery, on the hillside below Essex Castle, dismantled; Nunnery two 32-pdrs; Longy Lines along the cliff edge, consisting of a six-pdr carronade, one nine-pdr plus the Prince of Wales Battery with one 18-pdr, four 20-pdrs, two nine-pdrs, two 24-pdr carronades, two six-pdrs; behind these lines were the barracks and guardhouse, Clarence Battery with two 10-pdrs, and Kent Battery with two 32-pdrs.

With Napoleon's forces occupying most of Europe and western Russia, Artillery and Foot regiments were sent to the Channel Islands on regular tours of duty, mostly of about 12 month's duration, and Alderney received her share of these forces, often with a detachment of two or three companies of the regiments sent from one or other of the larger islands, usually Guernsey.

This more or less permanent garrisoning of the island created the need for more accommodation, a survey was carried out by Lt G. Cardew RE at the request of the War Office, in 1804, and the plan which he sent to accompany his report showed the situation and strength of the Batteries as they stood in 1797, (probably the plan drawn up by Mackelcan, detailed above).

About the beginning of 1806, Brigadier General J. R. Mackenzie was in command of the troops in Alderney, and part of his correspondence at the time has been preserved. Amongst documents to be found in the Mackenzie Papers, at the British Library; are estimates, dated 21 March 1806, for the erection; *of a Work proposed to be erected upon Touraille Heights in the Island of Alderney*. The cost was to be £4003 13s 0d of which the final item was £70 for the 'Oak Doors to the Tower, Locks and Bolts Complete'. The whole edifice was to take 81,886 cubic feet of masonry, 18,250 cubic feet of brickwork, and 4,560 square feet of granite paving. There were to be three grates in the kitchens, and one in the tower. Windows, ladders, floors etc. were all specified. The estimate was signed 'A. G. Lieut. RSC'. The contractor, Thomas Henry Jnr. undertook to carry out the works to the satisfaction of Lt General Doyle, and if the General

> ...on the part of the Government, Engages to furnish me with the Usual assistance from the troops in the garrison etc., in Consideration of which I undertake to complete the whole for the sum of Four Thousand Pounds sterling.

From this one can assume that he valued the entire labour of the troops in the building of the tower, gun platforms and magazine, at £3 13s 0d! It was apparently never built.

In a letter to his brother Henry dated 12 August, Mackenzie notes that the ships and packets from Weymouth sail on 10th, 20th and 30th of each month, and usually stay here 48 hours. He describes Alderney as:

> From this sterile place I can give you nothing entertaining.... There is but little Society ... but the place is healthy.

This letter bears three interesting postmarks from Guernsey, Alderney and Weymouth, illustrated here. '19' was the identification mark of the Alderney Post Office, see below.

A 'Return of the Construction and Occupation of the Barracks at Alderney'; made by Lt Hayman BSE dated 8 August 1806, gives an idea of the distribution of the troops in the island at that time.

Postal marks from Weymouth, Guernsey and Alderney on a letter written on 12 August, sent by the new steam packet service from Weymouth.

	Subalterns & Officers	Men & NCOs	Hospital patients	Occupied by Off, Men, Pts.	Corps	Rented from Per annum
Town		100		134	5th Btn Royal Veterans	Nicholas Robilliard £91
Crabbé	2	100	1			Gov. Le M. £120
Corblets	4	108	3	115	2nd Btn	Erected on Common Land
Longey	4	108	2	116	3rd Foot	Erected on Common Land}
Nunnery	3	72	3	57		
-ditto-				13	RA	Gov. Le M. £10.
Hospital in Town			13			Gov. Le M. £15
Jeffoine	1	32	1	33	5th Btn	Built on Common Land
Royal Veterans						
Longey Farm			40	27	Both units	Gov. Le M. £80

A 'Return of Ordnance Mounted Round the Coast, on the several Batteries undermentioned'; rendered by 1st Lt Rockrow RA on 21 August shows the siting of each type of gun, in the various batteries, which in total amounted to:

Iron cannons: 25 x 20-pdrs; 26 x 18-pdrs; 17 x 9-pdrs; 1 x 6-pdr.
Carronade:; 3 x 32-pdrs; 4 x 24-pdrs; 6 x 9-pdrs; 4 x 6-pdrs. Brass cannon; 2 x 5½-pdrs; 5 x 6-pdrs.
Total 93 pieces.

A 'Weekly Return of Meat issued to His Majesty's Land Forces in Alderney from September 9th-15th 1806', made by Nicholas Robilliard as agent for the contractor. A total of 3,764¾ lbs was supplied, to feed 471 men of the 2nd/5th Rgt, 74 men of the 44th Rgt, 68 men of Col Fahy's Company, 26 men of the RA detachment. A total of 639 men and an average of about six lbs per man per week. 92 lbs of meat were supplied to the Hospital, which apparently had no patients that week. Separate issues were recorded for the households of the officers. General Mackenzie received 127 lbs., Governor Le Mesurier

97 lbs. 211 lbs went to the officers of the 5th Rgt, and allowances of about 10 lbs each to the single officers. Also noted are 10 lbs to the 'Signal Master', and 2¾ lbs to the Signal Sergeant, suggesting that the telegraph was manned and operating at this time.

Robilliard, as well as being a Major in the Militia, had been acting as a contractor for the Army for some time. He built 'The Brick House', (later known as Val ès Portes, and now Le Val des Portes), around the turn of the century, from the profits of this trade. The carving on the portico offering a permanent reminder of the source of his wealth from privateering. He was also one of the founders of the Alderney Bank.

In 1807 the British Government voted £8,000 for the building of extra barracks and a hospital, for the 800 troops then here and, in 1808 the Alderney Court, somewhat belatedly, registered an act of the Royal Court in Guernsey passed in 1803, by which owners of boats were required to see that their boats are guarded whilst not in use, to prevent the escape of prisoners or deserters. Also in 1808 another similar Naval engagement gladdened the sight of the defenders on Alderney. Another letter from Col. Fahy to Sir John Doyle records:

> Yesterday a pleasant sight for our little garrison. 26 sail of French, principally gun boats, hugging the French shore from the South, bound for Cherbourg – followed by 60 sail, many of them trading vessels. Fortunately one of our Fleets of War came up The Swinge almost within Gunshot of Bray Harbour. Capt. Dunbar being warned immediately made a press of sail and in about one hour commenced firing at the van of the French Flotilla, when he was luckily joined by one of our Briggs, on which the French run in all directions to escape, but not until our vessels had captured 3 and drove many on shore.... The French shore was covered with troops, which fired shot and shell at our vessels

Sir John Doyle reviewed the Alderney defences on a number of occasions during this period, and in 1809 requested permission from the First Secretary to hire an additional 'Scout' for the sea-patrol around Alderney. He also rendered a report on Alderney to the War Minister:

> In addition to the general reasons as to the importance of the Channel Islands, the vicinity of Alderney to the French coast renders it an object of peculiar concern, as a descent might be made from Cherbourg on that island in three hours. in which operation the enemy have a great facility of transportation in the number of stone boats employed at the Coves and which from being flat-bottomed and strong are well calculated for landing troops, and if once possessed by the enemy, it could receive constant supplies and reinforcements from the French coast, add to which that, being masters of Alderney they would have the complete command of the Casket Lights so essential to our Channel Navigation, and so enabled to cut off trade from the other islands to England as well as to injure our Channel trade in general, by means of their privateers which would also give increased facility to an attack upon Guernsey, from which it is no more than seven leagues distant, and in time of peace be detrimental to the Crown from the smuggling that would be carried on from thence for which illicit trade that Island is particularly well adapted.

All these reasons made me feel it a duty to visit the I. at 1st opportunity after it was annexed to my command. I made a minute inspection of the several works, batteries and bays in that I. in which I had the good fortune to have the assistance of Lt Gen. Don, Admiral Sir Edmund Nagle, Brig. Gen. Robertson, Lt Cols. Humfrey and Mackelcan, the C.R.E.s of Jersey and Guernsey.

In these same years, the British government was making strong efforts to suppress piracy, and smuggling or 'fair trading'. The Blockade imposed for this purpose also had the effect of driving up the price of corn, and although once again Alderney fared far better than England, the wheat rentes increased from the steady level of the previous 30 years at 60 sous a bushel to 100 sous in 1808, and it was 1821 before the price fell to 60 sous again. The increase in England was almost four times as great, at the equivalent of 380 sous a bushel.

The Semaphore signal station on top of the new Telegraph Tower, which was built in 1811, by 'the ingenious Mr Mulgrave', near the site of a signal mast erected about 20 years earlier, on the orders of Captain Philippe D'Auvergne, the Prince de Bouillon, a Jersey-born, British Naval officer. This improved naval communications between the islands, but during the remaining period of the Napoleonic Wars, until Napoleon's final defeat in 1815, the Governor was frequently absent from the island, and Judge Le Cocq gives a list of 21 occasions when various persons were sworn, in the Court, as either Military Commander or Lt Governor during his absence. This situation continued after the end of the war, and a further 13 similar occurrences are recorded between 1816 and 1823.

Le Mesurier's attempts to delay the restriction on the *Fair Trade*, and retain both his personal prosperity and the island's, failed. The end of the Napoleonic Wars caused the

£1 note of the Alderney Commercial Bank of about 1820.

withdrawal of most of the garrison, with further losses to the incomes of the islanders, and in the face of these events, the Bank of Alderney, which had issued its own notes, crashed, leaving considerable liabilities for the investors

Doyle thought the estimates of the C.R.E. were extravagant, and that Le Mesurier's old batteries were better than those Brig. Gen. Este had put up some years ago, and that additional towers were wanted to secure Longis.

The Butes Barracks were built in 1813 for the Artillery, and were later turned into a military hospital in 1881.

This same Cardew referred to above, now a General, was the man who gave the approval in 1850 for the purchase of the land on which many of the Victorian Batteries were built, or existing batteries strengthened, including King's, Stoney, Reveland, Manize and Fort Hill, and the principal Powder and Ammunition Store at Longis.

Several 'Mutiny Acts' were passed by the British Parliament during the Napoleonic wars, each of which was duly registered and posted in Alderney, as noted in Le Mesurier's correspondence.

Despite all this activity, between 1793 and the Battle of Waterloo in 1815, no invasion of any of the islands actually took place. Alderney had received notice, registered in the Court, and made public at the Church door, on 3 March 1815, of the Treaty of Ghent, signed on 24 December 1814, which ended the American War, and at the end of the year, a letter from Governor John (III) Le Mesurier dated 18 December 1815, to Field Marshal the Duke of York, Commander-in-Chief of the British forces, congratulated him on the establishment of peace with France by the Treaty of London, but did not neglect at the same time, to promote with the Duke, his personal status as Governor and Commander-in-Chief of Alderney. This personal aggrandisement was likely to have been as a result of the considerable problems he had been having with Brigadier Este and other Military and Revenue officers, set out in Chapter 6.

These problems had obviously become less acute with the recent appointment of Brigadier General John Moore to command of the Alderney garrison. His letters to Under-Secretary of State John Beckett, show a much greater concern for the rights and status of all the local population, than had his predecessor. Moore was succeeded in 1816 by Major Henry Ross-Lewin, who acted as Lt Governor of Alderney for two years, during which time Le Mesurier was absent from the island. He held all the usual sessions of the Alderney States and Court, sitting next to the Judge, in the Governor's place, both with their headgear on, whilst the remainder of the Court were bareheaded. There seem to be no remaining records of any great causes of dissent during his administration.

The Militia in Alderney had largely been responsible for the manning of the coastal defences, with assistance and instruction from a small, regular, Royal Artillery unit, and this was continued, although the Invalid Battalion of the RA was officially disbanded in 1819. In 1824 the Master Gunner responsible for Alderney and Sark was George Anderson, who was assisted by two Invalids in each island. The Master Gunner was responsible for the condition and good order of all Ordnance, ammunition and stores, as well as training. Whilst in Alderney, his HQ was at Essex House, (once the Devereux House Country Hotel, in Barrack Master's Lane at Longis and in 2009-10 demolished and replaced by a large private house). This involvement of a few regular Artillerymen with local units increased throughout the British Isles, reaching a total of about 450 men in 1859.

Increasing discontent amongst the inhabitants, and disputes between the Court and the Governor, and the Military and the Governor, finally led to John Le Mesurier surrendering his patent to the British Government on 13 April 1825 in return for £700 sterling per annum for the remainder of his lease. This surrender is commemorated in a painting by John Linnell, bought at auction by the States of Alderney in June 1981 for £22,000, which now hangs in the Courtroom, (see colour section illustrations).

Regiments in Alderney

Research carried out by former States' member John Winkworth, and further reference to the various local newspapers of the time, has resulted in a nearly complete list of the various regiments which garrisoned Alderney over the 150 years following the Napoleonic period, information being obtained from the archives of the various units concerned, often with a contact in one regiment recommending another, in a different regiment. Information from 1782 to 1815, comes largely from the Le Mesurier and Mackenzie papers noted above.

Numbers in Brackets are the old designations of the Regiments of the Line prior to 1882, these are followed by their later names. Before 1752, the regiments had frequently been known by the name of their commanding officer. Some of the regiments' presence here overlapped, especially at crucial periods in the war and it has not yet been possible to trace all of the Regiments which garrisoned the island, thus leaving small gaps.

Dates		Regiment	
7/1782 – 6/1785	(18th)	Royal Irish Rgt	HQ in Jersey, 1/3rd in Alderney
1787 – 1788	(44th)	Essex Rgt	
		Uncertain	
2/1792	(8th)		
5/1793 – 9/1793	(27th)	Also Capt. Grant's Company of Invalids 9/1793 – 1/1794	
	(78th)	Came from Inverness	
1/1794 –	(80th)		
3/1794	(3rd)		
		Uncertain	
3/1804 – 11/1804	(1st/57th)	1st Btn Middlesex Rgt. The 'Steelbacks' so called because of the great amount of flogging used, and later known as the 'Diehards'. Three Companies in Alderney under Col. Inglis	
12/1804 – 1/1806	(2nd/3rd)	The Buffs (East Kent Rgt)	
1/1806 – 4/1807	(2nd/18th)	Royal Irish Rgt 7/1806 – 11/180 (2nd/5th)	

	Northumberland Fusiliers. CO Lt Col. John McKenzie, whose baby daughter is buried in the Stranger's Cemetery
11/1807 – 7/1810 (2nd/67th)	2nd Btn Hampshire Rgt
8/1809 – 3/1810 (2nd/44th)	1st Btn Essex Rgt
1810	5th Btn 'Royal Veterans still here
2/1810 – 5/1810 (2nd/18th)	2nd Btn Royal Irish Fusiliers
5/1810 - ? (2nd/11th)	Devonshire Rgt
5/1811 -10/1811 (75th)	1st Btn Gordon Highlanders
1811 - ? (2nd/63rd)	1st Btn Manchester Rgt Dates vague, Brighton 1812
3/1812 – 9/1815 (2nd/82nd)	2nd Btn Prince of Wales', S. Lancashire Rgt
1813	First record of 'deaths in the Hospital'
4/1815 – 2/1816 (2nd/15th)	East Yorkshire Rgt
6/1816 – 7/1816 (8th/15th)	Depôt Companies, East Yorks Rgt
1817 – 6/1819 (13th)	Somerset Light Infantry Btn in Guernsey, 1/2 in Alderney
7/1819 – 10/1819 (33rd)	Duke of Wellington's Rgt -ditto-
10/1819 – 3/1820 (79th)	Queen's Own Cameron Highlanders -ditto-
5/1823 – 3/1824 (72nd)	1st Btn Seaforth Highlanders -ditto-

The Barrack-Master in Alderney in 1819 was one William Hanmer, who would almost certainly also have had his HQ at Essex House in Barrackmaster's Lane.

From 1824 to 1852 there were no Regular Army units in the island, although a small detachment was sent from Guernsey in December 1847, after the 'Riots'. By the time of Queen Victoria's visit in 1854 a garrison had been re-established. Other units may have been sent on occasion, and during this period, a plan proposed by the Commanding Royal Engineer in Guernsey, to erect a new fort to house 250 men and 12 guns on Mount Touraille, to replace the Tower, was rejected by the War Office.

Despite this, there is a record dated 23 April 1825, of Thomas Cutmore of the Board of Ordnance, being blown out of the battery at Braye by the explosion of the gun he was loading. On 27 November 1826, the 85th Regiment arrived in Guernsey, but there is no record of a unit being sent to Alderney, and in 1832 Captain O'Hara Baines is recorded in Syvret's *Chroniques* as Town Major and CO of an RA regiment here. He was also acting as agent or deputy for the Lt Governor of Guernsey.

In 1831 the Channel Islands Militias were granted the title *Royal*. About this time the Royal Alderney Militia comprised approximately 150 men, of whom about 100 were Gunners, and the remainder 'Invalids' or foot-soldiers.

Despite the recent defeat of Napoleon, fears were still being expressed of the imminence of further attacks by the French, and in the Public Records Office from this time there are many letters written from the islands to the Secretary for War suggesting measures to counter the threat.

In a memorandum dated August 1832, Governor Ross comments:

My attention was forcibly drawn to the state of the harbour of Braye, (on the waterfront of St Anne's bordered by the Newtown of 1754)[1], the only one in which a decked vessel of the slightest tonnage can now lay with the least degree of safety. The harbour is a very bad and dangerous one, and there is not a single landing place for passengers except an open, loose sandy beach where with the least wind the surf runs so high that it is impossible to get out here until the tide leaves the vessel dry, unless recourse was had to a ladder 20 feet high, always dangerous but of which females and children cannot avail themselves.

In another, dated November 1832, he wrote on the Alderney defences in which he notes that the island is again threatened by Cherbourg and that the annoyance value of the Channel Islands to the French was well shown by the extraordinary success of their Privateers in the late war, but that with the exception of the Guernsey roadsteads, none of the islands affords any safe anchorage to larger vessels at all states of the tide. He suggested that Alderney needed a 'floating harbour', accessible at all tides to be a naval counterpart to Cherbourg, and appended sketches of The Race, Saye and Corblets Bays and Crabby and Saline Bays. He further added that; 'the military defences of the island are trifling', and that; 'its safety has mainly been due to the rocks and swift tides, but that after 17 years of peace, the pilots of Cherbourg are now conversant with the tides and currents, and in the worst weathers and darkest nights boats with illicit cargoes come and go'. He notes that the advent of Steam has increased the vulnerability, and they should not wait until war comes.

On 29 August 1838, a unit of the 8th Regiment arrived in Guernsey from Cork in the

Church and Parsonage 1830. Sketch by Lt Col. William Le Mesurier.

Frigate *Apollo*, again there is no record of part of this force coming to Alderney.

The 1851 census notes Lt Col. William Le Mesurier (62), wife, and two daughters, living at 8, Royal Square, and his occupation as 'Town Major'. Drawings made by him of the island, including a view of the church and parsonage from his window across the square dated 1830, still exist and on her visit to the Breakwater works in 1854, Queen Victoria records in her diary, that she was greeted by the Commandant, Col. Le Mesurier; 'a funny old man with a face like Punch', and that he dined on board the Royal Yacht. I cannot trace this officer with any certainty in the Army Lists for the period, nor his relationship (if any) to the late Governor.

With the decision in the 1840s to erect a Naval Base in each of the Channel Islands, euphemistically referred to as *Harbours of Refuge* in what can only be described as a futile attempt to disguise their true purpose. The Admiralty Breakwater at Braye in Alderney, and a very similar structure, St Catherine's Breakwater in Jersey, were built, but the proposed harbour in Guernsey was never started, and by the time the other two were completed, the need for them had passed.

With the building of the Breakwater in Alderney came the need to defend it from all sides, and a comprehensive and extensive series of Forts and Batteries was erected, almost ringing the island, to accomplish this aim. These are dealt with in Chapter 8.

The island entered a new period of expansion and prosperity when the Harbour of Refuge and the various Victorian Defences were built. The Acts which permitted the start of the project are relevant to begin a new Chapter.

This unsigned drawing of the old parish church and the Parsonage, *c.* 1810, includes the curate's house to the left, (possibly a former Almshouse and later the junior school) and, behind the trees, the (then) recently rebuilt Government House, now the States Offices and 'Island Hall'.

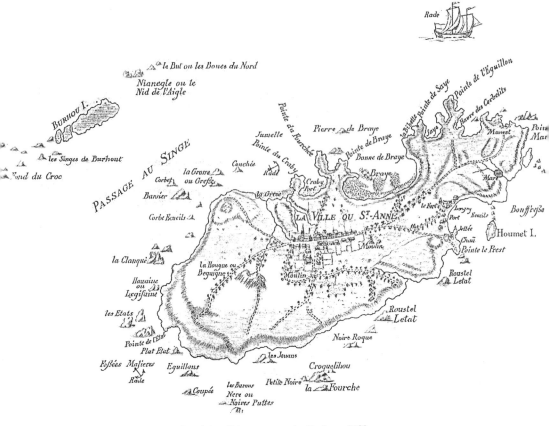

Les Isles d'Auregny et de Burhou. 1757.

Map of Alderney and Burhou by Jean de Beaurain, 1757.

5

1839-1940

With Le Mesurier's surrender of his patent to the Crown, the Governorship of Alderney had once more reverted to the control of the Governor of Guernsey, who appointed his own representative in Alderney, with the day-to-day administration of the island left in the hands of the Judge and States. The garrison had been withdrawn at the end of 1824, and except for a few RA Master-gunners who continued to support the Militia, was not replaced until after the *Alderney Riots*, which occurred at Christmas 1847.

The 1844 Act for setting up the Harbour of Refuge probably had the greatest effect of any law ever passed, on the economy of the island, and the lives of its inhabitants. Several schemes had been put forward of which more detail is given later, where the resulting huge increase in the population for about 25 years whilst the breakwater and forts were being constructed, and subsequently whilst the garrisons were maintained is fully covered.

In September 1846, Queen Victoria appointed two barristers, T. F. Ellis, and T. Bros to carry out an enquiry into the criminal law of the Channel Islands. In a report occupying over 300 folio sheets, they set out amongst many other things, the status of the Court and States of Alderney at that time, and some extracts are worth quoting. By the time the report was issued, the Harbour works were under way. There are some slight discrepancies with what has generally thought to have been the situation, but it seems reasonable to accept that two eminent lawyers would have made a proper investigation of the facts at the time.

> The Court in Alderney consists of a President who is called the Judge, and six jurats, two crown officers, called, as in Guernsey, the Procureur and Contrôle, the Greffier and the Prévôt. 'The judge receives his appointment from your majesty, (at a salary of £150 a year, which is certainly insufficient, now that Alderney, from its naval station and fortifications, has become of so much importance). The six jurats are elected for life by the ratepayers of the island; if from infirmity, they desire to resign, they apply to the States of Alderney, who transmit the application to the Royal Court of Guernsey, which decides upon it. The Procureur, Contrôle, and Greffier, also receive their appointments from the crown. The prévôt, is an officer named by the States of the island; he formerly held office for a year only; but within the last four or five years,

the Alderney Court of Chefs Plaids have passed an ordonnance making the office perpetual. The prévôté consists of twelve persons; these serve for twelve years, if they live so long; but, in case of death, the place is filled up. The twelve hold in rotation, the office of deputy prévôt for one year.

There are also two constables and two deputy constables, chosen by the court. They are annual officers, the two who have been chosen as deputy constables for one year, becoming constables for the year following.

The Procureur has an annual salary of £40. The Contrôle has no salary; and that office at present is not filled up, the Procureur being the only advocate in the island.

The jurisdiction of the court of Alderney, in matters of a criminal nature, is confined to a preliminary investigation into the fact of the crime. It may examine, and, if satisfied that the charge is without foundation, may dismiss the complaint; but it possesses no power of trial or punishment. When an offence is committed in Alderney, the party charged is apprehended by the constable, and brought before the judge, and at least two jurats. The witnesses are examined, and the interogatoire of the prisoner taken by the court. The examinations are then reduced to writing, and, if the court is of the opinion that there is sufficient evidence to put the prisoner on his trial, an act of court is made referring the matter to the Royal Court in Guernsey. This mode of proceeding is provided by an Order-in-Council of the 21st June 1585, which directs that the jurats of Alderney, 'shall refer criminal causes to the Royal Court, as was always the custom.' The prisoner is committed to the custody of the prévôt of Alderney, whose duty it is to convey him to Guernsey.

The court of Alderney also has the power of making local ordonnances, in the nature of police regulations, and for the repair and maintenance of the highways, obedience being enforced by a fine. The ordonnances must be made either at the Court of Chefs Plaids or at a meeting of the States. These are constituted of the same members; but the States meet whenever there is occasion; the Chefs Plaids only twice in the year, on the first Monday after Michaelmas, and the first Monday after the 15th of January. The body consists of the judge, the six jurats, the crown officers, and the Douzaine, which last is a body of twelve, elected by the ratepayers of the island for life, or until they obtain permission, for infirmity, to be discharged. The Governor also has the right of being present; and, when he cannot attend in person, he deputes some one who takes the oaths as lieutenant-governor for the occasion.

The constables in Alderney are mere officers of police, and have no place in the court sitting in Chefs Plaids, nor in the States.

The judge, and at least two jurats and seven douzainiers, with one of the crown officers, must be present to constitute the court, the bailiff, in the case of an equality of numbers, giving a casting vote. The crown officers and the members of the douzaine are, however, both consulted. The course is, upon a measure being proposed, for the judge first to ask the opinion of the crown officers. After they have been heard, the opinion of the douzaine is asked through the president, who is the senior member; after which the jurats decide on the proposition, which thereupon becomes law, and is binding on the inhabitants of Alderney.

An appeal against its enactment lies in the Royal Court in Guernsey, which has power to annul an ordonnance of the court of Alderney. It is however contended, in Alderney, that the Guernsey Court has no power to make an ordonnance binding on the inhabitants of Alderney, and that no one can be summoned before it for the breach of an ordonnance made by the court of Alderney, the jurisdiction of the Guernsey court in such cases being only apellate.

Besides the making of ordonnances, the taxes for the relief of the poor are raised, and the value of the wheat rents for the year are fixed at the court of Chefs Plaids.

It will be noted that the constitution of the Alderney Court was almost identical to that existing at the time of the *Status* in 1236. This continued until 1949. For a map showing the different designs for the harbout see Chapter 7, page 115.

The Forts were constructed between 1847-1861, and the western arm of the breakwater was completed by 1864, with maintenance work continuing until 1871, when the Board of Trade made the final decision to discontinue work on it. In 1872, a House of Lords Committee had the job of deciding whether to knock it down, abandon it, or maintain it. In view of the amount of money, around £1.5 million, by then expended, it was decided to reduce the length by nearly half, and hand the whole thing over to the War Office by the next important piece of legislation, The Alderney Harbour Transfer Act, 1874.

There was great rejoicing and a special parade on Butes of both the garrison and the Alderney Militia, for Queen Victoria's Birthday and Golden Jubilee in 1887.

Some years later, on 4 July 1895, after many years of debate and squabbling over the provision of a commercial jetty, the law covering its construction was finally passed,

Parade of the Army Garrison and the Militia on Butes for Queen Victoria's Golden Jubilee in 1887.

and work commenced in August. As a result, at about the time of her Diamond Jubilee in 1897, Judge J. A. Le Cocq, author of the notes quoted in the previous chapter, who had been against the project, resigned.

The establishment of this jetty actually gave a great boost to both Alderney's tourist and stone trade as well as greatly facilitating normal commercial traffic. Passengers and materials could now be loaded and unloaded directly from dry land and were no longer subject to either lightering or the tide, and passengers no longer needed to scramble down ladders onto the beach or into small boats or be carried ashore at low tide.

The history of the Army in Alderney from the time of the building of the Forts, until the garrison was withdrawn and the Militia disbanded in 1929, is dealt with in Chapter 8.

From 1895 until the start of the Second World War, the island ran quietly along, with little outside interference, from either Guernsey or the UK. It looked after its day-to-day needs, such as the law, the roads, and its very modest budget. Compulsory education was introduced in 1924, the last place in the British mainland and Islands to do so, despite the States having debated and agreed on the subject almost annually since the 1890s. The Mignot Memorial Hospital, was also opened in 1924 in Victoria Street. The principal single employer was its Stone Industry, but there were as many people working in the numerous small shops and pubs and the hotel and tourist business was increasing steadily.

In 1935 and 1936 laws were passed which set up the first Green Belt areas, principally involving the southern and western cliffs, and the lower eastern part of the island. Modified several times since the war they now include most of the coastline, and the former strip-farmed agricultural land. Although the first air services to Alderney were very much connected with the sea, using amphibian aeroplanes, in April 1935 the first Channel Island land-based airport to offer regular commercial passenger flights was established on the Grande Blaye, and another avenue for tourists was opened.

Alderney's Airfield and Air Services

Although not strictly relevant to a work on ships and soldiers a very brief record of this is included here, the earliest planes arriving in Alderney having been Seaplanes. The Guernsey Evening Press for 14 January 1935 announced that Alderney was soon to have an air link with England. This was the culmination of negotiations between Jersey Airways and some 60 Alderney farmers, who between them owned the 150 vergées of land on the Blaye needed for the airport. Much of the credit for the setting up of the airport must go to Jerseyman Harold Benest, who was at that time engaged in building the Blue Horizon, soon to become the Grand Hotel, on the Butes. The first sod was turned by Judge Mellish on 1 April, and construction of the two, 500 yard, grass runways was quickly accomplished. The official licence for the airport was granted on 12 October 1935.

Alderney's first contact with flying machines however went back many years before this, when on 5 October 1919, two Avro 504L seaplanes of the Avro Transport Company

Judge Mellish cutting the 'First Sod' to start the first airport in the Channel Islands, on 1 April 1935.

left Southampton for Jersey. One, registration G-EACC, piloted by Alan Storey reached Jersey safely, the other, G-EAFG, pilot Evans, ran into fog and landed on the sea near Alderney. In attempting to enter Braye harbour, it was wrecked on the Breakwater.

The first plane to actually land *on* Alderney however, did so at Platte Saline on the sloping shingle beach, at a somewhat acute angle, on 4 August 1933, only a few months after Lindberg flew the Atlantic for the first time. The plane was a single-engined Klemm monoplane with an open cockpit, carrying two passengers from Jersey.

On 6 April 1939 an RAF Handley Page *Harrow* made an emergency landing in a field near the airport, and bounced over a hedge onto the airfield. It stayed there until it was repaired in August, and flew off just before the war started.

The islanders obstructed the aerodrome with lorries and barbed wire before departing in 1940, rendering it useless for the larger planes which brought the first German troops, over a week later, but could not land. Apart from their initial landings the next day with two small planes, the Germans do not appear to have used the airfield during the occupation, and ploughed trenches across it to prevent landings, as well as placing other obstructions.

After the War, in 1946, the trenches were filled in, and the airfield was relaid with its three grass runways in the form of a letter 'A', by Army engineer Major Tudor and reopened after the war with the first commercial flight, on 18 June 1946. Since 1968 the principal carrier has been Aurigny Airlines who have run several different types

Cloud of Iona on Braye Beach in 1934.

Cloud of Iona was also one of the first to land at the new airport.

of aircraft, but are now firmly established with three-engined 16-seat Britten-Norman 'Trislanders' which have an enviable safety record, and in 1990 reached a peak, when they carried 116,719 passengers in and out of Alderney alone. Their routes direct from Alderney in 2013 are to Guernsey and Southampton only.

It is now time for this history to return to the sea. Fishing and trading vessels had been the mainstay of many islanders for centuries, but smuggling and privateering became of much greater importance after the suspension of the Bull of Neutrality, and became a principal source of the island's wealth for nearly a century.

The Windhover amphibian, built by Saunders-Roe, could also use both sites. It is pictured here, landed at the airport.

De Havilland biplane of Alderney Airlines.

6

Privateers and Smuggling

The traditional freedom from restriction of movement of Channel Island shipping between Britain and France, even in time of war, granted by the *Bull of Neutrality* of 1481, and the various freedoms and exemptions from English customs dues which were granted from time to time by monarchs from the thirteenth century on, were both exploited during the many wars between France and England, until the Bull was suspended by William III, in 1689, and never reinstated.

A number of instances of this Bull being invoked are still on record.

In 1513, during one of Henry VIII's wars with France, Amiral du Chillon, issued a licence to Guernsey and Alderney vessels to carry on trade with Normandy, and on 20 April, Loys, Amiral de France, Seigneur de Granville, granted the safe conduct already quoted.

The unknown author of *Les Us et Coutûmes de la Mer*, published at Rouen in 1671 states that the effect of the Bull was that

> ...the prize is not good if the prize be made in places of security and refuge, as are the Norman Isles, where the French and English, whatever war there be betwixt the two Crowns, ought not to insult, or in hostile manner pursue each other, so long and so far as they have the said islands in view....

It goes on to cite examples of ships captured in defiance of the bull which were ordered by the crown to be released without ransom.

The prosperity and employment of the islanders gradually went through a number of phases. The earlier association of many islanders with the sea, catching conger and mackerel, drying them at the *éperquérie* belonging to the Crown, and then exporting them to France and England, later gave way to a rise in the knitting industry. This was itself supplanted after the cancellation of the Bull by privateering and smuggling. The latter also gave rise to a busy coopering trade.

During the mediæval period wool and other commodities were often smuggled out of England, whilst later in the sixteenth to eighteenth centuries, during various periods of war, *Letters of Marque* were issued by the Sovereign to many Channel Island ship owners, permitting them to prey on the shipping of countries specified in the letter. There must have been a fairly fine distinction between these privateers, and the corsairs or pirates, for, in 1566, Richard Hitchens was forced into Alderney by ships from Guernsey and captured as a pirate. He was taken to St Martin's Point in Guernsey, and hanged in chains near the Low-water mark. Not long before that, in 1560, the defences of Alderney had been described as 'lacking, and unable to withstand rovers', after Captain Malesarde's short-lived occupation in 1558, already described.

The situation obviously had not improved greatly, some 60 years later, when another period of war with the French started in June 1627. (It has been said that Charles I went to war with France then because they had refused to recognise the neutrality of the Channel Islands).

Two English naval ships of 250 and 200 tons were sent by the Privy Council, to free the seas around the islands of pirates. Shortly afterwards two more were added to the fleet, but when that war finished, two years later, the naval force remained.

The increase in the knitting industry during the second half of the sixteenth century, had resulted from Queen Elizabeth receiving knitted stockings from Guernsey. The allocation of wool quotas to each of the islands to support this industry, at a time when exports of wool to France were expressly forbidden, gave rise to a demand which merchants in Guernsey and Jersey tried to satisfy, and some of the raw wool was illegally re-exported to France. Knitted garments consisted mainly of waistcoats and stockings, some from Jersey and Guernsey went straight to France, where they were much in demand. Virtually all of Alderney's small output however appears to have been sent to England then. The sheep population of the islands had fallen greatly around this period, when large areas of pasture were ploughed up to plant cider orchards, and supplies had to be brought in from England to sustain the industry. Licences for the export of wool to Alderney were first granted in 1619, and by 1660 Alderney had an annual quota of 200 tods (a tod is a bale of wool, 28 lbs in weight) of wool. This had more than doubled by the reign of James II (1685-89). Figures from the port records at Southampton, show that Alderney was sending stockings and waistcoats in some quantity, 530 items in 1680, 260 in 1681, 301 in 1682, and 873 in 1683.

By 1660, import duties of five per cent were imposed on a list of some 1630 articles, coming from overseas, and, by an Act of Parliament that year, Southampton became the only port from which wool might be exported to the islands. Cargoes from other ports had to be registered there before they could travel on to the islands. In February 1714 the Customs Collector of the port of Southampton attempted to impose a duty of 20 per cent on all goods and merchandise from the Channel Islands, as foreign produce, and impounded 40 bales of stockings from Jersey in May 1715, when payment was refused.

This caused the Greffier of Jersey, Jean Dumaresq, to appeal to the Crown on behalf of all the islands, and present a case based on the previous exemptions and charters. He was successful, and an Act of Parliament in 1717 restored to Guernsey, Jersey, Alderney and Sark, their right to export goods and produce from the islands to England, free of taxation, provided a certificate of origin from the Governor accompanied them. This included cyder and perry which had previously been exempted by Charles II in 1676. The stocking trade grew, to become of such importance to the economy, especially in Jersey, that in 1748, 14,022 dozen pairs from Jersey, and 5,529 dozen pairs from Guernsey, passed through Southampton.

The annual wool quotas were then 4,000 tods for Jersey, 2,000 for Guernsey, 400 for Alderney and 100 for Sark. From 1733 to 1773, about six vessels a year arriving from Alderney were recorded in the Port Books at Southampton.

The Nine Years' War from 1689 started another period of privateering, which reached a peak a few years later around 1713, during the Wars of the Spanish Succession. Thomas Le Marchant, a Guernsey merchant with interests in Alderney, with a number of other Guernsey gentlemen, mainly between 1692 and 1708, had a share invested in eight ships operating under Letters of Marque in the first war, and 18 in the second, mostly operating from Guernsey.

Not directly connected with the island, but nevertheless important in its nearby waters is the Battle of La Hougue, from 19-23 May 1692. The exiled James II was promised help in invading England by Louis XIV, and in April that year collected an army of exiles on the Cotentin. The French Admiral Tourlaville put to sea from Brest with 44 ships of the line, and was to be joined by the fleet from Toulon under the Comte d'Estrées. James had expected the English Commander-in-Chief, Admiral Russell to declare for him, but the English government sent troops to the islands under the Earl of Peterborough, and Rear Admiral Carter put into Guernsey with a fleet of 24 ships-of-the-line in April. Local privateers there agreed to act as pilots for this fleet, and the two fleets met between Alderney and the Cotentin peninsula, in fog, at dawn on the 19 May. Admiral Russell, acting under orders from King William, in company with a Dutch fleet of 36 ships under Admiral van Allemande, left Spithead on 18 May. About seven leagues off the Cape gunfire was heard to his west, and two of his ships sighted the enemy. The fog persisted and the action lasted five days, with ships drifting in and out of the mist. Twenty of Tourlaville's ships managed to escape through the hazards of The Race and reached St Malo. Four French privateers sailing with these were apparently intercepted in The Race by Daniel Tupper of Guernsey and the King later ordered a special commemorative medal struck for him and its inclusion in the family coat of arms. This was the most important of some 24 medals struck in connection with the battle.

Fifteen ships of more than 60 guns were beached or burnt close to James and his army, and the last ship of the French fleet was sunk off La Hougue St Vaast on the 23rd. Admiral Russell and his fleet later put into Guernsey roads in bad weather on 3 July, and whilst an Anglo-Dutch squadron went to survey the situation off St Malo, he returned to England with the remainder of the fleet. The event was commemorated by a set of Alderney postage stamps issued some three centuries later, on 18 September 1992.

The Port Books of Swansea and Neath record shipments of coal to Alderney. A total of 42.7 tons in 1712, shipped in 'chauldrons'. These were variable measures, which contained 45 cwts of coal if loaded in Newcastle, but only 27 cwts from London. The ship *Nicholas*, Master Peter Harwell, brought 13½ tons from Swansea on 25 June 1719.

There was a lull in privateering for over 25 years after these wars were over, which revived when war with Spain broke out again in 1739, increased during the War of the

Austrian Succession from 1744-8, and increased greatly when the American colonies rebelled in 1775. During this lull, Henry Le Mesurier reputedly built the 'New Pier' at Braye in 1736, presumably from the profits of the wartime prizes and smuggling.

The Seven Year's War started in 1755, and the English Fleet of 150 sail, under Commodore Howe in HMS *Essex*, anchored overnight off Alderney on 2nd June 1758 on its way to invade St Malo. The ships were carrying the Duke of Marlborough's Army of three Regiments of Guards and 15 Battalions of Infantry, totalling about 13,000 men, with 60 cannon and 50 mortars.

The Letters of Marque, which were elaborately penned on a large sheet of parchment bearing a portrait of the sovereign, were issued to a named Captain and owners, and vessel. Any changes in these particulars required the issue of a new letter, and they also specified the country whose shipping might be attacked. A captain required a separate commission for each country. For this reason the number of letters issued did not equate to the number of ships involved. The Admiralty required two bonds of £1,500 each to be put up as surety that the Captains would abide by the terms of their commissions, and as far as the Channel Islands were concerned, agents in London usually acted for them.

As has already been shown, the old island family of Le Cocq, headed by the Judge tried to prevent the establishment of the Le Mesuriers as Governors. They were also their rivals in privateering and smuggling. A Letter of Marque was issued in October 1744 to Thomas Le Cocq, Jnr. with Matthew Mauger and George Titoe of Poole, to operate the 45-ton *Bell*, Master, Peter Le Cocq, which mounted four carriage and six swivel guns and a carried crew of 45. On 15 January 1745 they took a 50-ton Frenchman, J. Le Coeur, Master, who abandoned his ship with his crew about two miles off the Cap de la Hague on the approach of the *Bell*. The prize was taken into Alderney by Peter Le Marinel, where Thomas, Peter and John Le Cocq acted as self-appointed local Commissioners for Prizes. The condemning was confirmed in London, as was another prize taken, and they received about £50, of which the crew were entitled to one-third. In September, *Bell* was granted another Letter under Captain Daniel du Frocq, but was not so successful and was eventually captured by the French on 14 May 1747, the crew at that time being mainly Jerseymen, with Philip Mauger of St Helier listed as the owner, although no new Letter had been issued as should have happened if the Le Cocqs had sold the vessel.

On 15 August 1746, *Hazard*, a four-tonner with six swivel guns and a crew of 20, Master, Amice Ollivier, which had been commissioned for John Le Mesurier, took a 15-ton French vessel *St Jean*, of Caen, in the Race. She was in ballast, travelling with other French merchantmen, and was sent in to Braye with a prize crew. Ollivier landed four of the French prisoners at Lulworth Cove a few days later, and they were sent to Weymouth. On his way back to Alderney he took a French fishing vessel *St Thomas*, with eight tons of oysters. He brought this craft and its crew into Alderney, and later applied to the Commissioners for Prizes to have his prizes registered, and the prisoners sent to London. The Le Cocqs refused to do this on the grounds that he had not registered the capture immediately, and later took the prisoners by force from his house. Ollivier thereupon went to Guernsey where he appealed to the official Commissioner, Peter Dobrée. His claim was substantiated by a member of the French crew and the Governor, and the two prizes were ordered to be condemned lawfully. Their value was about £40.

The following year Le Mesurier had 16-ton *Fly*, Peter Ollivier, Master, captured by the French off Quiberon, after she had been cruising for a couple of months. The French rated her at 10 tons, two years old, length 28 feet beam 10 feet three inches with a crew of 17, and she fetched 500 livres trs. somewhat less than £50. Sixteen-ton *Hawke* was granted Letters of Marque for Le Mesurier in March 1748, and took one prize.

From the 1760s several Beer and Seaton merchants were in partnership in various smuggling enterprises with Alderney owners, and in the 1770s several Alderney merchants were running contraband to Weymouth. An account for £14 5s 0d for goods supplied by Peter Le Cocq and received by W Matthew dated 24 April 1776 still exists. It list the goods as eight casks of Brandy @ 16/6d each, seven casks of Rum @ 15/6d, a flagon of brandy and one of rum @ 11/- and 24 lbs of tea.

During the period from August 1777 to May 1778, 35 Letters of Marque were issued to Channel Island vessels, one of them based in Alderney. By the end of 1778 there were 78 letters in existence against French and American vessels, 10 of which had been granted to Alderney craft. From January to November 1781 15 more were issued, four of them to Alderney vessels.

Alderney privateers were of some importance during this American War of Independence, and of the 715 letters issued to Channel Island craft from 1777-83, 26 were granted to Alderney vessels. Prominent in this trade were the Governor, John Le Mesurie and his sons, Nicholas Robilliard and his brothers, and Edward Anley and his family. The Robilliards were also the principal owners in the *Hope*, of Bridport in 1778, six more ships working out of Weymouth, and the *Endeavour* of Lyme Regis in 1781, at which last date England was at war with America, France, Spain, Holland, and the Republic of Batavia, simultaneously.

As already noted, on 12 August 1775, the 300-ton 14-gun Sloop *Atalanta* built for John Le Mesurier was launched at the Royal Shipyards at Sheerness.

Peter de Havilland, a member of an important Guernsey family with large shipping interests, is recorded as a principal owner of the 40-ton six-gun *Wren* of Alderney, commanded by John Mahy, in 1778.

Another member of an important Guernsey shipping family, Elisha Dobrée, kept a diary of the comings and goings of ships at the harbour, and other important personages at his family's house, *Beauregard*, from 1 January 1777, (he had his 21st birthday on 11 October 1777), until 9 December 1844, the day before he died. This may be found in the Priaulx Library, and has a number of entries concerning Alderney ships and the Le Mesuriers at the time. He notes that Governor Henry Le Mesurier dined at his family's home on 14 March and 23 November 1778, 30 July 1779, and 9 October 1781, and other Le Mesurier Governors on several subsequent occasions. He records the arrival at St Peter Port of a number of Alderney vessels with prizes; an unnamed craft on 8 July 1778, *Tartar* of Alderney with another on 3 October. On 15 September 1779, *Resolution* under Captain Gosselin (*see colour section*), captured two French prizes worth £120,000, 10 days after Samuel Dobrée had been in Alderney for the wedding of Peter to his cousin Mary, one of the Guernsey Le Mesuriers. This wedding was followed a month later by the marriage of Jean La Serre (b. 1759) to 19-year-old Judith, 7th and youngest daughter of Henry Le Mesurier. Her brother William married Eliza Le Marchant two weeks later on 18 October, and both Judith and William died barely 18 months later, in 1783.

Dobrée also notes the wreck of a French Indiaman, *Le Marquis de Marbonef*, on 15 November, after being captured by *Resolution*.

Brothers John and Henry Le Mesurier were joint owners of the best-armed vessel ever kept in the island. The 20-gun *Resolution* had a crew of 100, and in 1779, took prizes valued at £134,589 in total. Henry died that year, and by 1782, Governor John had eight privateers, mounting between four and 20 guns, and in that year took prizes worth £212,381. Le Mesurier's share of these sums of prize money after paying the Admiralty commission of 20 per cent, and the crew's share, would have amounted to about £185,000, the equivalent of about £7-10 million at 1994 values.

Several more Le Mesurier weddings were recorded in Dobrée's diary in the next few years; Peter's brother Havilland Le Mesurier to Eliza Dobrée on 27 June 1782, a Guernsey Le Mesurier, Abraham, to Rachel Le Cocq on 19 November, 1782, and Judith and William's brother Nicholas, to Mary Dobrée, known as 'Polly', on 13 July 1789. The diary goes on to record that *Resolution* left for Torbay on 6 July 1790 to join the 'Grand Fleet' under Admirals Barrington, Wood, Notham and Jervis. The fleet consisted of 21 ships of the line including one of 100 guns, three of 90 and six of 74, plus four frigates. He noted on 4 September, 'news has come of Peter Le Mesurier's bankruptcy', with no further explanation.

On New Year's Day 1791, two large Excise Cutters arrived at St Peter Port, and a month later tried to seize the lugger *Spider*, which promptly escaped. On 8 March, the sloop *Discovery* sailed from Guernsey on a round-the-world voyage which lasted until 1795, and on 3 April, an eclipse of the sun was visible from the island.

1792 saw a number of family deaths, including the Henry Le Mesurier, who was married to Mary Dobrée, and several marriages. 25 January 1793 brought news of the execution of the French King Louis XVI, this event immediately put the militia on night watch, and two weeks later an abandoned American brig with a cargo of 275 hogsheads of tobacco, and barrel staves was found by the brig *New Cornwall* and some of her crew brought the vessel into harbour.

From the beginning of March prizes were brought in more frequently, on 3 and 4 April the lugger *Brilliant* brought in two French ships loaded with wine, on 16th *Tartar* of Alderney brought in the 500-ton *Indispensable* loaded with sugar from Santa Domingo, whilst on the same day, *Brilliant* brought in another prize with 800 barrels of flour, and *Sprightly* seized a small brig loaded with corn. On the 20th, *Ranger* of Alderney sent in the American ship *Sally* loaded with flour from Baltimore, with a prize crew. *Brilliant* returned on the 25th with a French six-gun privateer and 25 prisoners, with *Sprightly* doing even better the following day capturing an eight-gun privateer and 40 Frenchmen.

Resolution arrived on the 28th with a 400-ton Frenchman *L'Heureux* loaded with rice, tobacco and timber. *Tartar* returned again on 1 May with the 200-ton *Choachen & Coco* laden with sugar and coffee from Guadaloupe. By the end of the month *Resolution* returned from another cruise in company with a London privateer, in which they had captured a large, rich, East Indiaman *St Jean de Lorme* from Pondicherry, and taken her to Plymouth. A week later she was back again with the brig *L'Union* bringing cotton and the red dye, anatto, from Cayenne, and left again the same day.

Over the next two months a prize was brought in every few days, and on 19 October, Captain James de Sausmarez in his frigate *Crescent*, with a crew of Guernseymen, took the 36-gun French frigate *La Réunion* off Cherbourg, killing or wounding 141 of her crew without loosing a man, an exploit for which he was knighted.

In 1792, Peter Le Cocq, Thomas Nicholas Robilliard and John and William Sandford of Alderney owned the cutter *Lively*, (Capt. Robert Chiles), built that year in Mevagissey. They owned several other vessels, some in partnership with the Beer and Seaton merchants, between 1790 and 1808. The loss of several of these including the *Lively* contributed to them going out of business in 1810. The Beer Customs Boatman, Jacob Good, had been particularly active in detaining small fishing boats at this period, including one belonging to John Sandford in 1806. Robilliard and the Sandfords had set up the Bank of Alderney (which issued its own notes) and the bank failed in that year bringing great hardship to its many Alderney investors. In 1804 the *Mayflower* which was owned jointly by John Violett of Seaton and John Robilliard of Alderney, was seized for smuggling at Southampton.

The situation in France was causing a great deal of activity in Guernsey, with naval vessels and troopships coming and going, the garrison reinforced and numbers of French prisoners arriving over the next few months, from St, Malo, Martinique, Guadaloupe, and Newfoundland, more than 1,000 all told. In the meantime Governor Brown had died of apoplexy, the military commandant, Col. Dundas was sworn in as Lt Governor in July, and *Resolution* recaptured a Welsh sloop which had been taken by the French.

The commanding officer in Jersey, Maj. General Craig was sworn in as Lt Governor of Guernsey following Dundas, but left again on 29 December 1793. The British had captured and burnt Toulon on the 18th, but had to withdraw again in January 1794, and a new Governor, Major General John Small was appointed on 10 March. The Dukes of York and Wellington were being victorious in their campaign in Flanders, Guadaloupe and Martinique were captured, and prizes continued to come in.

Governor John (II) Le Mesurier died on 12 December 1793, and in 1794, another Guernsey family, the Maingys (or Mesney ?) were recorded as the owners of a 20 gun ship *Resolution*, commanded by William Le Lacheur, and it is probable that this was the same vessel, perhaps owned in partnership. In the same year Maingys also owned the cutter *Brilliant*, which had done so well in 1793, master John Quiller, this may also be the same *Brilliant* referred to below. These two vessels took seven prizes between them, during the American War. Governor Small died on 17 March 1796, and was replaced by Sir Hugh Dalrymple.

Between 1793 and 1801, a total of 454 Letters of Marque were issued to Channel Island vessels, (about 10 per cent of the total number issued), three of them from Alderney, and later from 1803-14, two Alderney vessels were so licenced, one for action against French shipping, and the other against the Batavian Republic, out a total of 812 letters issued.

Two of the prize agents acting in London for the Channel Island owners were Governor John (II) Le Mesurier's sons, Paul (1755-1805), and Havilland (1758-1806). They themselves owned the 88-ton lugger *Phoenix*, Captain Daniel Hamon, which mounted 12 six-pdr guns and operated out of Jersey. She took 20 prizes in the period 1798-1801, and four more between 1803-6.

He married Mary Roberdean in 1776, niece of his London partner Noel Le Cras. During the riots in London in 1780 he formed the first Volunteer Military Association, which afterwards became incorporated into the Honourable Artillery Company. He was rewarded by being made a Director of the East India Company, a position he retained for the rest of his life. In addition he served for 12 years as MP for Southwark from 1784, was elected *Alderman* and in 1786 *Sheriff*, and became Lord Mayor of London in 1793 at the age of 38. He was chosen as Colonel of the HAC in 1794 and served the City so well during the period of the French Revolution that he received a vote of thanks from the British Government. He died at the age of 52. In 1808 his only son, yet another John, who does not figure in Alderney's history, but like his cousin John (IV), another only son, took Holy Orders. He became Chaplain to the Forces from 1812-1846 when he was made Archdeacon of Malta. His cousin John (IV) who built Alderney's present church,

Paul Le Mesurier an important member of the family became Lord Mayor of London in 1793 and Colonel of the Honourable Artillery Company in 1794.

consecrated in August 1850, eventually became a Canon and was Rector of Bembridge in the Isle of Wight.

In the same year 1793, Paul's brother Peter, who was Deputy Governor and Commander-in-Chief of the Island, reported to Captain de Sausmarez in Guernsey on 16 March that he had two 'Spy vessels', one, the cutter *Ranger*, Master John Lievre, with three pilots off the French coast, keeping watch, especially at night, which he might use if he wished. The same day he sent a message to the Commander of an English Ship-of-the-line, lying off Alderney, by the agency of Captain Chiles. This turned out to be Captain de Sausmarez in the Frigate *Crescent*, attended by the cutters *Drake* and *Cockatrice*. The following day he reported the presence of these vessels to Secretary of State Henry Dundas and that he had received signals from the French coast the previous night that an attack was imminent.

The following month, he paid off *Ranger* on 16 April, and issued a certificate for payment, dated 23 April, and addressed to Dundas, that John Sanford in the *Hope* Cutter

> ...had been employed by me as a Spy Vessel in the Government Service to cruize around this said Island to watch the motions of the enemy, from the 16th March to the 21st Instant, being one-Month and five Days, for which he is entitled to Seventy Pounds, at the Rate of Sixty pounds per Month. for the Hire of the said Vessel and Crew, as per agreement made with the aforesaid Mr Sanford on the aforesaid 16th Day of March, when the island was threatened with an attack.

Hope had returned to Alderney the previous day.

One wonders if this were not the same *Hope* operating 15 years earlier from Bridport for the Robilliards.

A month later still, Captain of the Invalids, John Grant, who was noted in Dobrée's Journal as

> ...going with his company of Invalids to Alderney in *Tisiphone*.

On 8 May 1794, he reported to Dundas that

> ...the Cutter *Ranger* now has a commission as a privateer and is cruizing for prizes in the Channel.

It was followed a few days later on 24 May, by a further letter to inform Dundas that *Ranger*

> ...returned to the island yesterday having been to Weymouth on the Governor's business, and is now cruizing out beyond the Casquets.

He asks that the vessel, 'whilst in Government service', should be 'placed under his direction, as Officer Commanding the troops in the island'.

This correspondence appears to have caused another of the frequent feuds between the Le Mesuriers and the military.

Other members of the rich Guernsey merchant families of Brock, Dobrée, and Perchard, as well as Jersey families also acted as guarantors in the same way as the Le Mesurier brothers and their Guernsey cousin, Benjamin (1767-1836), and became rich in the process. Peter Perchard, who was related by marriage to the Le Mesuriers, also became a Lord Mayor of London.

The various Privateers Acts of 1793, 1803 and 1805, laid down that strict valuations should be made in any case where there was a dispute, especially over the taking of a 'neutral' vessel. Where the prizes were of enemy shipping, they were usually 'condemned' without being contested, and after 1798, the Owners, Captain and crew were allowed the whole value of such prizes, without any share going to the Crown, unless the prize was adjudged a joint capture. Some quarter of all the prizes condemned to private vessels during this time had been taken by Channel Island craft.

Several such incidents are recorded in Alderney waters. Peter Le Mesurier reported to Dundas on 7 October 1795, that there were two Dutch prizes, *Vrow Johanna* and *Postillion* lying in Braye Harbour then and asked directions for their disposal, and on 1 January following, acknowledged orders to harry Spanish vessels, war having broken out again. In 1797 the 40-ton Guernsey sloop *Dispatch*, Master, William Le Lacheur, was captured by the French en route between Guernsey and Southampton, but was recaptured off Cap de la Hague the same day. The same year on Christmas Day, in another letter to Secretary Dundas, Peter Le Mesurier reported that a French privateer had chased the Cutter *Ann*, of Hastings, under one of Alderney's batteries which had opened fire with three shots just as she was boarding the *Ann*. One went through the sails and one killed a man on board. *Ann* escaped into Alderney Harbour and Le Mesurier quickly placed a force on board her under the Town Major, Hainel. *Ann* and another vessel in the harbour then gave chase and captured the Frenchman and brought her back to Braye, apparently without firing a shot. She was the *Epervier* out of Dunkirk, Captain Fierce, with a crew of 24, and mounting three guns and two swivel carronades.

In 1802 HM Brig *Liberty* being piloted from Jersey to Alderney, captured a large French Brig flying American colours. She was brought into Alderney and subsequently the Alderney pilot received £78 in prize money.

In 1804 the Dutch ship *Drie Gebroeders* was taken in the Alderney roads by the Alderney Privateer *Fly*. HM Cutter *Swift* was at anchor in sight of the island being becalmed. Her commander Lt Mounsey was ashore in Alderney, and she took no part in the action, it was nevertheless adjudged a joint capture by the Admiralty Court.

On 29 April 1810, the Cutter *Queen Charlotte*, Captain Thomas, a vessel mounting eight guns, with a crew of 25 was engaged in a two-hour battle off the coast of Alderney with a French privateer of 14 guns and 100 men. The engagement went in favour of the British ship, and the badly damaged Frenchman withdrew. The Cutter got into Alderney with her boatswain killed, and 14 men injured. A few years later in January 1814 the 80-ton Cutter *Brilliant*, one of the three maintained by the Government for communication between Southampton and the islands was captured en route from

Guernsey, by an American privateer, *Prince de Neufchâtel*. This was a large 325-ton vessel mounting 20 guns, with a crew of 180 men. *Brilliant* was 'despatched to the French port of La Hougue', under command of an American prizemaster. He, mistaking Alderney for the coast of France, gave the helm to one of her crew to steer into harbour. This man naturally did not point out the mistake, and brought her in, where she was immediately retaken. This event is also recorded in Dobrée's diary, where he refers to her destination as 'Grand Port', presumably Cherbourg.

The de Sausmarez family papers, formerly in the Priaulx Library, contain a list of the Guernsey and Alderney privateers, and during the American War, Guernsey and Alderney vessels took about 200 prizes with a gross value at that time of £981,300.

Privateering was finally abolished by the European powers, by the *Declaration of Paris*, on 16 April 1856, which declared that

Privateering is, and remains, abolished.

The Revenue Men

The Papal *Bull of Neutrality* dated 22 May 1480/1 had included Alderney in its exemption, and as a result a regular trade, effectively restricted by the small number of Alderney-based vessels, had been established over the centuries with both England and France for the transfer of goods, even during times of war. Examples of this are also noted in Chapter 15 on Commercial Shipping. The trade had continued because it was economically advantageous to both England and the Islands after the Reformation, which had effectively made it treason to invoke any Papal Bulls, and had, as has already been shown, been confirmed by later Sovereigns. When this Bull was suspended by William III in 1689, the suspension was only intended to be a temporary one, but had somehow become permanent. This was one of the factors which had encouraged the development of *free-trade*, Commerce de la Fraude, or smuggling, and the frequent wars with France and Spain encouraged the building of privateers, much to the benefit of Alderney.

Smuggling reached such proportions during the Napoleonic Wars, mainly due to the fiscal policies of Britain, that a number of laws were passed for its suppression, including several limiting the minimum size of barrels or casks in which wines and spirits might be transported. One of the most active smugglers on the Alderney run being John Rattenbury, (1778-1844), who operated from the late 1790s to about 1810 between Beer, Seaton, or Lyme and Alderney, and reputedly brought his cargoes in to the tiny Trois Vaux Bay where the barrels and balks of silk and cloth, were put at the top of the low cliff for transport inland. He loaded wines and spirits in small four-gallon waterproofed casks for the return trips. Wooden steps known as *Les Dégrés* were placed here to facilitate the transfer, and are marked on a map of about 1816.

He wrote a small book *Memoirs of a Smuggler,* which was published in 1837. In this he records many visits to Alderney to load wines and spirits in a variety of vessels. He and his family worked as fishermen, pilots, privateers and smugglers, the latter being his main occupation during 40 years or more.

He joined the crew of at least two privateers; *Alert*, a 117-ton Weymouth Lugger, granted a Letter of Marque on 28 April 1800. She had been built by Nicholas Booles and William Good of Bridport, sailed for Alderney with a crew of 45, to load wines and spirits and then went cruising for Spanish prizes round the Azores. She returned to Weymouth at the end of December without any luck. The next, 92-ton *Unity*, (Captain Timothy Head), was awarded her letter on 11 December 1804. Rattenbury was one of her crew of 35 men. She too sailed first to Alderney to take on a stock of spirits and stores and then sailed for Madeira. She returned at the beginning of August 1805, again without a prize.

Rattenbury immediately went back to smuggling. His small vessel *Fly*, (presumably not the one mentioned earlier) with Rattenbury on board was seized by the Poole Revenue Cutter, *Sea-Gull*, (Captain John Carter) on 7 August 1805. The Revenue men beached her on the Chesil Beach where she was broken up in a storm. He escaped and in the winter of 1805/6 made seven voyages to Alderney, five of them were successful, they lost their cargo on two. In the Spring of 1806, Sir John Doyle, Governor of Guernsey, offered a reward of £50 for the capture of the person or persons who had bored holes in the bottom of the Revenue Boat in Alderney on 22 February, presumably Rattenbury and his crew. They were captured by the Revenue Cutter *Duke of York* on their return journey, his crew were transferred to the cutter and a prize crew put on board. As they approached Dartmouth, Rattenbury jumped overboard, swam ashore and escaped again.

His many runs were not infrequently accompanied by the loss of his cargo which was thrown overboard when they were chased by Revenue cutters and oared-boats and several naval Brigs. These included HM Brig *Liberty* mentioned above, by which he and his crew were captured on 30 January 1807 and impressed. They were on the *Mary* of Sidmouth, a vessel he had hired in Alderney to take his cargo and crew home after being chased in his vessel *Trafalgar,* as he was attempting to land his sixth cargo of the month, by Lt Daniel Miller, leader of a press gang operating in the Beer area, in an oared boat. He got away and ran for Alderney, but *Trafalgar* was wrecked on the rocks as they approached the Le Mesurier pier. *Trafalgar* had already made five successful runs that month. He was captured on a number of other occasions. He frequently managed to escape before reaching jail or after being impressed into the navy, but served several sentences and lost a number of his boats through either seizure or wreck.

He made several more journeys to Alderney (as well as Cherbourg), landing his cargos at various places along the Dorset, Devon and Cornish coasts, and several times taking cargo along the coast from the point of original landing to a different delivery spot, in 1806/7. He was chased on one occasion by the Exeter Revenue Cutter *Alarm* (Capt. John Eales) and lost one cargo of kegs near Falmouth to the Revenue Sloop *Humber* (Captain Hill). Some of these trips were made in an eight-oared open boat formerly belonging to the Revenue Cutter *Alarm*. They had found this too slow to catch the smugglers and sold her off. Bought with several associates, as he was short of cash through recent losses of boats and cargos, he made several successful cross-channel trips in her, landing his cargo safely. In 1807 he bought a small vessel also called *Lively*, made three successful trips to Alderney in her but she was seized off Portland in 1807 and broken up at Bridport two years later. After her seizure, Rattenbury bought another small vessel, *Neptune* in which he made three good voyages to Alderney, but she was wrecked going into Alderney on the fourth trip.

During this year the Revenue Cutter *Lion* (Captain Blake) was based in Alderney. On one occasion she picked up 33 casks of Rattenbury's spirits, floating near the shore where he had abandoned them after sighting her.

After the wreck of *Neptune*, he had the three-masted lugger *Brothers*, built at Beer in 1807. On one run in 1808, about two hours out of Alderney, Rattenbury was in a 12-oared boat, belonging to his new smuggling boat, this was chased by the Revenue Cutters *Stork*, (Captain Thomas Amos) and *Swallow*, (Captain William Ferris). He made for Cherbourg, and then next day made for England, being finally caught near the coast. *Brothers* was seized by *Stork* and *Swallow* on 11 May 1808 with 135 small casks of spirits on board. She was then broken up at Cowes in 1809. Not deterred he bought yet another boat and made three more successful trips to Alderney in her.

The extension of the customs post to Jersey and Guernsey at this period made the islands less attractive and far more hazardous for the smugglers and for a period he gave up smuggling, married and bought a public house. The Robilliards closed their business in Weymouth at about the same time. Finding times hard he returned to smuggling and after another voyage to Alderney in 1812 was chased and fired on by HMS *Catherine*. Unable to outrun her, he surrendered, but they were still subject to a great deal of small arms fire. The cruiser was on convoy duty protecting Brixham fishermen from French privateers. She took Rattenbury's crew on board, placed a prize crew on his vessel and continued her escort towards Brixham. As she was passing close to the shore, Rattenbury, dived overboard, swam ashore, climbed the cliffs and escaped once more. He went back to the pub and for some time acted as a pilot to ships in distress off the coast, a service for which he was well paid by their masters. From 1814 on he had many similar adventures, after 1818 often in company with his eldest son William, then 16, lost several ships, spent a considerable amount of time in various jails, from several of which they escaped. William was soon smuggling on his own, was also caught several times and lost vessels, but their connection with Alderney seems to have ended after 1814. His father gave up smuggling after 1836 and wrote his *Memoirs*, but William continued for some time. John Rattenbury died in 1844 aged 65, having fathered eight children. Of the three sons, only William apparently became involved in smuggling, the other two stuck to legitimate fishing and coastal cargo carrying.

As early as 1650 the English Navigation Acts had laid down that only English ships could transport goods from the Colonies, and that all ships must call in at an English port to pay their dues before going on to a foreign port. Charles II had ordered the prosecution of Jersey vessels for failing to comply with these Acts in the late 1670s, and from 1679 an English Customs' Registrar had been stationed in Jersey to collect the 'Export Certificates', with Southampton being the only authorised port for export to the Islands, however impractical this may have been. He was also required to issue certificates of the origin of goods being sent to England, to prevent the avoidance of duty on foreign goods being sent via the islands. Lawrence Cole was appointed to this post in 1680, and in 1683 William Stevens was given a similar appointment in Guernsey.

From 1685 in Jersey, and 1687 in Guernsey, these officers were given powers to board ships and note cargoes, and search warehouses or stores. At this time the illicit trade in tobacco, now being brought from Virginia, was increasing, into both France and England. In 1688 James II rejected a petition from the islands to remove the restrictions, and despite another request William of Orange confirmed the various orders in 1690.

His suspension of the Bull of Neutrality in 1689 had given a new impetus to the free-trade, and at the same time, perhaps somewhat reluctantly, the Channel Islanders began privateering activities against the vessels previously welcomed in their ports, especially around Cherbourg and Cap de la Hague between 1693-7. That war ended in 1698, but was renewed in 1702, the smuggling of tobacco and wool revived strongly, and continued to do so after the peace of 1713.

A *Comptroller of Customs* was appointed in Guernsey in 1708 in addition to the Registrar. Local opposition caused the Crown to seek additional powers which included a prohibition on the export of prize goods. This caused the islanders, in 1709, to threaten to stop harrying the French unless it was withdrawn, and the British government agreed. The controller was also withdrawn when the war ended in 1713, leaving only the Registrar. By 1718 the tobacco smuggling had reached such proportions that the French Government ordered the arrest and seizure of any vessel found within two leagues of the French coast which was carrying tobacco.

Jersey and Guernsey boats more or less gave up that particular trade because of this order, but French boats continued to come to the islands, mainly to Jersey, to collect it. In theory Customs Duties were levied to discourage foreign imports, and promote home industry, but in practice the levies, on tea and tobacco especially, were fiscal in nature, in an attempt to pay the cost of the various French wars. The increase in demand for these items, both in England and France therefore caused the attempts to avoid paying the duty. The first Government enquiry had been held in 1733, when the principal bases of the smugglers were in the Isle of Man, and to a much lesser extent then, in the Channel Islands, which were both outside the British customs system. The Duke of Atholl sold the Isle of Man to the British Government for £70,000 in 1765, which brought it under the same controls as England. Jersey and Guernsey, and to a lesser degree Alderney, then became the principal bases for the free-trade.

Most of the vessels used in the trade were English, with Guernsey based merchants supplying the goods. The trade from Guernsey and Alderney was principally to the Hampshire, Dorset, Devon and Cornwall ports, whilst Jersey continued to trade with France. Sark seems not to have been greatly involved. Although Alderney was the lesser centre, at this time a higher proportion of the population than in the other islands was engaged in some connected activity, supplying tea, gin and brandy brought from Holland and France, and rum and tobacco brought from Guernsey.

This state of affairs prompted Captain Lisle of the Revenue Sloop *Cholmondley* to write in 1764, that in Alderney; 'no trade but that of smuggling carried on here'. The customs Registrars were withdrawn in 1767 after the Channel Island authorities arrested Captain Major of the Revenue Cutter *Lord North*, and the next 30 years were the heyday of the smugglers, with many small cutters from Lyme collecting cargoes in Alderney. It was to be almost 40 years before English Custom's Houses were re-established in the Islands, after the passing of the 1805 Act (see below).

An Order-in-Council of 13 February 1767 set up The Commissioners of the Customs of London, with powers to appoint Registrars at the ports, with the intent to examine and regulate the cargoes of all shipping in British waters, and ensure the proper collection of customs dues, but these powers had largely been in abeyance until, at the time when Buonaparte was master of Europe, an 1805 Act 'For the Better Prevention of Smuggling' was followed in 1807 by another similar Act.

These two acts, stimulated the merchants of Guernsey to form a Chamber of Commerce to help stop the illicit trade. The 1767 order, respecting examination and clearing of packages, had only been applied, as far as Channel Island vessels were concerned, to vessels at sea within a few leagues of the English coast, and had not affected the trade once landed, the sovereignty of the islands in this respect being complete, but the new laws extended to 100 leagues from the English coast, and thus affected everything arriving at or leaving the islands. A bonding system was introduced, which effectively put a limit on the legal trade of the islands and Registrars were appointed to control all cargoes. This produced a state of depression which had a considerable adverse effect on trade in Guernsey, until the Spanish broke away from their alliance with France, and trade was opened to the Americas.

The 1805 law was aimed at preventing smuggling, by making the minimum cargoes which could be carried in ships of less than 100 tons, 60 gallons of wine and 450 lbs of tobacco, and had imposed this on the islands.

On 3 November 1807, a special session of the Royal Court in Guernsey was held to revise the anti-smuggling ordinances which were not proving practical. In stating that they were not being observed *'tant en cette Isle que dans l'Isle d'Aurigny'*, it forbade the landing of any spirituous liquors, tobacco, salt and pepper, other than at Les Chausées (*causeways* i.e. the harbour jetties) in St Peter Port and Alderney, and at the Creux Harbour in Sark, except for the provisioning of the vessels themselves. It imposed confiscation of the goods and penalties of £20 sterling fine for each item, for anyone who assisted in the contravention of the ordinance. Except for the provisioning, it was forbidden to transport any such goods in times of war by any means at all, and imposed a fine of confiscation of the goods and any vehicles or animals used, and a fine of £20 sterling on each offender.

It was also forbidden to transport or store such items more than 200 yards from Braye in Alderney, or in any open places above high-water mark, or to move them between sunset and sunrise in any container of less than 30 gallons of wines or spirits, or bales of less than 450 lbs of tobacco, anywhere else in the island. Carts with up to three 30 gallon casks, and 50 lbs of tobacco were to be exempt.

It was further stated that all barrels and casks of less than 30 gallons would be assumed to contain spirits unless proved otherwise.

The Constables and Assistant Constables were authorised to seize any goods and vehicles or animals moved or stored in contravention of this act, and had to inform the King's Officers immediately. The ordinance would remain in force whilst the war continued, and the fines were to be given a quarter to the King, a quarter to the States, and half to the informers. The ordinance was to be cried in the Market, put up in the church porch, and read in church after the sermon, on the first Sunday after it was registered in the Alderney Court.

This Ordinance was debated again in the Royal Court on 3 December, after certain alterations or 'erroneous interpretations', had been made by the Alderney Court on 20 November. They had sent a letter of this date containing reasons why they had deferred registering the Ordinance. These concerned the fact that there was reason for the people of 'the Town' and of 'Craby' to be carrying water in either casks or little barrels at any time, by day or night, and that no-one had the right to stop them. It was quite obviously an excuse for ignoring the regulations, and carrying on with the lucrative trade, since the amount of liquor involved was vastly in excess of the quantity likely to be consumed by the local population. The Royal Court dismissed these reasons as 'illusory', and noted that the act was similar to that already registered in Alderney on a similar occasion in 1737[1], and ordered its publication and registration, 'without further delay'.

The Ordinance referred to was passed at the Christmas Chief Pleas in Guernsey, on 16th January 1737/8 to prevent the infringements of an Act of Parliament passed in the 12th year of the reign of Charles II (1672), entitled *An Act for the Encouragment and Increasing of Shipping and Navigation*. This Ordinance had resulted in a petition to the Privy Council 'on behalf of several persons qualifying themselves as Merchants, Traders, and Inhabitants, of your Majesty's Islands of Guernsey and Alderney', that 'the Ordinance was arbitrary and contrary to the law'.

On 30 November 1738, this petition was referred to the Committee of the Council for the Affairs of Guernsey and Jersey. Their reply was an order dated 1 December, sending the petition to the Royal Court for an immediate reply, and meantime to stop any action under the Ordinance complained of. The Royal Court's reply was finally sent on 24 April 1739, but the document notes that

...it does not appear that the affair may ever be submitted again for the consideration of the Council.

By another coincidence the delay in registering the 1807 Ordinance in Alderney may have caused an incident which is recorded in a book written by George Leabon an officer of the garrison, who was court-martialled because of it, although it is quite clear that this Ordinance had actually been registered long before the incident. Leabon was called in December 1807, from Ireland where he was in the recruiting service, to rejoin his regiment, the 67th Regiment of Foot, then in service in Alderney. He wrote:

> When I arrived in Alderney it was generally understood that the people of the former island [*Guernsey*] had transferred the illicit trade to the latter where they found agents to superintend this smuggling. About September 1808, I was appointed to the command of an outpost which, from the remoteness and convenience of its situation was then the principal scene of the smuggling trade....
>
> On 24th January 1809, a general order was issued to me to patrol, and send out patrols, as often as I might judge to be proper, to the creeks and landing-places within the limits of my post. On the night of 2nd March 1809, in the execution of my duties with a patrol I surprised a numerous party of smugglers shipping off spirits in the Bay of Jeffoine.
>
> On seeing the patrols they endeavoured to make their escape, leaving a considerable quantity of spirits on the cliffs, on which I immediately placed a sentry, and despatched a messenger for Mr Cole, the Registrar of the Customs, to take charge of the same. On his arrival, this he declined doing, but at the same time recommended me to keep possession until morning to prevent its being shipped-off in the night, and also suggested the propriety of depositing it in the barracks at Clonque.[1]
>
> At about the hour of six the following morning I reported the affair to my Commanding Officer Lt Col. Prevost, who waited on Brigadier General Hatton, commanding the forces, with my report; and in answer thereto Lt Col. Prevost informed me that the General expressed high indignation at my having interrupted the smuggling and that it was the General's orders that I should instantly give up the goods....

At about this period there was a flourishing coopering industry in Alderney reputedly involving some 200 people, making the small four-gallon casks in which much of the liquor was transferred. Many of the hoops, and probably the staves for this manufacture, were imported from Southampton, where they were made, but a little earlier, a permit dated 10 September 1801, issued by the crown, had allowed the transport of 25,000 barrel hoops from Rotterdam, direct to Alderney in a Dutch ship. The cargo of this vessel did not include staves, which were unlikely to have been locally made, as there were few oak trees in Alderney at any historic time, and must therefore also have been imported.

> Clonque Barracks was then sited on the low cliff above Hannaine Bay, just south of the causeway to the battery on Clonque Island, and the 'outpost' mentioned would almost certainly have been the Watchtower on the headland just above Trois Vaux Bay.

Leabon was Court-martialled for exceeding his duties, at which time, the Governor, his Chaplain, all the Jurats, and all the Douzaine agreed that he had grossly exaggerated the incident, and that his statements were devoid of all foundation! His appeal was rejected, clearly indicating that almost the entire military and civilian hierarchy of Alderney were involved in the trade. He was so disgusted that he later left the Army, and wrote about his experiences.

The kegs were waterproofed on the outside so that they could be weighted and sunk offshore if there was danger of detection or seizure and picked up later. The barrels were linked together in a chain, often of a hundred or more, and were later fished up by 'Tub-boats', open rowing boats using a grappling hook and 'creeping' until they hooked on. Customs officers and Revenue men often saw where the barrels were sunk from the cliffs through their telescopes, or noted where they were thrown overboard, whilst giving chase, and returned to the spot and picked them up themselves. Their subsequent sale made a good profit for the officers and crew and on a number of occasions, some part of their cargo was thrown overboard by agreement between the smugglers and the Revenue men, in return for being allowed to bring the rest ashore safely. The Revenue vessels usually stopped to pick up the floating kegs as evidence and thus the smugglers escaped.

One of the effects of the impounding and subsequent public auction of illegal cargoes, was that certain persons who had themselves smuggled goods to the island, could inform the authorities of the presence of these goods on the beach, or wherever they were left. They could then buy the spirits etc. at auction for around 2/- to 7/-, for a four-gallon keg, and thus get both the cargo, and half the money paid out, back. They then had a perfectly legal title to the items which could be sold, or exported legally to England.

Later the same year, on 29 July 1809, another special session of the Royal Court concerning smuggling, in Guernsey, Alderney and Sark, ordered that spirits may not be transported in barrels of less than 30 gallons between sunset and sunrise from 21

Grappling for kegs after sinking them overboard to avoid the Revenue Men.

September to 21 March, or between 8 p.m. and 6 a.m. from March to the following September, at the same time the fine was increased to £200 sterling, with the same allocation between the authorities and the informers.

On 25 November, the King's Officers noted that

> ...as there are still people in the Island of Alderney being so inconsiderate as to try to evade the said Ordinance, it was then forbidden to keep spirits in barrels of less than 12 gallons.

To encourage the informers, they were in future to have a choice, after a conviction, of receiving half the goods confiscated, or half the sum fetched when they were sold.

Another of the occasional, apparently quite arbitrary, acts of the Royal Court to try and control Alderney's affairs, took place the following summer. On 5 June, The States of Alderney, having passed an Act the previous day to levy duty, for the benefit of the States, on spirits brought in by any foreigner, not resident in Alderney, the Royal Court demanded an explanation of the authority by which they made such an order, and 'expressly forbids the said States to continue to raise the said duty'.

The last Ordinance in this series was passed in Guernsey on 2 May 1815, when, the war being over and the smuggling ordinances having therefore ceased, the Ordinance of 3 November 1807 was renewed for the time of peace, as the Court

> ...was convinced of the good effects which have come from this said Ordinance, and of the necessity of preserving the arrangement.

The fines were reduced again to £20, but the option for the informers to have half the cargo, or the money, was inserted in the new Ordinance.

The first customs officer appointed for Alderney was Richard William Cole, Custom's Registrar (the same referred to above by Leabon), appointed on 19 April 1808, who remained in this post until he died at the age of 52 in 1832. He was followed by John Holloway, who also died in his post at the age of 64 in 1838. At the same time a Customs Tender *Sea-Gull* was stationed in Alderney and regularly supported by a Revenue Ketch *Adder*, Captain James Needs, who died in Alderney on 6 November 1814 aged 39. Needs had previously captained the Dartmouth Revenue Cutter *Industry* in 1805.

There still exists in the National Archives a voluminous correspondence carried on between several of the Le Mesuriers and the various First Secretaries of State between 1782 and 1826, and there were frequent disputes between them and the officers of the Revenue Service, resulting in complaints and counter-complaints to Whitehall.

Starting about 1812, when the senior Revenue Officer in Alderney was Captain Needs of the Revenue cutter *Adder*, who claimed that his men had been assaulted on 2 September by a group of locals who apparently, as stated in a letter of Judge Peter Gauvain; 'rescued smuggled goods from an officer and boat's crew of the *Adder*', Need's claim, was open to doubt, and in this, John Le Mesurier's rebuttal was supported by Brigadier General John Moore then commanding the garrison. Captain Needs refused to give evidence or support his accusations in the Alderney Court and was said by Le Mesurier to; 'consider himself outside the control of the Court'. Another Revenue Officer in Alderney at that time, Captain Andrews, did appear before the Court as a witness.

Adder which was attached to Dartmouth, although based in Alderney, again appears in Le Mesurier's correspondence, by now commanded by Captain Richard Bowden, when he was fined by the Alderney Court on 24 June 1817 for sending his men to fish on a Sunday. The following day, in retaliation, he set about measuring all of the boats in the harbour to see that they were properly marked with their tonnage etc. and also invoked the law preventing open boats from 'going Foreign', which effectively stopped the inhabitants from taking their produce to France 'the only market open to them', in their fishing boats. The dispute continued and further complaints were made later that year. In November, Bowden seized a ship, arriving from Bere in Devon, as being a smuggler, and put the crew ashore without their belongings. They thus became a charge on the Parish to support them.

He also confiscated the entire stock of liquor, amounting to a trifling six bottles of wine, two of Hollands gin, one of brandy, and one of ale, from the Captain's cabin of Le Mesurier's three-masted cutter, (frequently referred to as his 'yacht'), when he arrived from Southampton, with a cargo of cows. Le Mesurier attempted to do something about this high-handed action, but as a result Bowden seized one of the two ship's-boats of this 65-ton yacht *The Vigilant*, Captain John Richard Le Cocq master. This was the smaller 17-foot boat, leaving the larger 24-foot boat used to supply the Casquets still free. He then seized Alderney's two pilot boats, one of which, owned by William Small, was also the Quarantine boat. He also enforced the law restricting the number of crew allowed on a vessel of this tonnage to six, in Le Mesurier's view quite inadequate to work a three-masted vessel.

Such ships, carrying greater numbers of crew, were liable to be seized as pirates. A couple of weeks later he again seized four bottles of Le Mesurier's private stock of wines and spirits on board. This rigid application of the law prompted Le Mesurier to complain to Viscount Chetwynd, the First Secretary, that he could not then even carry spirits on board to comfort his men against the chill. On Christmas Eve, Bowden seized the *Mary Ann* from Guernsey, as it arrived in Alderney Harbour.

From a flurry of complaints he made to various Government, Revenue Service, and Naval officials, Le Mesurier received little comfort, and finally an enquiry held by Admiral Thornbrough in Portsmouth, expressed itself 'entirely satisfied' with the Captain's conduct, and 'won't interfere' with the way he carries out his duties.

Bowden had a house in Braye Street, five of his children were baptised in the Parish church between 1822 and 1831, and two were buried in the churchyard, in 1819 and 1823. His wife Mary Harris Bowden died here on 14 November 1851 at the age of 66. Another officer, 'Writer' Robert Congdon, 'of the *Adder* Revenue cutter off this coast, stationed and living at Braye' to quote the Parish Register, had a son, John, baptised here on 23 July 1822, and Lt Francis Noble RN had three children born here up to 1830, indicating a settled naval and customs presence for at least 20 years. Revenue Cutter

Arrow was also stationed here in 1822-3, a child of her 1st Lt, William Petit, dying on 7 July 1822. Thomas Macklin RN. (45) captain of the Revenue Cutter *Jubilee*, was found dead in his cabin in the harbour on 4 July 1831.

In February 1818 further complaint was made to Lord Sidmouth, that these activities, and the recent Act of Parliament in April or May 1817, prohibiting the importation of Italian silks, foreign leather gloves, Crêpes and Tiffanies, which the Alderney Court had refused to register, until peremptorily ordered to do so by the Prince Regent on 18 December, were leading to a state of poverty amongst the inhabitants who were unable to support themselves without trading with France.

On 13 July 1819, a complaint was made to the Alderney Court, by Mr Petit, then the Mate of the *Adder*, that he had been assaulted by Henry Oliver, for seducing his sister. Petit claimed to be exempt from any attack on his person, 'because, as a King's officer, he was always on duty when in Alderney'. This affair sparked several Court hearings, during which another Revenue Officer, James Seoule, and Mrs Sarah Mesney were called as witnesses, to both the assault and the claim of seduction. A further stream of letters from the Governor to Secretary Hobhouse, eventually suggested that Petit should be 'made to marry the lady'. William Petit married 18-year old Anne Oliver in 1819. She was the 8th, and Henry the 6th, of 10 children of James Oliver of Kent, and Eleonore Ladd, daughter of Juse Ladd of Alderney. A child was born to them in 1820, and they had three more in Alderney, one of whom (mentioned above) died, before they sailed from Guernsey to Sydney on 8 May 1828. Lt William Petit RN became Harbour Master at Port Macquari, New South Wales, and died in New Zealand aged 82 on 17 May 1864. His wife then returned to Australia with her seven surviving children, one other having died in New Zealand.

In 1818 the Customs Tender *Sea-Gull* brought Admiral Sir James de Sausmarez, and the Bishop of Salisbury from Guernsey for an Episcopal visitation in which 264 people were confirmed, the first confirmation in Alderney since the Reformation.

Customs fees were abolished on 1 January 1820, and from this time the Revenue Service paid a salary to its officers in Jersey and Guernsey. For some reason, this did not include the Alderney officers, and Le Mesurier asked Secretary Lord Sidmouth to pay them.

In the following month *Sea-Gull* was sent to Guernsey for the Mail, because *Vigilant* was away on Le Mesurier's private business. Petit who had gone aboard her to collect the mail, refused to bring back the Governor's correspondence, although he was eventually persuaded to do so by the Post Mistress in Guernsey. This precipitated a further dispute about the personal use of his vessel, for which the Governor received payment from the Crown, as it was claimed, to be available for official purposes.

The presence of the Customs' Registrar obviously caused a few other problems, for we find in 1823, a request from the Alderney States' to the Treasury to instruct the Customs Officer to facilitate the export of sheep between the islands.

A few years later in October 1826, another item was brought before the Royal Court, when they were informed by the Alderney Court of abuses committed against a Customs' Employee,

...whose name doesn't matter, by an assembly of about 20 persons bringing illicit tea into the island.

The Alderney Court asked the Lt Governor for more Customs Officers to prevent this, but was instructed instead to take proper steps to apprehend all the offenders, and send them to Guernsey for trial if there was sufficient proof.

The tobacco trade in Guernsey was proving so profitable, and so many wealthy people were probably involved in it, that in 1833 these merchants petitioned the British Treasury to be allowed to take part officially in the tobacco smuggling and thus 'strike a blow against the French'. Not surprisingly, this petition was rejected.

Smuggling still continued and, on 19 April 1844, Captain Alexander, Acting Lt Governor in Alderney, (Governor John (III) Le Mesurier having resigned his office in 1824), received a complaint from the owners of an Alderney vessel that it had been captured, within the three-mile limit, by a French Revenue boat. He notes in his correspondence that

HM Receiver in Alderney has a son notorious to be engaged in smuggling, and it is therefore doubtful if the reasons given by the owners are true.

A letter from the French authorities in Paris, dated 21 June, notes that the fine of 1,100 Francs will be remitted, and the vessel released on payment of 55 Francs and the legal charges. It stated that the boat *L'Auguste* and the crew, Mr Nicholas Sebire, Martin Gauvain, and an English sailor named Digard, were then detained in Cherbourg. This event may well have seen the end of any significant smuggling from Alderney, which had fallen on hard times after the end of the war against the French caused the withdrawal of most of the garrison and the consequent loss of trade. Many families left the island at this time, some to France, others to the colonies, especially to Australia and New Zealand.

The decision only three years later to refortify the south coast, against renewed fears of a threat from France through the building of a huge naval base at Cherbourg and to establish a similar naval base at Alderney, soon re-established the prosperity of the island and there was a vast influx of troops and construction workers from 1847 onwards.

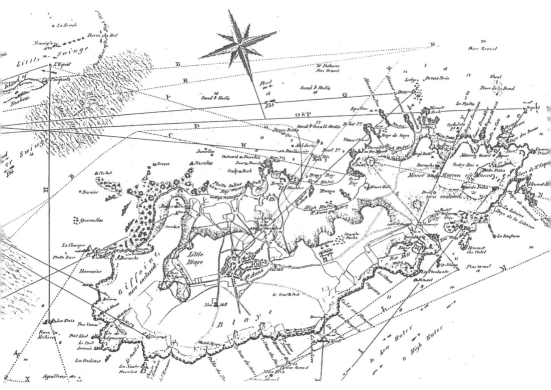

Chart of Alderney by James Wyld 1833.

7

The Harbours

1. Early Harbours

The position of Alderney's earliest harbour at Longis Bay, with its flat sandy shore, visible from the coast of France, and fairly sheltered with its south-west facing entrance, has already been described in some detail. This harbour which appears to have been used since prehistoric times, and was certainly the port during the Roman era, in general ceased to be used after the Le Mesurier Pier was built at Braye in 1736.

On most old maps and charts of Alderney, an anchor sign, indicating an anchorage, or the word *râde* meaning a haven, anchorage, or port, will be found in a number of the bays and roadsteads around the island. These are all places where a ship may drop anchor in a fairly sheltered spot, depending on wind and tide, and in a few cases, where smaller vessels may also conveniently be beached.

From a comparatively early period the small circular bay at Crabby, (Craby, Crabic, or Crabbie), with its narrow entrance sheltered from all sides except the north-west, has been used by small craft. The earliest reference I have been able to find to its use is by Revd Peter Heylin, who, writing in 1656 mentions 'the harbour at Crabbie, in the manner of a semicircle'. It is also mentioned in later works, and noted on the de Beaurain map of 1757 as 'Baye de Crabby, Port'. Here it would have been essential to use the ship's boats to gain the shore.

The *Manuscript History of Alderney* dated about 1770 and probably written by Frederick Williams, the Greffier, notes the following:

An act of the States of Alderney dated 1651, passed by the Lt Governor, George Michau, the officers of the law, and the Douzainiers, decrees that

...the due information which has been made that many vessels, foes of our country fitted out for war, making the coast of Normandy their appointed meeting place, that for the safeway and preservation of the island by the States of England, and to know our friends from our enemies, it is ordained that the Norman boats which frequent this island will come to the harbours of this island, and not in the neighbouring places of this island, and will make use of the said harbours when in their ordinary fishing time, under the penalty of sixty sous tournois to the State to whoever will act to the contrary, after a notice will have been made to them by the Officers of State that they must not land except at the harbours of Longis or Craby. It is moreover ordained that with regard to the complaints which have been made to the Governor, of the too great liberty permitted to strangers to go about the island with their arms, against ancient orders in use from time immemorial. It is said that henceforth strangers will not carry any arms in this island, under the penalty of a fine of sixty sous tournois to the State, to whoever will be found an offender after having received notice of the same.

It is moreover ordained that when the drum and bell will sound the alarm, each one will find himself without delay at the Windmill with his arms, which is the place of meeting, under a penalty of 60 sous tournois, *(half-a-crown)*, to those who will fail to be present unless they can offer a valid excuse for the first offence, and those who will be absent from home will be sent for by members of their family, and should anyone be found guilty for the second time will be sent to Guernsey as traitors and incorrigible.

The said ordinances will be registered and cried out after the services on a Sabbath-day, so that none may plead ignorance of the same and enable each one to fulfil his duty, or otherwise become answerable for not having done so.

The 'Craby Harbour' referred to in this, and other early documents, before the construction of the Breakwater cut it off from having a direct North-facing opening to the Channel, would have been in the position of what is now known as 'The New Harbour' or 'Little Crabby Harbour'. Constructed in its present form to shelter the shipping associated with the building of the Victorian Breakwater and used today principally for the fishing fleet, and the bunkering of visiting yachts.

Crabby Bay, as shown on de Beaurain's (*see page 72*) and other maps, is simply an anchorage or *râde*. Crabbic Harbour was referred to in a guide to Hampshire published in 1718, as the harbour at Alderney.

The MS History also notes that on 1 September 1660 George Michau had made an offer on behalf of Sir George de Carteret to expend £70 sterling to rebuild the bridge on the road to the harbour at Longis. The States decided to

> ...consult an engineer who would be competent to undertake this work, not wishing to take upon themselves the responsibility for beginning it without such a consultation.

There is no bridge at any point on this road today, and I have been unable to find any evidence of it on existing maps, but there must have been some access to the pier, the cliff immediately above the site being some 20-30 feet high, and it could possibly have been below the present cliff where the stream emerges, in a spot long since eroded. The archæological work at this spot of the 1920's gives good evidence of previous erosion of the coastline here. It is noted, from another source, that Michau offered £1,000 to rebuild the jetty there. At that time 1,000 L. trs. would have been equal to £72 sterling, and the two items may actually refer to the same thing.

Michau's connection with Alderney started in 1649, during the time of the Commonwealth, when he was appointed Lt Governor in Alderney by Governor Robert

Russell of Guernsey. He was sworn in again in 1654 under Josias King, and was acting once again after the Restoration as this document shows. It appears to precede by a week the date of the transfer of Alderney from Edward de Carteret et al. to Sir George de Carteret. Michau was again appointed de Carteret's agent, for three years from 7 August 1662.

On 3 January 1673/4, another ordinance was made that

> ...whoever will remove stones, large or small, or will demolish the Pier of the Laggue (Forth) at the Harbour of Longis, whether they be foreigners or inhabitants at whatever time it may be, will be fined 2/6d to His Majesty.

Old Alderney fishermen still referred in the 1980's to that part of Longis Bay as 'the Lagg', a word also used for a similar spot between Burhou and Little Burhou.

The Old Harbour

It has traditionally been accepted that what is now known as the *Old Harbour* or Le Mesurier's Pier, was built in 1736 by Henry Le Mesurier and the Douglas Quay was added later, and this is quoted in most books on Alderney.

There exists however in the National Archives the petition already mentioned, written on 7 July 1787 to Lord Sydney, the Principal Secretary of State at the time, by William Thomas Le Cocq. He was the grandson of Thomas Le Cocq, Judge of Alderney from 1 February 1703/4 to 7 May 1760, and claims in the second paragraph, that the harbour was constructed by his grandfather, which certainly appears to throw a different light on its origins, and is worth quoting:

> There being no harbour of safety in the said Island for the shelter of such ships as might be in distress upon so dangerous a coast especially in time of war, he at his own expence built an harbour there. To reimburse him his expences, the States by an Act of the Court of the said Island, set the revenues of the Harbour (as established by order of Privy Council) every year, up to public sale, for the purpose of repairing and maintaining the said harbour, as well as paying to the said Thomas Le Cocq the interest of the money he had thus laid out, until the year 1763 when John Le Mesurier Esq. nominal governor of the said Island appropriated the revenues of the harbour to his own use, and moreover upon renewal of his patent of the Island a few years after as [Sic] ffee farmer thereof, the inhabitants had the harbour as their property wrested from them and specified in His Majesty's Grant or letters patent of the Island unto the said Le Mesurier. The principal and interest due thereon amounts to upwards of One thousand five hundred pounds sterling, for which I have applied to the said Le Mesurier, who says the inhabitants must make it good, they are poor as well as myself, and law being very expensive, it is out of my power to sue either the Governor or the Inhabitants, notwithstanding he has had the general benefit of the harbour for a

The Old Harbour in 1890 with Fort Albert on the hill beyond. The lower level mentioned in the text starts at the left-hand edge of the photo.

considerable time, and the debt is registered on the records of the Court of the said Island.

Unfortunately he does not give a date for the construction, and of course, the Alderney Court records, which would have substantiated this claim, were destroyed during the Second World War. I have not yet traced the Privy Council order referred to in the letter, but it places a different light on the building of the Old Harbour from that which has generally been accepted for about two centuries.

The Douglas Quay, forms the lower level of the 'Old Harbour' jetty, and was added in 1840, according to a stone in the wall, probably on the orders of Sir James Douglas, Lt Governor of Guernsey.

Little Crabby Harbour

From the late 1840s, with the commencement of work on the 'Harbour of Refuge' a small harbour was built between Crabby Bay and Grosnez Point to house the ships and barges being used in the main construction. Now known as 'Little Crabby Harbour', This served throughout the many years of construction of the Breakwater and Forts for the shelter and berthing of many ships and subsequently as a shelter for the Alderney fishing fleet and cargo boats. It is a harbour which dries out at low tide allowing

Little Crabby Harbour (the New Harbour) in 1890.

maintenance work on the boat hulls but at the same time restricting the hours in which it can be entered or left.

The Germans used it during the Occupation years, mainly before they built the long deep water extension to the Commercial Quay. Today it is still used by the very limited number of Alderney fishing boats strill working here and by local resident's small craft and offers a chandlery shop and refuelling facilities to both locals and visitors. An annual ceremony of blessing the fishing fleet is still carried out here.

At periods of extreme spring tides the sea can come over the sides onto the surrounding roadway, where some local craft are lifted out for overwintering or maintenance work and in Alderney week, a 'Man-powered flight' competition is held from the outer retaining wall and the excellent acoustics in the shallow basin formed by the surrounding land are made use of for band or orchestral concerts with a large audience on the grass above, as well as round the harbour .

The Harbour Master was always a qualified mariner with a Master's certificate, or in earlier times a naval officer. Lt Holgate RN was appointed to the post by Lord Lincoln in 1844, a position he retained until his death in October 1859, when the work at the harbour was booming. He was replaced on the recommendation of the Governor of Guernsey, by Peter Le Ber, the appointment then being vested in the *Board of Woods and Forests*. The treasury agreed to the appointment, subject to the salary being reduced if the business at the harbour declined. There is however another record stating that the Harbour Master from 1855-77 was Andrew Brown. He was replaced on 16 March 1877 by F. Brice, formerly Chief Boatman to HM Customs in Alderney, and I have not been able to find records to explain the apparent four-year overlap.

Robert Allen, one of the Alderney pilots was appointed to the harbour master's job in

July 1896, and in January the following year, Woods and Forests voted £400 to be spent removing sand from the Old Harbour.

After much controversy, referred to elsewhere, the bells of the church were rung on 25 August 1895 to signify the start of work on the new jetty, and two months later Rowe and Mitchell were awarded a contract to place the land ties and piles for the new jetty and for fixing a large buoy. The work was progressing well, when, in December, the States invited tenders for cutting the road from Braye Street through to the new jetty.

Longis Harbour

Longis Harbour was still used by small vessels coming from France in the late nineteenth and early twentieth century, and continues to be used occasionally today by visiting yachts, and small fishing boats. Another sheltered anchorage exists in Hannaine Bay, where small vessels, mostly yachts, frequently drop anchor to wait for the tide in the Swinge to turn in their favour before making Braye. Telegraph Bay also makes an occasional mooring place for pleasure craft.

Cachalière Harbour

Around the turn of the century, contractor Matt Rowe-Buckingham had a pier built below the South Cliffs of the island at Cachalière, in order to be able to load the valuable blue granite which he started to quarry from the cliff here, directly into ships. The approach to the pier was hazardous, requiring careful navigation around the small offshore islets, and emergent rocks, and was impossible from the East because of a natural tidal causeway. Matt Rowe, (the Buckingham was soon dropped) came from Chicago, and the pier and adjacent quarry are frequently referred to locally as 'Chicago'.

The first ship to load at the new pier, was the SS *Ituna* on 12 July 1908. Both cut stone blocks, and crushed road-stone were taken from here in some quantity until about 1922, when, after the total loss of one of the ships, SS *Tyne* on 12 January 1922 after striking the Bonit Rock, it was later abandoned. The quarry was closed for a short time in 1919 following the death of the owner. This caused much hardship in the island at the time. Special running railway gear had been installed quite early on, to enable full trucks of crushed stone to automatically discharge into waiting ships. .

This was removed before 1930, and the Germans cut the pier in half and demolished the outer part to prevent its being used as a landing place in 1942. The remaining part still forms a feature of the South Cliffs, visible from much of their length.

A calm evening in Longis Bay, August 2005.

Cachalière Pier under construction, *c.* 1908.

SS *Tyne* loading stone at the pier, *c*. 1910.

The Harbour of Refuge

When 18-year-old Queen Victoria ascended the throne in 1837, 20 years or so after the decisive victory at Waterloo, there was little thought of war. Lord Palmerston, the Foreign Secretary from 1830-1841, however had an inherent mistrust of both the French and the Russians, even though from about 1830, Britain had nominally established an *Entente Cordiale* with France. He was also far from diplomatic in his relationships with other countries.

Victoria married her cousin, Prince Albert of Saxe-Coburg-Gotha, in February 1840, and Robert Peel became Prime Minister in 1841. He appointed Lord Aberdeen as his Foreign Secretary, and soon after set about reducing the taxes and duties on many commodities, which started a period of unprecedented trade expansion, one effect of which was to reduce the price of corn by 14/- in 1842/3. In 1846 the duty on wheat, oats and barley was reduced to 1/- a quarter, and the price remained steady at around 52/- for the next 20 years, a factor of benefit to the Channel Islands. In 1844 he managed to get the charter of the Bank of England modified and placed Britain on a *gold standard*, so that every note issued was covered by reserves of coin or bullion. Peel was defeated over the Irish question in 1846, and Palmerston once again became Foreign Secretary.

In the early 1840s, the French were enlarging several of their ports along the Channel coast, and in particular were creating large and well defended harbours at Cherbourg and St Malo. Despite the good relations which seemed to exist between the two Governments, there was concern that this might have an ultimate aim against the Channel Islands, and a similar programme of construction was planned for the

South Coast of England, and the Channel Islands, a programme supported and much influenced by the Duke of Wellington, who was convinced of the strategic value of the islands.

In the Summer of 1842 a commission under Capt. Edward Belcher RN, with Col. Cardew RE and Col. Colquhoun RA, examined potential sites for harbours in the islands. In Alderney they recommended Longis Bay as a suitable site, noting that, due to the force of the tides, 'no harbour could be constructed on its northern shores'.
In Jersey they recommended St Catherine's Bay, the eventual site of the Jersey 'Harbour', whilst the harbour proposed for Guernsey was never started at all. Another Commission was appointed by the Treasury, by an Act of 2 April 1844 to survey suitable sites for *Harbours of Refuge*, and the report was submitted by 7 August, recommending works at Dover, Seaford, Portland and Harwich. It made no mention of the Channel Islands.

Despite this omission, barely a year later, in September 1845, James Walker a competent Civil Engineer, was sent to the islands by Sir William Somerville at the Board of Admiralty, to purchase land at Braye in Alderney and St Catherine's in Jersey for the construction of the harbours, the sites of which by then had been decided upon and plans submitted. In November 1846 Lt General Napier was in correspondence with Somerville regarding the harbour construction works planned, and complaining about the standard of the postal services to the islands. Representation from the Bailiffs and Lt Governors of Jersey and Guernsey were passed to the Admiralty by Sir George Grey, who stated that it was the first he had heard of the plans, but the Admiralty were 'unable to find' earlier letters to them about the postal services. Grey acknowledged the letters in December and promised to give the matter his consideration, and later that month informed Napier that he had taken the matter of the mails up with the South-western Steam Navigation Company.

On 25 January, Somerville wrote to Gen. Napier saying that he had instructed the officer-in-charge of the Harbour Works to keep the Lt Governor informed of orders he received regarding them, and further instructions were given to Walker on 28 January 1847 by the Governor of Guernsey to liaise with his Lt Governor in Alderney on all matters relating to the harbour works.

The first task was to purchase the quarries for the stone with which to build both Breakwater and Forts, and in 1847, in Alderney, 125 vergées of land at Mannez was bought for quarrying, from 15 individuals and families, for a total of £1,493 8s 6d At the same time 34 vergées of land from Corblets to the Harbour was bought from 25 individuals and families for a grand total of £1,663 15s 3d for the railway, needed to carry the stone to the harbour.

It would be interesting to know how the negotiations were conducted, since Thomas Houguez and others received £215 9s 0d for four-and-a-half vergées at 'Valet Mélant', whereas Peter Houguez and family only received £137 9s 3d for just over five vergées at 'Rocqueret' half way along Braye Bay. John Herivel and others received a similar sum, £133 4s 6d for just over two vergées at 'Villain'. All of this land was classified as 'arable', and was required for the railway. The negotiations for the purchase of this land and the start of constructing the railway and opening the quarry must have been accomplished very quickly.

The Treasury records show that the various parcels of land were purchased from 1847 on, but, by the time of the official laying of the foundation stone on 12 February 1847, as Naftel's sketch, (page opposite), published in *The Illustrated London News* on 20 February, clearly shows, the line was already laid from the York Hill (and possibly from the Battery) Quarries.

At the end of 1846, Contractors Jackson and Bean had been appointed to carry out the work under the direction of James Walker, at both sites in Jersey and Alderney. Preliminary work in Alderney began in January, and the Jersey project commenced in July.

During Peel's administration France and Britain were both guided by men of similar outlook, and good relations were maintained, although the *entente cordiale* was never popular with the people of either country. Their differences really came to a head when the French sent formal notice early in 1846, that they would not accept the proposed marriage of the 10-year-old Queen Isabella of Spain with a prince of the house of Coburg, whom the British had been supporting, in opposition to the wishes of the French crown. The Bourbon King, Louis Philippe, wished to marry one of his sons to the young Queen. In August 1846, the French King announced the betrothal of his son to the Queen's sister, and of the Queen Isabella herself, to her effeminate cousin Don Francis. Palmerston could not accept this and persuaded Queen Victoria to make a strong protest to Louis Philippe, thus ending for a time, the period of collaboration between Britain and France.

Russia, Austria and Prussia got together in November 1846 to suppress Poland, and British support for the revolutionaries in Italy caused civil war to start in Sicily in January 1848. The disturbances and revolutions across Europe in that year overthrew both Louis Philippe in France, which once again became a republic, and Metternich in Austria, and there were revolutions in Hungary and Turkey. Louis Philippe took refuge in England.

The Alderney Breakwater

The *Harbour of Refuge* in Alderney was founded on 12 February 1847. A large party of officials from Guernsey came over on the SS *Ariadne*, and fired a salute as they came down The Swinge. As they approached Braye Bay, they were greeted by a tall mast with several flags, mounted on Grosnez Point, and a similar flag staff was mounted on the Bouillonaise rock in the sea about 400 yards away along the line the breakwater was to take. The Union Jack was flying on the Douglas Quay, and *Ariadne* anchored in the roadstead at 1.40 p.m. amongst flag-decorated shipping and with the town similarly bedecked. By 2 p.m. the Royal Alderney Militia, the Artillery under Capt. S. Robilliard and the Infantry under Major Barbenson, with many inhabitants, and the schoolchildren, were lined up on The Butes, overlooking Grosnez Point. By 3 p.m.,

THE FOUNDING OF A HARBOUR OF REFUGE AT ALDERNEY.

Laying the foundation stone for the Breakwater, 12 February 1847. Sketch by Paul Naftel.

Judge John Gaudion, the Alderney Court, the civil authorities of Alderney and Guernsey, including Col. de Havilland, were at the Point to lay the foundation stone. A large block of granite was waiting in a tipper truck on the end of the point, to which railway lines from the quarries now known as York Hill Quarry and Battery Quarry, had already been laid. Alderney's Minister, the Revd George Guille, blessed the undertaking, the Judge made a short speech, and the block was tipped into the sea, falling over the low cliff to an accompaniment of cannon and musket fire from the Militia.

The ceremony over, there was much feasting, with the workmen and the crew of *Ariadne*, about 150 people in all, being entertained at Braye, whilst the Court, the officials from Alderney and Guernsey, and the harbour officials, Mr Dickson the Engineer, and Mr Bisset, the Superintendent of Works, all dined at Baber's Hotel on The Butes. This was followed at 9 p.m. by a firework display on The Butes at which most of the population were present, a set piece firework display reading 'May The Harbour Prosper' ending the proceedings. A ball was then held for the 'Island Elite', bringing the day to a close.

Although the theory of a Harbour of Refuge is that it is a place of safety in which ships can seek shelter from storms, in practice it always has an offensive capability as well, and the three harbours planned for the Channel Islands could certainly have been expected to act as Naval Bases if need arose. In the event the one planned for Guernsey was never started, and the Jersey harbour began to silt up before it was finished. As eventually happened in Alderney, the western arm was completed, but the proposed, in Jersey much longer, eastern arm was abandoned after only about 400 feet had been built. The several different alternative plans for Alderney were each calculated for a given cost, but none of them were ever completed, and the project was finally terminated due to the excessive cost, by then well above the estimates, with only the western arm complete, and the first part of the eastern arm from Château à L'Étoc barely started, when it was abandoned in 1862.

As soon as the work was started, the French protested, despite their own similar activities. The British Government immediately denied any aggressive intent, and claimed that the bases were purely to provide protection and safe anchorage for shipping passing up and down the Channel.

This was perhaps a valid argument then, in the days of sailing ships, when they would have provided safe anchorages each side of the Channel, until the winds were suitable, and there are many records , in the surviving harbour records, of wind-bound vessels taking refuge inside the Breakwater in the 1860-70s. With the coming of steamships, which was just beginning, most such vessels could pass with equal facility in either direction, whatever the weather.

The Consultant Engineer, James Walker, (whose name does not appear in the *Illustrated London News* report of those present at the Founding Ceremony), had already designed, amongst many other projects, the East and West India Docks in London, Vauxhall Bridge, and the Victoria Pier in Jersey. The original designs for the two Channel Island breakwaters were similar, but events soon proved that the tidal forces exerted on the Alderney Breakwater were too great and the design was modified. Despite this, and the difficulties of construction causing an ever rising cost, the work went ahead.

As can be seen from the illustration below, taken from the Admiralty Plans, the original idea was to enclose about 25 acres of water with two arms, one starting from Grosnez Point, and the other from Roselle Point. The first design in 1847 was to enclose

Painting by G. S. Reynolds of the whole harbour works in 1852.

Detail of steam train from the Reynold's painting.

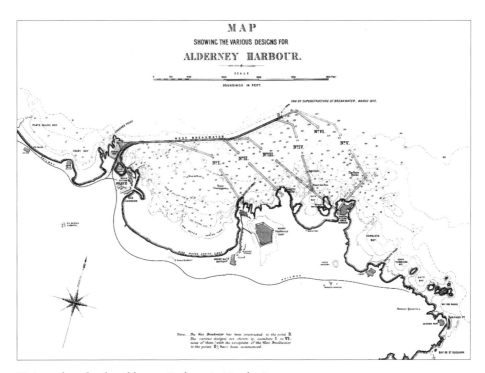

Various plans for the Alderney Harbour in March 1872.

25 acres over four fathoms, with only two acres of five fathom water and was estimated to cost £620,000, this was enlarged in 1854, and again in 1855, 1856, 1857 when four different proposals were put forward costing between £1.45 million and £1.7 million, each enclosing about 150 acres, and 1858. The final plan was eventually intended to provide sufficient anchorage for the entire Channel Fleet, enclose 163 acres including 65 acres of water with a depth above five fathoms, and to cost £2.5 million, but the continuous battering from the sea finally caused the construction of the western arm to be abandoned, about 1866, when it had reached 4,680 feet in length, at which point the water depth was over 130 feet, the depth and the currents making it impossible to form a stable rubble base, and no eastern arm was ever built from any of the several possible starting points proposed, apart from filling in a few small areas between tidal rocks at the shore end. (Another painting by Reynolds, showing the progress made by the Autumn of 1854 will be found in the colour section illustrations).

Parkes resigned as resident engineer at the end of 1849, and was replaced by Thomas Rhodes, with James May as his assistant. May took over in 1859 and Rhodes died in 1860. He continued in sole charge until 1870, when he went to superintend the building of the harbour at Alexandria. He was succeeded by L. F. Vernon-Harcourt a member of the Institution of Civil Engineers. The contractor's representative was Dickson from the commencement until 1857 when John Jackson took over until 1866, when the major construction work was finished. William Read then continued in charge until the end of the contract in 1872.

Walker died at the beginning of 1864 and his assistant, Burges, resigned shortly after. Mssrs McClean and Stileman were appointed chief resident engineers in February 1864. They resigned in July 1870 and were succeeded as Chief Engineer by Mr J. Hawkshaw CE.

The Breakwater had been visited on 9 August 1854, by Queen Victoria to see the work in progress, and this scene was also captured by Paul Naftel. His picture shows Queen Victoria stepping ashore from a rowing boat to be greeted by the important people of the island and their wives, the soldiers of the Militia and the Garrison and a huge gathering of islanders and visitors. (See colour section illustrations).

A similar painting now hangs in the Queen's Gallery at Buckingham Palace. The Queen and Prince Albert made a second, unexpected, visit in the Royal yacht on 8 August 1857, accompanied by a fleet of warships. They arrived in the evening and anchored in Braye Bay. Hurried preparations were made in the island, the Town Major, Col. William Le Mesurier and other officials dined on board the Royal Yacht and the Royal party came ashore after breakfast next morning. They travelled all over the island by carriage, and on the mineral railway in quickly adapted trucks, and departed that same evening.

By 1866, the construction had taken nearly 20 years, since it had only proved possible to work from about May to September, with some rubble tipping to enable the base to stabilise during the winter before the next year's construction work.

Meanwhile, the northern arm of the Jersey project at St Catherine's, about 2,500 feet long, had long since been completed, the southern arm, originally to be about 5,600 feet, and so much the longer of the two, had been discontinued after about 400 feet, and the whole project abandoned as it was already silting up.

About nine years had been spent in the construction and almost £250,000, excluding the land purchased, according to the Contractors reports. This sum differs considerably from the Admiralty report to the Board of Trade in 1866 which mentions a sum of £900,000 for the Jersey works.

Storms in 1864 and 1866 had caused extensive damage to the incomplete Alderney breakwater, and there was great dispute between the Admiralty, The Board of Trade and the Contractors, over liability for the cost of the repairs. This took more than a year to settle, and by this time the cost had already exceeded £1 million. When it was finally abandoned, the first arm had cost over £1,300,000.

After the storm damage in January 1870, civil engineer Mr J. Hawkshaw, who became President of the Institution of Civil Engineers and was later knighted, and Col. A. Clarke, RE, were requested by the Board of Trade to visit the site and make recommendations for the permanent securing of the breakwater. When Mssrs. McClean and Stileman resigned in July, Hawkshaw was appointed to continue the investigations and carry out the necessary work. That winter further breaches were made in the wall which were repaired in the spring, and survived the next winter.

More damage occurred in the winter of 1872-3 and the Government decided to resume maintenance and continue to repair the structure. Up to the end of 1864, when the main construction ceased, some four million tons of foreshoring stone had been deposited on the seaward side. From then until work finished in 1871 a further 332,000 tons of foreshoring was deposited, most of which had disappeared by 1873.

At the start of the project, cottages for the workmen had to be bought or built and much of the present Newtown originates from this time. Workshops, and a small hospital at the bottom of Braye Road, were built. The New Harbour, or Little Crabby Harbour was built, between 1847 and 1849, to accommodate the shipping, needed to transport the 2,000 or so tons of stone used daily for the foundations, out to sea. Earlier barges carried about 70 tons at a time, which was jettisoned at the correct place, by a mechanism which opened the bottom of the barge. They were towed from the specially designed loading jetty by a steam tug. The mechanisms which enabled the barges to be both loaded with blocks weighing up to seven tons, and emptied again, were designed on the spot by Jackson, of the construction company. The first barges (*below*) were replaced by several capable of carrying 100 tons, and one carrying 140 tons.

Early photo of the Breakwater building gear, *c.* 1870.

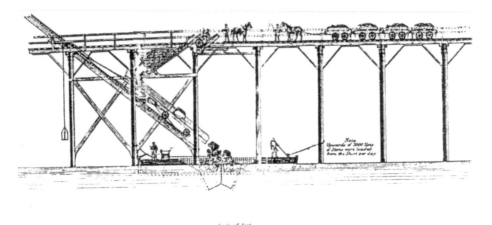

Jackson's barge loading chute.

Detail of Stone Barge from the Reynold's painting.

Cottages at Quesnard built by John Godfray for quarry workers, *c.* 1930.

A great army of workmen had to be accommodated, fed, and kept amused for five to six months each year, and the population of Alderney, in 1841 standing at 1,038, had increased by the Census of 1851 to 3333 of whom only 1671 were Channel Islanders, (the extra 600 or so islanders presumably coming in from Guernsey or Jersey to work). By 1859 it had increased to about 7,000 including Government workers and troops. In 1861, this figure had reduced to 4,932 (with 1,154 local residents), and 10 years later in 1871 to 2,738 including the Garrison.

John Godfray out at Quesnard built a block of 12 'back-to-back' cottages, each with one room up and one room down and a small porch, for workers in nearby Mannez quarry. Large water tanks were built beneath them to collect rainwater. The contractors threatened to dismiss any worker who went to live in one, and they remained empty for about 10 years. They were later used by other quarry workers until the Second World War, during which the Germans demolished them to open a field of fire for one of their batteries.

The Alderney Riots

The large band of workmen from time to time terrorised the inhabitants, extra police had to be brought in, and the street level window frames of some of the premises in Victoria Street and High Street still show the runners which accommodated thick wooden shutters erected at this period for the protection of both windows and inhabitants. Their presence led, in November 1847 to what became known as the 'Alderney Riots'.

Two workmen were put in jail, for assaulting the Constables during an affray in the High Street, the previous Tuesday evening, and released by mob-force on 25 November. Letters and a copy of an Act of the Alderney Court of the same date, were sent by the Alderney Judge to Government House in Guernsey. Copies of these were forwarded by Lt Col. W. I. Ward of the Engineers, acting on behalf of Lt Gen. Napier who was absent, to the Adjutant General on the 27th.

Alderney at this time had no garrison. Ward notes that he had had discussions about the incident with Lt Holgate, (the Alderney Harbourmaster then only on half-pay, who had been sent by the Judge with the letters), and did not consider it serious enough to justify sending troops to Alderney without the authority of the C-in-C. Col. Ward went on to suggest that

> ...whether, as the number of Workmen now employed in the construction at Bray Bay is about 400, and may be expected to increase; it may not be advisable to have a Detachment, not exceeding 1 Captain, 1 Subaltern and 48 rank and file stationed there for the preservation of the public peace, and which number can be accommodated in the Barracks at Longy.

The 'Act' referred to was passed by Judge John Gaudion and the Jurats at an extraordinary session of the Court, on account of an incident that morning when about 50 quarrymen had taken over the Town, with the intention of forcibly liberating the two prisoners. The Judge received warning of the attempt from an overseer at the quarries at 8 o'clock that morning. He had consulted with the Procureur, called out the Militia to surround and defend the Court, and placed another 35 men and a drummer in the School House, with orders not to use their firearms. The force was to be changed every 12 hours, in the hope that the Lt Governor would send sufficient troops promptly to keep the peace.

The Court had appointed extra Special Constables to serve in turns with the Militia, and ordered the tavern keepers and sellers of liquor to remain closed from 4 p.m. to 7 a.m. until further notice.

At about 9 o'clock, some 50 men, chiefly Cornish quarrymen, marched on the town to release the two prisoners, one of whom had been the ringleader of the riot in town the previous evening. The Judge's letter stated that; 'prudence forced me to consent to their release, as not having sufficient force to call upon to check them and avoid bloodshed'. He went on to say that he had placed a third of the Militia in a room in the centre of the Town who would keep the peace until the troops arrived. He also made the point that Longy Lines were two miles away, and the troops were needed in the Town to keep order, suggesting the Artillery Barracks on the Butes as being suitable accommodation. In a second letter of the same date to Lt Col. Ward, the Judge noted that the original affray was caused by; 'some 60 illiterate men knocking down and wounding some of the inhabitants', that the manager of the quarries was too scared to try and control them, and that Lt Holgate had his full authority to explain the situation personally.

On the 29th, Lord Fitzroy Somerset at the Horseguards sent a letter to Sir Dennis Le Marchant, the Assistant Secretary, to confirm the orders sent to the O/C Troops in Guernsey to send a detachment of infantry to Alderney, and a detachment of the 44th Foot arrived in Alderney on 4 December. On 13 December the Secretary of State, Sir George Grey sent a letter to the Judge requiring him to recapture the offenders and all connected with the riot if they were still in the island. In his reply, dated 20 December, the Judge stated that the prisoners and all concerned in the incident had left the island before the troops arrived. He went on to say that there had been further disturbances the previous Saturday on the monthly pay-day, but these had been contained by the Works Manager Mr Dixon, and 10 of his men, who had all been sworn as Special Constables, and the offenders apprehended and dealt with by the Court.

Le Marchant wrote again to 'the Acting Lt Governor of Alderney and Guernsey' (presumably Col. Ward) on 23 December saying that Grey thought the division of forces suggested by the Judge would destroy their efficiency if called upon to assist the Civil Power, and the whole force should be kept at Longy. He went on to say again that all concerned should be apprehended (if they are still in the Island) and brought to justice without delay. He further enclosed an extract of a letter which Mssrs. Walker & Co. had received from Mr Jackson the Contractor for the Alderney Works, stating that all concerned had been discharged and sufficient steps taken to prevent a repetition. He finished that; 'Sir George Grey Insists that the bringing the Offenders to Justice, and the precautions above alluded to, with the Military Force placed at the disposal of the Civil Authorities will be the means of securing the public peace in Alderney.'

The Judge's letter of the 20th was acknowledged on 24 December, but no further action appears to have been taken.

On 15 June 1847, Sir Walter Somerville had asked the Judge to have plans drawn up for a new Gaol in Alderney. It was approved in principal but Sir George Grey wanted details of the present gaol, and plans and proposals for the new one.

Lt Gen. Napier resigned his post on 9 January 1848, but 'plans for a prison for criminals and debtors, based on the Guernsey gaol; a gaoler's residence; Court House; and a records office and residence for the Greffier' were produced. These were submitted on 8 May 1848, by the new Lt Governor of Guernsey, Sir John Bell, to Sir Dennis Le Marchant, together with a letter from the Judge, and an Act of the Alderney Court authorising the construction. It was probably due to these incidents that a decision was taken to go ahead and build the new gaol in Alderney, as was stated in another letter dated 25 May, 'You cannot punish prisoners with no gaol'.

The works were to cost £4,021 15s 8d, and a request was made by the Alderney States to borrow the sum from the Treasury, and repay it, with interest at three per cent, at £350 per annum over 12 years.

Possibly stimulated by the difficulty of taking minor offenders to the Royal Court in Guernsey for trial, on 11 October, an Order-in-Council gave Alderney jurisdiction over petty criminal affairs in the island for the first time for several centuries.

There is much correspondence on the subject of the gaol in the Home Office papers. The Treasury felt that the gaol was too large, and there was no need for the residences. Bell's reply to this was that

> ...it is difficult in such a place without any precaution whatever for the proper control of a notoriously turbulent class of labourer, and does little credit to the authorities.

Judge Gaudion asked Bell for a copy of the 1846 Commissioner's report, on the laws of Guernsey to be sent to him, and this was forwarded on 19 June. Shortly after, Governor Bell wrote to G. Cornwall Lewis at the Home Office asking what was being done, and noting that the Judge was anxious to get it done before winter. He reported that the Breakwater and the new Church were progressing, and the plans for a '15-gun Tower to cost £8,000, were before Pall Mall'.

A letter from Daniel Tupper, Bailiff of Guernsey, to Sir Charles Trevelyan dated 19 August details the expenses of the Guernsey gaol, which were all paid by the crown, and recommends the building of the Alderney gaol as planned. He notes that 16 prisoners had been brought to Guernsey from Alderney since 1845, 10 of them since the new works started, generally for trivial offences, and stated that there was a garrison of 100 men there, and three steamers a week between the islands. The plans and estimates for the gaol were reduced somewhat in September, but in October, Bell was informed that there were no funds in the Treasury to finance the building. His reply supported the accuracy of a letter he enclosed from Judge Gaudion, and made the point that the crown should pay the costs of justice in Alderney as in Guernsey. The Judge had complained that many criminals go unpunished because of the heavy expense of sending them to Guernsey for trial, and blamed the government for having

> ...filled Alderney with a large number of people of the most unmanageable description.

Later that month Bell requested the return of the plans and estimates from the Home Office, and Lewis informed the Treasury that Alderney was building the gaol 'at their own cost'. Trevelyan then agreed to the crown paying for repairs to the building in future, the gaoler's salary, and the prisoner's maintenance.

The plans were eventually approved on 30 October 1848, and the construction was authorised by an Act of The States on 20 April 1849, with Captain David Fyffe of the 46th Regiment representing the Lieutenant Governor at the sitting.

In February 1850 Bell wrote again to Lewis, referring to his earlier letters, and stating that

> ...the extra staff needed for the new prison could be financed by abolishing the useless office of 'Public Executioner' who was paid by the crown. He also enclosed a sketch plan of Guernsey's 1811 prison.

By the beginning of April he was able to inform the Home Office that the building was nearing completion, and requesting a sum of £15 7s 4d to pay for the prisoner's bedding This was approved on 25 April, but had still not arrived in Alderney by the 20 June when he repeated the request. The building was finally completed and handed over to the Crown on 14 November 1851. (*See colour section*).

A force of Stone Masons, (despite the possible political implications, many of them French), were kept employed throughout these years dressing blocks of stone for the facing of the walls of the Breakwater and later for the Forts.

Quarterly reports of progress were submitted to the Admiralty, and on the outer face of the breakwater, the end of each year's work can be detected by a date carved into the stonework. This end section was specially reinforced to withstand the winter storms.

After much Parliamentary wrangling over several years, principally centring on whether or not to abandon the whole project to the mercy of the waves, a House of Lords investigating committee decided that such a vast expenditure could not be written off completely, and the facility should be maintained. Also to let it go would present a great hazard to shipping. All thought of constructing the eastern arm was abandoned.

About 2,000 feet of the outer part of the breakwater was reduced in 1870, leaving an undersea wall with only about 20 feet of water above it at low tide which still presents a potential, and occasionally an actual, hazard to shipping, projecting beyond the visible end of the Breakwater. This sunken arm has been the scene of many a temporary stranding, and one or two spectacular wrecks. The most recent of these was on 29 July 1980, when HMS *Sabre* collided with the sunken section at about 30 knots and ripped her bows off.

The 1870 reduction in length left the presently existing arm, 2,850 feet long.

In Jersey the completed and abandoned St Catherine's Breakwater was eventually handed to the States of Jersey, in 1877 , together with some of the other property purchased in 1847, property sufficient to bring in an income covering the maintenance costs, for nothing, after nearly 10 years of haggling about the price to be paid. During this time the annual maintenance cost had been around £100, and it has required only a comparatively small amount of upkeep to this day, a very different situation to that in Alderney.

In Alderney, the final three years were spent almost entirely on maintenance, and in building the slipway wall of dressed granite blocks. Almost 100,000 tons of stone were tipped along the length of the outerside of the breakwater in this period, to reduce the effect of the waves, and several huge breaches at places along its length, in particular the more distant end, around 4,000 to 4,500 feet, were repaired. A daily journal had been kept throughout the construction, and the last volume records that the winter of 1868/9 was

...the most stormy since the commencement of the works.

The nine volumes of these Journals also recorded daily details of the weather, tides, and shipping records, as well as the work done both on the breakwater and in the

A contemporary photo of the completed structure in 1870.

Aerial photo of the Breakwater, *c.* 1990, showing the dark line of the submerged part.

quarries. The last volume also recorded two unfortunate deaths; William Bowring (57), of Weymouth, who had worked on the project for 12 years fell into the sea with his horse from the top of the wall on 20 October 1868, and on 19 January 1869, Hugh Cameron (47), of Inverness, a night watchman at the Quarry was run over and killed after jumping off a moving train at the quarry end, in the evening. That same month it was noted that at 24 feet four inches above datum, the highest tide for 22 years was recorded, and on 29 March 1869, the low tide was one foot six inches below the datum line.

Some 600 stonemasons were still employed when, after the quarries had been 'cleaned out', the contract finally finished, on 30 September 1871. On 16 November, Sir J. Hawkshaw sent a list to the Board of Trade from the ledgers, giving details of all the land that had been used in the project, which had either been sold off or was to be sold by the contractors, or was let to tenants at the end of the construction work. This list also notes in many cases from whom the land was bought in the first place, and the date, price, and the use to which it had been put. Most of these purchases are of much later date than those already mentioned, and obviously had been made as the work proceeded, the last being dated in August 1860, when several parcels of land were purchased by the Admiralty from some 16 islanders. This ledger also notes whether the purchases were paid for in Guernsey or British currency. (In Guernsey, eight doubles equalled one penny, but the Pound Sterling equalled 21/- Guernsey money at this time).

It records for instance that Mssrs. Jackson and Bean had provided and maintained a Reading Room on the corner of Braye Street, where one of the 'Leading Lights' for the harbour entrance was sited, and that a Lifeboat House and Stables had been constructed on the site where the stone was stored. One also reads that, at the end of the contract Mssrs. Jackson and Bean were selling 23 cottages & gardens to the Board of Trade, and had already sold another seven cottages with gardens, and a house, outhouse & garden, to them for a total of £80, (with the cottages mostly priced at £6). By a curious coincidence, at the time of the evacuation in 1940, the 1942 Impey census shows that The War Office still owned 23 cottages, and the Granite Company had six cottages used as stores, near the harbour. Almost certainly the same properties.

Another *house, outhouses and garden* had been sold to the Admiralty for £2,000. The site over which the railway embankment commenced for the Eastern Breakwater passes, is noted, and also, that

> ...there passed from the Treasury to the Admiralty many years ago, a field; This piece of ground surrounding the old Telegraph Tower does not strictly belong to the Harbour Lands, having been formerly used by the Admiralty as a Telegraph Station – but if all the Admiralty Lands in this Island have been transferred to the Board of Trade, this piece must be included amongst them.

The copy of the plans and ledger entries was furnished by C. C. Trevor of the Harbour Department of the Board of Trade, to the Under Secretary of State at the War Office, three days after the passing of the Alderney Harbour Transfer Act 1874.

The Breakwater Workers in 1890.

Destroyers of the Channel Fleet in Braye Harbour in June 1906.

Foreshoreing blocks weighing several tons to protect the Breakwater wall.

One of the early engines on the railway *c.* 1893.

It was obvious that the small community of Alderney could not sustain the expense of maintaining its own *White Elephant*, as it came to be called, but strong pleas were made by the islanders, that, since their previous harbour had been spoilt by the new construction, having rapidly silted up after the breakwater was built, the new one must be maintained, and eventually, on 25 October 1874, The Alderney Harbour Transfer Act, 1874 (passed in Parliament on 20 October), was signed at Balmoral by the Queen. This transferred the harbour and its immediate appurtenances from the Board of Trade, the Admiralty, the Treasury and the Commissioners of Woods and Forests, as appropriate, to the Secretary of State for the War Department. The full details being recorded in the documents above.

The Admiralty moorings were to be reserved exclusively for Admiralty vessels or those authorised by them, and they, and the War Department, were given powers to exclude the public from any part of the area, when it was considered necessary. Henceforth the maintenance would be the responsibility of the War Department. For the next 114 years, except for the 1940-45 period, a small force was maintained constantly on Alderney by the British Government to maintain it, and until the evacuation in 1940, stone from the quarries was still cut almost daily for this purpose.

In the First World War, searchlights and gun batteries were maintained on Roselle Point to protect the Harbour entrance, and the remains of these can still be inspected. (See recent photo in the colour section).

The UK Government offered to give the Breakwater to Alderney in the summer of 1922, on condition that it continued to be maintained by the Granite Company, and that certain taxes, landing fees, etc. were imposed on the island to help pay the cost. This was accepted by the States without reference to the people, and raised strong protests, resulting in a public meeting on 27 September in which Alderney born surgeon, Sir Henry Gauvain took an active part. An act to reform the Alderney States was already under consideration which later, when it was passed in 1923 included 'People's Deputies' for the first time as members of the States, and the delay in introducing this Act was much quoted in the debates on the Breakwater scheme. The scheme was eventually abandoned, and it continued to be maintained by the British Government until the island was evacuated in 1940.

In the Second World War, during the early part of their occupation, the Germans were forced to import labour from Guernsey and Sark to carry out essential repairs and maintenance of the Breakwater, and several Batteries and searchlights were mounted for its defence, at Fort Grosnez, Fort Albert, The Arsenal, along Braye Beach, and on the Breakwater itself. Guernsey paid the cost of the maintenance work, which involved, on the first repair alone, some 7,800 tons of stone, and hoped to recover its expenses from the British Government after the war.

After the island was freed in 1945, the work of maintaining the Breakwater was carried on by the Ministry of Works, later to become the Department of the Environment. The first post-war work commenced on 6 November 1948, at which time there was a huge breach at sections 46/7, the railway was washed away at section 32, the high wall was washed away at sections 54/5, and many minor breaches and damage were found along the remainder of the length.

R.F.A. *Robert Dundas* arrived on the 9 November with a quantity of new plant, including an RB 33 crane *(page opposite)* which had to be reassembled, (a job which took a fortnight). The German locomotive and an old RB 19 crane were taken away when she left on the 13th. Over the next few months *Robert Dundas* and SS *Radford* each made a number of calls with new plant and equipment for the breakwater, quarry and railway, and on most occasions took away old equipment and machinery when they left.

The railway was unusable so tipper lorries were brought in to move the stone, and a gang of men were set to cleaning out the quarries of the loose stone and rubble. The new crane was moved up to Mannez Quarry on 27 November and another old RB 19 there, was adapted for use as a shovel.

In December the weighbridge at the quarry was restored, and the foundations for a new crusher laid. By the following March, Fort Albert was being prepared as a hostel for the gang of breakwater workers. Roofs had been repaired, a new canteen floor laid, and the buildings decorated, with new hot water systems, drains and plumbing being installed, by a gang of 10 craftsmen brought from England. The breakwater and quarry workers reached a peak of about 40 in number then. In the same month, new beds were laid in the Electricity shed (used until the late 1990's by Alderney Fuel Services), for new generators to be installed.

A new excavator was installed at the quarry, a Pegson stone-crusher was assembled there, with various size screens, and could produce about 20 tons of crushed stone

The old Sheldon-Cowan crane, working in Mannez quarry in 1946.

Sheldon-Cowan steam crane working on the Breakwater in 1950.

Wartime damage to the Breakwater before repair in 1948.

Breakwater damage from a storm in January 1962.

The Breakwater in a storm in August 1989.

Rushton generators at the Power Station in 1950s.

a day. The railway line was having the cuttings excavated to a width of 11 feet, to enable new track to be laid. The old 'Jubilee' rails on the breakwater, installed in 1935, were excavated from the stone deck and relaid. By May the pre-war Ruston-Hornsby locomotive was repaired ready to be shipped back to the UK when a new locomotive arrived, and the railway could be reopened. Night shifts were started on the breakwater in June to take advantage of the tides, the Alderney Light and Power Company laid on floodlights, and work on repairing the breaches continued, moving 7-800 tons of stone in the tipper-lorries each week.

Civil Engineer R. W. Bishop was appointed to superintend the repairs from 1 April 1949 to the end of September when they were finished. Some further damage occurred that winter which was repaired in 1950.

From June to September 1949, R.F.A. *Robert Middleton* made a number of visits loaded with hundreds of concrete sleepers, and new rails, to enable the track to the quarry to be relaid, and cement for the breakwater, and departed with old rails, plant, and spares. By October the new rails were being laid to the quarry, and the shuttering around the biggest breach at section 47 was being removed, although it took almost two years to complete all the repairs to the storm damage which had occurred during the war, during which the Germans had done only minor maintenance. Also during this month, the hostel at Fort Albert was disbanded and the stores and furniture shipped out.

Once the railway line was relaid the steam engine *Molly* was brought in, new tipper, wagons were imported, the steam-crane was also fully mobile between breakwater and quarry, and daily drilling, blasting, and loading or crushing work was carried on at Mannez.

Molly 1, which was probably the only steam engine in the British Isles at the time to be equipped with a lifebelt, was involved in two accidents with cars at the level crossings in December 1957, and the expenditure on the Breakwater that year was noted as £23,000. During the following year the railway was improved, a loop was built at Mannez, and a turntable installed. A new Diesel Locomotive, later named *Molly II* arrived on board MV *Jersey Coast* on 4 November, and took about two weeks to assemble and fit a lifebelt. Its first trial run to the quarry pulling 75 tons of wagons took 40 minutes due to the drive chain being too tight. Adjustments were made, and the next day the run was accomplished in 10 minutes. During the early part of 1959 about three months were spent converting and rebuilding *Molly I*. The cab was demolished and the funnel shortened. Much of the track was again relaid that summer, and on 30 October had its '1,000 mile service' started, which took 10 days to complete. The last blasting at the quarry for some time took place in March 1960, the stockpiles of stone continuing to be used, and two-ton blocks being 'cleaned' from the quarry face, with the crusher making about 20 tons a day. Some 700 tons of stone blocks a month continued to be shifted to the breakwater.

Blasting was recommenced, and the base for a new crusher laid in December 1961, with the crusher being erected, tested, and adjusted, only two days before another enormous breach 120 feet long, was made in the wall at the landward end in a storm

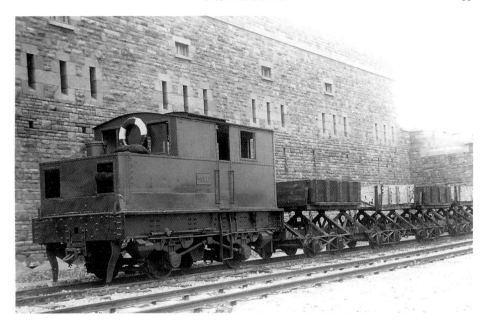

Steam engine *Molly 1* with stone wagons at Fort Grosnez in 1955. Note the life belt.

on 11 January 1962, which became extended a few days later. Whilst repairs were being carried out, on several occasions the day's work was washed away overnight, and the breach was extended again on 5 April, and the slipway ripped up. The January breach was finally closed on 2 May. To make these repairs a new technique using precast blocks which were made with cement and the crushed stone, at Grosnez using special moulds, at the rate of about five a day, was tried, and some 400 such blocks were used to close the breach. Further storms on 19 May washed newly placed blocks in other damaged sections, into the harbour. A new RB 33 crane arrived on 26 May, and on 23 June fell into the harbour. It took about a week to get most of it out again, with some parts still being recovered in September. Another new crane was delivered on 14 August. Meanwhile the last of the breaches had been closed, and the repair completed on 25 July.

Work continued daily, with about 25 men being fully employed on the project, and there were regular visits from the Department of Works supervisors. A 'Jumbo Crane' and a new Land-Rover were delivered by Landing craft on 28 June 1966 and R.F.A. *Robert Dundas*, still in service some 20 years after its first visit, brought new dumper trucks and two loads of Boom Defence Nets in July and September 1967. The nets were used to try and contain the foreshoring material, by packing them with smaller rocks and lowering them into place, since the hot-asphalting foreshoring techniques tried in the early 1960s had not proved very successful.

It is estimated that the amount which has been spent on preserving the structure since then is at an annual figure in excess of £100,000.

In 1988, as her contribution to the Defence costs of the British Government,

Loop extension to railway at Mannez Quarry, winter of 1958.

The RB33 crane after assembly following its delivery in 1948.

Molly 2, after the 1960s rebuild, towing the steam crane along the Breakwater.

Guernsey agreed to take over the responsibility for all future maintenance, expecting this estimated annual figure to be the likely cost to their budget, and the ownership of the Breakwater was transferred to the States of Guernsey. Alderney was to contribute £15,000 a year as her share of the costs, and receive a peppercorn rent of £1 a year for the buildings used by Guernsey.

With the quarries not functioning after the 1960s, much of the repair work has been done since then, with four-and-a-half-ton precast concrete blocks, probably similar to many made during the original construction, which were placed in the foot of the wall on top of the rubble base, although some of the huge pile of stone left at Mannez at the end of the quarrying is used from time to time. It is worthy of note that many of the stone blocks used at the turn of the century are noted as weighing from 60 to 180 tons on contemporary photographs, well beyond the lifting capabilities of the machinery in use. These were cast on top of the breakwater on rollers opposite their required position, and pushed over the side, since there never was any equipment in Alderney capable of transporting them. The present permanent workforce employed numbers eight men.

The Mineral railway was restored to good order in the late 1970s and early 1980s, by the Alderney Railway Society, which runs trains as a tourist attraction during the season, and is still available for transporting stone to the breakwater if needed. A steam locomotive *J. T. Daly* was used to pull converted wagons in about 2000. This was later sold and replace by the diesel-esngined *Elizabeth* which had been in a shed at Fort Grosnez for years. Elizabeth is still functioing in 2012 and can now be assisted by *Molly 2* which was stored in another shed until it was completely overhauled in 2010. Either engine is now used, mainly during the Tourist season and at Christmas to pull two old London Underground Northern-line coaches which have been refurbished by the members from the Quarry to the Harbour and back.

Hurricane force winds from the North-west, on 11 January 1962, which continued for several days, lashed the waves to a height of more than 200 feet above the wall, a large section of the coping and upper deck was washed away half way along the arm, and on 1 March the upper wall at its junction with Fort Grosnez was washed away for a distance of about 40 yards, and a hole punched right through the Victorian foundations of the breakwater and beneath the roadway, at the junction with the slipway. This place was immediately below the wall erected to repair the 1962 gap, but that wall held firm. The breach was about 15 feet high and 30-50 yards long. The estimate for the repair of the latest damage amounted to £500,000, but the work took above eight months,

Steam Engine *J. T. Daly* towing converted wagons, *c.* 2000.

Diesel-engined *Molly* 2 after a refit in 2010. She was also fitted with a life belt in 1959.

with a specialist team from England being brought to assist, and the final cost was around £1,000,000. This firm have continued the maintenance work ever since. The saga of mounting costs looks set to continue well into the next century. Meanwhile the Breakwater continues to form a dominant part of Alderney's landscape whether viewed from land, sea, or air, and an essential protection for the large number of visiting yachts now using the Harbour during the season.

In 1992 the States of Guernsey decided to investigate the possibility of reducing the length and turning the end inwards towards the beach, in the hope of reducing maintenance costs. Models were set up for tank tests on the feasibility, and a report was expected in 1993. Money to carry out the survey was not voted until late 1994 and there was no change in the situation by the end of 1995, with contractors still carrying out a continuous repair and maintenance programme.

In the meanwhile another of the several schemes considered in recent years by the States of Alderney to construct a yacht marina has had to be postponed pending the outcome of these tests and the subsequent decisions. It was finally announced in July

2012 that a scheme to build a deep water marina inside the brakwater from the old Blacksmith's shop to about opposite the tip of the newly rebuilt commercial jetty had been approved and was expected to start shortly. It remains to be seen!!

The Commercial Quay

The Commercial Quay, built in the late 1890's after much debate and disagreement between pro and ante 'jettyites', to replace the 'Douglas Quay' which had silted up and made it impossible for all but the smallest ships to tie up alongside, thus forcing passengers to be lightered ashore and cargo such as coal, building materials and cattle feed, to be transferred in small boats, greatly to the detriment of both Alderney's tourist and commercial trade.

The benefit of the new quay, opened fully in May 1897, was immediately obvious. Passengers and freight could be landed directly instead of using lighters or carrying

Two views of the German Jetty, taken when the island was liberated in May 1945.

The cranes were removed and long in use at St Sampson's harbour in Guernsey.

The newly widened and extended Commercial Quay in 2011.

The former Napoleonic Braye Battery. A German photo from 1942.

things ashore when the boats were grounded at low tide. A regular flow of tourists began. and in the last six months of that year 21,685 tons of stone were exported. A period of rapidly increasing prosperity resulted.

The Commercial Quay had served the island well for more than a century, had been greatly extended by the Germans during the 1940-45 Occupation, with deep water berths for up to six ships, (*above*) but the extension had, probably mistakenly as events turned out, been completely demolished in the late 1950's.

The original quay, after many years of the minimum maintenance expenditure, was completely rebuilt, widened and improved in 2009-10, with several delays and a huge increase over the originally estimated cost, but can now accept the berthing of larger cargo ships and oil tankers on either side, if necessary with both berths in use at the same time.

8

The Forts and the Garrisons

1. The Victorian Defences

Coinciding with the decision to erect the Breakwater, came the need to defend it. Batteries flanking the 'Old Harbour' in Braye Bay were already in position from the time of the Le Mesuriers, and the Telegraph Tower, Fort Doyle and Platte Saline battery had also been constructed, but it was considered that these were not sufficient, and that the entire island needed to be defended.

As has been shown in Chapter 5, there was no regular garrison in Alderney between 1824 and 1852, when the 11th Field Company Royal Engineers arrived. By this time several of the forts were almost completed. Fort Grosnez was the first to be completed, at a cost of £37,000, had 29 guns and accommodation for four officers, and 150 men. The first foot soldiers to come after this, were the 72nd Regiment of Foot, in 1856, (whose name was later changed in the reorganisation of 1882 to 1st Btn Seaforth Highlanders). Coincidentally, they were the last unit to have been in garrison in the old Forts from May 1823 to March 1824

It was not so long after that, in 1830, that the common lands were divided up among the inhabitants to alleviate their financial distress, caused after the Garrisons were withdrawn when the French wars finished. The War Office had then retained a 100-foot-wide strip on some beaches and cliffs, particularly on the north and east of the island, and some other land, including a 300-foot-wide strip along the beach at Longis, where rifle butts were later erected, and along the east coast. They did not have sufficient land however to build the chain of forts which was envisaged and between 1847 and 1853, numerous parcels of land were purchased from their many owners.

Land at the Rochers, for another quarry, (now known as Battery Quarry, and the Island's principal Water Reservoir), totalling just over 100 vergées from 22 families and costing £4,559 was bought in various parcels between 1847 and 1851. Five vergées from four owners to extend the railway to Saye to facilitate the erection of Château à L'Étoc, and to provide access to the proposed starting point for the eastern arm of the Breakwater, cost £243 5s 0d, whilst the 15½ vergées of pasture forming Mount Hale, cost £588 14s 6d from seven owners in 1852 and 1853.

Last to be bought at this time, was the land for Fort Tourgis, 16½ vergées bought from seven families for £1,005 19s 0d in 1853, in which same year, Fort Grosnez, the plans of

A hundred feet above high water mark Boundary marker on the track to Fort Clonque.

which were authorised on 24 April 1850, with its 29 guns, defending the Breakwater from its western end, was completed. The entire force of Gunners in the Militia was needed to operate these pieces alone.

The general unrest throughout Europe had already decided the British Government to refortify the Channel Islands, and establish harbours from which the Channel Fleet could operate in both Alderney and Jersey.

These events had led to the building of the Breakwater, and the purchase of some of the land needed to build the defending forts, which would be essential if the Harbour of Refuge was to be of any use in a time of war. Similar Harbours of Refuge were built at about the same time at Portland Down, Dover, and Harwich. By the time the Crimean War began, these, and their supporting Forts, were almost complete, but with Britain and France now close allies in the war against Russia, were hardly likely to be needed.

As well as the original plans, War Office records contain considerable detail about the materials to be used in the construction of the Forts, and each individual item of the construction was priced, with premiums being paid over these prices, of two per cent for the work done on Rochers, four per cent for the Batteries round the coast, and five per cent for work done at Corblets, Longy, Nunnery and Clonque. There existed at this time a set of standard books which the military engineers and masons used to follow. For instance, in the *Schedule of Contract for Mason's Work for the Service of the Honourable Board of Ordnance in the Island of Alderney*, we see that

The stone in masonry steps, landing sills, coping, flagging, hearths, channels and sinks to be placed with the grain, or natural quarry bed of the stone, horizontal; in arches the grain radiating to their centres; in all curbs the grain to be vertical.

The common mortar to be composed of one part Devonshire limestone, kilned in Alderney, [2 lime kilns were built at the 'New' Harbour for this purpose], to four parts of either screened land gravel, free from loam, or coarse screened Plat Saline gravel. The blue lias mortar, of one part of Lyme Regis limestone kilned in Alderney to two and one half parts of either screened land gravel free from loam, or coarse Plat Saline gravel.

All the masonry shall be fronted with hot lime until the cavities are filled up, from the foundations to the finishing course.

Salt water or sea sand is on no occasion to be used in any process or part of the manufactures used, without instructions in writing from the Superintending Officer.

The Roman cement to be of the best quality, fresh, that would set within a quarter of an hour, and subject to the approval of the Superintending Officer.

Much more, similar detail, was set out for the Mason's work, and other schedules were prepared for the other craftsmen to follow. The Carpenters were required to; 'conform minutely to all designs, drawings and instructions in writing', the sources of supply of the various timbers were specified, and the nails, ironmongery and screws to be according to the Engineer's pattern book. The Bricklayers were to use bricks that were; 'first quality Guernsey, sound, hard, well burnt, of a proper shape and size, with no four adjoining courses to exceed 12 inches in height', and the pantiles and mortar were specified.

The slaters were also supplied with minute detail; the slates were to be; 'Delabole or Bangor, nailed with iron nails dipped in boiled oil, two strong nails to each slate'. If laid on battens the slates were to be 'plastered with one coat lime and hair mortar against the underside of the slating', and the mortar itself was to consist of; 'Two parts of lime to three parts of sand from Longy Common or Plat Saline, as may be ordered, with one pound of dried and well beaten ox-hair to three cubic feet of lime'.

The roofs of both the Officers' and Soldiers' Barracks were to be

...fireproof, of iron girders carrying 9 inches arches of stock brickwork in mortar, filled in concrete, trowelled off with a coating of fine concrete in which rain water channels were to be formed to discharge points through the wall and the whole;

to be covered with two thicknesses of half inch each of Claridge's best Seyssel Asphalte, breaking joints carried up the parapet wall and chimney shafts at least 9in. and over the top of the parapet, the joints to be well raked out to receive the Asphalte, and the surface to be well gritted and lime-whited, twice done....

The Forts, except for the first erected, Fort Grosnez, were all designed by Captain William Jervois, (later Lt General Sir William Jervois, who was later still appointed Governor-general of New Zealand), most with a somewhat mediæval appearance, including drawbridges, arrow slits and crenellations, and the construction of each was supervised by a junior officer. Jervois was then aged 32, and newly married when he came to Alderney in June 1852. Fort Touraille, later renamed Fort Albert, the largest, and the last to be built, was of an unusual hexagonal shape to conform to the contours of Mt. Touraille, and was completed in 1858, with the supporting Arsenal and Mount Hale Battery; Château à L'Étoc in 1854; Fort Corblets was completed in 1855, and Fort Quesnard in 1853. This latter fort is of particular interest, in that its construction was supervised by Lt Gordon who later became General Gordon of Khartoum fame.

Of the four island forts, Fort Les Hommeaux Florains, (1858), and Fort Houmet Herbé, (1853), were to have flat roofs of wood with boarding and asphalte on the barracks, and slates on the Artillery Stores, whilst Fort Rat Island (1853), (as Fort Raz was invariably referred to in all the documents), and Fort Clonque (1855) were to have the same fireproof vaulted roofs as the larger forts.

Fort Tourgis, authorised on 15 April 1853 with an estimated cost of £22,026 3s 2d, was completed in 1855. The windows of this Fort were to be

...provided with bars and Iron Shutters having long horizontal loopholes in them formed by being left 4 inches shorter at the bottom than the window itself.

When the ring of Victorian Forts were completed, after six years, at a cost in excess of £272,000, their full complement of armaments was to be 140 guns which was obviously beyond the capabilities of the island to service. Queen Victoria came to visit the Breakwater in 1854, and the entire Militia was on parade in its two units. Shortly after, the infantry unit of the Royal Alderney Militia was disbanded, and their activities fully concentrated on the Artillery defences, thereafter, an Artillery Garrison was maintained. Islander Philip Mesney erected his house and buildings (the ruins of which can still be seen), near the Longis rifle butts in 1860, and in May the following year was complaining bitterly to the Court, of the danger to his home being caused by firing practice there. They do not seem to have been greatly sympathetic, because the butts continued in use into the present century. A long, tall, stone wall was however built close by during the Victorian era,, which could have been intended to provide the necessary protection. Known locally as *the Hole in the Wall* because of a large circular hole, made in the middle, possibly by a shell, during the Second World War and only filled in again in 1992.

A further defensive strategy was put forward in about 1863. A record of this is to be found under the heading of *England's Broad Stone of Honour* on pp. 427-439 of a book I have so far been unable to trace as to Title and Author, having only a copy of this Chapter. After an extensive review of the defences so far constructed and the progress of the breakwater into deep water at that moment, with the expected commencement shortly of the Eastern arm, the author goes on to say that all the forts on the eastern part of the island could be quickly reduced by the guns of a mail-clad steam frigate.

In brief, the idea proposed was to cut a half-mile Canal across the island between Saye and Longis Bays. The author states that if a wide trench were cut, it would be quickly scoured out by the action of the sea, leaving a steep cliff on the side opposite the detached promontory. This would reduce the length of coastline to be defended by almost a half, and do away with the necessity of keeping up five forts.

The author continues with a fairly accurate review of the other defences, both natural and Military of the island, its agriculture, its population, and its strategic importance. He notes that the Telegraph cable is once again out of action, and states, somewhat less accurately, that the expenditure on the harbour and forts had already reached £8 millions.

Not surprisingly, since to separate part of Alderney in this way would offer a potential base on which an enemy could establish himself, the scheme was never adopted.

The armaments of the various forts in 1866, by which time they were well established and garrisoned, (by this time there were both rifled muzzle loading (r.m.l), and breech loading (r.b.l.) guns, in addition to the original smooth bore (s.b.) armaments), in brief summary, amounted to:

Fort Grosnez:
> 2 x 68-pdr s.b., 2 x 64-pdr r.m.l., 2 x 40-pdr r.b.l., 3 x 32-pdr s.b.,
> 5 x 8-inch s.b., 2 x 8-inch s.b. howitzers.

Bray Battery:
> 9 x 68-pdr s.b.

Mount Hale Battery:
> Nil

Arsenal:
> 1 x 64-pdr r.m.l.

Fort Albert:
> 4 x 68-pdr s.b., 7 x 64-pdr r.m.l., 4 x 8-inch s.b., 1 x 7-inch r.b.l., including
> 2 x 64-pdr at Roselle.

Château à L'Étoc:
> 4 x 68-pdr s.b., 2 x 64-pdr r.m.l., 4 x 8-inch s.b., 1 x 7-inch r.b.l.

Fort Les Hommeaux Florains:
> 1 x 68-pdr s.b., 2 x 32-pdr s.b.

Fort Quesnard:
> 4 x 8-inch s.b.

Fort Houmet Herbé:
> 3 x 68-pdr s.b.

Fort Rat Island, (Ile de Raz):
> 4 x 64-pdr r.m.l.

The Nunnery:
> Nil

Longy Lines:
> Frying Pan Battery; 1 x 64-pdr r.m.l.
> Other batteries; 3 x 8-inch s.b., 1 x 10-inch howitzer.

Fort Essex:
> No armaments, used as a hospital and barracks.

Fort Clonque:
> 1 x 68-pdr s.b., 4 x 64-pdr r.m.l., 1 x 8-inch s.b.

Fort Tourgis; 4 x 68-pdr s.b., 4 x 64-pdr r.m.l, 2 x 24-pdrs s.b, 6 x 8-inch s.b.

Plat Saline Battery:
> 5 x 68-pdr s.b.

Fort Doyle:
> 2 x 8-inch s.b.

There were four nine-pdr bronze smooth bore guns and 2 x 24-pdr bronze howitzers stored in the Butes Gun Shed, and six 40-pdr rifled breechloaders in store at Fort Albert. The projected Redoubt on the summit of Les Rochers overlooking the entire harbour area, was never built, although two small magazines were earlier built near there, and are still in evidence, incorporated into houses.

Despite this heavy load of artillery, once again, as so many times in the past, with the various cannons which had been deployed in Alderney, and as was later to be the case in the First World War, and (with a few exceptions, principally shortly after D-day in 1944), by the defences erected by the Germans in the Second World War, not a shot was ever fired in anger by any of these weapons. By the time the First World War started most of the ordnance had been withdrawn, and there were only two six-inch r.b.l. guns and two rapid fire 12-pounders left guarding the harbour, and some carriage-mounted field guns stored at the Butes Arsenal.

The 15th Regiment (East Yorkshire) may have returned for a time in 1852, and the first regular unit of the Royal Artillery, the 1st Company of the 9th Battalion, under Captain Telwin, arrived in June 1853.

From 1856, the island was garrisoned continuously, there are still a few uncertainties as to the exact dates and order in which some of the infantry regiments were here, and there must also have been a continuous presence of the Artillery personnel, some of whom are recorded after the table below, but as far as details have been ascertained, the tables on the following pages give the sequence of occupation by the infantry units:

Date	Regiment	
8/1856 – 4/1857	(72nd)	1st Btn Seaforth Highlanders, HQ Guernsey, half strength in Alderney.

From 1857 to 1863, no regular garrison was maintained in Guernsey.

1857	(73rd)	2nd Btn Royal Highland Rgt, The 'Black Watch'
1858	(36th)	The Hereford Rgt, later became 2nd Btn The Worcestershire Rgt
4/1859 – 5/1860	(1st/15th)	East Yorkshire Rgt
6/1860 – 5/1861	(30th)	The Cambridgeshire Rgt HQ in Jersey. Later became 1st Btn, East Lancashire Rgt
3/1861 – 6/1862	(55th)	2nd Btn The Border Rgt, HQ in Jersey.
6/1862 – 2/1863	(2nd/18th)	The Royal Irish Rgt, HQ in Jersey,

After which, until 1873 there were usually detachments in both Guernsey and Alderney, from units with their HQ in Jersey.

8/1863 – 8/1864	(61st) 2nd Btn		The Gloucestershire Rgt
8/1864 – 7/1865	(2nd/1st)		The Royal Rgt (Scots)
7/1865 – 7/1866	(1st/6th)		Royal Warwickshire Rgt

Date	Regiment	
7/1865 – 3/1867	(69th)	South Lincolnshire Rgt. Later became 2nd Btn Welch Rgt
3/1867 – 4/1868	(66th)	2nd Btn The Berkshire Rgt
4/1868 – 4/1869	(43rd)	The Monmouthshire Light Inf. later became 1st Btn, The Oxfordshire Light Infantry.
4/1869 – 7/1870	(2nd/17th)	The Leicestershire Rgt
7/1870		8th Battery RA brought to relieve the 2nd Bty
7/1870 – 5/1871	(2nd/15th)	The East Yorkshire Rgt
5/1871 – 7/1872	(1st/22nd)	The Cheshire Rgt
7/1872 – 8/1873	(1st/9th)	The Norfolk Rgt, HQ in Guernsey
7/1873 – 9/1873	(84th)	2nd Btn Yorks and Lancs Rgt, HQ in Jersey

From this time on, the HQ of the Alderney detachments returned to Guernsey.

Date	Regiment	
9/1873 – 7/1874	(1st/15th)	The East Yorks Rgt
7/1874 – 6/1875	(2nd/6th)	The Royal Warwickshire Rgt
6/1875 – 6/1876	(61st)	2nd Btn The Gloucestershire Rgt
6/1876 – 5/1877	(104th)	104th Bengal Fusiliers (British troops raised by E.India Co.) later became 2nd Btn The Royal Munster Fusiliers
5/1877 – 5/1878	(75th)	1st Btn The Gordon Highlanders
5/1878 – 4/1879	(105th)	Light Madras Infantry (British troops) later became 2nd Btn The King's Own Yorkshire Light Infantry
4/1879 – 9/1879	(64th)	1st Btn Prince of Wales North Staffordshire Rgt HQ in Jersey
9/1879 – 7/1880	(107th)	107th Bengal Fusiliers later became 2nd Btn The Royal Sussex Rgt
7/1880 – 4/1881	(87th)	1st Btn The Royal Irish Fusiliers
4/1881 – 11/1882	(1st/22nd)	1st Btn The Cheshire Rgt

After this date the British Army was reorganised and the regiments were, with a few exceptions, given the name of the county from which they originated and where they had their Depôts. When in the Channel Islands, the Alderney contingent usually had its HQ unit at Fort George, in Guernsey.

Date	Regiment	Notes
11/1882 – 9/1884	1st Btn The Middlesex Rgt	
9/1884 – 12/1885	1st Btn The Royal Irish Rifles, (late 83rd County of Dublin Regiment)	
12/1885 – 8/1887	2nd Btn The Gordon Highlanders	

9/1887 – 4/1888	2nd Btn The Border Rgt	
4/1888 – 2/1891	2nd Btn The East Surrey Rgt	
2/1891 – 5/1893	2nd Btn K.O.Y.L.I.	
5/1893 – 11/1895	2nd Btn The Royal Fusiliers	
11/1895 – 5/1897	2nd Btn The Somerset Light Infantry	
5/1897 – 9/1897	2nd Btn The Northamptonshire Rgt	HQ in Jersey
9/1897 – 9/1899	2nd Btn The Wiltshire Regiment	
9/1899 – 1/1900	1st Btn The Worcestershire Rgt	
1/1900 – 4/1901	3rd Btn The Suffolk Rgt	
4/1901 – 7/1901	4th Btn The Norfolk Rgt	
7/1901 -12/1902	3rd Btn The Lincolnshire Rgt	
12/1902 – 9/1904	2nd Btn The Leicestershire Rgt	
9/1904 -10/1907	2nd Btn The Manchester Rgt	
10/1907 -10/1910	2nd Btn The Middlesex Rgt	
10/1910 -10/1913	2nd Btn The Royal Irish Rgt	
10/1913 – 7/1914	2nd Btn The Yorkshire Rgt	(The Green Howards)
7/1914 – 9/1916	4th Btn The North Staffordshire Rgt	Officer Training unit

The regular battalions sent to Guernsey, consisted of about 25 officers, and 800 men, in eight companies, and the Alderney detachment generally had about nine to 10 officers, 15-18 Sergeants and around 320 junior NCOs and men, in three or four companies. Companies were interchanged with those in Guernsey about halfway through the posting.

The Royal Artillery

The various units of the Royal Artillery noted in diaries and newspapers, are as follows, with some notes about the movements of the infantry:

21 January 1859. The building of the RA Arsenal under Fort Albert commenced.

April 1859. Captain F. J. Vernon RA, CO of 6th Company 3rd Btn RA presented 94 silver medals sent by the Sultan of Turkey to veterans of the Crimean War. The medals were inscribed on the rim 'La Crimea 1855'. The RA company in garrison, consisting of four officers, seven sergeants, six cpls. six bombardiers, two trumpeters and 108 men, will soon leave for Limerick.

Whit-Monday 1859. The Army parade and drill at Platte Saline, followed by a cricket match there in the afternoon.

25 July 1862. Private James Weir (22) of the 18th Regiment shot himself.

4 May 1885. Captain Edward Charles Lethbridge Walter of the Royal Irish Rifles was killed in an accident, whilst driving a Tandem horse-drawn carriage in Longis Road. A stone inscribed E.C.L.W. and the date still marks the spot.

18 September 1887. 5th/1st South Irish Division RA relieved the Scottish Division in Guernsey and Alderney, transported on the South-western steamer.

January 1889. Captain Campbell Royal Fusiliers, sworn in as Lt Governor's representative in Alderney.

30 July 1889. Cricket match between the Island and the East Surrey Rgt on Longis Common. East Surrey's won by 82-45.

June 1890. Visit of Prince Henry of Battenburg, towed into harbour in his yacht *Sheila* by SS *Courier*, stayed over night. Followed next day by the Lt Governor to inspect Fort Tourgis.

26 March 1895. Four privates of the Royal Fusiliers were arrested for breaking windows and assaulting shopkeepers in Victoria Street. They got two months in prison, one month at hard labour, and one in solitary confinement on bread and water. As a result a nightly 'Picquet' was put on patrol in the Town.

April 1895. Major C. D. M. Gall, OC Royal Fusiliers, sworn in to represent Lt Governor. Captain Parker, RA returning to Regimental duties after five years as adjutant to Royal Alderney Artillery Militia.

17 April 1895. Two privates were arrested for breaking windows at the home of C. S. M. Hammond of the Militia.

17 November 1895. Four Companies of the 2nd (Prince Albert's) Btn of the Somerset L.I. arrive in the Clyde Steamship Company's SS *Aranmore*, 400 men and 43 women. The Royal Fusiliers departed in the same ship next day.

14 March 1896. SS *Sir Redvers Buller* brings stores, and 12 Artillerymen to dismantle the remaining guns at Fort Albert.

June 1896. Visit of Army C-in-C. Lord Wolseley.

July 1896. Sixteen men from RA in Guernsey arrive to take the guns to Woolwich in *Sir Redvers Buller*.

17 October 1896. Funeral of Crimean War veteran Sgt Maj. Beale RA.

January 1897. *Sir Redvers Buller* brings more stores and removes the condemned stores and guns from the inner harbour. Sgt O'Flanagan of the Somerset Light Infantry (33) died of consumption on the 24th, and was buried with full military honours.

February 1897. Telephone wires laid to connect Fort Albert, the Post-Office and the signal hut on the Judemarre, using the Gower-Bell system.

May 1897. *Sir Redvers Buller* brings more stores from Woolwich, and the Somerset L.I. leave for Worthing, in SS *Frederica*. 41 men under Capt. Chandler left behind.

August 1897. Telephone installed to Fort Albert.

11 September 1897. SS *Frederica* brings eight officers and 295 men of the 2nd Btn the Wiltshire Regiment. She is the first English Mailboat to tie up at the new Jetty.

October 1897. Ten men of No. 10 Company Western Div. RA leave for Guernsey, to be replaced by No. 6 Company.

November 1897. Twelve men of No. 6 Company arrive and are quartered at Fort Tourgis. Later the same month Major G.H.F Talbot, RA, came from Guernsey to inspect the Forts.

25 December 1897. Cpl. William Croft, 2nd Btn Wiltshire Rgt died from a brain hæmorrhage after being assaulted by one of the soldiers, who was duly arrested after the inquest.

30 December 1902. Death of Crimean hero William McMurray (66). His funeral was made a great affair.

Funeral of Crimean veteran William
McMurray, 30 December 1902.

September 1905. Major Baldwin of 2nd Btn Manchester Regiment at Fort Albert, came
to inspect the Wireless Telegraphy Station and apparatus at Essex Hill.

In 1905 there was a reorganisation of the Alderney Militia which was from then on
known as *The Royal Alderney Artillery and Engineer Militia*, under its Commanding
Officer Capt. L. J. A. Langlois. This is fully described in the next chapter, but it is
relevant to note here that Capt. Langlois was promoted to Major on 29 January
1906, and made Adjutant by the War Office in 1913 after another reorganisation.
He continued to command the Militia until it was disbanded and he was made Lt
Colonel on retirement. He was appointed Crown Receiver of Alderney in April 1914,
a post he continued to hold until the island was evacuated in 1940, and then from the
return until 1947. He died in December 1953 aged 84.

II. Defences 1914-1939

(i). The First World War

The Garrisons in Alderney just prior to the First World War at the end of the list above,
were:

10/1913 – 7/1914	2nd Btn The Yorkshire Rgt	(The Green Howards)
7/1914 – 9/1916	4th Btn The North Staffordshire Rgt	Officer Training unit

The Green Howards were withdrawn when the war started, and an Officer Training
Unit of the North Staffordshire Regiment replaced them.

During the 1914-1918 War the Island Garrison usually consisted of troops of low medical
category from several infantry units, (apart from the O.T.U.). Although a large part of them
had volunteered and left the island in two batches on 20 and 27 March 1915, the defence of
the island was entrusted solely to the remaining members of the Royal Alderney Militia in
1916 and 1917, and the 167th. Protection Company of the Royal Defence Corps in 1918. At this
time, the mounted batteries consisted in total of two six-inch guns and two 12 pounders, with
the Searchlight battery, defending the harbour, all normally served by the Militia.

A group of volunteers embarquing on SS *Sir Redvers Buller* on 20 March 1915.

Alderney Militia Volunteers at the bottom of Victoria Street marching to the harbour, 27 March 1915.

Despite the traditional exemption of Channel Islanders from military service out of the islands, and the fact that most men of military age in the Militia had already volunteered, on 19 July 1916 the States of Alderney in a special session, agreed to introduce compulsory military service for all fit men between 18 and 41 years, as had already been done in Jersey and Guernsey. They sent a message to King George V in the following words:

> We, the members of the States of Alderney, descendants of the men who, for a thousand years have sworn allegiance to, and fought for, your ancestors, place in Your Majesty's hands all our available resources to be used as you think best for the honour of the Empire, and its Defence.

After the war was over, the units posted to Alderney generally only comprised a single platoon of a unit nominally posted to Guernsey, but frequently deployed elsewhere, including Ireland, and during the General Strike in 1927, in England.

From about 1929 the visits to Alderney were usually of short duration.

In sequence, the units posted here were:

1919   2nd Btn The North Lancashire Rgt (The Loyals)
1920   The Royal Irish Rgt
1922   1st Btn The Manchester Rgt
1924   2nd Btn The Duke of Cornwall's Light Infantry
1927   2nd Btn The Queen's Own, Royal West Kent Rgt
1935   2nd Btn The Sherwood Forester's
1938   1st Btn The Irish Fusiliers.

The withdrawal of the permanent Garrisons after 1929, inevitably meant a large drop in the revenues of the people and the island for the next 10 years. The Sherwood Foresters spent a short time here in 1935, and the 1st Battalion, the Irish Fusiliers, had come to Alderney on an extended training exercise late in 1938. They departed in June 1939.

(ii). The Second World War

Shortly after the war began, towards the end of September 1939, a training unit of the Machine Gun Battalion was sent to Alderney as a garrison, and Forts Albert and Tourgis were opened up again, repairs carried out, and a mass of stores and equipment moved in.

The 341st Machine Gun Training Centre consisted of 100 Territorial officers and Royal Army Reserve members from machine-gun units of several different regiments. They came to Alderney in the RMS *Courier* after spending a few days in Guernsey. Major (at the time Capt.) J. Harley recalls that the officers were taken to the Grand Hotel which became their mess, and the troops also put Château à L'Étoc in order for their own use. They had only one old staff car, brought from Jersey for the CO, Col. P. R. Worrell CBE, DSO, MC, of the Devon Regiment.

G Troop, 341st Machine Gun Battalion, Alderney 1940.

Over the next month a further 100 experienced officers and men, and an assortment of vehicles arrived, and a month later, the first intake of 200 recruits arrived in two batches of 100 men, the maximum *Courier* could carry at one time. These monthly intakes continued to a total of 800 recruits, by which time they occupied Fort Albert, The Arsenal, Fort Essex, and lastly Fort Tourgis. The married quarters at Whitegates and Coastguards were also occupied, and the extra 1,000 men on the island placed a considerable strain on the island's resources to repair buildings and roads, and feed the men. They nevertheless found time to have a special Christmas card printed with a small map of Alderney inside. At the same time of course the two units had brought a degree of prosperity back to the island, and the shops were once again well stocked.

Capt. Harley was sent over to Fort George in Guernsey in February 1940 to establish a

By mid-June 1940 as Hitler's forces swept across France, there seemed little hope that Alderney, with only the small garrison of the Machine Gun Training Centre, mostly raw recruits, and a population of about 1,400 civilians, would be able to defend itself against the victorious German Armies.

The island, so strongly fortified against possible invasion by the French, at various times since the Napoleonic Wars, with the mighty Victorian Forts ringing it, and its huge *Harbour of Refuge*, could not hope to withstand the weapons of modern warfare, and the vast numbers of troops available to the enemy, nor, in the event of it resisting, could it be kept adequately supplied with food and ammunition, in such close proximity to France and the long range guns, and superior air power of the Germans.

By this time the Germans had reached Paris, declared an open city, and were advancing on Cherbourg and all down the coast to St Malo. On 15 June it had been decided to withdraw the Machine Gun Training School from Alderney and divide it to defend the Airports in Jersey and Guernsey. Capt. J. Harley was already over in Guernsey supervising the battle training of the recruits sent over from Alderney after their arms instruction.

Another young officer here at that time, John Everett, who kept a diary of daily events, noted that on Saturday, 15 June 1940 he was Orderly Officer and spent the morning supervising the laying of another telephone line from Fort Albert to The Arsenal. He visited Château à L'Étoc to inspect lunch and tea meals, and during the evening paid two visits to the Airport at 9 p.m. and midnight to check that all was quiet, despite the depressing news of the French collapse.

The following morning Sunday the 16th, at 6 a.m., he met the RAF high-speed launch at the harbour, which brought news that the troops in Alderney were to be evacuated immediately. Captain Harley confirms that orders were received in Guernsey late on Saturday evening, to move the Machine-gun Centre from Alderney, and to use these troops to defend Jersey and Guernsey Airfields. Some were taken off on *New Fawn* within a few hours of the order arriving, Everett noted in his diary:

> The M.G. companies went today, one to Jersey and one to Guernsey, and at L'Étoc we got all packed up and ready to leave tomorrow. We saw the *New Fawn* leave, weighed down to the Plimsoll, maybe they'll get there by 1 a.m.

The first body of troops left around midday on the 17th, sailing along the side of Sark to Jersey on MV *Joy Bell III*, a further party left on the morning of the 18 June. John Everett saw *New Fawn* arriving with this party, at St Helier, about 11 a.m. and went to the harbour to help unload, and to recover his bicycle. He spent the day helping the unloading, and guiding officers and men to their billets. On the same day, SS *Courier* took the families of the soldiers to Guernsey.

Churchill made a stirring speech to the British people the following day, but by then the decision had already been made to demilitarise the Channel Islands.

On the morning of the 19th, the Jersey party received orders to reload all the stores and depart for England. In an atmosphere of chaos SS *Malines* with part of the unit and stores left only three-quarters loaded, the Jersey Militia evacuated on *Hodder*, and boatloads of civilian refugees were leaving. The ferry *Autocarrier* came in, stayed an hour, and went with only about 40 passengers and none of the transport. The Train ferry arrived at 10 a.m. and loading of stores and trucks continued until after midnight. They finally left Jersey at 8 a.m. on Friday 20 June 1940, the last military to leave, and with scores of refugees on board, arriving at Southampton about 8.30 p.m.

Meanwhile in Alderney, the last party had left in *Courier* on Wednesday 19th, leaving large quantities of stores, vehicles, fuel and food, and including the equipment for a complete Military Hospital on the Quay, and all the movable barrack equipment locked up in Fort Tourgis. By the time they reached Guernsey, the order to evacuate the Channel Islands on the 20th had arrived and they were transferred at 5.30 the next morning to SS *Biarritz*, which left at 8 a.m. leaving most of the equipment behind.

Trinity House Vessel *Vestal* had arrived on the night of Friday 21 June, to take off the keepers and their families from the Channel Island Lighthouses. From Alderney this included Kathleen Mary (Mrs Richard) Allen from the Riduna Stores, Robert and Florence Anderson from the Casquets with Paul (2), Thomas Davies with his wife and three children, Assistant Keeper at Quesnard, retired keeper John Jones (b. 1868) with his daughter and son-in-law, Mrs A. Duplain, Patrick Hodnett a retired keeper from Quesnard, Mrs J. N. Holeman, with two daughters and her mother and sister, Henry Howgego and his wife, and Griffiths Humphreys with his wife and daughter from Quesnard. *Vestal* returned to Alderney early on Saturday, to drop-off Nick Allen the pilot. The Judge sent a message by them. In it he asked the Admiralty to send ships to evacuate the inhabitants.

The ships arrived the following day, Sunday 23 June 1940.

Within a few hours almost the entire population of Alderney, some 1,432 souls had embarked on the six small ships, and abandoned their homes and their island for an uncertain future. They all arrived safely at Weymouth. (See the next chapter.)

It is not the purpose of this volume to deal with the life of the Alderney exiles in Britain and in Guernsey during the war, the Occupation period in the island itself, nor the defences erected by the Germans during their time here. These are well covered in the several books available about the island's history between 1940-45, and the dreadful hardships endured by the slave-workers in Alderney. These include; *Alderney – Fortress Island*, by T. X. H. Pantcheff (Pub. 1981) and *The Island of Dread in the Channel* (Pub. 1991), *Alderney at War* (Pub. 1993) both by the present author and reprinted as paperbacks in 2008 *The Fortifications of Alderney* by C. Partridge & T. Davenport (Pub. 1993). *Festung Alderney, The German Defences of Alderney* by Trevor Davenport (Pub. 2003) and *A Peculiar Occupation* by Peter Tabb (Pub. 2005).

The military part of our history therefore continues at the evacuation of the islanders on 23 June 1940 in Chapter 9 and later, in Chapter 16, the return of the islanders after the German surrender of the island to Brigadier Alfred Snow's Force 135 on 16 May 1945.

Apart from the transition period of just over a year before the civilian population was more or less re-established, there has been comparatively little military activity in the island in the last 45 years. Various units of the Royal Corps of Signals or the Royal Engineers come over for two weeks camping most summers and perform much needed repair work, such as the steps to Telegraph Bay and other heavy work. The Signals were awarded the Freedom of Alderney on 29 May 1989. and have made many more visits since.

9

The Evacuation Ships

In 1995 to coincide with the 50th anniversary of the return of the islanders on 15 December 1945, I researched details of the ships which were actually concerned in the Evacuation in 1940, which those of the islanders who were involved were, in general, too concerned about their fate to pay any great attention and about which no definitive information has been available until recently. Many months of research and letter writing finally resulted in correspondence with Lt Cmdr. Newby, the Commodore of the little fleet which evacuated Alderney on 23 June 1940, at long last giving definitive details of the names of the vessels involved.

The details about the ships, their later history and the photographs, have come from several other people, all over the world, to all of whom I express my thanks.

MV *Stork,* the flotilla flagship, was under the command of Lt Commander T. G. Newby. He was rushed by car from Southampton to Weymouth on the evening of 22 June 1940 to take command of the flotilla. He reached Alderney at dawn on the 23rd and went alongside the jetty at 7 a.m. As *Stork* was the most comfortable vessel, most of the pregnant mums were put on this which was the first to leave. Despite the later rumours, no doubt stimulated by the name of the ship, no babies were born during the voyage!!!

All ships were loaded and left by midday. Cmdr Newby returned on the *Alnwick*, reaching Weymouth late in the evening. He caught the 10 p.m. train and was back home by 12.45 a.m. *Stork,* 787 tons, 214 feet long capable of 10½ knots was built in 1937 for the General Steam Navigation Co. Ltd of London. On 19 May 1940 she was attacked by German aircraft whilst anchored off Boulogne during the evacuation from France. The gunlayer shot one down with her 12-pounder gun and was awarded the BEM. Her master Capt. R. J. Carey and two members of the crew received commendations. She was sunk off Portugal by German submarine U201, whilst travelling in Atlantic convoy No. OG 71 on 23 August 1941 when her master, Capt. Williams and 18 men were killed and one wounded.

MV *Suffolk Coast*, 535 tons, 175 feet long with a top speed of 9½ knots, was built in Holland in 1938 and named *Marali*. She was acquired by Coast Lines Ltd the following year and renamed. She was sold in 1951 to Tyne-Tees Shipping Co. Ltd and again in 1963 to Luigi G. Melloni of Savona, Italy and renamed *Melania*.

MV *Camroux IV*, 590 tons, 170 feet., capable of nine knots, was built in Holland in

1938 for the Newcastle Coal and Shipping Co. Ltd of London. She was presumably the collier in which many of the evacuees reported they had travelled. She was sold to Osborn and Walter of Bristol in 1942 and renamed *Salcombe*. sold again in 1969 to George Dapenois of Torquay and renamed *Friars Craig* as she is shown in this photograph. She was resold in 1974 to the Red Rose Shipping Co. of Rochdale and again in 1980 to John Grace and Charles Peterkin and used in the West Indies. In the late 1980s she was stripped of all useful fittings and sunk off the coast of Florida to serve as an artificial fish reef.

MV *Alnwick*, 508 tons, with a speed of nine knots was built at Newcastle in 1936 for the Tyne-Tees Shipping Co. Ltd. She was renamed *Cyprian Coast* in 1946 under the same owners when they became part of the Coast Lines group of companies.

MV *Empire Jonquil*, 369 tons, 140 feet long, was built in Holland in 1939 as *Begonia*. She was aquired by the Ministry of War Transport in May 1940 and was managed by Monroe Bros. In 1948 she was sold to H. P. Marshall of Middleborough and renamed *Marton*. Sold again in 1951 and renamed *Galtee* as shown here. She was sold to F. Maggiani of Viareggio, Italy in 1961 and became the *Vittorio Bogazzi* sold again to Capt. Figlie of Viareggio in 1970 and renamed *Enrico Effe*. She was finally broken up in Italy in 1976.

MV *West Coaster*, 361 tons and 148 feet, also built in Holland, in 1938. Owned by British Isles Coasters Ltd of London, she was sold to the General Steam Navigation Co. Ltd in 1943. She was sold to A. L. Cole of Cowes in the Isle of Wight in 1964 and renamed *Allard*. Converted to a sand suction dredger in 1968 under the ownership of E. Cole & Sons Ltd She was sold four more times to Southampton and Portsmouth owners, before finally being broken up at Gravesend in 1984.

As a contribution to the celebrations for their return I prepared a large display board.

This was done on behalf of the Alderney Chamber of Commerce and was on view in Advocate Kay-Mouat's window until 20 December 1995.

A photograph of this display of photographs of the day of the return and what they found here, with photographs of the six evacuation ships is included in the colour section of this book.

Subsequent to this I received copies of a two-page letter written to Cmdr. Newby, two days after their arrival in England, by one of the evacuees Mr R. L. Moffett, expressing the thanks of the group for their safe deliverance from certain German occupation for an unknown length of time.... These, and photographs of the ships involved, are reproduced below.

MV *Stork,* the flotilla leader.

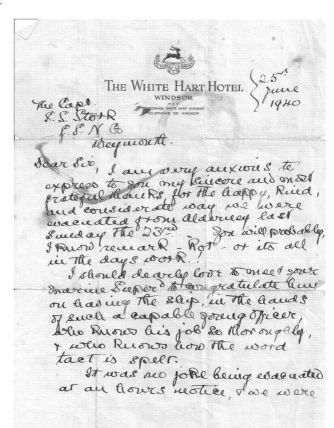

Letter of thanks dated 25 June 1940 to the flotilla Commander from Mr R. J. Moffatt.

MV *Suffolk Coast.*

MV *Camroux IV.*

MV *Alnwick.*

MV *Empire Jonquil.*

MV *West Coaster.*

10

The Alderney Militia

The early history of the Alderney Militia has already been covered in part. The Militia probably attained its peak of importance as a major part of the defences of Alderney during the rule of the Le Mesuriers, and much of this chapter is devoted to their activities, especially during the Napoleonic wars.

Subsequent to the construction of the Victorian Forts, the Militia played a primary defensive role as an artillery unit to support the regular garrisons. Service was compulsory except for a few exempt categories of men, until 1905, when it was turned into a volunteer force, and its history from then until it was disbanded in 1929, forms the final part of this chapter.

(i). The Le Mesurier Period

First, a brief reminder of the period between 1729 and 1782, greater details of which will be found in Chapter 6.

When Henry Le Mesurier became Hereditary Governor in 1729, on the death of Ann Andros, he also assumed the command of the Militia, but this passed to John (II) Le Mesurier when they exchanged estates. John fled from the island to Guernsey, in fear of his life from threats made by Judge Thomas Le Cocq in 1747, after he had prosecuted several of Le Cocq's relations for smuggling wool to France. Le Cocq then, by a Commission dated 25 November 1745, obtained fraudulently from the King, had his son Thomas appointed Commander-in-Chief with the connivance of the Governor of Guernsey.

Thomas promptly appointed his father as Deputy C-in-C. The affair was investigated by two of England's top lawyers of the time, the Attorney-General Sir Dudley Ryder, and the Solicitor-General Sir John Strange. They concluded that Le Cocq had obtained the commission for his son

> ...at a time when part of the Kingdom was in open Rebellion, [Bonnie Prince Charlie's uprising], by artful misrepresentations to his Majesty.

As has already been recorded Le Cocq was eventually ordered by the Privy Council to treat Le Mesurier with proper respect, as Governor and Commander-in-Chief, and not

1 Grant of States of Alderney's Coat of Arms registered on 20th December 1993.

2 John Le Mesurier's 20-gun privateer *Resolution*, which played a large part in establishing Alderney's prosperity in the late eighteenth century.

3 Both sides of the seal, used on a document dated 1793.

4 Seal of
the Court of
the Island of
Alderney.

5 Judge's seal, unknown date.

6 New seal made in 1989 to replace the one
lost during the Second World War.

7 Fort Grosnez from Platte Saline, 2010.

8 Fort Grosnez interior with Alderney Militia, c. 1890.

9 Fort Albert from Braye Meadow, 2010.

10 Living quarters in Fort Albert, c. 1960 before internal demolition.

11 The Arsenal and Squash court (in left foreground) from Fort Albert.

12 The Arsenal and Mount Hale Battery form part of the Fort Albert complex.

13 Fort Tourgis at sunrise in 2006. A very occasional sight, apparently in pink stone.

14 Interior and main gate of Fort Tourgis, 1989.

15 Fort Corblets and Corblets Bay.

16 Fort Essex and Longis Bay.

Above and below: 17 and 18 Fort Clonque and Fort Raz Island both have tidal causeways which flood daily.

Above and below: 19 and 20 Fort Houmet Herbé also has a tidal causeway and can flood inside in a storm.

Above and below: 21 and 22 Fort Quesnard (Duck Point) and Fort Les Hommeaux Florains (Flowery Islet). The latter took such a beating from the waves on its tiny islet that it was abandoned a few years later.

23 Château à L'Étoc.

24 One of the smaller barges (detail from the Reynolds painting on page 127).

25 View of Casquets from near Butes' telescope rest, using a long telephoto lens.

26 The remains of the First World War searchlight position on Roselle Point.

27 Lloyd's concrete telescope rest on the south-west corner of Butes, trained on the Casquets lighthouses.

28 Essex Castle walls, built in around 1530, and the 'Pepper pot' added in 1812.

29 Sail training ships *Tormentor* and *Lord Nelson*, Fleet Auxilliary 142 (at rear), etc. in Braye Harbour, July 1994.

30 The Danish brig *Astrid*, another training ship makes occasional visits to Alderney.

31 Sail training ship *Lord Nelson* is also a frequent visitor.

32 HM Queen Elizabeth II disembarking on the breakwater.

33 Royal Yacht *Britannia* in harbour during HM Queen Elizabeth's visit in 1999.

34 President Jon Kay-Mouat giving the annual address at the Hammond Memorial in May 1992. The Junior Militia provides the guard of honour. The striped flag of Les Amicales is on the left of the flagpole.

35 RNLI *Roy Barker 4* entering Braye Bay to take up permanent station there on 22 December 2008.

36 Left to right: Alderney rib, *Cap de la Hague* lifeboat, *Mona Rigolet*, Alderney lifeboat, RAF Rescue Helicopter.

37 *Louis Marchesi* escorting new Trent Class Lifeboat *Earl & Countess Mountbatten of Burma* into Alderney.

38 Trent Class lifeboat *Roy Barker*, 1 July 1994. Alderney's current lifeboat, supported by a RIB & RAF helicopter.

39 2nd CIAS plane, a Britten-Norman Islander also called *Lion's Pride*.

40 *Lion's Pride 3* visiting Alderney a few days after it was commissioned in September 2010.

41 A Norman Britten Trislander over Alderney.

42 Cruise ship *Aurora II* visited twice in 1992.

43 Cruise ship *Caledonian Star* in Braye Harbour in June 1995.

44 MV *Norona*, another visiting cruise ship in 2011.

45 The vicar blessing the fishing fleet at the harbour, Easter 2000.

46 50th anniversary display of photographs and details of the six evacuation ships of 23 June 1940.

47 The Mayor and Mayoress of Weymouth unveiling a plaque on the 50th anniversary of the evacuation.

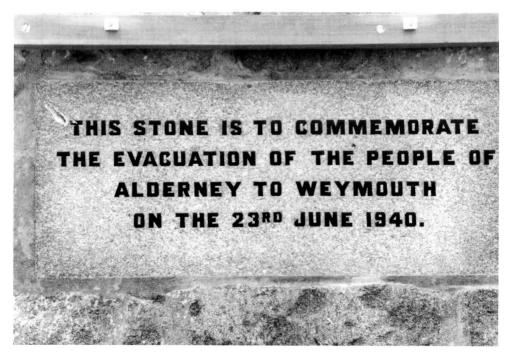

THIS STONE IS TO COMMEMORATE
THE EVACUATION OF THE PEOPLE OF
ALDERNEY TO WEYMOUTH
ON THE 23RD JUNE 1940.

48 Close up of the Commemorative Stone Plaque on the wall below the Sailing Club premises at the harbour. Father Bradley, for many years the Catholic Priest on Alderney, blessed the stone at the ceremony.

49 Little Crabby (The Inner) Harbour and Fort Grosnez, 1993.

50 A Trimaran service between Alderney and Guernsey began in 1993 but was discontinued in 1995.

51 Wave-piercer MV *Condor 9* started a short-lived service in 1990.

52 Alderney States and Courthouse in 2009. The police station and jail are on the right.

53 Training ship *Royalist*, a frequent visitor to Alderney.

54 Portrait of John Le
Mesurier, Alderney's
last hereditary governor,
c. 1820. It hangs in the
Alderney courtroom.

55 Governor John (IV) Le Mesurier resigning his office in 1824. Painting by John
Linnell, also hanging in the Alderney Courtroom.

56 This painting also by Reynolds shows the progress made by the autumn of 1854.

57 Arrival of Queen Victoria to view progress of harbour works, 9 August 1854. Painting by Naftel.

58 Alderney's governor, Peter Le Mesurier, *c.* 1790. He died in 1803.

59 Mannez Lighthouse. It still looks exactly as it did in 1913.

60 Pistols and muskets from the wreck of SS *Liverpool* before conservation.

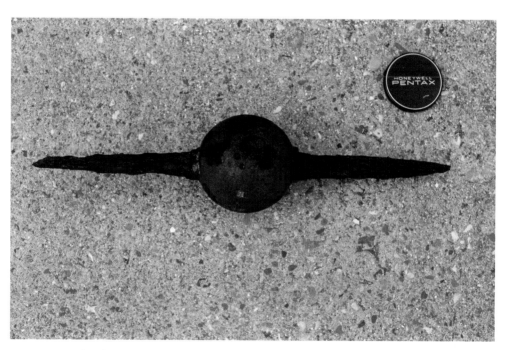

61 Bar shot from the wreck of SS *Liverpool*. The lens cap is two inches diameter for scale.

62 The cannon, recovered from SS *Liverpool,* still in its concretion in a transport box for conservation at the York Museum.

63 One of the SS *Liverpool* cannons after conservation, mounted on a replica of a contemporary gun carriage.

64 The first cannon raised from the wreck of SS *Liverpool*, being landed at the quay.

65 Model of a crew member of SS *Liverpool*, in contemporary dress and armaments, in the Alderney Museum.

to hold meetings of The States without his presence. The letter, signed by the Duke of Bedford from Whitehall on 16 August 1750, ordered Le Cocq Junior to: 'return the warrant obtained by surprise, contrary to the rights of John Le Mesurier', immediately.

In 1770, Governor John passed the command of the militia to his son, Colonel Peter Le Mesurier, and some of the troubles which later arose between the officers of the King's Garrison and the Commander of the Militia have already been mentioned. By 1770 the Militia consisted of about 200 men. When Peter Le Mesurier took over the command, they were an ill-trained and ill-equipped band. He brought it up to the same degree of proficiency as existed in the other islands, and 200 stand of arms was requisitioned from England. An Ordonnance of 7 June 1777 introduced standards of discipline and penalties for infringements, including absence. A Uniform was first introduced in 1781, paid for themselves, by those who could afford it, and by the Governor, for those who could not.

The uniform was to consist of white breeches, a red coat with facings and a black hat.

A voluminous correspondence between three generations of the Le Mesuriers and the various First or Principal Secretaries of State (later to be known as the Home Secretaries) is preserved at the National Archives, from 1782 to about 1830.

Within these are many references to the activities and needs of the Militia during this period, and many reports of the activities of the French navy from Cherbourg, who created much alarm in the island every time they were sighted, usually escorting merchantmen through the Race.

The first of these, from John (II) Le Mesurier to Thomas Townshend, dated 28 July 1782 contains an urgent request for the powder ordered a month earlier, and a request for instructions regarding the fate of seven Swiss soldiers of the Waldness Regiment in Cherbourg, who had wounded two French Artillerymen in a quarrel and fled in an open boat without sails or provisions. They had been picked up by an Alderney fisherman, and wished to serve England. He was instructed that they were to be sent to Weymouth, where they were to be enrolled in His Majesty's forces.

In November he gave details of the wreck of a Portuguese ship on the Casquets, which does not seem to have been noted in any of the lists of shipwrecks published in the islands in the last hundred years. The proclamation of peace on 14 February 1783, followed by the Treaty of Versailles, was; 'received with satisfaction in the island and published to the inhabitants'.

Lord North was appointed Principal Secretary in 1783, and in October Le Mesurier acknowledged receipt of copies of the recent peace treaties with France and Spain. Lord Sydney replaced Lord North in August 1786, and was sent a congratulatory letter, followed later, on 3 November 1787, by a long letter to say that he was now recovering from the gout, but had nevertheless been attentive to the needs of the island for defence, and that; 'all guns were now mounted round the island, and storehouses provided with 20 rounds for each gun. The Militia had ball and cartridges, and there were now 60 artillerymen with an officer appointed.' He enclosed a further request for powder, and a long list of other stores needed. Considerable detail was included of the position of the various guns, and he stated that La Platte Road and Bay to the NE was defended by a fort of four 18-pdr and two nine-pdr cannons and another redoubt of two nine-pdrs, both emplacements being close to the water's edge, and advised that two more 18-pdrs should be put there. He acknowledged that the weakest part of his defences was 'The Castel, [Longis] where the French boats usually come', which had 'only four nine-pdrs constructed during the late war'. A fortnight later, having received notification in a letter of 31 October, of the declaration of mutual disarmament made between the King and the Court of Versailles, he cancelled his requisition for stores, and requested instead; nine flags for the forts, two cwt of paint, two gun carriages for the brass cannons numbers 180 and 181, and clothing for the Militia.

This last request started a long running series of letters to Lord Sydney, and to Evan Nepean the Under-Secretary, which was supplemented by letters from Paul Le Mesurier the London agent, supporting the requisition, and later to William Wyndham Grenville, who replaced Sydney in June 1789, repeating the request for the gun carriages, flags and paint. The requests for stores were repeated with a list dated 6 April 1790 which included all the above, and 1,000 Tack Nails and 600 six-pdr flannel cartridges. This was followed on 6 May by a detailed inventory of clothing needed which provides an account of the appearance of the uniform then. The request included 320 each of;

Coats, faced dark blue, (the colour of the coat not mentioned, but presumably red as previously decided and issued)

Waistcoats, white

Canvas trousers instead of breeches

Black stocks

Belt plates (298)

Bayonet Slings or Cross Belts (298)

Musket Slings (298)

Caps (68)

Sashes (20)

Side Arms & Belts (30)

Epaulets (18) (These last four items presumably for the Sergeants and Officers.)

Cocked hats and Cockades (252 ordered)

Pouches and Shoulder Belts, with a badge enclosed in an oval (298)

January 1791 saw a request for 800 quarters of corn to feed the inhabitants, the garrison being adequately supplied through army channels. This was accompanied by an Act of the States requesting the supply, and in February a rather sad note asking if there was: 'any progress with the clothing' pointing out that the militia had clothed themselves at their own expense in 1779, with he providing for the poor, and had had no replacements. In March that year, Peter Le Mesurier made a personal call on Nepean to urge the immediate consideration of the matter. This seems to have had no more effect, and in June 1792, Peter again wrote the same request to the New Secretary, Henry Dundas, 'on behalf of his father who was ill, and unable to attend to matters himself'.

The French Revolution caused an influx of French priests and other emigrés to the island in February 1793, and considerable correspondence ensued on their disposal, on the precautions to be taken in the event of an attack, and reports from various spies and ship patrols on the activities of the French warships at Cherbourg. The priests were eventually sent to England at the expense of the English government. Peter Le Mesurier drew up an agreement in March, with Francis Bot, to carry up to 45 of them to Portsmouth in his vessel *Sally*, for £16 10s 0d. Bot returned on 12 April with a certificate from the Portsmouth Custom House of his landing 32 people there on 25 March. Similar agreements were drawn up with David Fougére to carry up to 25 in his ship *Tartar* for £10, and with Stephen Bedbrook to take up to 50 in *Fly*, also for £16 10s 0d. He landed another 36 at the same time as Bot, they returned together and were paid by the Governor.

Meanwhile John (II) Le Mesurier had been to Guernsey in February, and agreed signals with Colonel Dundas, commanding the garrison there, using the new signal mast, in the event of Alderney being attacked. In informing Secretary Dundas of this, he also noted that 15 Frenchmen now in Alderney had applied to be allowed to purchase a boat to enable them to return to France. He suggested he should instead treat them as prisoners-of-war, and take them to Cherbourg under a flag of truce to exchange. He enclosed a list of vessels now fitting out there as privateers. These were a 40-ton Brig described as a *Chasse Marée*, a six-ton schooner, and five cutters, two mounting over 30 guns, two of 20 guns and one of 18 guns, joined soon after by the 64-gun *Brilliant* as a guard-ship in the Cherbourg Roads to replace *Triton*. In the letter about the guard-ships he also noted that; 'a rascally fellow named Digard, who used to come here after tobacco, commands a French Privateer of about 44, and has publicly offered to conduct an expedition of boats against this island, not only for the sake of plunder, but in order to cut the throat of every Priest here'.

A couple of weeks after this letter, two Alderney boats detained in Cherbourg, *Pigeon*, (Master, Charles Herivel), and *Nation*, (Master, Jean Gaudion), were released with their crew and equipment, by Duperraic, Chef de la Marine at Cherbourg, with a safe-conduct valid for six days. In March Le Mesurier reached an agreement with the Mayor of Cherbourg for the release of Jurat Edward Gauvain, his boat and crew of two, and six English prisoners, in exchange for the 15 Frenchmen. They were released, on the grounds of 'Justice and Humanity' by the signatures of the Mayor, Amice Asselin, and six of the Municipal Officers. A pass was issued to the Cherbourg Harbour authorities, and a guarantee of safe passage, for them to be brought to Alderney on Gauvain's boat, escorted by Citizen Prosper Eyries, Commandant of the Marine at Cherbourg, in the boat *Les Coeurs Reunis*, (Master Captain Cartier). Eyries carried letters to the Governor from the Mayor and the safe conduct, which are now at the National Archives. One of the English prisoners released, John Edwards, an Engraver, of The Strand, London, who had been teaching English in the house of Auguste Jubé, Chief of the Legion of the National Guard, and Commandant at Cherbourg, swore an affidavit before the Alderney Court on 20 April that the French had been preparing to attack Alderney, and this had only been stopped, when a revolt in Brittany caused a Company of Cannoneers, and two Regiments of Infantry, to be sent from Cherbourg to suppress it.

Peter Le Mesurier seems to have maintained a number of spies in France, especially around Cherbourg and received frequent reports or signals from them. These were most likely smugglers who had had regular contact with Alderney before the Revolution, and wished to keep their trade open. He wrote to Nepean at 7 a.m. on 17 March, that signals from Cherbourg indicated an imminent attack on the island, he had set two cutters to cruise in the Race to give warning, and acknowledged; 'receipt of the clothes for the Militia, recently sent'. Persistence had finally paid off.

He duplicated his letter to Captain de Sausmarez, the Naval commander in Guernsey, and to the Captain of a Frigate off the coast of Alderney. This turned out to be de Sausmarez in *Crescent* accompanied by the cutters *Drake* and *Cockatrice*. On the previous day signal fires had been seen from near Cherbourg around 2 a.m., by Joseph Lorani, Lieutenant of the Militia, Cpl. Edward Simon, and Privates Jonathan Ozard, Lewis Main, and Thomas Herivel. Other signals were seen about 2.30 a.m. by Lt Nicholas Barbenson of the Militia and a French servant Lewis Garnier, who were setting nets in Longis Bay, indicating that a French attack was imminent. They were answered by a fire lit at 'the Fort'. This incident caused the Alderney Court to sit on the 22nd and carry out an enquiry into the events, taking depositions from all the witnesses. The same day he reported that two sloops and two brigs were now stationed off Alderney to keep an eye on the French.

As a result of all these alarms, two companies of Invalids, intended to be 170 men and a few women were sent on 24 April by the British Government, and John (II) Le Mesurier was asked to provide barracks for them. The accommodation that he provided was to fit up two of his own warehouses at Braye, which he proposed to rent to the government.

Their commander, John Grant, Captain of the Royal Independent Invalids, wrote another series of letters to Henry Dundas which detailed a running feud between himself and the Colonel of the Militia, (Peter Le Mesurier). Grant considered Le Mesurier's defences and guard posts to be totally inadequate; for instance at the Nunnery, the guard was one corporal and six men at night, whom he accused of being asleep on duty, he considered that the post needed two sergeants, two corporals and 40 men at night. He also accused the Governor of using his cutter *Ranger*, which was supposedly employed on Government service, for his own ends, and stated that she had just been given a commission to act as a Privateer, and was then cruising in the

Channel looking for prizes. In fact *Ranger* had been sent to Weymouth with despatches and returned a few days later, when Grant reported that she had just returned, and was now cruising 'off Beyond the Casquets.'

He asked that the command of the island should be given to him, and he threatened to leave the service after 35 years, if it was given to Peter Le Mesurier

> ...as I cannot with any comfort serve under the Command of a Man who has never been an Officer, and of Course is totally ignorant of every mode of Defence.

He went on to complain that he could not buy any provisions for the troops in the island, who were starving and required supplies from England, asked that *Ranger* should be put under command of the O.C. troops in the island, and that increased allowances should be made for the officers, as rents here were much higher than in Guernsey, and his pay was £20 per annum less.

Le Mesurier wrote the following day to Dundas threatening to leave the island with all his family if Grant was given the command, and, in another letter of the same date, 25 May, complained that Grant had seized all the Militia stores and magazines belonging to the island, and brought an order from the government to provide two barracks at Longis. This had arrived aboard the frigate *Perseus* which sent its boat ashore 'at the back of the island' because Le Mesurier was refusing to carry Grant's mails in his vessels. A week later Grant ordered his sentries at Longis not to allow the Militia's nightly horse patrol of an officer and two men, who patrolled the bays all night, to pass without giving the countersign, (which of course he had failed to supply them). The feud gathered momentum when Grant challenged his right to act as Governor of the island, on the grounds that the lease of the island fell to the heirs, administrators and assigns of John (II) Le Mesurier at his recent death, and that therefore under Alderney Law it should be divided equally between all his children.

This last attempt backfired on the Captain, Whitehall sending a letter to Peter Le Mesurier in June 1793, confirming his Patent and Title, and instructing that he was to command, except if there were a regular officer holding the rank of Brigadier General or above in the island, or one sent with a special commission to command the troops. He was to receive the regular returns of the state and conditions of the garrison and the defences, from the CO of the garrison, but must not interfere with the details of Military Regulations, duty or discipline.

Grant's reply to this was to complain that the barracks for 75 men, fitted up at Longis in his Barn by Le Mesurier, in response to the order, were; 'contrary to my desire, and therefore he is an unfit person to command'. He refused to pay for the bedding supplied until after a survey which he had convened. This survey found that the beds erected were 6 feet 5 inches x 2 feet 4½ inches, each to serve for two men, (standard practice at the time), with 32 men in the lower chamber and 33 in the upper. The building was 25 x 14 feet and each room had only two 2 x 3 feet windows. The committee of enquiry ruled that these beds were suitable only for berths on ships, and not for barracks. He further complained that there were no quarters for the officers, and that Le Mesurier had gone to England again on the 12th without telling him. Copies of these complaints were sent by Whitehall to Le Mesurier, who expressed himself as 'astonished'.

The feud continued, with Grant refusing to sit on the Court Martial of one of his men who had been found asleep on duty, and eventually on 16 August, on orders from Whitehall, Le Mesurier sent part of the Invalids force back to Guernsey, leaving only 70 men in Alderney. At the same time he wrote to Dundas requesting payment of the £400 he had expended on setting up the barracks for the Invalids, and requesting two companies of 'Regulars' to replace them. Lord Amhurst, Secretary for War, ordered another two companies of Invalids to be sent instead ! These eventually arrived on 7 November in the *Mary Ann* from Portsmouth. Two companies under Captains Lausdaines and Murray, with two ensigns, eight sergeants, 109 men, 30 women and 25 children.

There were frequent sightings of large French fleets escorting merchant ships to and from Cherbourg through the Race during this period, each meticulously reported by Le Mesurier, who does not record any problems with the new garrison, but on 9 April 1794 he slipped and fell whilst helping to mount a battery, and suffered two broken ribs, a broken right thigh, and compound fractures of the left leg, which put him out of action. He reported on 16 June to the Duke of Portland, who was then First Secretary, that he was partly recovered and going to Bath, leaving Captain Waugh of the Invalids in charge.

French privateers had taken some prizes in local waters, Josiah Noyce, from Chichester, who had been living in Alderney with his family since 1790, Master of the Sloop *Tommy*, was captured with four other small vessels, by the French Frigate *La Légère* in February 1794, when returning from Hurst in Sussex. He managed to escape from a prison camp at Valognes to Cherbourg in July, and got to Alderney in a Danish ship. He attested before the Alderney Court in November, that there were other Jersey and Guernsey men in the prison, and an Alderneyman, John Gaudion; 'who voluntarily had run away to France' was described as having offered to; 'take the island if the French would give him a 40 gun ship and 500 men, as he knew a bay defended by only a single gun where they could land'.

1797 was a comparatively quiet year for correspondence, and there did not seem to be any dissension in the island worth reporting. In January, following the grant of new clothing for the Jersey and Guernsey Militias, the Governor requested a similar favour for Alderney, and this was granted in February. On 31 August he asked for 200 quarters of corn and flour to be sent for the inhabitants, extra to the quota already supplied. There seems to have been a bad harvest expected, and he notes that the military had no difficulty over their own supplies. This was agreed on 23 September.

The division of the Militia force into two units, artillery and infantry was well established by the end of the eighteenth century. In February 1793, a General Review of the Militia had been held at Braye; at this time there were present, the Colonel, Major, Chaplain and Surgeon, two divisions of artillery comprising 130 officers and men; the infantry comprised a Grenadier company, a Light Infantry company, The Colonel's company, Capt. Leroy's and Capt. Simon's companies, totalling 214 officers and men,

22 men of the Invalids under Samuel Le Cocq, 10 recruits and a storekeeper, a total of 377 men. In 1798 there were two Captains and seven Lieutenants of Artillery, under Capt. Pierre Gauvain, and three Captains and nine Lieutenants of Infantry under Major Nicholas Robilliard. Le Mesurier wrote to Dundas in Whitehall to inform him that he had increased the defences of Alderney by four new nine-pdrs and two six-pdrs on travelling carriages, which had all been purchased by public subscription. From 1803-1815, a mounted section of Light Dragoons was formed under a Cornet, with a Sergeant and 12 men.

1799 saw the appointment of Colonel Charles William Este to the command of the troops in Alderney with the local rank of Brigadier General. This event was the start of several years of conflict between Le Mesurier together with the other civil authorities of the Island, and the military command, which soon became a feud.

A letter from Robert Brownrigg, an Under-secretary of State, informed Le Mesurier, (who held the honorary rank of Colonel), of this appointment on 20 June, and this of course evoked the situation envisaged in the letter of 1793, of an officer senior to the Governor commanding the garrison.

A few weeks later, in August, Le Mesurier was ordered by Lord Portland, the Principal Secretary, to apprehend one Richard Oliver for the murder of Humphrey Glinn on the Cornish coast, and other persons for the murder of a Custom House Boatman at Lymington, and with severely wounding another boatman William Lynne. Portland's information was that they had made for Alderney in the vessel *Lottery*. Le Mesurier's reply was that no such person or vessel was known in Alderney, the only English boat in and out of Alderney at the relevant time being the lugger *Elizabeth* of Folkestone, Francis Carskett, Master, which had left Alderney on 8 July, returned on the 11th, and gone back to Folkestone on the 14th.

In September he wrote to Portland, drawing his attention to the fact that, whilst Guernsey and Jersey each had a quota of corn granted to them annually by Parliament, no fixed quantity was granted to Alderney. He made the point that any increase granted to them should also be applied to Alderney, because of the influx of wives and children of the garrison, and requested an additional 200 quarters. This was granted on 17 September. At the beginning of October, in a letter to the Alderney Court, Le Mesurier appointed the *Contrôle du Roi* Jean Le Ber, to represent his civil affairs in Alderney whilst he was away, and agreed with the Brigadier that he would act as Commander-in-Chief of the Militia, during his absence.

A few days later Brigadier Este informed Whitehall that he had been sworn in as Deputy Governor in the Alderney Court, whilst Le Mesurier was in England for the winter. In fact Peter Le Mesurier was in Guernsey then. He returned from 19 January to 1 February 1800, to attend the Christmas Chief Pleas and collect his dues, after which he seems to have been almost continuously out of the island for at least two years, during which time relationships continued to deteriorate, with a long series of complaints and counter-complaints sent from both Este and Le Mesurier to Whitehall, and occasionally directly to each other, and a battle royal between Este and both the Alderney Court and the Royal Court in Guernsey. This developed to such an extent, that Frederick Williams the Deputy Procureur du Roi and Greffier, who had been in post since 1785, asked Le Mesurier in August 1801, to be allowed to resign his offices.

Este was supposed to have been sworn in as Commander-in-Chief of the Militia in Le Mesurier's short absence, and had asked to see the form of oath the previous day. When he arrived at the Court he refused to take that oath, and demanded to be sworn in instead as Deputy Governor. His actions and words were so violent that, despite Williams' opposition, the Court finally administered the other oath. The following day he sent for the Court Book to see how it had been registered, and finding that the oath he had sworn included his promise to obey the directions of the Governor, flew into a rage, and, to quote Williams' letter to Le Mesurier:

...taking Pen in hand he instantly blotted your Name out of the Book....

The following day he called the court into session, denied taking the oath as recorded and accused Williams and his son, the Deputy Greffier, of falsifying the records. A few days later Este called the court in session again and presented three ordinances which he demanded they should pass; 1. to cut a road through the Parsonage garden to shorten the way for the Town Guard; 2. to forbid the inhabitants to pile up manure on their dunghills, (which would mean that they could not fertilise their land); and 3. to prohibit Nicholas Lilian from keeping his Tavern at Longy, though he had paid £10 sterling for his licence.

A few days later, he also opposed Le Ber's existing appointment as Le Mesurier's civil agent on the grounds that it was against his own rights. The Court failing to pass his ordinances, he threatened to arrest them all and take them to London.

Le Mesurier wrote a series of letters from Guernsey, in December, in answer to those of Este which complained of his actions. Este wrote a note relinquishing his powers on the Governor's return in January, but before leaving again, Le Mesurier agreed that, although it was not his normal practice, for the good and peace of the island, he would appoint Este as Deputy Governor during his ensuing absence, and not just Commander of the Militia.

During the next year or so, Este continued to interfere with the traditional rights and customs of the island, and its people; bringing charges against several inhabitants who tried to exercise those rights. He demanded to be treated as the Governor, and given control of the taxes and revenues, claiming that; 'Governor Le Mesurier ought no longer to be continued in the receipt of dues, apparently belonging to my situation'. This particularly concerned the charges made to ship owners for issuing a pass to allow them to leave the harbour. He wrote numerous complaints to the Duke of Portland (First Secretary), refused to allow proper trial of a Lieutenant Gouch of the 'Basilicks', who had been wounded, after stabbing a local man.

He issued orders limiting the islanders fishing hours and fired both guns and muskets at Mannez on an Alderney boat, belonging to Edward Gauvain, fishing close to the shore between 6-7 p.m., damaging the boat and refusing to give its owner, who was a Jurat, any satisfactory explanation the following day. On at least three occasions he broke up the assembly of the Court of Chief Pleas, because they insisted on carrying on the traditional business of collecting tithes and paying homage, before conducting the legislative part of the assembly, which did not therefore take place.

Meantime he apparently allowed his troops to terrorise the inhabitants, burgle their houses, steal their animals and crops. In a series of 39 affidavits sworn before the Alderney Court in June 1801 by the victims, a total of 310 sheep, 37 lambs, 33 hens, 94 bushels of potatoes, many sacks of greens, and a great deal of personal property was claimed to have been stolen, with another 100 lambs unaccounted for, in the period since Le Mesurier went out of the island in October 1799.

In sending these affidavits to Lord Pelham, Le Mesurier stated that not a single sheep had been stolen in the previous 20 years, and burglary was virtually unknown in the island before the arrival of these troops. He asked for £500 compensation for the people, from the King, and in another letter a few days later, he requested the removal of Este because of his total disregard for the laws and customs of Alderney.

In October 1801, Captain John Gauvain of the Militia resigned his Commission after Este had tried to force the Militia to build a new, 12ft. wide road up Hannaine Hill, and they had refused, to a man, to do so. This incident had occurred the day after news reached Alderney of the signing of the preliminaries of Peace with France, and the following day, Este strenuously opposed the States' plan to hold a 'General Illumination' to celebrate the peace. Despite his opposition a large bonfire was lit on the Butes. He then tried to convene the Court to fine all the militia men who had refused to build the road, but was defeated in this as the Court stated that it could not be convened, because the Michaelmas session of Chief Pleas had not been held.

There was a wreck on Burhou on 10 November 1801. Este wrote to the First Secretary reporting the incident and its results. The vessel, which was not named in Este's account, went to pieces in two or three minutes, but the Master and seven men were saved. A few days later planks from the ship, and candles, part of its cargo, came ashore at Quesnard, and were placed under guard by Este. The Master stated that the whole valuable cargo was insured for £30,000. Le Ber claimed the rights to the wreck on behalf of the Governor, Este represented the interest of the Crown, but as the master and crew had survived they also laid claim to the vessel on behalf of the owners. Meantime, as reported by Este, 19 Alderney boats had gone out to the wreck and salvaged what they could, much to his annoyance.

Periodic shortages of *specie* (coin) in the islands, resulted in changes in the value of the available French money in the Bailiwick being decreed by the Royal Court. On 23 March 1802, the Alderney Court under Juge Delégué John Ollivier, confirmed their order that in future the 6 livre pieces should be exchanged at the rate of 5/3d instead of 5/-, and the 3 livre coins at 2s 7½d, and forbade anyone to refuse to accept them in payment at this value. Este immediately forbade this, put up a proclamation to that effect, and issued an order to the troops to demand payment at the rate of 5/-. This was immediately torn down, and a similar fate was accorded to further proclamations he issued on the same subject, and others in which he threatened to imprison anyone who removed his proclamations.

The Judge and Jurats finally appealed to the Royal Court about his actions and he was ordered in April 1802 to explain his conduct in stopping the course of justice in Alderney. He failed to respond adequately to this, and instead initiated proceedings against Le Mesurier whom he alleged to have appropriated a piece of public land to his own personal ownership. This had been agreed by the States to replace the Crown land Le Mesurier had given up in September 1799, for the creation of the Stranger's Cemetery at St Michel in Longis Road. This subject was debated at Alderney Chief Pleas on 7 June 1802, in front of Le Mesurier, who had by then returned to the island. Le Mesurier claimed that he would not have given up the piece of ground unless the equivalent area had been promised to him personally, and the Douzaine was ordered to investigate the matter on the site.

Este, whilst in London in July, wrote to Sir George Shee, setting out his own version of all these various complaints. He requested the suspension of the Deputy Procureur, admitted 'breaking up' Chief Pleas on four successive occasions; 'because they had not conducted their proceedings as he had directed', and complained bitterly of the Chief Pleas system which he described as; 'a Burlesque, neither Dignity or Reverence being observed on the [sic] Occassion'. He justified all his actions; 'on the Propriety of my Conduct from the Nature of the Power held out to me', and described the proceedings of the Royal Court as 'vexatious and oppressive'. He added:

> The Court of Guernsey has proceeded to pass an Act pronouncing my Conduct to have been Arbitrary, Illegal and tending to subvert and annul a Custom until then inviolable, and ordering the same to be also registered in the Records of the Court of Alderney, which Proceeding I hold a libel on my Character.

It was probably the result of all this turmoil which led the Crown the following year, to consider resuming the Patent, and to appoint a Military Governor instead. Lord Pelham was now the Principal Secretary, and Havilland Le Mesurier, Peter's Uncle wrote a letter to him, and to the Under-Secretary John King, supporting the continuance of the grant, on the basis of all the earlier grants, which he quoted, giving detailed accounts of the family expenditure of the island, and the revenues received from it, which had been certified by the Alderney Court at his brother's death in 1793. The expenditure to that time had amounted to about £2,500 with an additional £500 for the Mill, built in 1760, and a further £12,657 6s 6d since that date, up to 1800. The revenues from the tithes had amounted to approximately £500 each year, with the Manor House and gardens valued at an additional £200 yearly.

During part of the period of Este's presence in the island, from the middle of 1799 to Christmas 1800, a total of 83 men, presumably in most cases with their families, had been recorded as 'leaving the island to settle elsewhere'. The Court records of these departures list the occupations of the men concerned. Six Merchants are listed, but the majority were craftsmen of one sort or another, with 55 of them listed as 'Coopers', (probably making barrels for the smuggling trade). About a dozen were described as 'Labourers'. It is possible that this may have had a connection with the clampdown on smuggling which started about this time. Although there is little evidence to support any mass migration from Alderney to the New World, the suppression of smuggling in Guernsey about five years later led to an emigration to the Wills Creek Settlement in Ohio, which was later renamed Cambridge, Guernsey County, with about 50 Guernsey families residing there. It is also worth remembering, that Sir George de Carteret, to whom the grant of Alderney in 1660 had been transferred, was also granted land in Carolina in 1663, and had been granted the area between the Hudson and Delaware rivers by the Duke of York in the following year, an area which was renamed New Jersey after the third Dutch war of 1672-4. In 1680 the Governor of New York was the same Sir Edmond Andros whose earlier grant of Alderney later descended to the Le Mesuriers. The children of the poor families sent out of Alderney by Captain Nicholas Ling in February 1669, had also gone to this area, and since then there had been a steady trickle of Channel Islanders to New England, and Canada, mostly from Jersey.

Este was eventually replaced by Brigadier General J. R. Mackenzie in 1806, followed by Brigadier General John Moore in December 1812.

Peter Le Mesurier had died on 9 January 1803, mainly as a result of the injuries he had received when the cannon fell on him, and on the 21st, his son John (III) was sworn in as Governor and Commander-in-Chief of the Militia. In the end he was to be the last hereditary Governor of the island.

The annual return of the Militia and their equipment made to the new Commander in March, by Major Robilliard shows that the strength then was; 1 Major, 2 Captains, 14 Lieutenants, a Chaplain and a Surgeon, 22 Sergeants, and 276 men, of whom 16 were on leave and 15 were sick. Judging by the clothing and equipment recorded, (presumably

John and Peter Le Mesurier's tomb in Old Church.

from the items in store, and not issued), above half of it in poor condition, the headgear was distinguished as 'Artillery and Battalion hats' and 'Grenadier and Light Infantry Caps'. Of coats, waistcoats and trousers there were about 25 of each in good condition, and 130 unserviceable. Their arms were noted as 79 serviceable muskets and bayonets, and 88 of each in poor condition.

Another return made by Major Robilliard, dated 25 September 1806, now in the British Library, shows a strength of one Major, two Captains, 14 Lieutenants and a Chaplain, 20 Sergeants, seven Drummers, and 339 men of whom 68 were on leave, and 32 sick. It notes the addition of one lieutenant since the previous return. The 14 lieutenants were employed; four on field artillery, with five sgts and 58 men; three on battery artillery, with four sgts and 60 men; three grenadiers, with three sgts and 44 men; three with the light infantry, with three sgts and 74 men; and one on battalion duties, with four sgts and 34 men. There was one Sergeant and 12 men noted as 'Troopers', 29 'Invalids', and 28 recruits in training.

Major Robilliard's ration return for the troops of similar date, for whom he acted as contractor was noted in Chapter 6.

Most of the remaining correspondence from the Le Mesurier family at the National Archives is concerned with the state of poverty of the inhabitants, and various suggestions and attempts to relieve it, which culminated in the division of the Common Lands in 1830.

(ii). The Victorian Period

The granting of the title 'Royal' to the Channel Islands Militias in 1831 has already been recorded, and the change about 1854 to an all Artillery unit improved the effectiveness of the unit. In order to give them a depôt and drill hall, a property on Ollivier Street belonging to the Le Mesurier family, was bought by The States in 1860 for £600, and turned into the Militia Arsenal. Here they were able to store their weapons and the Band Instruments, and practice their gun-drill, and a library was established. The building also served as a station for the hand pumped Fire-Engine, which dates from 1859, and was recently restored.

The parade room was also used for dances and concerts. The Militia was disbanded in 1929, but the Militia Arsenal was still used for social purposes until 1940. The building was allowed to remain in disrepair after the war, although the sittings of The States were held there from 1946 until the Court House was restored in 1953/4. It was eventually demolished in 1954.

In 1881 the three Channel Island Artillery Corps of the Royal Militias were reorganised as Coast Artillery, and formed into garrison companies to defend their own islands. In Alderney thanks to its small size mobilisation could occur, if needed, within an hour.

Despite the earlier change to an all Artillery unit, once again there were infantry sections active during this period.

An interesting insight into the working of the Militia from about 1886 to 1929, is

The Militia Arsenal in Ollivier Street, *c.* 1952.

The old 1859 hand-pumped fire engine in Marais Square after restoration, *c.* 1990.

provided by a Scrapbook of newspaper cuttings and other mementoes kept by L. J. A. Langlois, many of which refer to the doings of the Militia, of which he was at first a junior officer, and finally the CO, retiring as Lt Colonel when it was disbanded.

Almost every week's entries bore reports of parades, target practice, shooting and sporting competitions and scores, parades for the Sovereign's birthday etc. Some extracts are given here:

3 November 1894. Officers; Artillery; Commander Major P. T. Hérivel, Adjutant Lt J. Christian RA, Captains R. G. May, L. J. A. Langlois, Lts. T. A. G. Barbenson, G. S. Cosby. RAAM shooting cup given by Gov. Lt Gen Sir Redvers Bulwer won by No. 2 Company.

17. November 1894 Col. Barton, RAAM (Royal Alderney Artillery Militia), gave his own portrait to the Militia library, to hang between Lord Beaconsfield & Mr Gladstone.

January 1895, at Chief Pleas, OC Militia asks for £24 10s 0d for the Regiment, including £6 for Band instruments. Laws relative to Artillery Practise strongly opposed & rejected. Request for exemption of Militia officers from service as Constables was rejected.

February 1895. No. 1 Company, the 'Red Indians' Company drill at 5 p.m. Monday and Thursday evenings. No. 2 Coy., the 'Brave Bulgarians' Company drill on Tuesday and Friday.

March 1895. 2/Lt Cosby has passed his exams and been appointed Lieutenant.

April 1895. Capt. Parker RA appointed as Adjutant to the Militia for the last five years, is to return to his Regiment when the vacancy is filled. Major P. T. Hérivel acting CO and CSM was William Hammond.

15 June 1895. Lt Governor comes to Alderney to witness a mock battle with the Militia and the Royal Fusiliers, then in garrison. The alarm was to be sounded at any time in a three day period. It came much later than expected; three guns fired from Fort Albert, a red/white flag raised there, and the Church Bells rung. Lt Langlois was the first on parade on The Butes where the Militia assembled. The regular unit mustered at Fort Albert. The enemy was reputed to have landed on Rat Island (Raz), and dummies were set up on the causeway. These were quickly demolished by 64 pounders firing from Fort Albert, and 9 pounders from Essex, and the infantry wiped-out the remainder with rifle fire. The war lasted 3½ hours, and they all went home to supper at 6 p.m.

July 1895. Shooting match for the Lieutenant Governor's Cup held at Longis. No. 2 Company won. Royal Alderney Artillery, United Rifle Club meets regularly at Longis at 5 p.m. on Saturdays.

1 September 1895. Captain Gilbertson RA arrives, to be the new Adjutant.

30 September 1895. Chief Pleas vote another £6 for Band instruments and £10 for Shooting Prizes. Law regarding shooting practice made. Shooting to be between 21 May and 30 September. A red flag to be hoisted at Grosnez the day before, and a notice placed at the Post-Office. Anyone having cattle, boats or property on WD ground in the way of the firing to be cautioned, and if they did not remove the obstruction fined 50/-.

January 1896. Col. W. Barton resigns after ten years. Chief Pleas vote £15 for accommodation at the Militia Arsenal, and £20 15s 0d for Militia expenses.

February 1896. A board put up at the Militia Arsenal for men to claim exemption from service, five men claimed.

March 1896. Major P. T. Hérivel promoted to Lt Col. and becomes new CO. New clothing issued for the first parade on Easter Monday.

17 April 1896. Lt T. J. Robilliard resigns and Lt L. J. A. Langlois promoted to Captain.

June 1896. Adjutant Capt. Gilbertson dies of consumption after a six-month illness. Midsummer day parade on Butes.

July 1896. Lt J. Christian RA appointed Adjutant and promoted to Captain. Parade for Lt Governor's visit.

December 1896. Militia no longer to have 'M' on their shoulder straps.

January 1897. 10/- voted for Militia at Chief Pleas. Training Schedule for 1897 decided, as follows:

Easter Monday, 19 April, Squad & Company drill 10 a.m.

Monday, 3 May, No. 1 Company, Carbine and Company Drill, Butes, 5 p.m.

Tuesday, 4 May, No. 2 Company, the same.

Wednesday, 5 May, No. 1 Company, the same.

Friday, 7 May, No. 2 Company, the same.

Wednesday, 19 May, Regiment, Battalion Drill, Butes 5 p.m.

Monday, 31 May, No. 1 Company, Gun Drill Mounting and Dismounting exercises, Butes, 5 p.m.

Tuesday, 1 June, No. 2 Company, ditto.

Whit Monday, 7 June, Regiment, Battalion Drill in The Square, 10 a.m.

Wednesday, 9 June, No. 1 Company, Gun Drill mounting and Dismounting exercises, Butes, 5 p.m.

Friday, 11 June, No. 2 Company, ditto.

Thursda, 24 June, Regiment, Colonel's inspection in The Square, 10 a.m.

General's Inspection – when and where ordered.

Stretcher Bearer's Class. Instruction at 7.30 p.m. in the Militia Arsenal, on 6, 7, 13, 14, 20, 21, 28 and 30 April.

There were also parades for Easter and the Queen's Birthday, and frequent Rifle practise.

June 1897. Midsummer Day Parade, Artillery practise from Fort Grosnez, 40- and 9-pounders firing at rocks beyond Burhou. Visit of Lt Governor and OC of the RA in Guernsey.

11 August 1897. Militia returns arms and uniforms at the end of the season.

September 1897. Rifle shooting 'Wimbledon', on Longis Common.

4 October 1897. Chief Pleas vote £10 for carbine shooting prizes. OC Militia to furnish an annual balance sheet in future.

13 November 1897. Seventeen-year-old recruit Jack Quinain fined 1/6d for being absent from Drill.

January 1898. Chief Pleas vote £20 10s 0d for Militia expenses.

January 1899. A packed meeting at the Militia Arsenal heard the Militia officers call for unmarried volunteers to serve in South Africa.

6 September 1899. Presentation of a clock to CSM T. Judge, RA, a former NCO of 21 Company in Jersey, retiring after serving in the RAAM for the past eight years. The clock was of marble with bronze pillars, surmounted by a bronze figure of Britannia, and with an inscribed silver plate affixed.

In November a *Transvaal War Fund* was set up in Guernsey for the relief of sufferers from the South-African War. The collectors in Alderney were to be Major Hilton of the Worcestershire Regiment, The Judge, The Vicar, Revd Le Brun, and The Procureur, with a committee consisting of Revd Le Brun, Lt Col Hérivel and Capt. Langlois of the Militia, and C. R. Le Cocq and N. Simon, the Constables.

1899-1905. Many reports of Rifle competitions with visiting Army and Navy teams.

6 June 1900. 'Pretoria Day'. The arrival of Lord Roberts in Pretoria, to a day of holiday and rejoicing. At least 15 Triumphal Arches were erected across the streets all round the town, some illuminated at night. Each bore a legend recalling the names of various battles, and personalities such as Baden-Powell and 'Bobs'. The Riduna Club (formed in October 1899 over Nicholas Gaudion's Tobacconist's shop in Victoria Street, as a place to discuss war news, with Judge Barbenson as President and Mr

The Pretoria Day arch erected in Little Street on 6 June 1900, to mark Lord Roberts' entry into the town.

Price as the treasurer), had an illuminated motto 'Riduna Rejoices' on its front. A 'Grand Cavalcade' processed from the Butes round the town in the morning. The Militia engaged the Army in a tug-of-war, in the afternoon, and beat them, and at night most of the States buildings, and the principal private residences were illuminated with lanterns, fairy lights and intricate displays and designs made up of gaslights. Mr May's house, 'North Star', in Victoria Street sported a 30 feet long illuminated battleship, HMS *Powerful*. A torchlight procession, followed by a bonfire on York Hill, and a firework display lasting an hour brought the rejoicing to a close.

1 August 1900. The barracks in the island received their annual inspection by the Chief Medical Officer of the Southern District, Surgeon-General C. McD. Cuffe, CB. who arrived on board SS *Courier*. The Militia was paraded for his inspection, and later carried out gun practice with the 68 pdrs at Fort Grosnez, demolishing the target with two simultaneous direct hits.

September 1901. Militia gets four Maxim machine guns, and two double-barrelled Gardner Guns.

27 September 1901. Capt. Arnold RA, Adjutant RAAM, on sick list, his duties to be performed by Capt. Langlois.

15 March 1902. Capt. Langlois and Lt J. P. Price leave for Militia exercises in the Isle of Wight.

30 June 1902. King's Birthday parade held, (in the pouring rain) on the Butes. A very short parade with few spectators.

30 August 1902. Alderney born Lt C. L. Price DSO of the Royal Scots, returns from South Africa where he had gone in November 1899. He was recommended for a VC for conspicuous gallantry at Bermondsey, in the Transvaal, on 16 May 1901. Militia officers took the horse from his carriage, and pulled it from the harbour to his parents house in Braye Road.

12 November 1902. Distribution of prizes, in the Militia Arsenal, for the annual shooting competition. The winning team, Gunners T. & H. Le Vallée, Cpls. Simon & Tourgis, and Gunner Le Cocq, each received 2/6d.

On 30 December 1902, William McMurray, 66-year-old Crimean veteran died, and was buried with honours. The Militia turned out in full strength, and were supported by the unit of the Leicestershire Regiment, then in garrison. (*photo page 156*).

September 1903. A team from the Corps of Royal Engineers in Guernsey erected an electric searchlight battery on Roselle Point.

May 1904. CSM William Hammond RA, retiring after 21 years military service, the last few of which were in No. 1 company of the Alderney Militia. He was presented with a tea service, and intends to remain in Alderney.

5 August 1905. The Court House was packed with the members of the Militia to take the oath of allegiance to the new King, Edward VII. First to take the oath was the CO, Captain Langlois.

September 1905. Capt. Langlois commands Guard-of-Honour for visit of the Duke of Connaught, following the reorganisation described below. Twenty-one Long

Service Medals were presented by the Duke to members and former members of the Militia.

A *Law Relative to the Royal Militia of the Island of Alderney*, was passed by the Privy Council on 10 May 1905, which set in motion a complete reorganisation of the force. This first set out the various conditions and requirements for the compulsory service, which had formerly been customary in both war and peacetime, and the long list of persons exempt from service, including States, Court, and Government officials, Clergymen, Schoolteachers, Doctors, Vets., Pharmacists, the Constables, etc. etc.

Under the new law, the Militia was to be reduced to a Regiment of Artillery of 100 men in peacetime, and 180 during a war, with a first reserve of 80 men who had already served, and a second reserve of all males 16-60 years of age. It became a voluntary force. If insufficient men volunteered the numbers were to be made up by drawing lots from the lists of eligible persons aged 16-45, which the Constables had to draw up annually in October. An oath of allegiance to the sovereign was specified, and discipline was to be in accordance with the British Army Act of 1881.

The Lt Governor of Guernsey was appointed as Commander-in-Chief.

The officers had to provide their own uniforms for which they received an initial allowance of £20, and the men were to be responsible for the maintenance of their uniforms, arms and equipment, provided by the Crown, with the Crown bearing the cost of accidental damage to

arms, which remained Crown property. When needed the Constables had power to requisition horses, carriage, carts and panniers, the owners of which were liable to a fine of 5/- for each horse and carriage they failed to provide.

The Government would pay the costs of all pay, training, subsistence and rations. The Commanding Officer in Alderney was to receive £150 per annum, and all other members were to be paid on a scale per day served, according to their rank. These are fully set out in the law.

There was a minor amendment regarding the powers of the Lt Governor in times of war dated 8 June 1916.

Following the reorganisation, in September 1905, Field Marshal, HRH the Duke of Connaught, visited Alderney and the Official Programme records that The Royal Alderney Militia, and half a Company of the Royal Garrison Artillery lined the Pier. A banner inscribed 'The Key of the Channel Welcomes You' was erected over the dais at the top of the Slipway, whilst the 2nd Btn The Manchester Rgt then in garrison, provided the Guard of Honour.

He inspected the newly completed works at Fort Grosnez, 'reconstructed for the accommodation of The Artillery and Engineer Militia under the new scheme'. He also inspected Fort Tourgis, Fort Essex, near which was the recently erected Wireless Telegraph Station and the site of a proposed new 9.2-pdr Battery. From there he went to Fort Albert, where he inspected the 6in. Battery, the Quick-fire 12-pdr Battery, and the 'Electric Light Emplacement' at Roselle Point.

Lunch at Scott's Hotel, was enhanced by another Guard of Honour supplied by Capt.

Arrival of the Duke of Connaught at Braye Harbour in September 1905.

Niven RA and 110 men of the Royal Alderney Artillery and Engineer Militia, led by Capt. L. J. A. Langlois, who had tripped over a railway line on the arrival of the Duke and injured his knee.

Many of the houses were decorated and illuminated by gaslights, and an special display was made by Mr John Gibbons at Val-ès-Portes. The departure of the Duke was followed later in the evening by a torchlight procession through the streets with illuminated floats and a Bicycle Brigade, all led by the Rechabites Drum and Fife Band.

This visit is recorded in the extracts in the Langlois Scrapbook, together with some faded photographs taken at the time. Other extracts note the following occurrences:

18 December 1905. Presentation, in the School Room, of a gold watch to Sgt Maj. R. J. McClernon of RAAM on retirement after 16 yrs.

29 January 1906, Capt. Langlois promoted Major.

20 May 1910. Funeral Service for the late King, with 1,200 people packed into the church. 68 gun salute fired on The Butes.

23 November 1911. Coronation Medals, (King George V), presented to Major Langlois, and the two longest serving men of the Militia, L/Cpl Stubber RE, and Gnr. Batiste RA, who had all attended the ceremony.

30 January 1914. The Annual Militia Dance was held at the Skating Rink.

9 April 1914. Major Langlois appointed Crown Receiver in Alderney, (a post he occupied until after the second world war, when it was abolished.

During the First World War, a detachment of Volunteers from the Alderney Militia left for Guernsey on 20 and 17 March 1915 in SS *Courier* and the War Department Tug, *Sir Redvers Buller*, to train with the Guernsey volunteers. In November 1916

Guernsey decided to waive the exemption for Channel Islanders to serve the crown out of the island and introduced the English conscription act. Compulsory service was introduced in Alderney on 13 December 1916, (at which time the Militia was temporarily disbanded). A Service Battalion of the Royal Guernsey Light Infantry was formed as a unit of the British army. After training this unit was sent to England for advanced training and joined the 29th Division, in France in September 1917. Their first action was at Cambrai where 505 officers and men were killed. The strength of the unit was made up with men from other regiments and early in 1918 they fought at Passchendale. By the end of this battle only four officers and 55 men were left of the 503 who entered the fight. The survivors acted as guard troops at Field Marshal Haig's HQ for the remainder of the war.

During that war 41 men from Alderney lost their lives, their names are recorded on the War Memorials in Victoria Street and in the Parish Church, and are listed in the Appendix. The Militia was reinstated on 16 March 1921, and continued until 6 March 1929, when it was finally disbanded after existing for about 800 years.

A list of many of the Militia Officers will be found in the next chapter.

The memory of the Militia was briefly revived on the occasion of the Silver Jubilee of King George V, on 6 May 1935, when, as part of the celebrations a pageant included two units of the Militia wearing nineteenth century military uniforms, (which look somewhat different from the actual Militia ones). There was a gun carriage and limber drawn by six horses, and an Infantry section. This part of the parade was led by a Mr Le Mesurier from Guernsey. Two photographs from this event are annotated, but not dated, on the reverse in a handwriting which seems to be that of Colonel Langlois, who notes that he was 'just ahead of the gun carriage, but the photographer cut me off !'

A large part of the history of the people of Alderney has been bound up with the Militia and the sea, over the centuries. The 'Hereditary Governors', the Le Mesuriers played a large part in the activities of the Militia in what was potentially the most perilous period in Alderney's history, the Napoleonic Wars. At the same time, they took full advantage of the opportunity to enrich themselves through privateering, nevertheless ploughing a considerable part of their profits into buildings of lasting benefit to the whole population.

They built, or at least completed, the 'New Peer' (now the 'Old Harbour') in 1736, built the warehouses in Braye Street between 1736 and 1756, the first 'Court des Héritiers' in Rue des Sablons (now Victoria Street) in 1742, rebuilt Government House (now the Island Hall) in 1763, built a Market House in 1772, and a hospital or almshouse, built Mouriaux House as their private residence in 1777, extended and altered the original church by adding a side chapel, a gallery, and the Bell Tower, at various time between 1760 and 1790 and later added the clock in 1808. They built and endowed the public school in 1790, and the 'Pepperpot' on Essex Castle was added by them about 1812-15. (See colour section illustrations).

They also entertained visitors, officers of the garrison, and various dignitaries on a lavish scale, and provided much work for the poor people especially during the winter periods.

The war memorials in the Memorial Garden in
Victoria Street.

The Militia Artillery reformed for the Silver Jubilee parade for King George V, 6 May 1935.

The Militia Infantry on the same occasion.

The 'Island Hall', formerly 'Government House', *c.* 1990.

Mouriaux House built by the Le Mesuriers in 1777, photographed in 1975.

The period of their rule was also a time when other islanders were able to profit from trade and smuggling. Especially notable were the Robilliards, who were a Guernsey family, from St Peter-in-the-Wood, first brought to the island by Thomas Le Mesurier about 1684. They built their fortune on this trade, and later acted as victualling contractors to the various garrisons, particularly in Napoleonic times. They built 'The Brick House' in the late 1790's, which soon became 'Val-ès-Portes' and is now known as 'Val des Portes', and has been the private residence of the Kay-Mouat family from the 1930s until today. Jon Kay-Mouat who died in 2011 was a former long-term President of the States of Alderney.

The Robilliard family also provided many Militia Officers, Nicholas Robilliard was made a Jurat in 1794, and the family maintained a seat on the Court bench almost continuously until 1908. They established the Alderney Bank, albeit that it crashed at the same time as several other Channel Island Banks around 1810, and they lost a fortune.

As a final act of generosity of the Le Mesuriers, the Revd John (IV), son of the last Governor, the eleventh 'John' found in the direct line of succession in the family since 1331, and the fourth with connections to Alderney, built the present Parish Church, probably the finest in the Channel Islands, at his own expense, and gave it to the people of the island in 1851, in memory of his parents.

The huge influx of labour associated with the Harbour and Fortification building made the existing facilities quite inadequate. Extra clergy were brought in to serve the needs of the Garrison, and some Chapel facilities were provided in Fort Albert, but

The Old School, built 1790, and the clock tower of the old parish church.

The Revd John (IV) Le Mesurier who built the new church in 1850 and gave it to the island.

Parish Church of St Anne from the west, *c.* 1851.

partly to deal with this, the present Parish Church, designed by Giles Gilbert Scott, (later Sir Giles), to seat 843, was erected by Revd John (IV) Le Mesurier for a sum of around £8,000. Its foundation stone was laid on 24 September 1847, and it was consecrated on the 21 August 1850, by the Bishop of Winchester.

The Reverend John had written to the First Secretary, Sir George Grey offering to build the church at his own expense, and this letter was forwarded by Grey to the Bishop of Winchester, on 4 March 1847, and shortly after on the 18th, Sir William Somerville at the Home Office wrote to the Lt Governor of Guernsey, Gen. Napier, stating that neither the Government nor the Bishop had any objections to the proposal and had approved the plans.

Correspondence of the same date from Somerville to Napier, concerning the resignation of Alderney's vicar, the Revd Vincent William Ryan who had been appointed Bishop of Mauritius, recommended approval of his suggested candidate the Revd George de Carteret Guille. On the 22nd another letter informed Napier that he needed no further authority to install the Revd Guille in the Alderney living. Later the same year on 2 August authority was given for the payment of £40 per annum to the clergyman selected by 'the perpetual curate of Alderney', to perform divine service for the government labourers and their families at Braye, and to establish a school for their children.

The *Illustrated London News* dated 5 October 1850 contains an accurate, unsigned engraving of the new building, and brief details of the church, then referred to as dedicated to St Ann, (no 'e').

> It is built of island stone with Caen Stone finishings, is 116 feet long internally, has a hot air heating system, and 400 proprietary seats, out of a total of 660 seats for adults and 183 for children. The stained glass windows are by Mr Wailes of Newcastle. The sculpture over the South Porch represents 'The Good Shepherd' with a lamb on his shoulder. The Superintendent of Works for the building was a young man named Stephen Hunt, from Durham, who died whilst the work was in progress and is buried in the Stranger's Cemetery of St Michel in Longis Road. His brother finished the work.

An entry in the Parish Register dated 26 July 1848, records that Matthew Hall or Hull (50) from Somerset, was killed whilst excavating the foundations for the new church.

The old Parish Church, enlarged by John (II) Le Mesurier in 1761, with the Tower added 1767, and the Gallery built inside in 1790, to increase its capacity to 400, ceased to be used, and all except the clock tower was pulled down in 1851, after the new church was taken into use. The clock in the tower, with an unusual escapement, restored by Mr Martin in 1989, was originally built and installed by A. Harvey in 1808.

The donor, Revd John (IV) Le Mesurier, was Vicar of Bembridge in the Isle of Wight from 1851-91, he was made an Honorary Canon of Winchester in 1878, and died at Yateley in Hampshire on 26 February 1903, aged 84.

The Alderney Church Plate, with two chalices dating from 1713 and 1740, and later items given by Le Mesurier, with the new church in 1850, was described and illustrated in the *Transactions* for 1917 (*on right*). Except for the pewter flagons, which cannot now

Alderney Church plate

Pewter jug

Flagon 1849

Pewter jug

Alms dish 1849

Platter 1841

Paten 1849

Paten 1849

Chalice 1713

Chalice 1740

The Church silver, dating from 1713 to about 1740. Photo taken about 1917.

The steps formerly in The Terrace but now a slope, *c.* 1900.

be found, it survived the war, and is all still in use.

At the same time Frederick Le Mesurier gave part of the curtilage of the Government House (now the Island Hall) at the upper end of La Vallée, to the church. This part is now known as The Terrace and was made an open space for the recreation of the people about 1900, during the time of Judge Barbenson as head of the island's administration. By Ordinance of the Alderney Court, the gates were to be open from 9 a.m. to sunset, and were much used as a place to stroll in the early part of this century.

Although not greatly used now, The Terrace is still open today. The death of the row of large Elm trees due to Dutch Elm disease in the mid-1970s, resulted, in the late 1980s, in their being felled. The largest, from the rings on the stump was 183 years old, taking its planting back to approximately the date of the battle of Trafalgar. Much had happened in the island during its lifetime, and the author secured, planed and polished a thick slice, which he mounted with a chart of the history of the island linked by strings to the annual rings on the trunk, in the Alderney Museum where it creates considerable interest amongst the visitors.

(iii). The Junior Militia

Long after the return of the islanders to Alderney in 1945, a new local Militia was formed on 1 September 1983, as a unit of the Army Cadet Force, (The Junior Militia), later to become the Royal Alderney Militia (ACF). I am indebted to Col. Peter Walter, MBE, MC & bar, founder and Commanding Officer, for the information from which this next section has been compiled.

Early in 1982 Peter Walter, a retired army officer, and a Major in the HAC, who had been living in Alderney for some time, was approached by a group including the Vicar, who were concerned to do something for the youth of the island. He suggested forming a unit of the Army Cadet Force. After approval by the President and the Lieutenant Governor, the MoD and the Home Office were approached. This culminated in approval for a one year pilot scheme for 12 cadets being given, with all necessary uniforms and equipment being provided by the MoD. This was later extended, and in 1987, it was agreed that the scheme should continue and the MoD would continue to pick up the bill, up to a fixed limit, so long as the recruits were of high quality, but they now have to pay for their own uniforms.

President Jon Kay-Mouat suggested the title of the *Junior Militia*.

Negotiations were later conducted to continue the title and traditions of the old Militia, and the unit became a Regiment in its own right, wearing replicas of the old Regimental titles, buttons and badges, paid for by the unit. They also followed the old tradition, mentioned above, of the women manning the guardhouses by day, by allowing girls to join the ACF.

From the initial 12 members the unit grew to a peak of 47, and now averages about 25-30, with two adult officers and five or six adult instructors. The members take part in a range of activities including preparation for the 1-4 Star Army Proficiency Certificates, the Duke of Edinburgh's Award Scheme, St John's Ambulance First Aid Certificates, Marksmanship, including participation of some members in the inter-services competition, and other competitions, including an annual shooting competition in 1983-5, against the surviving veterans of the Royal Alderney Militia disbanded in 1929. Some sort of training activities for various groups are held on four nights a week and Sunday mornings, with weekend exercises with other visiting units, including SAS, Parachute Rgt and Jersey TA units, approximately every two months, quarterly visits from UK Cadet Training teams, half-yearly weekend survival exercises, an annual camp, and a MoD Annual Inspection.

The Annual camps include mountaineering, and have been held in 1983 in Alderney; 1984, Bavaria/Austria and Dartmoor; 1985, Leek, Staffs; 1986, Penhale, Cornwall; 1987, Berlin; 1988, Dartmoor; 1989, Penhale; 1990, Dartmoor.

There is an annual visit from the GOC SW District, at which the prize giving takes place.

In addition to their military activities, the instructors and senior cadets form the staff of the Civil Emergency Bunker, and are trained to operate sundry monitoring equipment, and a radio link to the UK. The Militia also take part in various community activities to help the old, and keep the island tidy. They paraded for HM Queen Elizabeth, the Queen Mother, on her visit in 1984, for the Duchess of Kent in 1987, and mounted a Royal Guard of Honour for the visit of HM The Queen in 1989.

The unit takes part in the annual Remembrance Day Ceremony at the Alderney War Memorial, and their bugler sounds the last post. They also participate in the annual ceremonies each May at the Hammond Memorial honouring those slave-workers who

The German underground hospital now the island's Civil Emergency Bunker.

died in Alderney during the war (see colour illustrations and text on next page).

Lt Col Walter was appointed Honorary Colonel of the Royal Alderney Militia (ACF) in the Supplement to the *London Gazette* of 1 January 1989.

The Junior Militia was having some difficulty in attracting the young people of the island and at the same time former military officers who took part in the activities were retiring or leaving the island and it was disbanded, on orders from the parent unit in Hampshire about 2006/7.

The stripes on the flag are a reminder of the clothing worn by the prisoners in the SS Camp and the organisation; *Les Amicales des Anciens Déportées d'Aurigny* was formed by the group who were sent back to France in May 1944. Former prisoners attended many of the annual services such as the one shown above, with gradually decreasing numbers due to old age or infirmity. The first President of Les Amicales, M. Albert Eblagon came until he was past 90 in 1992, when there were only four survivors of the group. The next President, M. David Tratt made his last visit to Alderney, accompanied by his son, on 28 October 2004 when I took this photo, but now there are none left fit enough to attend the annual ceremony which is still held on the Sunday nearest 14 May.

The military part of our history therefore continues at the evacuation of the islanders on 23 June 1940 in Chapter 9 and later, in Chapter 16, the return of the islanders after the German surrender of the island to Brigadier Alfred Snow's Force 135 on 16 May 1945.

Apart from the transition period of just over a year before the civilian population was more or less re-established, there has been comparatively little military activity in the island in the last 45 years. Various units of the Royal Corps of Signals or the Royal Engineers come over for two weeks camping most summers and perform much needed repair work, such as the steps to Telegraph Bay and other heavy work. The Signals were awarded the Freedom of Alderney on 29 May 1989. and have made many more visits since.

David Tratt, President of Les Amicales des Anciens Déportés d'Aurigny, in 2004.

11

Officers of the Alderney Militia 1650-1929

The records of the Royal Alderney Militia seem to have vanished during the Occupation, if indeed they were still in Alderney at that time.

The following list, which is by no means complete, has been made up from various Almanacs, such official records as are extant, entries in the Parish Registers, the National Archives correspondence and contemporary Newspaper reports.

1650	Captain	Nicholas Ling (died 1679)
1711	Captain	Pierre Barbenson
1718	Captain	Jean Le Cocq
1722	Lieut.	Jean Simon dies aged 92
1745	Commandant	Thomas Le Cocq jnr.
	Deputy	Thomas Le Cocq snr.
1750	Colonel	John (II) Le Mesurier
1770	Colonel	Peter Le Mesurier sworn-in
1790 & etc.	Major	Nicholas Robilliard, Acting CO
	Captain	Simon Le Cocq
	Lieuts	?. Simon. ?. Le Cocq

1793, 19 February, a general review of the Militia at Braye, under Col. Peter Le Mesurier. The force consisted of:

The Colonel, a Major, a Chaplain and a Surgeon

Artillery	2 divisions totalling 130 officers and men
Infantry	A Grenadier Company, a Light Infantry Company, the Colonel's Company, Capt. Leroy's Company, Capt. Simon's Company, totalling 214 officers and men

YEAR	BRANCH	RANK	NAMES
1793 cont.	Invalides		(War veterans) 22 men under Samuel Le Cocq
	Recruits		10 men and a storekeeper.
			A grand total of 381 officers and men.
1794		Captain	John Waugh, Acting as Deputy Governor/ CO

From now on more frequent records are found in correspondence and press.

YEAR	BRANCH	RANK	NAMES
1798		Colonel	Pierre Le Mesurier
		Major	John Le Mesurier Deputy CO
	Artillery	Captains	Pierre Gauvain, Jean Sanford
		Lieuts	Phillipe Brine, Joseph Lorani, Amice Ollivier,Nicolas Ollivier, Nicolas Robilliard, Jean Rogers, William Sanford
	Infantry	Major	Nicolas Robilliard (Commandant)
		Captains	Pierre Le Cocq (Adjutant), Jean Gauvain, Thomas Nicolas Robilliard
		Lieuts	Nicolas Barbenson Snr.,Nicolas Barbenson Jnr., Pierre Gauvain, Jean Le Ber, Thomas Le Cocq, Samuel Le Cocq, Jean Le Mesurier, Pierre Simon, Frederick Williams
1800	Infantry	Captains	Thomas Le Cocq. He was ADC to the Commandant, Jean Ollivier was Adjutant, the other officers remaining the same
1801		Captain	Jean Gauvain resigns through Brig. Este's interference
1803		Colonel	John (III) Le Mesurier sworn-in on death of his father
	Infantry	Major	Nicholas Robilliard.

Light Dragoons Section formed (lasted to 1815)

		Cornet	Name unknown, plus a Sgt and 12 Troopers

Total Strength then 20 officers, 22 Sgts, 276 men

YEAR	BRANCH	RANK	NAMES
1805		Colonel	Le Mesurier, John (III) (until 1824)
	Artillery	Captains	Pierre Gauvain, Jean Sanford
		Lieuts	Thomas Barbenson, Stephen Bradbrook, James Gibson, Isaac Hocart, Joseph Lorani, Jean Robilliard, W.Joseph Sanford
	Infantry	Major	Nicholas Robilliard (Commandant)
		Captains	Nicolas Barbenson, Thomas Nicolas Robilliard, Thomas Oliver Le Patourel
		Lieuts	Pierre Gauvain, Jean Le Ber (Quartermaster), Pierre Le Cocq, Thomas Oliver Le Patourel, Nicolas Ollivier, Pierre Simon.
		Surgeon	Benjamin Foster

Total strength then included these and 20 Sgts, seven Drummers, 339 men

1807			
	Infantry	Lieut.	Jean Gauvain
1813			
	Artillery	Captain	Isaac Hocart
		Lieuts	Jean Gaudion (Adjutant), Thomas Barbenson, Thomas Fudge, Jean Pierre Gauvain, Pierre Le Cocq, Pierre Le Lievre, Jean Richard Le Cocq
		Quartermaster	Pierre Le Lievre
	Infantry	Major	Thomas Oliver Le Patourel
		Captains	Lucas Le Cocq, Pierre Le Cocq, Jean Gauvain, Pierre Simon
		Lieuts	Pierre Gauvain, Jean Le Ber, J. Tilbury
	Cavalry	Lieut.	William Le Cocq, fils Jean
		Quartermaster	Jean Le Ber
1816			
	Artillery	Captain	Isaac Hocart
		Lieuts	Jean Gaudion (Adjutant), Thomas Barbenson, Thomas Fudge,
	Infantry	Major	T.O. Le Patourel Jean Pierre Gauvain
		Captains	Pierre Le Cocq (Adjutant), Lucas Le Cocq, Pierre Gaudion, Pierre Simon, Frederick Williams
		Lieuts	Jean Gauvain, J. R. Le Cocq, Pierre Gauvain,

YEAR	BRANCH	RANK	NAMES
1816 contd.			Pierre Le Lievre, J. Tilbury
		Quartermaster	Jean Le Ber
1821			
	Commandant	Major	Thomas Oliver Le Patourel
	ADC	Lieut.	William Le Cocq
	Artillery	Captain	Isaac Hocart
		Lieuts	Jean Gaudion (Adjutant), Thomas Barbenson, Jean P. Le Cocq, Pierre Le Lievre
		Major	Lucas Le Cocq
		Captains	Frederick Williams (Capt. des Invalides),
	Infantry		Pierre Le Cocq Jnr.
		(Adjutant),	Pierre Gauvain, Lucas Le Cocq, Pierre Simon
		Lieuts	Jean Pierre Gauvain, Jean Gauvain, William Le Cocq, Pierre Robilliard Gauvain
		2nd Lieut.	William Sanford
		Quartermaster	Jean Le Ber
1826			
	Commandant	Major	Lucas Le Cocq
	Artillery	Captain	Jean Gaudion
		Lieut.	John Richard Le Cocq, Samuel Lauga Robilliard
	Infantry	Captain	Jean Gauvain
		Lieut.	Pierre Robilliard Gauvain
		Quartermaster	Pierre Le Lievre
1830			
	Commandant	Major	Lucas Le Cocq
	Artillery	Captain	Jean Gaudion
		Lieuts	J. R. Le Cocq, Pierre Le Lievre Samuel L. Robilliard
	Infantry	Captain	Jean Gauvain
		Lieuts	Pierre R. Gauvain, William Sanford
	Cavalry		Mentioned in weapons return dated 4th March
1832			
	Infantry	Captain	William Sanford
		Lieut.	Thomas Nicholas Barbenson
1837			
	Commandant	Major	Lucas Le Cocq

YEAR	BRANCH	RANK	NAMES
1837 contd.			
	Artillery	Captain	Jean Gaudion
		Lieut.	Samuel L. Robilliard
	Infantry	Captain	William Sanford
		Lieut.	Thomas N. Barbenson
1838			
	Infantry	Major	William Sanford
		Captain	Thomas N. Barbenson
1840			
	Commandant	Major	William Sanford
	Artillery	Captain	Samuel L. Robilliard
	Infantry	Captain	Thomas N. Barbenson
		Quartermaster	Richard Sanford
1843			
	Artillery	Lieut.	Lucas Le Cocq
	Infantry	Lieut.	William Robilliard
		Quartermaster	Jean William Robilliard
1844			
	Infantry	Major	Thomas N. Barbenson
1846			
	Infantry	Captain	William Robilliard
1847			
	Artillery	Captain	Thomas Nicholas Robilliard
1849			
	Commandant	Major	Thomas N. Barbenson,
	Artillery	Captain	Samuel L. Robilliard
		Lieut.	Jean William Robilliard
	Infantry	Lieut.	Richard Sanford
1850			
	Infantry	Captain	Robilliard, William T.(ex Durham L.I.)
		Lieuts	Frederick John Cottle, John MacDougall

YEAR	BRANCH	RANK	NAMES
1851			
	Commandant	Major	Thomas N. Barbenson
	Artillery	Captain	Thomas Nicolas Robilliard
		Lieuts	Jean William Robilliard, Alfred Willis
	Infantry	Captain	W. T. H. Robilliard
		Lieuts	Frederick John Cottle, Philippe Mesney

With the building of the string of Forts between 1848 and 1853, the island was garrisoned with regular infantry troops, and the Militia Infantry unit was disbanded after Queen Victoria's visit in 1854. The Infantry men were retrained, and the entire Militia became an Artillery Force. The facings on the uniforms were changed to scarlet with gold lace. Only a few Officer's names have survived from this period.

YEAR	BRANCH	RANK	NAMES
1854		Quartermaster	J. G. Bichard
1855		Captains	Frederick John Cottle, Philippe Mesney
1856		Surgeon	N. J. Bisson (Asst.)
1857		Lieuts	W. Gauvain, Alfred Willis, Jean Le Ber, J. N. Le Bair
1858			
	Commandant	Major	Thomas N. Barbenson
		Captains	Frederick John Cottle, Philippe Mesney
		Lieuts	Alfred Bisson, Jean Le Ber, Alfred J. Cottle, James S. Paint, John E. Paint
1858		Surgeons	N. J. Bisson, Thomas Shoreland
1859			
	Artillery	Captain	Alfred Willis (Quartermaster)
1860			
	Commandant	Lt Col.	Thomas N. Barbenson
		Lieut.	Nicholas P. Barbenson
1861		Lieut.	Jean Renier (Adjutant to 1878)
1862		Lieut.	Andrew Langlois
1864		Lieuts	Thomas John Despré, Peter T. Herivel

YEAR	BRANCH	RANK	NAMES
1867		Captain	Nicholas P. Barbenson
		Lieut.	William Gauvain
1869		Surgeon	N. J. Bisson
1870	Commandant	Lt Col.	Thomas N. Barbenson
		Captains	Nicolas P. Barbenson, Frederick John Cottle, Philippe Mesny
		Lieuts	William Gauvain, Pierre Herivel, Jean Renier, James Andrew Langlois
		Quartermaster	Alfred Willis
1871			Surgeon George H. Turnbull (Asst.)
1874			Surgeon Dr Henry Skey Muir MD
1876/7	Commandant	Lt Col.	Thomas N. Barbenson (rank since 1860)
		Captains	Philip Mesney (rank since 1855), Frederick J. Cottle (1855), Nicholas Barbenson (1867)
		Lieuts	John Renier, Adjutant and A.I. (1861), Peter Hérivel (1864), Thomas John Després (1864), William Gauvain (1857), James A. Langlois (1870)
		Quarter-Master	A. Willis
		Surgeon	Dr H. S. Muir (1874)
1878		Lieut.	J. Weeks (ex RA)
1879	Commandant	Lt Col.	Thomas N. Barbenson
		Major	Pierre Herivel
		Captains	J. Weeks (Adjutant),
		Lieuts	William Gauvain, J. A. Langlois, Alfred J. Wills, Charles Francis John Skyring
		Quartemaster	Robert McClernon
		Surgeon	J. A. MacMunn
1883		Captain	Charles Francis John Skyring
1886		Lieut.	T. J. Robilliard
1887	Commandant	Lt Col.	W. Barton (ex Royal Guernsey Artillery)
1888		Lieut.	R. G. May
1890		Lieut.	Thomas A. Barbenson
1894	Commandant	Lt Col.	W. Barton
	Adjutant	Captain	W. Parker (RA), J. Christiam (RA) acting
		Major	Pierre T. Herivel (Honorary)
		Captains	R. G. May, C. F. Skyring,
		Lieuts	T. A. G. Barbenson, L. J. A. Langlois,,

YEAR	BRANCH	RANK	NAMES
1894 contd.		Captain	T. J. Robilliard
		nd Lieut.	G. S. Cosby
		Surgeon	Captain H. E. Mann 1895
	Acting CO	Major	P. T. Herivel
	Adjutant	Captain	Thomas Gilbertson (RA) replacing Capt. Parker
		Lieut.	L. J. A. Langlois,
		Lieut.	G. S. Cosby
1896	Commandant	Lt Col.	Pierre T. Herivel, (Col. Barton resigns)
	Adjutant	Captain	Thomas Gilbertson (RA) dies of consumption after six months' illness. Lt John Christian promoted to replace him
		Captain	L. J. A. Langlois, (Lieut. T. J. Robilliard resigns)
		Surgeon	E. W. Livesey
1897	Commandant	Lt Col.	Pierre T. Herivel
		Adjutant	Captain J. Christian (RA)
		Captains	L. J. A. Langlois, R. G. May
		Lieuts	T. A. G. Barbenson, G. S. Cosby
1897 contd. Surgeon		Captain	E. W. Livesey
1898		Lieut.	J. B. Price
1901	Adjutant	Captain	Capt L. J. A.Langlois standing in for Capt. W. R. Arnold (RAA) on sick list
1902		Captain	L. J. A. Langlois,
		Lieut.	J. P. Price
1904	Adjutant	Captain	Oswald C. Niven
1905			

Compulsory service in the Militia ends after some 800 years. Reorganisation of the Royal Alderney Artillery and Engineer Militia into a volunteer force

1906		Hon. Major	L. J. A. Langlois,
	Adjutant	Captain	Frederick J. N. Smyth

YEAR	BRANCH	RANK	NAMES

1907

	Artillery section		
	Commandant	Lt Col.	William Grant de Jersey (appointed 1.7.04)
	Adjutant	Captain	F. J. N. Smyth RA
		Captain	L. J. A. Langlois, (Hon Maj. since 1.1.06)
		Lieut.	1
	Surgeon	Captain	E. W. Livesey
	Engineer Section	Lieut.	1

Uniform; blue with scarlet facings

1911	Commandant	Lt Col.	W. Grant de Jersey
		Major	L. J. A. Langlois, (Honorary)
		Captain	F. J. N. Smyth (Adjutant, Lt Charles Fellows from 1/8/11)
		Lieut.	C. Gibb Mitchell
		2nd Lieut.	K. E. S. Stewart
1911	Surgeon	Captain	E. W. Livesey
1913		2nd Lieut.	L. M. T. Griffin

Honorary Colonel of Royal Guernsey, & Royal Alderney Militias

| | | Maj. Gen. | M. H. Saward RA (appointed 10.6.14) |

1914-1918: armaments in Alderney consisted of; 2 x 6 inch and 2 x 12-pdr guns

1914		Major	L. J. A. Langlois, (Substantive)
		2nd Lieuts	H. ff. Ozanne, Herbert W. Bainbridge
1915		2nd Lieuts	L. A. C. Robins, F. C. Bowden, S. A. Hankey

A large contingent of the Militia, and other able-bodied men, left the island in two batches on 20 and 27 March 1915. Many served in the Guernsey Section of the four battalions of Channel Islands Light Infantry in the First World War, and their battle honours include Ypres 1917, Passchendale, Cambrai 1917, Estaires and Hazebrouck.

1916: After the Compulsory Military Service Order, the Alderney Militia continued at greatly reduced strength, supported by a small contingent of low medical grade regular troops.

YEAR	BRANCH	RANK	NAMES
1916	Commandant	Lt Col.	W. Grant de Jersey
		Majors	Fellowes, L. J. A. Langlois,
		Captain	C. Gibb Mitchell
		2nd Lieut.	C. A. Fenwick
1917	Artillery Section		
	Commandant	Lt Col.	W. G. de Jersey
	Adjutant		1
		Major	L. J. A. Langlois, (appointed 7.7.14)
		Captain	C. G. Mitchell RE (appointed May 1915)
		2nd Lts.	L. M. T. Griffin, H. ff. Ozanne W. H. Bainbrigge (Hon Lt in Army, L. A. C. Robins, F. C. Bowden,C. A. Fenwick (Artillery Instructor)
	Surgeon	Major	E. W. Livesey (promoted 1.4.13)
	Chaplain	Captain	Revd W. A. Price (appointed 1.4.13)
	Engineer Section		1 Lieut.

1919 From the Army List May 1919

	Commandant	Lt Col.	W. G. de Jersey
		Major	L. J. A. Langlois
		Captain	C. G. Mitchell, (Hon Capt in Army)
		2nd Lts.	L. M. T. Griffin (Hon Lt in Army), H. ff. Ozanne MC, RA, W. H. Bainbridge, (Hon Lt in Army), L. A. C. Robins, F. C. Bowden, C. A. Fenwick
1919	Engineer Section Lt		1. No name given

Uniform noted as Blue with Scarlet facings

1920	Commandant	Lt Col.	W. Grant de Jersey
		Major	L. J. A. Langlois
		Lieuts	W. H. Bainbridge, C. A. Fenwick, S. A. Hankey, L. A. C. Robins

The Militia was officially reinstated after the First World War, on 16 March 1921.

1921	Adjutant	Major	David A. Strachan
		Major	L. J. A. Langlois
		Lieut.	M. P. Le Brun
		2ndLts.	H. F. Ozanne MC, W. H. Bainbridge, L .A. C. Robin, F.C. Bowden, C.A. Fenwick, S.A. Gaudion

1923		Captain	W. R. Thompson
		Lieuts	M. P. Le Brun, S.A. Gaudion
1924	Commandant	Major	W. R. Thompson
	Adjutant	Major	Patrick J. T. Pickthrall
		2nd Lieut.	T. M. Y. May
1925		2nd Lieut.	A. A. Fletcher-Jones
1926	Commandant	Major	W. R. Thompson
	Adjutant	Lieut.	H. G. T. de Sausmarez
		Lieut.	S. A. Gaudion
		2nd Lts.	J. M. V. May, A. A. Fletcher-Jones
1927			

Honorary Colonel Royal Guernsey, & Royal Alderney Militias

| | Maj. Gen. | M. H. Saward RA (appointed 10.6.14) |

Artillery Section

Commandant	Captain	W. R. Thompson (Lt Col. retd., appointed 1.2.23)
Adjutant	Captain	H. G. T. de Sausmarez (& of R. Guernsey Militia apppointed 28.9.25, promoted local Captain 19.12.25)
	Lieut.	S. A. Gaudion (appointed 1.2.23)
	2nd Lt	A. A. Fletcher-Jones, (appointed 13.9.25

Engineer Section

| | 2nd Lieut. | J. M. V. May (appointed 1.5.24) |
| Chaplain 4th class | | Revd J. Le Brun, (appointed 25.7.21) |

Uniform again noted as 'Blue, Facings – Scarlet'.

1928	Commandant	Lt Col.	W. R. Thompson
	Adjutant	Captain	H. G. T. de Sausmarez
		Lieuts	S. A. Gaudion, T.M.Y. May
1928 contd.		2nd Lt	A. A. Fletcher-Jones
1929	Commandant	Lt Col.	L. J. A. Langlois

The Alderney Militia was finally disbanded on 6 March 1929 after about eight centuries in existence.

6 May 1935
A special parade of former Artillery and Infantry units under Lt Col. Langlois for the Silver Jubilee of King George V.

Captain Lionel Langlois in 1900. He later rose to become a Lt Colonel in the Alderney Militia and was its last Commandant before it was disbanded.

April 1938
Another special unit under Lt Col. Langlois was reconvened to provide a Guard of Honour for the visit of the Bailiff, who lunched at the Marais Hall.

Following the end of the Second World War, the idea of having a militia force in Alderney was revived with the creation of a 'Junior Militia', details of which were given in the previous chapter.

12

Wrecked Around Alderney

Introduction

The treacherous waters, the swift tidal races of *Le Passage au Singe*, (The Swinge) and *Le Raz de Blanchard*, (The Race), where currents run at eight knots, the many sunken reefs and projecting rocks around Alderney, and also those stretching from Cap de la Hague to the Casquets, have been the death of many ships both small and large over the centuries.

Examination, over several years, of the Alderney Parish Registers, the records of the MoD Hydrographic Survey Department, and many contemporary documents and Newspapers from Record Offices and Libraries, has produced a list of over three hundred ships to date, wrecked or stranded, including a small number of wartime casualties, sunk by enemy or Allied action, as distinct from nature's hazards. Doubtless many more were lost in olden times without any record of them being kept in any surviving documents, and small fishing vessels have often disappeared without trace.

There is a legend that the *Blanche Nef*, the *White Ship* carrying Prince William, the only son of King Henry I was wrecked on the Casquets in November 1120. This legend has been perpetuated through the centuries by repetition in many published works, and is still included on the Trinity House leaflet about their Lighthouse. The general opinion now is that the vessel, which was of the latest construction at the time, single-masted, and rowed by 40-60 oarsmen in three tiers, was late leaving Normandy with the King's household on board, because of the Crew's carousing.

In attempting to catch up with the King's ship *Royal Tiger*, it struck a rock and foundered off Barfleur. There was reputedly only a single survivor, a butcher from Rouen named Bèrault, who reached Southampton four days later, and informed the King of the tragedy.

As a result of the loss of his heir, and with no obvious successor, a situation which still existed when Henry died, in 1235, after 29 years as Duke of Normandy and 36 years on the English throne, there were nearly 20 years of anarchy in England, following his death.

An Elizabethan warship was probably wrecked about half a mile off the island in 1592, the possible identity of this has only recently come to light some 15 years after a musket from the wreck was first found. It was protected in 1992 under the Bailiwick

Historic Wrecks Law, and moves instituted by the States of Alderney to ensure its proper excavation.

In February 1993 it was reported that two bronze cannon from the wreck of HMS *Dragon* off the Casquets in 1711 had been brought up and sold in France for £40,000. This vessel was then also declared an historic wreck and an exclusion zone declared of a half nautical mile around the Casquets.

From the *White Ship* legend, until the first record of a wreck in the Alderney Parish Registers in 1665, over four centuries later, there is nothing recorded, although from the frequency of catastrophes after that date, it is certain that many vessels must have been lost during this period. Except for a section on the Elizabethan wreck, this chapter thus starts after the Restoration of Charles II to the English throne, and thus to the Dukedom of Normandy.

Since the end of the nineteenth century, photographs have been taken of many of the wrecks, some of the more famous are included in the illustrations. Following many of them, a number of local pilots and fishermen made brave, and frequently successful, attempts to save the crews of the vessels involved, often at great risk to themselves, and to bring them safely to Alderney.

Stories of the Wrecks

The Elizabethan Wreck

Probably sunk in 1592

The most exciting discovery in marine archæology in Alderney's history was made as the result of an accidental find in 1980. Local fisherman Bertie Cosherill brought up a heavily concreted musket when lifting his pots just to the west of Le Grois Ledge, off Château à L'Étoc. Little interest was shown at the time by the Alderney museum or local historians and he left it against the wall of his house for some time. When he eventually broke off the iron and sand concretion the wooden stock and iron barrel of a long musket was revealed.

This was left outside for a couple of years and later disintegrated. Fortunately Bertie had taken transit marks on the position of his pots and eventually returned to the spot with local diver Fred Shaw. Fred went down to the bottom in almost 100ft. of water and landed right on top of two large cannons about eight feet long and an anchor. He picked up some bits of pottery a few yards away on two more dives and then abandoned the site.

Ten years later he returned to the spot with three other divers. After three dives they located a few ship's timbers but failed to find the anchor or the cannons. Next year (1991) in the late spring, several more local divers joined the search and found two more cannon and, about 100 feet away from these, relocated the original find. In the next few weeks many small artefacts were brought up, mostly heavily concreted. After chipping away the concretion the stocks and barrels of several muskets, some cannon balls and other items, were found and placed in a tank with running fresh water in the author's garden to preserve them temporarily.

Many smaller items were found in the surface layer of sand at the site including a lot of French, German and Dutch pottery shards of the period about the end of the sixteenth century. Two round flattish discs turned out to be lead pan weights when the concretion was removed. These were marked with the crowned initials EL with a dagger alongside and weighed almost exactly 1lb. and 2lb. Investigation showed this official mark to have originated in the City of London in 1586.

A hardwood powder flask and several brass 'apostles' (single charge powder containers) with their caps were found. Surviving examples of these are extremely rare and were of great interest to the Tower of London armoury. A pewter bowl with *A De Pouce* (probably the owner's name stamped on the bottom, a pewter spoon and a pewter flask stamped with a round mark of a Centaur with a drawn bow and arrow on the base. About a dozen peasecod breastplates and back plates, some with their leather padding with brass rosettes still attached and several burgonet and cabocete helmets. All were carefully extricated from the concretion.

More matchlock muskets of two different types and a larger swivel musket were found. A gun port cover with its hinges, an iron pump handle, parts of a wooden pump and associated lead piping. Parts of several swords with leather scabbards, a leather

A 1 lb. pan weight dated about 1586 from Alderney's Elizabethan wreck.

Twelve copper 'Apostles', a pair of guilded stirrups, wooden powder flask and a pewter bowl.

shoe, quantities of 3-inch cannon balls, star shot and chain shot were brought up. A clay 'ladle' pipe, later dated to about 1590, a rare pewter pipe and a complete ceramic hand grenade emerged, followed by a pair of brass stirrups with traces of gilding still remaining in the chased parts.

The area of the wreck was marked out in five-metre squares and all the finds carefully recorded. A total of nine cannon about eight feet long were noted, at least one with the remains of a wooden gun carriage still beneath it. The whole area was then placed under the protection of the Bailiwick Wreck and Salvage Law 1986 and further diving prohibited without a licence from the Alderney Receiver of Wrecks, the Clerk of the States. The quantity of arms and armour being found suggested that this vessel might be a supply ship.

Much of the pottery, some 500 items initially and some of the other material was identified and dated by Bob Burns, Assistant Curator of the Guernsey Museum who made several visits to Alderney during this period.

The interest aroused locally attracted the attention of the national press in England, and in June 1991 a colleague of David Keys, archæological journalist working for **The Independent** researching the period at the Public Record Office found a reference in the papers of Lord Burghley, Elizabeth I's Chief Minister, to the loss, off Alderney in 1592, of a warship carrying supplies to Paimpol for Sir John Norreys' army in Brittany. It seemed at least possible that this might be that vessel.

A halt was called to any more work on the wreck whilst the artefacts already recovered were investigated by archæologists and a start made on conserving some of them.

In 1993, some 400 years after the loss, a combined unit of about 20 archaeologists, students and divers from the Oxford University Marine Archaeological Research Unit MARE, under its Director Mensun Bound and from the North Wales Maritime Studies Unit at Bangor University, under Michael Bowyer their Maritime Historian, who had been appointed project director by the States, came to Alderney for several weeks in June and July. A large tank was set up in the former DOE Stables building by the harbour, to contain the artefacts recovered and the material already collected was placed in it. A predisturbance survey was started on the wreck of what appears to be the only Elizabethan warship ever to be discovered, and thus of immense historical and archaeological significance. Much underwater camera work, both still and video was carried out and many more small artefacts lying on the surface were logged and collected.

Every item brought up was carefully catalogued and drawn by expert artists forming part of the team. The Old Stables were opened to public view. Some of the artefacts already conserved were also placed on display in a special case in the Alderney Museum. It was decided to set up a trust to control the work and raise funds for both the recovery and subsequent preservation of the unique material discovered. This was finally achieved in December 1993 when the Alderney Maritime Trust was formed with a number of eminent trustees appointed. Island born schoolmaster Royston Raymond was appointed to represent the local community on the Trust. Their area of responsibility is for all historic wrecks round Alderney and not just the Elizabethan vessel.

The divers worked in difficult conditions at about 100ft. in an area of strong swirling tides. The whole area was carefully marked out, triangulation points established and the area mapped and photographed. The vessel appears to have been a three-master about 100 feet long, probably of 100 tons or more and carrying 12-24 cannon.

The Alderney Journal published a reprint of all the articles concerning the Wreck from its issues between August 1991 and April 1994, a booklet which will no doubt be followed by other collections in due course. The profits from the sale of these were promised to the Trust.

In the meantime documentary research at the National Archives suggested that the vessel might possibly be the *Makeshift*, a pinnace which formed part of Drake's squadron which had defeated the Spanish Armada in 1588, which disappeared from the records about 1592.

The unit returned in greater strength in the summer of 1994 and carried on with the surveying and recording work, assisted by the local divers who had been responsible for much of the original work on the site. This included a considerable amount of underwater video and still photography. The climax came when, on the evening of 20 July, the canon on its carriage was raised and conveyed to the Old Stables amidst the cheers and congratulations of a large part of the population of Alderney.

A press briefing had been held at the sailing club earlier that day, when TV, Radio and Newspaper correspondents from UK National press and the Channel Islands media representatives were briefed on the work carried out so far by Michael Bowyer and Mensun Bound. They were then given an opportunity to examine and photograph some of the artefacts already conserved. This resulted in several newspaper articles over the next few days and nation-wide TV coverage on both BBC and ITV.

A few days before the end of the diving season here, two more cannon were found to be still mounted on carriages, possibly in a better state of preservation than the one already raised. These await another season's work. Subsequently a Side-scan Sonar survey was carried out by American Jon Jolly, an expert in this type of underwater exploration and Nick Winder, a local man, currently working in Archaeology at Cambridge. The resulting computer prints from these surveys seem to show the outline of the hull and give further information about the area surrounding the wreck.

Later in 1994 year the cannon already raised was sent to the National Exhibition Centre in Birmingham for the 'Dive 94' exhibition, where it aroused much interest.

From there it was taken to the Museum at York for conservation work to be carried out by Dr Ian Panter. This took about three years and cost £10,000 before the canon was returned to Alderney.

After the concretion was removed and the gun and carriage separated, the barrel was found to have its wooden tampion still in place and a lead plug in the touch hole. In order to remove the tampion, which could not be removed complete, holes were drilled in it and it was sawn across. The hemp wadding used to keep the ball in position was dry and in good order, this was withdrawn but the ball was too tight a fit to remove at this stage. The immediate heating up of the barrel gave fear of the possibility of the powder, inside the bone dry barrel where it had been for 400 years, exploding and propelling the ball through the wall of the laboratory. Unfortunately the use of water to cool the barrel and prevent this happening also soaked the powder and has effectively prevented an accurate analysis of the mixture used at the time from being made.

The carriage was in two halves, one each side of the barrel, with the trunions of the cannon still resting in their grooves, any connecting iron work, axles etc. between the two parts having been eroded over the centuries. Some of the tarred rope which was used to secure the cannon to the carriage and also to run it in and out of the gun ports has been well preserved inside the concretion. The remaining wood however is iron hard and after freeze-drying and other conservation processes, will be in good condition although the lower parts of the carriage have rotted or been worn away. This makes it difficult to decide whether the carriage had two wheels and a skid at the rear, or four wheels. Further investigation may resolve this. Experts from the Tower of London who have examined the barrel think it might have been a 'sakar', made about 1586. At the end of 1994 the MARE team was withdrawn from the project by their executive committee and the work was continued in 1995 by the Bangor team. The 'predisturbance' survey was continued, after divers had driven specially made pegs into the rocks to locate the grid and a number of other artefacts which had come to the surface of the site, including a rapier complete in its scabbard, were brought up for conservation. (See colour illustrations). Since then much conservation work has gone on the artefacts, more canon and other items have been raised and an excellent display created in the Alderney Museum, including one of the cannon mounted on a reproduction contemporary style gun carriage in a mock up of part of the ship's deck kindly made by the Jersey Museum Service. Part of this display has been loan to the Tower of London for an exhibition during 2010 and will be returned soon.

Since about 2007/8 the MARE team under Dr Mensun Bound have now been officially placed in charge of the work by the States of Alderney and a decision was made to leave most of the remaining artefacts where they are but to bring up and conserve such items as from time to time become exposed to avoid their possible permanent loss.

No contemporary details of this wreck have survived in Alderney and it was to be another 73 years before the first mention of any wreck is found in the surviving Parish Registers. Details of some of the many other wrecks are given in the following pages.

Other, Later Wrecks

Mary

Wrecked in June 1695

Only the barest details of this tragedy have been recorded, but it gives a terrible example of the hazards facing mariners in olden times. *Mary* was wrecked on the barren rocks of the Casquets in June 1695 with a crew of 22 men. The survivors managed to reach the rocks where they were marooned for weeks. They first ate the ship's dog, and then, after drawing lots, two of their shipmates. When the 10 skeletal survivors were finally picked up by a passing ship bound for Southampton, they were in such a poor state that two of them died before they reached port.

Michael

Wrecked on 5 January 1701

Michael was a sailing ship of 330 tons, registered in London, which struck the Casquets en route for Lisbon to get a cargo of salt.

Her Master, Richard Hutton had set sail 'out of the Downs' and had passed the Isle of Wight about 4 p.m. the next day. The wind turned into a N.E. gale, with sleety rain, and they were forced to shorten sail, finally running under the foresail only. At 2 a.m. the bowsprit ran into the rocks and the mainmast broke, forming a bridge onto the rocks. Five of the crew managed to drop ashore from this, and four more used the foresail's yardarm. The ship quickly broke up and the master and six more crew were drowned.

Those who had managed to scramble onto the Casquets, in the days before there were lights there, had no food, little clothing and few shoes between them. They made two little wooden huts from bits of broken planks from the ship, which sheltered them a little from the wind, but not from rain or spray. At low tide they managed to find limpets and seaweed to keep them alive. After five days they found the ship's dog on a nearby rock, who could not eat these things, so was killed and eaten raw. This continued for two weeks, by which time they were almost starved to death, although they had plenty of fresh rainwater.

During this time they sighted one ship which they thought was the *Express,* but were not seen, most ships keeping well clear of the hazardous area.

A young lad, sailing on board his father John Taskard's ship, out of Lymington, had a dream in which he was responsible for saving some shipwrecked mariners from the Casquets. He told his father about it, but it was laughed off. The next night he had the same dream again, and in the morning, as they approached the rocks from Guernsey, bound for Southampton was sure he saw men on them. His father laughed again, but being persuaded to use his telescope, was astonished to see one of the survivors on top of the rock waving his cap. They reached the rocks about 4 p.m. on 20 January, and rescued the nine men, arriving at Southampton the following day. Here they were well treated by the Mayor and Townspeople, and when they had recovered, seven of them went on to London.

The men rescued were the Mate, Thomas Mead, Stephen Hutchins, John Mow, John Baldock, John Boulter, Ambrose Rawlinson, Nathaniel Freeman, William Trotter, and the cabin boy, Isaac Leader. It was generally agreed that their rescue had been a miracle.

HMS *Dragon*

Wrecked on 15 March 1711

The Frigate *Dragon* was launched in 1647 at Chatham, and subsequently rebuilt twice, in 1690 and 1707. At the time of her loss, she was of 414 tons, carried 38 guns and was lost off the Casquets.

Early in 1993 a report was received in Alderney that two bronze cannon from the wreck had been brought up and sold in France for £40,000. As a result the wreck was immediately placed under the protection of the Bailiwick Wreck and Salvage Law 1988, and an exclusion zone declared around the area. Under legislation currently being considered by the European Union, which it is proposed to make retrospective, it is possible that Alderney might be able to be reclaim them at some time in the future, and the persons who plundered the wreck prosecuted if they can be identified.

One of *Dragon's* cannons is reputedly used as a shore mooring point at the Inner Harbour.

HMS *Victory*

Wrecked on 4/5 October 1744

At the time of the wreck of Admiral Balchen's flagship, the 'Casket Lights' had been burning for 20 years. HMS *Victory*, a 110-gun 'First Rater', and at that time the largest ship in the world, with a fleet of 21 sail, was convoying 200 merchant ships. They relieved the French blockade of the Tagus, visited Gibraltar and, passing through the bay of Biscay were dispersed by a tremendous storm. Eventually all except the Flagship reached Spithead. Some days later news was finally sent from Alderney that fishermen had heard guns booming after midnight on 4 October, but were unable to go to the assistance of whatever vessel was in distress because of the conditions. Wreckage, including spars marked 'Victory' were washed ashore on Alderney in the next week or so, and it was eventually established that she must have struck *Roque Noire* one of the Casquets group. All 1,100 men on board were lost, and not a single body was ever recovered.

Various imaginative paintings of the wreck were created and later postcards showing the wreck 'Off the Casquets' were on sale for many years.

In 2008-9 an American salvage vessel searching for this wreck, eventually found it about 60 or more miles west of the Casquets, in deep water. Their sophisticated underwater mobile cameras produced some excellent and conclusive photos that this was indeed the Victory. The wreck was far removed from Alderney which probably

72. LOSS OF H.M.S. VICTORY, OFF THE CASQUETS 1744.

Artist's impression of the wreck of HMS *Victory* in October 1744, published as a postcard.

explains why no survivors or bodies were ever found but their guns just might have been heard on that night.

Santissimus Sacramento

Wrecked on 10 November 1782

The details of this wreck come from a letter in the National Archives written by John Le Mesurier to Thomas Townshend, Principal Secretary of State, the following day, and do not seem to have been recorded elsewhere.

At 3 a.m. the 600 ton, 36 gun Portuguese ship, Master, Captain Johan Lobo, carrying a valuable cargo of masts struck the Casquets en route from Riga to Lisbon. Nineteen members of the crew were rescued from a ship's boat by a ship coming from Guernsey, which then went to the wreck and brought the Master and thirty-seven men to Alderney. The next day she was still just afloat, held up by her spars, and was towed off by local vessels. She broke away near Braye Harbour in the evening, and by next morning had drifted 3-4 leagues N.E. of the island. A second attempt was made to take her in tow, but the local vessels were driven off by a 10-12 gun French Privateer which was already towing a loaded sloop she had captured. One of the four-oar Alderney boats trying to regain the wreck was also captured by the Frenchman. The Captain had told the Governor that there was a box containing £5,000 in Spanish dollars on board, as well as the masts.

Le Mesurier's letter requested the Admiralty to at once send HM vessels to attempt to gain the wreck before she sank or drifted towards France, in order to acquire the valuable cargo and the gold.

HMS *Amethyst*

Wrecked on 29 December 1795

Amethyst, Captain F. T. Affleck, was a 1,029-ton 5th Rater, launched in 1793, carrying 38 guns and a crew of 300. The Guernsey Society Review for 1984 carries an interesting story of the wreck from an Edinburgh paper, *The Evening Courant* of Thursday 7 January 1796.

The Frigate *Amethyst* left Torbay in company with HMS *Trusty* on Monday afternoon of that week, and missing the

'Commodores' [? Casquets] lights in a severe gale, struck on the 'Hannouaux Rocks near Guernsey' [Hanois], at 4 a.m. on Tuesday. '...having got off thence, was driven upon the island of Alderney and at half past nine ran on shore in the Bay of Praye [Braye] in that island. It was luckily near high water, and by waiting till the water was low, the crew were safely landed without losing a man. The three masts and bowsprit are gone, but if the weather proves moderate the stores will probably be saved.'

It appears that in attempting to assist, a boat with six Alderneymen was capsized and two were drowned, the others being saved by a human chain from the shore. The extract concludes:

Having their pockets full of money very little regulation can take place among them [the sailors] so long as it lasts.

Elsewhere HMS *Amethyst* has been recorded as wrecked in The Swinge, but in either case her armaments were salvaged, and mounted at the expense of the States of Alderney, for the defence of the island, the ammunition and gunpowder to be provided by the War Department. One cannon was reported in *Le Bailliage* on 30 October 1897 to have been lying 'half buried in sand at the far end of the old jetty [the Le Mesurier Pier] for at least 100 years', and was removed in that year to join others in use as bollards on the new jetty. Another of the cannons, found in a garden in St Anne after the Second World War, has been mounted on a carriage and is now in the Alderney Museum.

At the enquiry, her Captain was held responsible for the loss.

Unnamed Vessel

Wrecked in November 1801

The details of this wreck are contained in a letter from Brigadier General Charles William Este Commanding Officer of the garrison, to Lord Portland, First Secretary, on 10 November 1801.

The vessel was wrecked on Burhou, and broke up in a few minutes, the previous Wednesday. The Master and seven men were rescued. On the day of his letter, planks and bales of candles came ashore at Quesnard and were placed under guard. The Master said the cargo was insured for £30,000. There was then a very considerable amount of dispute between Este, Le Ber, representing the Governor, who claimed the salvage rights were his, and the Master of the vessel, over the ownership of the cargo which could be salvaged, and a series of letters and Alderney Court hearings quickly followed. It was held that as the Master had been saved the vessel was still his property, but by then 19 boats from Alderney had gone out to the site of the wreck and picked up everything they could, much to the disgust of the General, who wanted to prosecute the persons involved.

Cimoni

A Greek warship wrecked in November 1825

One of the less savoury aspects of any wreck has always been the reactions of the local population to the occurrence. Many stories are told of the killing of survivors, and the pillaging of the cargo, of ships driven ashore in any land. Although Alderney folk have never been averse to personal gain from these disasters, [even in very recent times when the MV *Corinna* was wrecked {*qv*}], in general the crews of the vessels have been treated very well, and over the years many Alderneymen have lost their own lives trying to save others.

The crew of this Brigantine, wrecked on our East coast, were not so fortunate. The crew of 40 managed to gain the shore but they were robbed and the vessel pillaged. The captain was reported to have said:

> Had I been cast upon the shore among Turks I should have expected death and met it; among Christians, from them I expected pity and protection. I have met with robbery instead.

The Lt Governor of Guernsey, Sir John Colborne was informed of the situation and travelled to Alderney. The seamen were each given clothing, food and £5, and taken to Guernsey. The British Government later sent HMS *Aurora* to convey them to Portsmouth. No-one was ever punished for the affair, but it could well have been this incident that led to troops being sent to guard the cargo of the next recorded wreck eight years later.

Jupiter

Wrecked on 4 January 1833

The Danish Brigantine *Jupiter* which came ashore at Mannez on the N.E. coast of Alderney, a frequent area for wrecks in the days before the Alderney Lighthouse was built in 1912. She carried a valuable general cargo including casks of liquor. Three of the crew were drowned in the wreck, but the remainder got safely ashore. The Captain requested a military guard for his cargo, and this was provided. In spite of these precautions many islanders managed to get aboard the ship and carry off portions of her cargo and liquor. Some were too anxious to sample the latter, and as a result were caught, arrested and jailed for looting.

Bonne Famille

Wrecked on 8 March 1850

Not far from the scene above, the French Chasse Marée *Bonne Famille* ran onto L'Enfer Rock. Her crew spent the night on the rock from which they were rescued in the morning. The Government Mineral Railway from Mannez Quarry was built by this time, and the crew were taken on the train to Braye. They were well cared for and the ship, which was not badly damaged, was later patched and refloated and taken to Guernsey where she was rebuilt at St Sampson's and renamed *Alice* in 1851.

Boadicea

Wrecked on 6 January 1857

Boadicea, a 415-ton Barque of N. Shields, sailing to Antwerp from Alexandria, ran onto Tauteney Rock between The Casquets & Herm, and was seen by the Brig *Diolinda*. When she arrived in Guernsey and reported the wreck, a couple of hours later HM Revenue Cutter *Eagle*, the Pilot Cutter *Blonde*, and the Steam Tug *Watt* owned by Captain Scott of Alderney, went to her assistance.

Three of the crew were saved by the Guernsey boats, and taken to *Watt*, but nine lives were lost in this tragedy. The RNLI made awards to the Guernsey sailors, as reported in the *Guernsey Star*. Some time later, a report in *Le Bailliage* on 12 February 1868 records a presentation being made to Captain Scott, [who was also the owner of Scott's Hotel, Braye Road, Alderney], for his bravery in rescuing members of the crew of *Boadicea*.

Although Guernsey had had an official States pulling lifeboat since 1803, it appears never to have been launched. An appeal subsequent to the loss of *Boadicea* resulted in the purchase of another pulling boat, *The Rescue*, but, four years later, and with a further 13 vessels lost or stranded in Guernsey waters, she too had never been launched.

Carioca

Wrecked on 18 October 1866

By the time the French Sailing Barque *Carioca*, en route between Le Havre and Rio de Janeiro, was wrecked off Château à L'Étoc at about 3 o'clock in the morning, the four Forts on this part of the Alderney coast were completed and occupied, in the event a fortunate circumstance for her crew. Sailing up The Race in storm force winds, she was dismasted by a sudden shift of wind, and driven onto rocks near the Château. Some of the crew managed to get ashore near the fort by climbing along the fallen rigging, and roused the soldiers who, assisted by men from Fort Corblets, finally managed to rescue 21 members of the crew in difficult conditions. One of the gunners from Fort Corblets, Gunner Moore, had risked his life climbing over the rocks in the storm to find them. Only five sailors were lost, and Gunner Moore received a silver Medal and £1. from the RNLI, and a medal and another £1 from the French Government. Two other men, Sparks and Fox received a vellum certificate and £1 from the RNLI, and a medal and £1 from the French, who also gave awards to 14 other men for their part in this rescue.

Shealtiel

Wrecked on 19 February 1894

The collier *Shealtiel* caught fire in Braye roadstead. *Le Bailliage* for Saturday, 24 February 1894 has an amusing tale of this wreck.

Under the heading; *'The boy stood on the burning deck, eating apples by the peck.',* I quote the news item which followed:

> ...or as we should say here, by the dundrel[1] (I don't know whether that is spelt right Mr Editor), but that did not prevent the *Shealtiel* (owner Mr Bird of Guernsey, with 240 tons of coal for Mr Després), from burning away merrily right inside the Admiralty harbour. How she ever got there is a mystery. Early on Tuesday morning last she was discovered to be on fire near the foremast. She was then in the roads. The captain ran her for shore, and there she lay, lazily burning all Tuesday. The fire engine ran down to have a look at her, but found itself powerless to subdue the flames. It is of course a question for experts to decide, whether a fire can or cannot be put out, but it seemed to us that if a company of soldiers had been asked for and the fire engines from Forts Albert and Tourgis had been brought down, something might have been done to save some of the coal.
>
> The crew amused themselves by throwing their belongings into the water whence they were fished by innumerable boys. Later on it was a beautiful sight to see the masses of flames rising from the hold, and the smoke pouring from the forecastle in dense clouds, the flames every now and again catching the lower part of the shrouds and running nimbly up, and then eating through the stays until the foremast went with a crash over the side.
>
> It is interesting to note that this unfortunate ship is occupying the exact site of the *Courier's* berth in the Admiralty harbour!

SS *Behara*

Wrecked on 22 March 1895

The issue of Guernsey Newspaper *Le Bailliage* dated 30 March 1895, carries brief details

---

[1] *A dunerel is a basket measure of one sixth bushel*

of another wreck, fortunately without loss of life. *Behara*, was a screw-driven collier from Glasgow. Sailing from Sunderland to Bilbao with 2,000 tons of coal, in thick fog at midnight on Friday 22 March, she drove onto the little island of Les Hommeaux or Houmets Florains (Island of Flowers), then, as now, almost entirely covered with a Fort.

Her Master, Captain Russell started to back off, but, finding the ship filling with water, he drove her back onto the rocks on the other side of the gully. The crew took to their boats, but Mr John Godfray who lived nearby, hearing their cries ran to the beach and held up a lantern which they saw and pulled towards him. As a result all landed safely. Next day it was seen that the cargo of coal was all slipping out through the holes in her side and she was a total wreck. The crew were taken to Guernsey on *Courier* on the Sunday, and within a week, she had broken up. By 1 April, *Behara* had vanished completely. Her boats and gear were sold at a public auction on 15 April.

SS *Marie Fanny*

Wrecked on 14 December 1896

Another issue of *Le Bailliage,* this time for 19 December 1896 carries an account of the foundering, on rocks on the north side of Burhou, of the 436-ton French steamer from La Rochelle, *Marie Fanny* Her Master Capt. Aoustin, had left Bayonne for Rouen with a general cargo almost a week before, and had lost his compass and most of the deck fittings in a storm which arose on Sunday afternoon. Towards midnight he saw the Casquets light, and turned towards Cap de la Hague. Not long after, the ship struck the rocks and immediately split up. He managed to cling to a spar and was washed up on the island where he lay all night badly battered. At dawn he saw the hut and dragged himself to it and passed out. By great fortune two men were on the island rabbitting. They were woken by a noise at the door, and according to another report written in Alderney were too scared of ghosts to open the door at first. When they eventually did so, they found the Captain, and the ship's dog which was also washed ashore and survived. When the boat came out from Alderney next day to collect the two men, they were very surprised to find the third man and the dog.

Wreckage was washed ashore on Alderney in large quantities over the next few days, but none of the 14 members of the crew survived. Le Bailliage report says that none of their bodies were found that week, the next issue recorded four bodies being recovered during the following week, but the Alderney reference says that nine bodies were recovered the next morning, and were buried in St Anne's churchyard. The Parish Death Register shows no entries at all for this period, but that is not particularly strange, as the extant records are very limited in this respect, those which have survived appear to be hand written extracts from the originals, made at an unknown date.

SS *Ville De Malaga*

Wrecked on 14 August 1897

Le Bailliage for 21 August carries the story of the wreck of this 868-ton French steamer, belonging to Mssrs. Huline of Rouen.

Carrying 1,751 tons of coal from Dunkirk to Brest, she passed-by the Alderney Breakwater at 2.45 p.m., and not long afterwards struck the Pommier Reef N.W. of Casquets. She sank in three minutes. According to this report, 23 members of the crew and the Captain's sister were clinging to spars and planks in the water. The Casquets keepers signalled to Alderney by Telegraph and the signal was seen by the Lloyd's signalman at the station on The Butes, Mr Paling. He notified Judge Barbenson who immediately sent the SS *Courier* to the scene. Meantime a fishing boat *Mayflower*, had picked up four of the crew. *Courier* picked up 11 men and the woman and returned to Alderney. Later that evening another man was seen to be on rocks near the lighthouse. The keepers again signalled and *Courier* returned and rescued him. In this tragedy seven drowned, but thanks to the vigilance of the Lloyd's signalman Mr Paling, 20 were rescued.

Brigantine *Hasparren*

Wrecked on 29 November 1897

Once again I am indebted to *Le Bailliage* for a contemporary account of the wreck of the 603 ton, 2-masted, French Brigantine *Hasparren*. Registered in Bayonne she was on her way from St Malo to Lisbon in ballast. In 'boisterous weather' N.W. of the Casquets, at 9 a.m., she sprang a leak near Pierre au Vraic. The ballast shifted and blocked the pumps and she was filling with water. The Captain and crew of nine took to the boats, and pulled towards Alderney where they reached the end of the Breakwater in about two hours. Crossing the sunken part, the boat capsized and four men were drowned. The rest clung to the upturned boat and were seen by Thomas Batiste. He and Mr A. Bliestel got a boat and went to their assistance. The Harbourmaster R. Allen in a rowing boat with four other Alderneymen also went to their aid. When the seas swept Batiste past the survivors without his managing to catch hold of them, Allen and his crew managed to pick them up. The six men were taken to his house and cared for, being much exhausted, but despite his care, and the attentions of Dr Steadman, 23-year-old Garnier-Théodore François died next day, and was buried in St Anne. The survivors were taken to St Malo in the SS *Courier* the following Tuesday. Just how *Hasparren* got to the Casquets en route from St Malo to Lisbon was not mentioned.

SS *Blanche*

Wrecked on 22 March 1898

The Guernsey Press of 24 March records another shipwreck due to the Breakwater. In a N.N.E. gale SS *Blanche*, a 320-ton coaster in light ballast, and coming to Alderney for stone was blown onto the end of the Breakwater, she foundered in the roadstead. The crew of nine were all saved but the vessel was an old one and it was thought not worth raising. Being however a considerable obstruction where she sat with her masts out of the water she would have to be blown up.

One of the earliest mentions of this trade was a year earlier, in March 1897 when it was recorded 'several vessels have been loaded with stone in the last 10 days and the trade is rapidly increasing'.

Blanche was one of a number of steamers carrying stone between Alderney and London at that time. Between them they moved 21,685 tons of stone in the period from April to October 1897. (This compared with a previous export of about 100 tons a year). The other ships concerned in these shipments, were the steamships; *Fal*, *Westbury*, *Vanda*, and *Mount Park*.

SS *Stella*

Wrecked on Good Friday, 30 March 1899

Stella was perhaps the most famous of Alderney's wrecks because it involved the greatest loss of life in modern times. The London and South-western Railway Company running from Southampton, and the GWR whose port of departure was Weymouth, at this time were competitors for business on the steamer routes to the Channel Islands, and the captains of the vessels were always keen to get there as quickly as possible. L&SWRs 1,059-ton *Stella* ran into thick fog on this crossing just before reaching the Casquets, but despite this her Master, Captain W. Reeks, only reduced speed, and sounded his foghorn for about 10 minutes, he then increased speed again, and as a result ran into Black Rock one of the outliers of the Casquets group, and the same as that on which *Victory* was thought to have foundered, at about 20 mph according to one survivor. The ship sank in eight minutes during which time only five of the lifeboats and a collapsible boat had been launched.

The Guernsey Mail and Telegraph, in hourly editions the next day carried a full account of the tragedy, interviews with the survivors, and lists of passengers saved and drowned. *Stella* left Southampton just before midday with about 180 passengers and 35 crew aboard. She was eight years old, and had a top speed of 18 knots. After striking the rocks Captain Reeks organised the launching of as many boats as possible, and was still on the bridge when she sank, stern first. One of the dinghies took a boatload of ladies in tow, but the remainder disappeared in the fog. Fortunately the sea was calm, although with a swell. This boat rowed all night, until about 6 a.m. they spotted a sailing ship, and almost immediately saw the GWR Steamer *Lynx* approaching. *Lynx* picked up the two boats and 41 survivors. About the same time *Vera* came up with 62 survivors from two other boats. Survivors from one of these said that a fifth boatload of passengers had been sucked down by the vortex as *Stella* sank, and only one man survived and got to their boat.

When *Lynx* arrived at Guernsey with her survivors there was already much anxiety about the overdue *Stella*. L. & S.W.R. cargo steamer *Honfleur* was immediately despatched to The Casquets, but only found the two empty boats whose passengers had already been recovered. They collected the personal possessions from these and went on, searching without success for other survivors. Judge Barbenson from Alderney had already been out searching in his steam launch, but had also found no-one. A French boat had picked up the small collapsible lifeboat with nine people on board and taken them to Cherbourg, from whence a tug had immediately been sent to search the area.

Several eyewitness accounts from survivors were later published as small pamphlets, and talks were given to women's meetings in England. Such a pamphlet, was the text of an address given by Miss B. H. Angel at the Bedfont Hall Middlesex on 16 April 1899. The address contains little in the way of details of the wreck, but much in the way of thanks for divine intervention in her deliverance.

One of the children to survive the wreck, picked up from the sea by the small boat, who was taken to Cherbourg, and many years later returned to Alderney was Benning Arnold, by then Major Benning Arnold DSO, RA, living in the house called Red Tiles near Coastguards. He was the father of Peter Arnold, founder of The Alderney Pottery, and erected a beacon and light on the rock near which he was rescued, which was kept in good order for many years. Benning Arnold's brother was drowned in the wreck, and his body washed up on Alderney next day. His watch had stopped at 4.05 p.m. His mother had been seen in the water being put into a lifebelt by a Mr Carrington, but neither survived or were recovered.

In this tragedy there were 105 persons drowned, including the Captain, Chief Steward, Steward, and the three Stewardesses, but a total of 120 people were rescued.

Some three weeks later the Dieppe Steam trawler *Duquesne* picked up the body of 38-year-old Richard Lamerton, the Second Steward, from St Luke in Jersey, floating in a lifebelt some 12 miles off Point d'Ailly. French fishing vessels brought in seven corpses altogether. They were buried at Dieppe.

The British Vice Consul in Dieppe, Henry W. Lee Jortin, arranged for his burial and invited all the members of the 'English Colony' in Dieppe to attend the service at All Saint's Church on 24 April. A few days later he wrote a letter of condolence to the widow in which he described how the body was identified from the contents of the pockets and the arrangements made for the funeral.

The Consular flag and those of all ships in the harbour were at half mast. The service was attended by Mr and Mrs Lee Jortin, Captain and Mrs Wallis, General Ruddell, Colonel and Mrs White, Mr Palmer Lambourne (the German Vice Consul) and his wife, Mr and Mrs Taylor, and most of the principal English residents of Dieppe. Captain Wheatley and many officers and crew of the London, Brighton & South Coast Railway steamer SS *Rouen*, and others attended in uniform. After the service, the coffin, draped in a Union Jack and with a large cross of Arums and white Tulips surrounded with Laurel leaves, placed on top by the consul's wife, was taken to Dieppe Cemetery in a two-horse hearse.

Amongst the personal effects described by the Vice Consul was 'an Amber pipe mouthpiece' and photographs of his two children. The photographs accompanying this article show SS *Stella* in St Peter Port Harbour in the 1890s, which was printed as a Christmas card, and Richard Lamerton and his wife, shortly after their wedding in

1889. The cigar holder in his left hand may well be the item described by the Consul.

Notice of the recovery of the body and some of the details from the Vice Consul's letter were published in the Jersey Evening Post that same week. A Certificate of his death by drowning from the wreck of SS *Stella* was issued by the Registrar General of Shipping and Seamen, in London on 26 January 1900.

There is a memorial window in Liverpool Cathedral to Mrs Mary Rogers, 'A Noble Woman' who gave her lifebelt to a passenger, refused a place in a lifeboat and was drowned.

The keepers on the Lighthouse were totally unaware of the wreck, although they said they had 'heard a steamer' the previous afternoon when questioned by *Honfleur*. Those who survived had nothing but praise for the calm way the crew behaved, although there was criticism of the lack of compasses, food or water in the ship's lifeboats.

The next day L&SWR sent over *South-western*, a former Mail-boat, then used for cargo, to search for more wreckage and survivors, she finished up going ashore on the Cap de la Hague and had six feet of water in her hold, but no casualties.

The wreck of SS *Stella* was found some years ago and still sits upright on the gravel sea bed about three-quarters of a mile south of where she struck on the Black Rock. Various small items have been recovered from her by divers, including some of the crockery from her kitchens. It is now within the protected zone of the Alderney Wreck and Salvage Law.

As with HMS *Victory* a number of imaginative paintings of the sinking were created and more than one turned into postcards. An example of these is shown here.

Artist's impression of the wreck of SS *Stella* off the Caskets, 30 March 1899. Also a postcard.

SS *Mercure*
SS *Hermann Koppen*

Both wrecked on 5 February 1900

The *Guernsey Evening Press* on 5 February 1900 records another double tragedy in The Swinge on the same day, the crews of which were both rescued in a single operation by Captain Petit of the steam Pilot-boat *Volage*. Expecting a steamer in, he was getting up steam to go and meet it, when he saw lights of a ship going down The Swinge in a dangerous position. They went after her and found by the time they arrived *Mercure* wrecked on Barsier Rock, about a mile N.E. of Fort Tourgis. Her lights were still showing. Capt. Petit sounded his whistle, and immediately saw flares further west. He steamed towards them, and picked up a lifeboat with 18 survivors from the German Steamer *Hermann Koppen*, they turned back to the first wreck, that of the French Steamer *Mercure* and picked up another lifeboat containing 15 of her crew. They got back into Braye with difficulty because of their load, the strong N.E. wind and the hazard of floating wreckage. At high water next day, the *Mercure* was submerged and the *Hermann Koppen* nearly so. No note is made of any crew members of either ship failing to be rescued.

Two Naval wrecks

Although there were frequent visits from Naval vessels after the Breakwater was completed, often Torpedo-boat destroyers in twos and threes, the whole Channel Fleet visited Alderney for maneuvers in 1891 and 1901 and lost two ships during the 1901 visit. (two of the few times in its history when the **Harbour of Refuge,** built and maintained at such enormous cost was actually used by the entire Channel Fleet). There were further visits in 1904 and 1906 by squadrons of Royal Navy T.B.Ds.

Torpedo Boat No. 81

Wrecked on 1 August 1901

This vessel was entering the harbour at low tide, and ripped its bottom out on the submerged part of the Breakwater. She sank in the harbour, but there were no casualties. She was dragged alongside the recently opened Jetty slung between two other torpedo boats on one side and an old merchant ship *Staperayder* on the other. Later as the pictures (below) shows, she was raised between two pontoons and salvaged by the Admiralty Tug *Camel*. She was patched and towed to Portsmouth by *Camel* and after repairs survived the First World War, finally being broken up in 1921.

Less fortunate was the next vessel.

Torpedo boat Destroyer 81, at her sea trials in 1900.

TPD 81 kept afloat between two smaller boats after sinking.

HMS *Viper*

Wrecked on 3 August 1901

HMS *Viper,* a 350-ton Torpedo Boat Destroyer (T.B.D.) was the world's first Turbine-driven Warship. She was two years old, and with a top speed of 37 knots was also the fastest ship in the world at the time. During the maneuvres she ran onto the Renonquet reef just W. of Burhou, travelling in fog.

During the course of the maneuvres, on turning the ship to starboard, rocks were seen dead ahead, avoiding action was taken, but the ship drifted sideways onto the reef at about 10 knots. The Alderney Pilot Boat *Volage* saw the distress flares and went out and towed the two ship's boats into harbour. The fog lifted almost immediately, and *Viper* was found to have capsized and broken in two. The crew had scrambled onto the rocks and no lives were lost. Within the next few weeks most of her armaments and some of the torpedoes were recovered by the Navy. The turbines had to be left.

Many years later, a group of Alderney divers led by Fred Shaw, acquired the salvage rights, and using John Allen's fishing boat, started to salvage items from the wreck. They soon found one torpedo tube still loaded and two other torpedoes, one beneath the wreck. Although it was unlikely that they would have been carrying explosive warheads on manoeuvres, Navy divers came and blew these up, but in doing so further damaged the wreck. Over the next few years various trips were made to the *Viper* and items recovered, both small and large, mostly pieces of bronze.

Shaw's group later formed the **Seasalter Divers**, and carried on recovery work when they could, raising quite large pieces of material. Another wreck stopped their activities for a time. On 14 October 1971, *Seasalter* broke her moorings in Braye Harbour, and was thrown onto the rocks near the Douglas Quay and badly holed. She was thought likely to break up in the next northerly gale, and left there.

Although Alderney has continued to receive regular and quite frequent visits from Naval vessels, ever since that time, including the Naval escorts for Royal visits, and has also had two ships named after her during these years, (see Chapter 11), a submarine, and currently a fisheries protection vessel, no large scale visit has ever taken place since then.

HMS *Viper* at her sea trials in 1900.

The wreck of *Viper* showing the several propellers.

HMS *Alderney* given the Freedom of the Island in 1989.

States President Jon Kay-Mouat presenting the Freedom scroll to RPO Chris Wellstead.

SS *Liverpool*

Wrecked on 22 February 1902

Liverpool was a 3,400-ton four-master, with a length of 333 feet two inches, one of the largest sailing-vessels afloat, when in thick fog, with all sails set, she ran gently into the small islet of Les Hommeaux Florains, crowned by its Fort. That morning, John Godfray who lived only a few yards away and had just gone to work in the Quarry near his house saw the ghostly ship with its white masts glide by. Later he and his friend George Sharp heard voices in the fog. They ran for his little boat in the creek in front of his house, and pulled quickly out to the ship. They were able to tell the crew who were taking to the boats that they could walk ashore over the island, using the little bridge between two rocks and the shore of Alderney. The Crew walked ashore, and there was no loss of life.

Liverpool, owned by R. W. Leyland, was en route from Antwerp to San Francisco with a cargo of cement, steel girders, marble, and foodstuffs, silks, olive oil and wines. Islanders were given permission to help unload the cargo. Her sails were taken down and the yards removed. All of this took some weeks, and the great ship sat there on the rocks. Trips were run in *Courier* and other vessels from Guernsey and Weymouth to view the wreck. As the second picture shows, she eventually broke up and sank. The part of the cargo that did not disappear into the homes of the islanders was sold for £10,000. Some of the marble was later used to make a flight of stairs in the Town Hospital in St Peter Port, where it remained until the building was converted into the Police Station in 1992/3.

Sailing Ship *Liverpool*, wrecked on Alderney in February 1902.

SS *Liverpool,* wrecked on Alderney in February 1902, after her sails were taken down.

Remains of the *Liverpool* some months later.

SS *Leros*

Wrecked on 29 May 1906

Leros was a 7,500-ton German Steamer which ran onto Fret Rock off Burhou in fog, and became stranded on Burhou itself. Part of her cargo was Sewing Machines in boxes of four. Despite the crew refusing assistance at the time, E. M. P. Audren, usually known as 'Bender' who was the first on the scene, later managed to 'salvage' a number of cases of these machines which he sold in the island for 5/- each. The crew later took to their boats, but had forgotten to put in the bungs, and began to sink, so they had perforce to accept assistance. They were all rescued, and much of the cargo saved. Some time later *Leros* was blown up so that her engines could be removed and salvaged.

Between the SS *Leros* above, and SS *Rhenania* below, in this six-year period 13 more ships were lost on the coasts of Alderney and Burhou, all apparently without loss of life.

SS *Rhenania*

Wrecked on 7 April 1912

Rhenania was a 1,600-ton Dutch steamer which struck Noir Houmet, also off Burhou, and also in fog, carrying a general cargo including some cattle. The crew and most of the animals got onto Burhou where the cattle remained for about three weeks in the care of the mate. The crew also managed to salvage the cargo. No human lives were lost, although some of the cattle were drowned in the hold before they could be got out. Like *Liverpool* before her, *Rhenania* became a tourist attraction, and excursions were run from Guernsey.

Recorded losses due to enemy action in the First World War were comparatively small round Alderney despite U-boat activity, and only two lives are known to have been lost.

SS *Pascall*

Sunk by enemy action on 19 December 1916

A German Submarine surfaced close to the Troop Transport *Pascall* near the Casquets and ordered her to stop. The Captain tried to outrun the submarine, but was shelled and his steering gear put out of action. The crew took to the boats and pulled away and the ship was sunk by a torpedo. The submarine then machine-gunned the boats, two sailors were killed, and others wounded. The submarine left them and they rowed to the Casquets. The pilot boat came out from Alderney to pick them up. The two who died were buried in St Anne's Churchyard, and included the 2nd Officer Howard Dutson Boulton, to whom an impressive 'broken mast' headstone was erected.

Fortunately the ship was not carrying troops at the time.

The Lifeboats were sold and used as fishing boats, one by Arthur Jennings, which was renamed *Fleur de Lys*, and in this boat many years later he and his son Arthur took the Post Office documents and the Postmaster to Guernsey on the day Alderney was evacuated in 1940. The other one was bought by Jack Quinain Snr. and renamed *Sunrise*. She was used for fishing for many years, and, as Jack was one of the Alderney pilots, also as the pilot boat. *Sunrise* also went to Guernsey during the last war, where she suffered further damage during an air raid.

Returning to Alderney after the Second World War, *Sunrise* again was used as a pilot boat by Jack Quinain, and also by his son Jack Quinain Jnr., another qualified pilot until about 1960, when she was replaced by *Sunrise II*. *Sunrise* still lay on the quayside in Little Crabby Harbour for many years after that and her prow was cut off and kept in Quinain's garden until he died in 1994.

Agnes Cairns and an unnamed French Ketch, both sunk by enemy action on 26 April 1917

Agnes Cairns was a Brigantine, a true sailing ship without an auxiliary engine. She was on passage from Portsmouth to Guernsey with a cargo of coal. Her Master was Joseph Penhaligon, and she carried a crew of four men. About eight miles N.E. of Alderney she was shelled by a German submarine which brought down the mainsail. The crew took to the boat, and were pulling away, but were stopped by machine gun fire, and taken onto the U-boat. Delayed charges were set in *Agnes Cairns* and she was sunk. A French ketch was nearby and her crew also took to their boat and managed to escape, but the submarine sank the ketch. The crew of *Agnes Cairns* were questioned for some time, and then released and put back into their boat. A French Torpedo boat then came on the scene and the submarine submerged. They picked up the English crew, and returned to pick up the Frenchmen. The T-boat brought the English crew into Braye where they found the American Tanker *Illinois* at anchor, riddled from stem to stern with shell holes. She had encountered the same U-boat a little earlier.

The crew of *Agnes Cairns* were later taken to Guernsey on SS *Courier*.

The Twenties and Thirties were a comparatively quiet time for the island as far as wrecks were concerned and there were only a dozen ship casualties recorded in the 20 years up to the start of the Second World War.

After the evacuation of Alderney in 1940, with Britain standing almost alone against the entire German armed forces, there was not much Naval activity recorded in Channel Island waters until early 1942. At about this time British ships began harassing convoys of enemy supply ships, and several were sunk both by submarines and by surface action, principally by M.T.Bs. In February 1942 two British destroyers sank two German supply ships, *Hermann* and *Schleswig Holstein* carrying troops and supplies between Cherbourg and Alderney. Harassing of other convoys passing up The Race caused the Enemy considerable problems, and troop movements were made by land to St Malo, and thence to Guernsey and then on to Alderney, the stages usually being carried out at night, and causing considerable delays.

German troops stationed in Alderney often had to wait a couple of weeks before they could get on or off the island, and supplies were interrupted to the point where the Germans attempted to build up at least a three month stock of food, fuel and ammunition.

The massive fortifications being built required constant supplies of cement and workers, and the sectional iron jetty built to deal with this was in constant use. Several British owned vessels had been taken over, and one of these was SS *Staffa*.

SS *Staffa*

Sunk in harbour, on 12 March 1941

Staffa, had been making regular runs between Guernsey and Alderney before the war, and was taken over by the Germans when they occupied Guernsey. They continued to use her until she sank close to the landward end of the stone jetty, apparently sabotaged by her crew. She remained in this position throughout the war, and was eventually cut up for scrap about 1950.

Several other German ships, or at least German commandeered ships were sunk in Alderney waters including the harbour during the last war. Wartime photographs also show a derelict dredger against the west side of Little Crabby Harbour at least from early 1944, but I have been unable to ascertain her eventual fate.

SS *Staffa* sunk in the harbour by her crew 12 March 1941. Photo 1945 after the German surrender.

Xaver Dorsch

Sunk in harbour, on 1 April 1943

The 515-ton MV *Xaver Dorsch* was named after the Berlin Director of the Organisation Todt, by which she was used as a transport. She broke her moorings on the Iron Jetty whilst loaded with Russian slave-workers too weak to continue working, who were being shipped back to France, and grounded on the rocks near the shore in the centre of the curve of Braye Bay, in a severe storm on 1 April 1943.

Some of the prisoners had already died through overcrowding below decks whilst waiting several days for the ship to sail, and more were drowned in the wreck. There are still the keels and other remains of three ships, including the boilers of two of them which can be seen at this spot at low tide, but it would appear that *Xaver Dorsch* is not one of them, because she was eventually reported sunk by Allied aircraft off Lezardrieux on 29 April 1944.

One of these remains is certainly that of another German supply ship, the 300-ton *Henny Fricke*. The wreck at the left, viewed from the shore is often spoke of in Alderney as that of *Staffa*, although it is actually that of the *Voorposten boot VP 703*, lying on its side, one of the small German harbour guard ships. At very low spring tides the port side of this vessel still emerges from the water. The third keel and the other boiler is that of SS *Burton* which sank there in 1911.

The last recorded German casualty off our shores during the war was the German Minesweeper *M 83*, sunk in a surface action between Alderney and Cap de la Hague a few days after D-day, on 14 June 1944.

Despite modern navigational aids, there have still been many wrecks since the war, several large vessels, some fishing boats, and increasingly small yachts and motor cruisers belonging to leisure sailors. Whilst more than a few have been totally lost, many of these last have broken down, sprung a leak, or been swamped, and have been towed into harbour by local fishermen, or since the establishment of the Alderney lifeboat station in 1984, (see the next Chapter), by the lifeboat.

SS *Edirne*

Wrecked on 29 January 1950

The Turkish steamer *Edirne,* from Istanbul, was another casualty of the reef just North-east of Burhou. A 3,653-ton cargo vessel carrying 50 crew, she had gone aground on her way to Denmark. The St Peter Port Lifeboat *Queen Victoria* reached the scene about four hours later. Twenty of the crew had already taken to their boats, and the lifeboat picked them up. The remaining 30, and the ship's dog, had got onto Burhou. They were ferried out to the lifeboat in the ships boats, and the open lifeboat took all of the crew, and with the two boats and a dinghy in tow tried to return to Guernsey. They had to cut the boats adrift, because of the bad weather conditions, but got safely into port without loss of life.

Later on, an attempt was made to tow off the badly holed *Edirne*, but she subsequently foundered, and sank in deep water.

Constantia S

Wrecked on 23 January 1967

A Greek Tanker of 8,686 tons, *Constantia S* was on her way from Rotterdam to Gibraltar with a cargo of fresh water, and in terrific seas fetched up on the Casquets. RMS *Sarnia*, and other vessels stood by, and the crew managed to scramble up nets and ladders onto the rescue vessels from their two ship's boats. Ten of them were taken to Weymouth on *Sarnia*, and the remaining 20 men got to the THV *Burhou*, usually at Braye to act as a tender for the lighthouse, which had been despatched by the Harbourmaster, who had received the distress call. The Captain was later lifted off the rocks by a French Helicopter, and taken to hospital in Guernsey, after giving the direction of the ships boats, which had been unable to reach him, and were by then off to the south, to the rescue vessels.

In November that year, Captain S. P. Herivel CBE, DSC, President of Alderney, presented awards from the RNLI to the crew of *Burhou*, Pilot Nick Allen, who received a Vellum, and framed letters of thanks to the crew, Jack and Harry Quinain, John Allen, and Alan Johns. Captain H. Walker, Master of the British Rail *Sarnia*, and First Officer C. P. Baker also received awards. The awards had been brought from England by Lt Commander Teare, SE Divisional Inspector of the RNLI, in the American all-steel lifeboat 44-001, the first of the new Waveney Class lifeboats, of which Alderney's former lifeboat 44-019, *Louis Marchesi of Round Table* is a member.

SS *Constantia S* wrecked on the Casquets, 23 January 1967.

The *Constantia S* later broke up and sank in 80 feet of water. Some three years later the Seasalter Divers team of Fred Shaw, Ron Smart, and Peter Oselton brought up the seven-and-a-half-ton aluminium alloy propeller and conveyed it safely to Alderney. MFV *Sea Salter* was a 450 ton, converted Oyster Catcher which took part in the evacuation from Dunkirk in 1940, but was later wrecked in Braye Bay in a storm.

MV *Armas*

Wrecked on 25 November 1973

MV *Armas* was a 2,500-ton Greek Cypriot cargo vessel built in Lübeck in 1953. She was 347 feet long and had a laden draft of 29½ feet. She was originally named *Steckelhörn*.

Travelling in ballast from Nantes to Le Havre, she grounded on a rocky ledge just west of the Nannels at the eastern end of Burhou at 2.40 a.m.

Alderney Pilot Jack Quinain heard the alarm, relayed by St Peter Port radio and went out in his Fishing Vessel *Tol*, and the St Peter Port Lifeboat was also launched. Quinain located the stricken vessel at 4 a.m. but owing to the weather conditions was unable to get alongside. RFA vessel HMS *Engadine* carrying Sea King helicopters happened to be just off the Casquets, and two of these lifted off all the crew, 13 from the ship and nine from the rocks off Burhou which they had reached in a lifeboat. Only one seaman was lost.

At low tide next day the ship was seen to be balanced amidships on the ledge with stem and stern over deep water, the double skin of her hull beneath the engines was ripped out. The few valuable items and papers were recovered from the ship, and over the winter she broke in half and the bow section sank. The gales of January and February 1974 gradually broke her up and the stern too disappeared. Only small non-ferrous parts were salvaged. The engines are still visible from Alderney for much of the day, and the prow can also be seen at low tide.

MV *Armas* wrecked on the Nannels, 25 November 1973.

Oil Barge No. 406

Wrecked 25 November 1974

This gigantic 300 foot oil rig barge, being towed from Stavanger in Norway to Florida USA fouled its towline in the propeller of the tug *Gulf Fleet 8*, and was drifting towards the Race, the tug managed to keep it inside the shelter of Château à L'Étoc and they drifted backwards into Braye Bay, where it was moored. In the night it broke loose and fetched up high and dry on Bibette Head. At high tide that afternoon the tug managed to pull it off and moor it alongside the German jetty. A force eight gale raged for several days but finally on the afternoon of 30 November assisted by a second tug from England, the barge was towed off to be inspected and repaired at Southampton.

The inhabitants of Alderney were treated to a spectacle which was to create interest for months to come, when another wreck occurred in 1975.

MV *Point Law*

Wrecked on 15 July 1975

1,500-ton Shell Tanker *Point Law* with a crew of 12, drove straight into Le Puits Jervais a rock formation just west of Alderney's favourite swimming beach, Telegraph Bay, shortly after midnight, in a midsummer gale. She sat hemmed in on both sides with her bow well on the beach. By good fortune she was in ballast, but there was some oil spillage from her fuel tanks. St Peter Port Lifeboat *Sir William Arnold*, and Alderney MFV *Christmas* with pilots on board, were quickly at the scene, later assisted by a French Rescue Helicopter, and the Alderney Fire Brigade Cliff Rescue team.

When it got light, *Sir William Arnold* managed to transfer six men, one of whom was injured, from the tanker, one at a time, using two rubber dinghies, and took them to Braye Harbour. A French tug tried, but failed, to pull the tanker out on the rising tide. The remaining crew and three of the Cliff rescue team were then lifted off singly by the helicopter. The tanker began to break up into three, disintegrated, and was later sold for scrap. Members of the lifeboat crew later received gallantry awards.

Mv *Corinna*

Wrecked on 11 February 1985

Corinna was on a regular run between England and the islands with a mixed cargo of furniture, gas cookers, food and liquor. She fell foul of the rapid currents over the Brinchetais Reef, and was swept onto the back of Houmet Herbé islet with its ruined Victorian Fort. Perched high and dry at low tide the crew walked to safety, and she gave an easy access to the islanders who salvaged a considerable part of her cargo. Much of the liquor was locked up in the old town Jail for security, and over the next few weeks various salvage attempts were made, as the vessel was not badly damaged. She defeated all attempts for almost six months, until a particularly high tide and some powerful Dutch tugs combined to release her, and she was towed off, and repaired.

MV *Point Law* wrecked in Le Puits Jervais on 15 July 1975.

Some time later *Point Law* broke into three parts.

MV *Corinna* ran aground on Houmet Herbé islet on 11 February 1985. She was eventually towed off.

An interesting sequel to the number of new gas cookers that appeared in island homes was that they wouldn't work. Intended for use on town gas, the jets were unsuitable for the bottled gases used in Alderney. One lucky possessor of a box of odd parts, found that he had the entire supply of conversion kits for the cargo of cookers, and is reputed to have done very well out of his find, selling the kits to possessors of the useless cookers. This wreck too provided a tourist attraction for months .

MV *Perintis*

Wrecked on 13 March 1989

Perintis was a 1,796-ton Indonesian freighter with a deck cargo of containers, en route from Antwerp to Indonesia. She foundered and sank just N.W. of the Casquets in a storm, midmorning on 13 March. The containers on her deck floated away as she sank, and, as a number were floating barely out of the surface, they presented a hazard to shipping. Various ships went to her assistance, and to remove the containers, including a French Naval vessel which took a container with six tons of the poisonous agricultural chemical **Lindane** in tow to Cherbourg.

Somewhere along the way, the tow parted and the container disappeared. The French ship did not appear to know where it was, and since the chemical could pollute a large area, and kill marine life or at least render fish and shellfish unsafe to eat, a tremendous hunt was set up with underwater television cameras, divers and echo-sounding

Rescue Boat *Spirit of Alderney*, 1977.

Brede class lifeboat *Forester's Future* 1984.

Waveney class lifeboat *Louis Marchesi of Round Table*, 1992.

Second Channel Island Air Search plane *Lions' Pride* – a Piper Aztec, 1980.

equipment. Fishing was banned over a considerable area of the English Channel, and a general panic was caused amongst conservationists. The container was never found, but monitoring of the water in the area failed to detect the chemical over several weeks.

Another container was towed into Braye on 15 March by MFV *Golden Promise* (skippered by Pierre Dupont). It proved too heavy for the Alderney cranes to lift out full of water, so was opened. It was found to contain a very valuable cargo of banknote printing paper, and after the container and contents had been landed the paper was repackaged and the doors welded up for security.

In recent years the vast improvement in navigational aids on both ship and shore has helped to reduce the toll taken by the sea. There is still however much work for the Channel Island Lifeboats, now with an official station of the RNLI on each of the three larger islands.

The great increase in pleasure sailing and small motor cruisers, often run by inexperienced people, but all equipped with two-way radio, has caused a huge increase in the demands on the rescue services. Much of this work needs no more than escorting or towing small vessels into harbour, and loss of life has become much less frequent, but the crews of the Lifeboats are still willing to hazard their own lives in the service of others.

In the next chapter we will look at the history of the rescue services in Alderney, and to some extent in Guernsey, which covered both islands until comparatively recently. Some of the more recent rescue craft used are shown here and in the colour illustrations.

The new third *Lions' Pride* at Alderney in 2011. Like the first, an Islander, but greatly modified.

13

Lifeboats and Rescues

The pilots and fishermen of Alderney have traditionally been, and still are, greatly concerned with helping fellow mariners in trouble. They have saved many lives, and lost not a few of their own in the process.

In Victorian times when the great activity of building the Harbour of Refuge and the Forts caused a huge increase in the sea traffic for 30 or more years, and with none of the modern navigational and communication aids, it is not surprising that there were many wrecks, and considerable loss of life in the dangerous waters around the island.

Lifeboats were brought to the Channel Islands from a number of specialist builders at that time, but almost without exception they remained on the quaysides, unable to find proper crews, and when needed, rescues were still carried out by the fishermen and pilots.

The first Alderney lifeboat *Mary and Victoria*, was brought to the island by the British Government, towed by the 300-ton HM Steamer *Sea-Mew*, Commander Barrett, from Weymouth on 20 October 1869. It was housed in a shed built by the contractors where the stone was stored near the harbour. The first Guernsey boat had arrived in that island in 1803, bought by 'The States'. As far as has been recorded, neither of these boats was ever used, and *Mary and Victoria* a pulling and sailing boat with 10 oars, was eventually towed by SS *Wonder*, to Jersey to replace their boat, on 2 April 1884.

The National Institution for the Preservation of Life from Shipwreck, founded in 1824, became the Royal National Lifeboat Institution in 1854, and later Guernsey boats, after the first official RNLI station was opened there in 1861, when the RNLI took over *The Rescue*, (the boat bought by public subscription after the wreck of *Boadicea* off Alderney). This, and the various pulling and sailing lifeboats which followed it, only went to 17 wrecks out of the 135 which occurred in Guernsey waters in the next 125 years!

The history of the Guernsey station is well documented in *Mayday! Mayday!* by Guy Blampied, but it is worth noting that the first power driven Lifeboat to be stationed in Guernsey was RNLB *Queen Victoria* in October 1929, replacing the 10-oar *Arthur Lionel*, in service since 1912.

The Steam Pilot boat *Watt* owned and operated by Captain Scott of Alderney in the 1860s, took part in a number of rescue operations both in Alderney and Guernsey waters, some of which have been noted in the list in Chapter 9.

Rescues around Alderney continued in the main to be carried out by local fishermen and the pilots, using their own boats, but the official services which have developed since the Second World War form an important part of Alderney's maritime history.

One of the first post-Second World War rescues carried out in Alderney waters by the Guernsey Lifeboat *Queen Victoria*, was when the freighter *Edirne* was wrecked on Burhou in 1950. This lifeboat continued in service until 1954.

Her successor was *Euphrosyne Kendal*, which first saw action in Alderney waters on 10 September 1954, when she came to the assistance of the Alderney cargo and passenger boat *Island Commodore* which had broken down off Burhou and was drifting. The Lifeboat towed her into Braye Harbour.

The next St Peter Port Lifeboat, *Sir William Arnold* attended the wreck of *Armas* on The Nannels on 26 November 1973, but the crew were lifted to safety by helicopter and her services were not needed. Later, her services in connection with the wreck of the Shell tanker *Point Law* near Telegraph Bay on 15 July 1975, resulted in several awards to her crew.

Some of the rescues involving Alderney boats have already been described briefly, in particular those of the two *Couriers*, and as is noted above, the original Alderney Lifeboat, *Mary and Victoria*, was withdrawn and sent to Jersey in 1884, after 15 years without being launched, due to the difficulty experienced in finding crews. In the intervening century, there have been many more instances of local fishermen and pilots towing in broken down or damaged craft from Alderney waters, and both these and the Trinity House Launch *Burhou*, stationed in Alderney as a tender for the Casquets Light, took part in many rescues from ships actually wrecked over the years. Alderney people have in the last 20 years or so been generous in their financial support of, first the Guernsey boats, and now Alderney's own boat, and regularly top the poll for the whole of the UK for contributions per head of population to the RNLI Flag days.

This generosity was carried still further when, in November 1977 Alderney resident Graham Lawson provided and maintained *Spirit of Alderney* as a Rescue boat for the island. Capable of 22 knots, she was equipped with stretchers and medical facilities, and was placed at the disposal of the Harbour Master Dave Allen. When needed in emergencies, she was skippered by Jack Quinain or one of the other pilots, with a volunteer crew. She was kept in service for about five years. (*See photos pp. 235-7*).

The good work done by the Alderney seamen, and the increasing calls on their services led Dr John Ayoub to gather public opinion to the point where the RNLI agreed to station a Lifeboat at Alderney for a limited period as a trial. The Brede Class Lifeboat *Foresters Future* arrived on station on 29 January 1984. Partly purchased by a generous donation of £60,000 from the Ancient Order of Foresters, after trials, it was dedicated on 10 March. In a comparatively short space of time this boat proved its worth, being launched on 34 occasions and saving 15 lives in its trial year. The station was then made permanent.

In September 1986, *Foresters Future* was replaced by the larger Waveney Class vessel *Louis Marchesi of Round Table*.

Public subscription resulted in sufficient funds being raised to build a proper crew room, and boat house for the inshore inflatable launch, with a small shop to generate funds. A fine new stone-faced building was erected on the Quayside in 1987. It was opened on 18 July by Dr John Ayoub, who had done so much to ensure the establishment of the permanent station in Alderney. The lifeboat itself is moored in the harbour.

At the firing of the maroons as a warning to the volunteer crews, the Lifeboat can be fully manned and underway in less than 10 minutes. (See colour section photos).

Regular exercises are carried out in conjunction with helicopters of the RAF Rescue service from 845 Squadron RAF based at Yeovilton in Somerset, and the Helicopters from here, and occasionally from the French service controlled by CrossMa, have been responsible for a considerable number of rescues in recent years.

During her time of service in Alderney, *Foresters Future* took part in 104 missions, and rescued 91 people. Her crews received a number of certificates for bravery.

From coming on station, to the end of November 1992 *Louis Marchesi of Round Table* attended 131 emergencies, rescued 108 people, and her crew received several more commendations.

On 15/16 August 1992 the prototype of a new series of FAB (Fast Afloat Boat) lifeboats paid a visit to the Channel Islands to enable the local crews to have a brief trial on her and comment on her performance. On 4 October she paid another visit to Alderney for rough weather trials, and some of the local crew were able to participate.

As a result of these and other trials, at the end of the year the RNLI announced that two new classes of Lifeboat, the Trent and Severn were being built.... These were to be faster and have better propeller protection, the Trent was to be 45 feet 11 inches overall length, weigh 25 tons and have a speed of 25 knots from its two 808hp engines, whilst the larger Severn was to be 55 feet nine inches long weigh 37.5 tons and produce the same speed from its larger 1,050-hp engines.

The prototype Trent lifeboat 14-01, was allocated to the Alderney Station and was named *Earl and Countess Mountbatten of Burma* by the Countess at the RNLI Depot on 17 June 1993. She made her first visit to the island on 21 August on an eight-hour stage at full speed, of her 300-hour engine trials. She returned to Falmouth next day. During her trials her engines were changed to the 800-hp Rolls Royce engines used in Chieftain tanks, but these were found to be less reliable than the 808 HP MAN diesels which were replaced.

Not long after, as the result of a legacy of £6.5 million to the RNLI from Jersey resident Roy Barker, it was decided that Alderney would actually receive a production vessel of this class, which will be named *Roy Barker-1,* as her permanent vessel when completed and this was expected to come on station in Alderney later in 1994.

In February 1994 the crew went to England for a period of familiarisation with and running in the *Earl and Countess Mountbatten of Burma*. Whilst bringing the vessel to Alderney when this was completed they answered an emergency call. The Lifeboat was slightly damaged in the process and its arrival delayed by about a week.

She arrived, on time, at 4 p.m. on 3 March and was officially welcomed by President Baron and former President Jon Kay Mouat. Coming to Alderney via the Scilly Isles in very rough weather, she was met in the Swinge by *Louis Marchesi of Round Table* and after a display of manoeuvrability off Platte Saline, was escorted into Harbour. 14-01 remained on station until the production vessel was delivered. (See colour section photos).

The new Lifeboat answered its first emergency call on 10 March, (one of the rare days of light winds and a smooth sea), to a boat with engine failure in the Swinge. When they arrived to take the vessel in tow, one of the crew members was very surprised to find that the casualty was his own vessel, MFV *Tudor Rose*. She was towed into harbour without difficulty.

The Duchess of Kent paid a visit to Alderney to inspect the Station on 24 March 1995. She met the crew and took a trip in the new vessel, afterwards meeting many of the schoolchildren.

The new permanent vessel 14-04, named *Roy Barker -1* arrived on 19 July and after familiarisation trials took station on the 21st. She was soon in service with seven call-outs in the first six weeks. The Duchess paid another visit on 18 September for the official naming ceremony, which took place in the Inner Harbour in heavy rain.

Channel Island Air Search

Sterling rescue work in recent years by RAF helicopter crews, was often aided by the Channel Island Air Search plane, based in Guernsey and crewed by volunteers and maintained entirely by public donations.

This type of service was first started in 1972 in Alderney by Graham Lawson, as a personal contribution, using his own twin-engined Apache. He operated the aircraft for his own personal affairs, but was always ready to go on search and rescue when needed. He sold the aircraft in 1977, and put the money to purchasing the Rescue Boat *Spirit of Alderney* mentioned above.

C.I.A.S. as it exists today was started in Guernsey in 1980, as Guernsey Air Search, by the founder of Guernsey Airlines, Roger Dadd; Sqdn. Ldr. Andy Blake, a former RAF Search and Rescue pilot; and David Keys a former Fleet Air Arm navigator, using the airline's Piper Aztec plane, available about four days a week. In 1984 the present plane was bought by the Lion's Club of Guernsey to enable a full time service to be offered, and the service was renamed. It is now manned by a crew of 18 volunteers who offer a round the clock, throughout the year, service, six pilots, six navigators and six search directors. Despite various problems caused by lack of sufficient funds from time to time, it still continues in 1992 and is expecting to do so into the next century. In addition to calls from the local harbourmasters, they respond to the French Coastguard Stations at CrossMa on the Cotentin, and CrossCo near Brest.

This aircraft was a twin-engined low-wing monoplane Piper Aztec called *Lion's Pride*. It was capable of 170 knots but usually flew much less than this at 120 knots. The plane was equipped with sophisticated Radar, Navigational and Radio facilities, and could drop flares and lifejackets if needed.

The crews wear immersion suits and lifejackets in case the aircraft ditches, and the plane carries a dinghy for the crew should this happen.

Over the 10-year period an average of 17 sorties a year have been flown, with a peak of 36 sorties in 1989, and a number of lives have been saved as a result.

In 1991 an appeal was launched for sufficient funds to purchase and equip a twin-engined Britten-Norman Islander, with all the necessary gear, to replace the ageing Aztec. By June the aircraft had been purchased and was being overhauled at a cost of £300,000, before going to England in 1992 to be painted, fitted with some special equipment and to receive its air worthiness certificate.

On its return run to Guernsey in September, for final fitting out before coming into service, the plane's pilot spotted a three-and-a-half-mile oil slick in the Channel. They traced this to an American owned, Panamanian registered tanker *Dawn Redwood*, which was bound for Key West in Florida in ballast, and was discharging the oil. A full report was submitted to both British and French Coastguards who passed it on to the American authorities for appropriate action to be taken.

This plane was expected to be named by Jersey's Lt Governor, and taken into service, in November 1992, but by the time the sophisticated locating instruments were installed, it was eventually given its Air worthiness Certificate on 13 March 1993. Soon after it was given the same name *Lions' Pride*, as the previous aircraft by Lady Mills, wife of the Lt Governor of Jersey.

It paid a courtesy low level flight around Alderney the same afternoon. (See colour section and p. 256.)

In September 1995, the Barclay brothers, who were building a mansion on Brecqhou and whose helicopter and pilot were based in Alderney, offered the use of the machine for Air Search duties when it is not otherwise engaged. Its first mission was when it took part in a search off Jersey in October that year

Fifteen years later in September 2010, yet another plane with even more sophisticated equipment was taken into service and also named Lions' Pride. Also being supported by the Lions' Club of Guernsey and voluntary donations.

14

Alderney's Lighthouses

The Guild Fraternity or Brotherhood of the most Glorious and Undivided Trinity, and of St Clement in the Parish of Deptford Strand, in the County of Kent, now known as The Trinity House Corporation, and controlled by eight Elder Brethren who are all Master Mariners, was given authority to regulate Pilotage by a Charter of 1514. Its responsibility for lighthouses was set up by an Act of Parliament in 1566, and it received its Patent from Queen Elizabeth I on 11 June 1594, to erect Lighthouses and to maintain Seamarks.

In these early days a tax per ton was levied on all shipping passing the lights either inward or outward bound. The tax was to be double for foreign vessels, and at a fixed rate per vessel for all coasters for each time they should pass. All Officers and Ministers in Ports, Creeks, Harbours and Havens in England, were required to assist in collecting this tax from vessels calling in their jurisdiction. A tax on shipping called *Light Dues* is still levied to pay for the service, at all ports in the UK, Eire and the Channel Islands.

1. The Casquets

The Casquets Lighthouse, about seven miles West of Alderney, spelt variously over the years as Caskets, Casketts, or Casquettes, was first lit on 30 October 1724, and at that time consisted of three towers of roughly equal height, set in a triangle. Each was equipped with a coal burning fire in an armourer's forge, enclosed in a glazed lantern. The fires were maintained by bellows, which in those days had to be worked more or less continuously by hand. The three towers were named St Pierre, St Thomas and Donjon, Dudgeon, or Dungeon. Perhaps this is a corruption of St John?

As long ago as 1685, Philippe Dumaresq, in his book, *A Survey of the Island of Jersey*, in a description of Alderney and its surroundings, had written:

And here I cannot forbear to mention, how worthy it would be of His Majesty's conideration, to have a light set up upon Casquet head, so much feared of all Vessels that go up and down the Channel; it being upon the entrance of those dangerous Islands and tides; and there is ground enough to build a convenient house and Tower, that might in all ordinary times be supplied from Alderney....

A petition was made by ship owners, and submitted to the Crown by Thomas Le Mesurier in 1709 for a light to be placed on these dangerous rocks, which mark the extremity of a long sandstone reef extending due east for 20 miles to the Cap de la Hague with many barely submerged, or emergent parts, including Burhou. It was 14 years before Thomas Le Cocq, Alderney's Judge, who owned the Casquets Rocks obtained a patent from the Masters, Wardens and Assistants of the Trinity Brotherhood, which had been granted to them by George I on 3 June 1723, to establish three lights, the pattern of which they determined, '...to distinguish it from other lights in the Channel Islands and on the nearby French coast, and to keep *lights continuously burning therein during the Night Season'*. In the intervening period HM Ship of War *Dragon*, and several more merchant ships, with their crews and cargoes had been lost on the rocks.

The first station was built in barely a year, and a lease was granted to Le Cocq in 1724, for a period of 61 years at a rental of £50 per annum. He was to collect a halfpenny per ton from the owners of every British vessel which passed the light in either direction, and one penny per ton from Foreign Vessels. Coasters were to pay sixpence each, every time they passed by. He obviously had difficulty in collecting the payments, since this problem was put before the Trinity House Brethren, who, on 20 July 1725 petitioned the King for an Order-in-Council, (which would have the force of a law in the Channel Islands), requiring the authorities in each of the islands to collect the dues from Foreign Ships entering their ports, as well as from local vessels.

Alderney Parish Registers record the death on 20 September 1750, of Pierre Baudoin; 'Keeper for some years at Casquets'.

Sketch of the Casquets Lighthouses, 1815.

Le Cocq was assisted in his endeavours to obtain the patent by Sir Thomas Hardy, and in return

> ...he made him a compensation of one quarter part of the emoluments of the said Lights, which the Corporation of Trinity House claimed from the heirs of Sir Thomas Hardy at his death, as their right, and have held ever since.

The above letter is written in an immaculate Copperplate hand by Le Cocq's grandson William, to Lord Sydney, the First Secretary, on 30 July 1787. Le Cocq continues his plea for assistance:

> The lease of the said lights terminated in the year 1785, previous to which I made various applications to the Corporation for the renewal of the lease, which they would not think proper to grant, in consequence of which I am, with a large family, involved in real distress. I have lately made several applications to the Corporation, craving from them some relief, or recommendation to any of the public Offices for the place of a Clerk, and notwithstanding that they gain a Thousand pounds a year nett by the termination of the lease, they will not even listen to the words of my prayer. At the death of the said Thomas Le Cocq, the three quarters that was his share became divided amongst four, consequently but a small stipend to support and bring up a numerous family, besides suffering a variety of losses in trade. I should my Lord, lay a state of my case before His Majesty, for his most gracious consideration, but am at a loss how to contrive its coming into his royal hands, unless your Lordship will be so humane and charitable as to put me in the way of doing it.

Le Cocq gave further details of his distress and probable need to leave the island to seek work, and repeated his request for a position in some public office. A Samuel Le Cocq died at the Casquets on 12 February 1788.

The armourer's forges were replaced in 1779 by oil lamps in a copper lantern, but when the lease reverted to Trinity House in 1785 they decided to improve it further, and in 1790, replaced these with Argand lamps in metal reflectors. Later still, the revolving apparatus, powered by clockwork which needed winding every hour and a half, was fitted in 1818, giving one flash every 15 seconds. The lighthouses were badly damaged and the lanterns smashed in a great storm on 31 October 1823.

The Argand oil burner was invented by a Swiss, A. Argand, in 1784, and consists of a wick between two concentric tubes with a draught up the middle. It was enclosed in a glass chimney which increased the draught and improved the illumination.

Robert Stevenson, on his third inspection of lighthouses, arrived at the Casquets on 23 August 1818. He noted in his diary that; 'The towers are about 100 feet apart, and each has a revolving apparatus with eight reflectors of silver and copper upon each frame. The light rooms are of timber with small panes of glass, and at the western and middle towers you enter the lightroom by the tower stair. At the eastern one you enter only by the parapet which has indeed two doors to suit the weather, but still I am of the opinion that this light cannot be kept burning in stormy weather.

Casquets lighthouses in 1833, from James Wyld's map.

Everything except the reflectors was clean but some of these were in such a state as to seem as if they had not been cleaned for weeks, being quite furred-up with sea-gum. The Governor of Alderney is said to be the agent for the lights – and contractor indeed ! Be this as it may, this important lighthouse establishment is very unlike a public one and seems to be little attended to in keeping or putting up.

The whole of these three light rooms and revolving apparatus is in charge of one man and his family with a girl who acts as servant, but is rather in the character of a nun. She has been here five years and said she had been a very bad girl and had come here to reclaim herself. The keepers are said not to remain here more than seven years, when they expect a pension. The present man and his family have been here only a few weeks. When they want beer and other stores, they make signals by a telegraph to the island of Alderney for the attendant boat or vessel according to the state of the weather. The lightkeeper has £52 per annum and his victuals.

We observed the lights as we sailed away and they had a tolerable appearance till we got off about 10 miles when they became languid and less brilliant. They appeared too close, and indeed exhibited only two lights. The light rooms are intended to be all of the same height from the sea, – perhaps 130-150 feet, but were too low so the lights were hid by the diameter of the towers.

In 1834 the three revolving lights (which were not synchronised, and rarely showed more than two lights at the same time), each contained eight of these burners rotating horizontally, whose total annual consumption of oil was over 1,000 gallons, and had a range in clear weather of about 12 miles. A bell was used as a fog signal. The Keeper then was John Le Bair (or Le Ber) who lived on the rock with his family. He received an annual salary of £52 10s 0d, and an additional £101 13s 5d a year was allowed for victuals for himself and his family. The Trinity House agent for the area was paid £80 a year, and was supposed to make a monthly visit of inspection to each light in his jurisdiction. Charles Williams was assistant keeper in 1850, Elias Morris was keeper in 1854, and Jeremiah Godfrey in the following year.

In 1854 the height of each tower was raised by another 30 feet, increasing the range. The lamps were then of 184,000 candlepower, and gave three slow flashes every half minute.

In 1877 the light was converted to a single lamp in the N.E. tower, the height of which was increased again, with a quick flashing signal five times every 30 seconds. In 1952 the lighthouse was converted to electricity, and the power increased to 2,830,000 candlepower. The light was now at about 120 feet above sea level and it had a range of 14 miles. Unlike most other lighthouses, the reflectors rotate in an anticlockwise direction.

The other two towers were shortened and the East tower now contains the foghorn, whilst the S.W. tower has a helicopter landing pad. There is a second landing pad on a flat section of rock not very far above high tide level. In 1989-90 a third, larger, pad was built level with the courtyard, well above the waves' reach, except in the most severe conditions, in preparation for the light going automatic later in 1990. A 400 Mercury discharge lamp has been installed which should last at least six months. It

Sketch of Casquets Lighthouses from *Illustrated London News*.

had a number of filaments, and was rotated automatically should one fail. The light now flashes continually throughout the 24 hours, to avoid the surges of power when the lamp is switched on and off which greatly reduce their life, and has a range in clear weather of 28 miles. The Foghorn gives three two-second blasts every two minutes. The final changes were completed on 29 November 1990, when the continuous occupation by keepers, and in earlier times by their families as well, of over 265 years, ceased.

The Casquets Light and its keepers and their families have figured in many a novel, romance, poem, and painting over the years. In former times the keepers remained on station for many years and a vegetable plot made in three terraces with soil brought from Alderney in the sheltered east facing cleft just outside the courtyard helped to support them.

Over the years the servicing of the lighthouse and the relief of the keepers was carried out by the Trinity House Vessels. Previously carried out by various sailing vessels, in the 1880s and 90s this was done by the Trinity Steam Yacht *Irene* which made an annual visit of inspection. This paddle steamer was launched in 1852, sold in 1890 and replaced by a twin-screw steamer the second of that name, which often acted as a Royal Escort and continued in service until the First World War. THV *Triton*, built in 1901, made regular visits with barrels of oil for the light and usually took several days to complete the transfer.

On 26 October 1895, the Alderney vessel *Maggie* was used to relieve the men on the light. She took 19 young men out to the rock and because of weather conditions had to stay overnight.

When SS *Ville de Malaga* was wrecked in 1897, most of the crew and passengers were rescued thanks to the vigilance of the Lloyd's signalman Mr Paling who saw the signals from the Casquet's semaphore and sent vessels to help. After the Second World War, before a radio telephone was installed, signals were exchanged between the lighthouse and an Aldis lamp operated on the Petit Blaye each day at regular times so that any urgent needs of the keepers could be met.

At the same times it was possible for the keepers to send advanced information on the names of ships passing up The Channel near enough for them to see, to Paling using their semaphore arms. This information was vital to Lloyds and kept them ahead of their rivals in the shipping business. For many years Paling passed it on to London using the electric telegraph installed in the hut on Butes where he lived in a small compound leased from the States. To simplify his job a large concrete pillar with a groove cut along the top onto which his telescope fitted was trained directly on the Casquets.

This pillar is still there, but the direct view of the Casquets is now blocked by a house built some years ago. (See both pictures in the Colour section).

For more than 50 years now, three large ships all named *Patricia* have serviced the light in succession, aided by *Siren*, *Mermaid* and the smaller tenders *Burhou* and *Lita*.

The first *Patricia*, bought in 1918, was formerly an armed merchant ship named *Miranda* built in 1908. She was modified and renamed after Lady Patricia Ramsay,

Trinity House Vessel *Patricia,* 1920-39, launched in 1908 as *Miranda* and renamed *Vestal* in 1939.

daughter of the Duke of Connaught, then Master of Trinity House. She was brought into service in 1920. After serving as the principal ship for many years, in 1939 she was downgraded and renamed *Vestal,* (the fourth of that name), allowing her name to go to a new vessel launched in 1938 as *Patricia II. Vestal* remained on the East Cowes station and, under Captain McCarthy, evacuated the Channel Island lighthouse keepers, and a total of 121 people from Guernsey and Alderney on Saturday 22 June 1940.

The new ship was powered by Diesel-electric motors and at 1,415 tons displacement was by far the largest vessel in the fleet. She had an eventful wartime career being damaged in several air attacks, laying marker buoys across the Channel for the D-day operations, and having the dubious honour of accidentally causing a British Anson which flew low over her, closely followed by the guns mounted on board for war service, to hit the water. Boats from *Patricia* picked up the crew unharmed. She was finally sold to German buyers in May 1982 after 44 years service.

THL *Burhou* was stationed for many years in Alderney. She was built in 1945 with a wooden hull of carvel planking and displaced 28½ tons. She originally had a 60hp diesel engine which was replaced in 1955 by a 70-hp and again in 1964 by a 127-hp Gardner six-cylinder diesel. She then had a speed of about eight-and-a-half knots. A new, larger, aluminium deckhouse was fitted in 1982. She was withdrawn from Alderney about 1987 but was still in service for some years after that.

In recent times most of this work has been done by helicopter, but THV *Patricia* (the third of that name, launched in 1982), is still a frequent visitor to Alderney, and carries spares and much of the fuel needed to run the generators and formerly the compressor

Trinity House Launch *Burhou*, built in 1945 and stationed in Alderney for many years until *c.* 1987.

for the foghorn. THV *Mermaid*, (also the third of that name), was brought into service in 1987, to replace the THV *Siren*, which was last in Alderney in 1982, and also makes occasional visits.

Legends of the Casquets

The origin of the name of the Casquets, is that they are supposed to resemble a casque or 'helmet', but it is more likely from the Latin 'cado-'to fall', descriptive of the cascades around the rocks. Over the centuries, they have been marked on maps and charts from the very earliest times, with the spelling changing over the years from Casquettes, or Caskets, this century, Casket Lights (1816), Caskett (1739), Casquetes (1693), Quasquettes (1570), Casquet or Casus Rupes (1540), Quiasquit (1436), to the earliest known chart, the Pinelli Walkenaer map of 1384, where the spelling is Quaquet. One old Norman record not mentioned elsewhere gives the name as Les Cattes Razes.

Other rocks in the surrounding group are known as; Le Biblet. A single rock, possibly from the Norman-French *bibet*, a 'small thing' or 'pimple', L'État aux Guillerete, L'Étacq aux Guilmots (Dobrée). L'Étac au Guilmet. 'Rock of the Guillemots', Le Noire Rocque Black rock. Site of the wreck of *Stella*, 1899

(i). The Formation of the Rocks

Long ago, one of the Seigneurs of Jersey, a warrior, and a giant of a man, had a beautiful wife. A wealthy Auregnais, out fishing in Jersey waters, saw her walking on the shore, whilst her husband was off fighting in France. They fell in love and used to meet often.

One day, whilst with her lover, the lady heard that her husband was on his way home, so they got into the fishing boat, and sailed for Alderney. When the husband arrived, he found his wife gone, and the boat almost over the horizon. His helmet had magic powers, and he threw it violently after them, at the same time laying a curse on them, that they should never reach land.

The helmet (or *Casque*) carried a great distance, and fell over the fishing boat. It turned into the dangerous helmet-shaped rock which has ever since been feared by all passing ships.

(ii). The Shipwreck

The legend of the loss of the *Blanche Nef* or *White Ship* on the Casquets in 1120, has already been given in Chapter 12.

(iii). The Miraculous Dream

The saving of the crew of the sailing ship *Michael*, wrecked here on 5 January 1701, has also been told in Chapter 12.

2. The Alderney Lighthouse

On the 'mainland' of Alderney the Alderney Lighthouse otherwise known as the Mannez Lighthouse or Quesnard Lighthouse, was built in 1912, on the N.E. coast between Forts Quesnard and Les Hommeaux Florains after a remarkable succession of wrecks nearby. A plot of land sufficient for the purpose was deeded to Trinity House by the British Government and work commenced. The lighthouse, which was constructed by William Baron who almost bankrupted himself in the process, was first lit in 1912. Later the same year the tower was painted black and white in its present distinctive way. This paint is stripped off so that any cracks in the structure can be detected and the whole tower repainted every few years, most recently in 1996. Until 1954 the Baron family had continued to maintain the structure since it was built.

At first the 458,000 candlepower lamp was powered by paraffin using a Hood petrol vapour unit, (now preserved in the Alderney Museum), and the reflectors turned by clockwork, wound by a simple hand crank requiring 350 turns every one-and-a-half hours, this was motorised in 1952, and on 2 June 1976 the whole light was converted to electricity. It then had an output of 1,000,000 candlepower and a range of 17 miles. The

Mannez Lighthouse under construction in 1911.

Above left: Mannez Lighthouse completed in 1912, before painting.

Above right: Mannez Lighthouse stripped for a complete repaint in 1996.

tower is 109 feet high, and the signal is four flashes every 15 seconds. The Foghorn gave four two-and-a-half-second deep blasts every 90 seconds.

Alderney Light controlled the Casquets Light as well as the Channel Light Vessel which was already its responsibility, and Point Robert Light on Sark. For some years in the 1990s It eventually became the base station for telemetry which included the Hanois Light off Guernsey. Alderney Lighthouse became automatic in 1996 or 1997 and ceased to be manned, at which time most of the UK and all of the Channel Island lights became controlled from a central station in England. Further developments in early 2011 because of the huge increase in oil prices, resulted in the revolving light being replaced by solar powered white LEDs with a range of about 12 miles and the foghorn has been switched off as no longer necessary, since virtually all vessels now have efficient Radar and Satellite communications. For its appearance today also see colour section.

15

Commercial Shipping

1. The Thirteenth and Fourteenth Centuries

As has already been demonstrated, following the loss of mainland Normandy the frequent wars with France between the thirteenth and sixteenth centuries, caused much movement of military personnel and stores, both between the islands, and between England and the islands. Portsmouth and Southampton were the ports commonly used, with Weymouth used on occasions such as that when John Mautravers was re-appointed Warden in 1352, and the Bailiff of Guernsey was instructed to send two of their best ships to Weymouth to fetch him. The Assize Rolls of 1309 record an incident when a ship from Portsmouth went to Alderney where one islander was seized, and taken to Sark where he was robbed. The Calendar of Close Rolls of this same year contains an instruction to certain collectors of customs, at Southampton, Weymouth, Lyme, and Dartmouth, <u>not</u> to treat men of Guernsey, Jersey, Alderney and Sark as aliens; 'as the King regards the inhabitants of these islands as of his realm'. Further instructions on the same subject were given to the collectors at Southampton in 1311.

During most of these wars the islands were regarded as safe havens on the route between England and Gascony, and in 1325, a Southampton merchant Richard Bragg was granted a safe conduct for one year, enabling him to go to the islands of Jersey, Guernsey, Alderney and Sark for corn and victuals, although he seems only to have gone to Guernsey for this purpose. Shortly after, in 1328 the King received a petition from Guernsey asking that the Bailiwick might be; 'quit of customs in selling and buying merchandise in England in the same manner that English people are', which was later granted, and confirmed in charters. It would seem from this that the 1309-11 instructions had been ignored by the customs collectors.

The Guernsey Extente of 1331 cites a toll called the *Grand Custom* of 27 sols trs. on vessels over 40 tons, and 22s 6d trs. on vessels under 40 tons, dropping anchor in any harbour in the islands, including ships visiting Jersey, Sark and Alderney, whilst the Rolls for 1329 had recorded a 'full custom' of 54 sols trs. and a 'half-custom' of 27 sols trs. being collected on ships trading between Poole and Southampton, and Guernsey, Jersey and Alderney. The trade from Southampton to the islands and France was well established when, in 1335, Edward III complained to the French King of ships from that port being pillaged and destroyed in the Seine, as well as the attacks on the islands and southern England already recorded, on the pretext of his war with Scotland.

Rumours of activity in the northern isle caused John Gant, the King's Receiver of Guernsey, Sark and Alderney to claim 5/- in 1352 for the payment of a boat sent from Guernsey to Alderney to 'find out what was happening there'. Another facet of these same wars was the 'arrest' of all ships over 12 tons burthen ordered by the Crown in 1370, including any such ships in ports in Jersey, Guernsey, Sark and Alderney, in order to use them to attack France.

2. The Fifteenth to Eighteenth Centuries

During the fifteenth century, trade between Alderney and England was increasing, one Alderney vessel appears in the Port records at Dartmouth, and 31 in the records at Poole. In June 1448 Colin Bot was Master of the ship *Thomas* of Alderney. Was this perhaps the Jurat Colin Bot commemorated in the street name in St Anne? In 1460 a large Alderney ship *Mary*, Master, Stephen Le Ber, took cargoes of Breton canvas and other items there, and brought back English cloth. He is recorded in the port as Master of several different vessels between 1461 and 1472. The following year John Le Ber, was trading in and out of Poole, and he is also recorded there, as Master of various other ships between 1471 and 1492.

Small ships, variously described in the records as *scapha* (a sort of pinnace), and *batella* (a carvel) were active in the conger trade which had become quite an industry in the 1470s and 80s, and during 1487/8, 15 visits were made by Alderney ships including six by *Dolphin*. Other vessels from the island were *Thomas, George, Jelyan* and *Jenette*. These ships each took between one and four tons of conger, and returned with one to eight tuns of ale and the occasional horse. This was an all-year-round trade, busiest in October, but less between November and February. One William Galliott of Alderney is recorded in the port records of Exeter at this time, and his vessel is described as 'spinaca vocata Barke', (a pinnace known as a Barque).

The trade in congers continued to expand in the sixteenth century, when knitted goods, as well as sheep, lambs, salt and kelp were also taken to England from Alderney, with an occasional Alderney vessel taking goods, mostly canvas and linen, direct from Normandy and Brittany to England. In 1590, another ship *George* from Alderney is recorded as landing 26 tuns of Bordeaux wine at Poole. The salt was created from sea water at Platte Saline (Salt flats), an industry which was assessed at a rent value of £12 a year to the Crown. The conger trade from the Channel Islands to Poole almost stopped in the seventeenth century, with only one or two vessels a year, all from Alderney, being recorded.

In the later part of this century vessels from all four islands were sailing regularly to Newfoundland for the cod trade, which became of prime importance to the Jersey and Guernsey economies, although it was never of very much significance to Alderney. From about 1690, Guernsey concentrated on other trade, as recorded in *The Quiet*

Venturers by Turk. The cod trade collapsed from about 1874, and caused great distress in Jersey. It was finished by 1886.

Shipping from Alderney was still bringing wool from Southampton at the start of the eighteenth century. In 1700-1 a total of 386 *tods* of wool was shipped. In July 1700 the ship *Nathaniel* of Alderney, John Olliver, Master, carried 20 tods home, and in August, the *Elizabeth* of Guernsey, Daniel Perchard, Master, brought 30 tods for Peter Cock [Le Cocq] of Alderney, as well as leather, candles, malt and hops, charcoal and soap. In the same month another *Elizabeth* this one of Alderney, John Cook [?Le Cocq], Master, brought 100 tods from Southampton to Sark, on the account of Philip Carteret & Co. The records of Weymouth in 1753 show Alderney craft bringing cattle and hides, and returning with sailcloth and coal, whilst Southampton records for the 1750s show a regular trade of hides and stockings brought in, and wool, building materials and household goods taken back to Alderney.

The hides from the islands were taken to England for tanning, and the dressed leather formed part of the return cargoes.

As well as the smuggling trade in the late 1700s already dealt with, legitimate cargoes were brought to Alderney by a number of vessels. One record in September 1790 shows that the *Betsy*, Master H. Wate, brought a cargo from Bristol, consisting of; two boxes, six bags, one grate of iron, one balk, four boxes, two parcels, one grindstone, two crates earthenware, one bag blankets, two barrels tierce, four kegs paint, two bunches of mops and brushes, sugar, five balks of tinware and two half-barrels of gunpowder, consigned to Guppy and Co.; four boxes and one of glassware for Stevens & Co.; 7,344 empty bottles for Lawson & Co.; and sugar for Thomas Keene.

3. The Post-Office Cutters

The early postal services to Alderney were very much the concern of the Bailiwick and Island administration and the military. Personal mails were sent by any available vessel, usually through a port agent in England or France, who forwarded them to a similar functionary in the islands, but official communications were sent by a limited number of routes on vessels chartered for Government service.

The small number of days which usually elapsed between the passing of an Order-in-Council, and its registration in the Royal Court or the Alderney Court, testify to the speed and frequency with which these communications reached the island, and the voluminous correspondence between the Governors of Alderney and the Crown Officers, or between the War Office and the Military commanders here, in the eighteenth and early nineteenth centuries regularly acknowledge communications dated only two days previously.

The Le Mesuriers had their own agent in Southampton, (in 1720 Thomas Le Cocq), for handling their correspondence and also had their own office on Alderney.

At the turn of the eighteenth century such agents were J. Ahier and N. Robillard at Weymouth, and Seward of Southampton, who also had an agent at Calais. Most of

Alderney's mail from France came via Cherbourg. The name of the Alderney agent there does not seem to have been recorded. The usual charge for a letter at this time was 3d or 6 sous. This last became three decimes after 1799 when France adopted the decimal system of currency, and the penny and the sous were then equivalent, the coins being of virtually the same size and weight. The fee was divided with 1d going to the agent at each end, and 1d to the captain of the vessel.

During the American War of Independence, packets were needed for Government communications with the islands, and one, the cutter *Express*, was removed from the Dover Station to Southampton in 1778. In carrying despatches to and fro, it was natural that civilian mails should also be carried, but this service was discontinued in 1783 when the war ended, and she returned to the Dover-Calais packet service. Hostilities with France broke out again in 1793, and the following year the service was renewed, this time from Weymouth, the nearest port to the islands.

A Southampton to Alderney Packet boat of 30 tons under Captain Le Ray, with a crew of three was running in the 1780-90s.

Official Post-Offices were established in Jersey and Guernsey by an Act of Parliament dated 28 March 1794, using Weymouth as the packet station, and established the rate of 2 pence for carrying a single letter up to a quarter of an ounce. To this was added the 5d charge for carrying the letter from London to Weymouth. The first packet boat had actually sailed in February, carrying a Post Office Surveyor, who appointed a postmaster each in Guernsey, (Mrs Ann Watson, a relative of Paul Le Mesurier, at that time Lord Mayor of London), and in Jersey, but it was not until 6 October that the Act for Granting Rates of Postages etc. was registered in the Royal Court in Guernsey. Jersey refused to register this act, but nevertheless took on the service. Letters had to be collected from the Post Office. Mrs Watson regularly collected an average of £265 a month in fees, representing about 4-5,000 letters handled. She continued as postmistress until 1814 when she retired, and her son Nicholas took over.

Letters carried from the Olive Lodge of Freemasons in Alderney between 1802 and 1810 via Guernsey bear a number of frankings. The earliest surviving example is a circle with the letter 'G' and the date 'Jan 10 1803'. The letter with this also bears the mark 'Weymouth 134'. Several other letters bear the Weymouth mark, and two went via Southampton.

The Government Scout *Speedy* with eight guns and a crew of 20, was in regular use from 1808-14, between Guernsey and England, and in 1814 was also running between Southampton and Jersey.

Sir John Doyle, Governor of Guernsey at the time of Napoleon's major threat to the islands in 1812 agreed with Le Mesurier to use his 'Scouts' for communication with Alderney, and the Postmaster-General sanctioned the carrying of both official and private mail by this means, in a communication transmitted to Doyle by the Post Office Secretary, Francis Freeling on 28 April. They would not agree to a direct service to Alderney on account of the expense, but directed 'the Postmistress in Guernsey to make up sealed bags, and deliver them to any person she cared to appoint for the purpose, who will of course be responsible to her for the postage'. When peace was restored in

1815, the service returned to private hands, presumably controlled once again by Le Mesurier.

Although Alderney did not have its own official Post-Office until 1843, in 1794 and 1795 *Betsy*, Captain John Bazin was employed taking mail between Guernsey and Alderney, making 68 voyages in 1795. In August 1823, the States of Guernsey authorised the setting up of a Foreign Post Office to deal with mails between Guernsey, Alderney and France, with Syvret and Barbet in High Street as the official agent for all letters from foreign ships calling at St Peter Port. They paid the masters of the ships 1*d* for each letter, and collected 2*d* from the addressee. This was repealed in October, and repeated in greater detail in December, remaining in force until it was finally repealed in January 1841.

Privately owned vessels were hired on an annual contract, and the Dover packets employed on this service in 1794 were *Royal Charlotte*, (Captain Wood), and *Rover*, (Captain Bennett), both of some 80 tons burthen. The sailings were weekly on Thursday evenings. *Royal Charlotte* was replaced in 1795 by *Earl of Chesterfield*, and the weekly service was maintained. Another *Royal Charlotte*, a Paddle Steamer of 90 tons, was bought by some Jerseymen in 1819, (she was later described as a sailing/steam yacht), and also carried mails between the islands in November 1821, and from Weymouth in September 1823. She eventually foundered off Cap de la Hague in October 1823. In 1806 an attempt was made to improve the service, and a third packet was added to the Weymouth station when a twice-weekly service was started. Passengers on the service paid £1 7s 6d for their passage, and had to provide their own food. It was the custom to take food and drink for 10 days, in case the passage was delayed, and the customs allowed the residue of this to be taken ashore without paying duty, which provided an opportunity for small-scale smuggling.

Stimulated by this official traffic, private individuals began to set up in competition, and, as already recorded one of these, *Chesterfield*, was taken by the French in 1811, and another, *Brilliant*, in 1814.

4. The Post Office Steamers

The Post Office began to introduce steamers to their cross-channel services about 1821. The first steam vessel to reach Guernsey was probably the PS *Medina*, built at Cowes in 1822 and noted in Elisha Dobrée's journal as arriving at St Peter Port on 10 June 1823.

She left the following day on an excursion to Jersey with 130 passengers, and the St Peter Port Town Band. She returned that evening with over 200 passengers, and made the crossing between the islands in four hrs 12 mins. She returned to Southampton the following day, and this appears to have been her only visit. 300 ton, 3-master, PS *Royal George* on her way to Cadiz, called at Guernsey on 6 September 1823.

Two of the Post Office Cutters were lost in 1826, *Hinchinbrook* off Alderney in February, and *Francis Freeling*, which disappeared with all hands after leaving Weymouth in September.

PS *Watersprite* started the first Steamer service on 7 July 1827, and at the same

Paddle-steamer *Medina*, the first Post Office Steamer on the
Guernsey run in 1823.

time stimulated the introduction of privately owned steamer services to the islands.
162-ton *Watersprite* was of a mere 60 hp, cost £8,770, and had a crew of 12. In 1835
she and her two companion steam-cutters *Ivanhoe* (Captain Robert White), and *Flamer*
carried a total of 7,218 passengers to and fro, the service having been increased to three
times a eek in 1829. *Meteor* (Captain Connor), which had joined *Watersprite* on the run,
foundered off Portland Bill on 23 February 1830, and was replaced the following year
by *Flamer*, 165 tons, and also 60 hp. This ship had larger 100-hp engines fitted in 1837,
and was renamed *Fearless*. *Watersprite* was renamed HMS *Wildfire*, also in 1837, and
continued to carry mails to 1845. She saw service in the Baltic, during the Crimean War,
and was finally broken up in 1888.

Wooden paddle steamers had been introduced on the route from Southampton to
Jersey in 1824, PS *Ariadne*, (Captain Bazin), 197 tons, with two 36-hp engines, which
also had three masts and sails reached Guernsey on 8 June, and the slightly smaller PS
Lord Beresford, (Captain Masterman), 160 tons with the same engines, but only two
masts, came later that month, on her return trip from Jersey.

J. T. Cochrane in his *Guide to Guernsey* (1826) notes that the sailing cutters,
Experiment, Capt. Simon, and *Frederick*, Capt. Le Cocq, were trading weekly with
Guernsey. According to Louisa Lane Clarke, *Experiment* was still operating in 1848. Also
from 1826 privately owned passenger and (unofficial) mail services were running, the
PS *Sir Francis Drake*, 113 tons, began operating a service to the islands from Plymouth
on 9 June, (which it continued for 32 years), followed in 1831 by PS *Lord of the Isles*,
(Captain William Hide), running from London, and calling at Brighton en route. This
vessel was built on the Thames, for the London, Guernsey and Jersey Steam Passenger
Company, she was of 345 tons and 120 hp, had berths for 74 passengers, and made the
journey from London in about 33 hours. Her first season ended with an unfortunate
incident. Running short of coal in a headwind off Alderney on her passage from London,
she turned for Southampton, and ran into and sank the schooner *Julia*, anchored off
Lymington without any lights. She resumed the service from London Bridge in May
1832. *Lord of the Isles* remained on the run until August 1839, when she was replaced
by *Triton*, which made her first trip from Guernsey with 50 passengers on the 30th,
under Captain James Goodridge, in 27 hours.

In 1835 the 350-ton 100-hp PS *Lady de Sausmarez* owned by the British and Foreign
Steam Navigation Company started a run from Southampton, followed in 1836 by
the 400-ton 120-hp PS *Atalanta*, owned by the South of England Steam Navigation

Company, who also owned *Ariadne*. B. & F. tried to cut the competition out by reducing their fares to 5/- for a Chief-cabin and 3/- for a fore-cabin, instead of the regular fares of 21/- and 15/- with 10/6d charged for deck passengers, sailing every Tuesday and Saturday at 6 p.m. for Guernsey, Jersey and St Malo. After the winter of 1836, the two companies got together, raised their fares to the previous level, and operated alternate sailings.

The first official services were the responsibility of the War office, but were transferred to the jurisdiction of the Admiralty in January 1837, after a number of Mail Packets had been lost or wrecked. Some alternative vessels were employed whilst the older ones were being refitted, and a more powerful ship, HMS *Fearless*, built for the Admiralty in 1831 was put onto the run for the winter.

The first vessel specially built for the Channel Island route, the Paddle-steamer HMS *Dasher*, of 275 tons, with 100-hp engines, was introduced to the service on 15 April 1838, under Lt William Roberts. She continued to carry the mails for seven years, until the service ceased altogether in 1845. This caused the Lt Governor, Lt General Napier, to complain to the Home Office in October 1846, and again in January 1847, about the service, and the manner in which it was performed. These letters were acknowledged by Sir J. G. Sinclair, but the service obviously did not improve, for there were further complaints sent in December.

Postage stamps had been introduced by Sir Rowland Hill in 1840 with the 'Penny Black', but the first known hand cancellation from Alderney consists of a Maltese Cross cancelling British Penny Red and two-penny Blue stamps from 1843-8. By 1848 the Alderney Post Office had its own cancellation stamp under the authority of the British Post Office, with the cancellation number 965. In 1851 the Alderney Post Master, John Tilbury died at the age of 65. He was also a watchmaker and had his premises in La Grande Rue.

In 1859 a petition was sent to the First Secretary, Spencer H. Walpole for Alderney to be granted a direct mail service, because of the huge increase in the volume of mail due to the government works, but it was considered that the cost would be too great, and mails continued to be routed via Guernsey.

Courier, Ellen and others brought the mails to and from Guernsey from 1876 and James Odoire, postman 1875-1905, carried them up from Braye on his back. His son William used a horse drawn van for the same purpose for 19 years. 'Big' *Courier* continued to carry the mails, until Alderney was evacuated in 1940, and carried the Royal Mail Ship insignia on her side for many years.

A military cancellation mark of 1907 is known, an oval stamp in a ring, with a cross each side, and 'Post Office/ RE Office/ Alderney', on three lines between them. (*See below*).

HMS *Dasher* returned to Gorey, and was based in Jersey from 1851 to 1884, to protect the valuable oyster fisheries, which had been found in 1797, and were later almost exhausted by 1872, through over-fishing. *Dasher* took over these duties from HMS *Cuckoo* which had been on station in Jersey from 1847-51. This vessel of 234 tons, and 100 hp had been built as *Cinderella* in 1831, and renamed at the same time as the others in 1837. She had carried the Alderney Mail for a short time in 1848. In 1854, *Dasher* was

HMPS *Dasher* was built for the Guernsey route in 1838 and accompanied Queen Victoria in 1854.

Above left: Alderney's postal identity mark cancellation stamp 965, introduced in 1848.

Above right: A military postal cancellation stamp used by the Royal Engineers in 1907.

used for a time to convoy French troops through the Baltic during the Crimean War, and took part in the great Spithead Review of 1856. This vessel was described by Queen Victoria in her diary, on her visit to Alderney in 1854, as: 'a very slow, useless, steamer which could not keep up with us at all'.

From 1841, the Post Office allowed letters to be sent from the islands via Southampton if suitably endorsed; 'to Southampton by private steamer', and letters reached London in 24 hours, better than the average service today.

5. The Railway Steamers, the Stone Trade, and others, 1840-1940

The coming of the railway to Southampton in 1840, with the journey from London taking three hours, gave further impetus to the cross-channel traffic competition, and five years later the government closed the steam-packet station at Weymouth and transferred the mails to the South-western Steam Packet Company on contract. In 1847 the twin funnel Paddle Steamer *Courier* and two similar vessels *Dispatch* (which in the 1890s was turned into a store barge), and *Express* (wrecked off the Corbière in 1859), were put into service, being leased in the following year to the South Western Railway Company.

The railway reached Weymouth in 1857 and both the London and South-western, and the Great Western, Railways established new steamer services from that port to the islands, with iron ships *South-Western* and *Wonder*, supplementing, and soon supplanting, the wooden-hulled *Camilla* and *Atlanta*. These last three, and the PS *Courier* were all broken up in the 1890s, whilst *South-Western* was turned into a Barque and sailed on the China run. An advertisement in the first issue of the Alderney *Parish Magazine* in 1859, offers

...communication between Weymouth, Alderney and Cherbourg, by the well-known Fast Iron Paddle steamships *Aquila, Brighton,* and *Cygnus,* (weather and circumstances permitting).

The fares were 30/- First Class, 20/- Second Class and the ships were advertised to leave Alderney at 11.30 a.m.

Also in 1854, the Jersey Steam Packet Co., who were running regular services between Jersey, St Malo and Granville ran summer excursions to Alderney and Sark in the PS *Rose*. In 1857 the iron PS *Venus* and in 1859 the iron Screw-steamer *Dumfries* were added. The Company went into liquidation in 1862/3.

During the time the Breakwater was being built, contractors Jackson and Bean ran the 100-ton PS *Princess Royal*, which they had bought from the Jersey Steam Packet Company, from 1847-53; *Queen of the Isles* (81 tons, built 1853, and used between Guernsey, Alderney and Cherbourg from November that year until July 1872) and the Steam-Tug *Watt* (1856), all commanded at various times by Captain Scott, who opened

Paddle-steamer *Queen of the Isles*, built 1853 for Captain Scott, had
a figurehead of Queen Victoria

Scott's Hotel in Braye Road to accommodate the new tourist trade which this brought.
Jackson and Bean also used the Steam-Tug *Bolton* on the Alderney works. *Queen of
the Isles* was able to carry 70 passengers, and had 25 berths. The return fare in 1859
was 3/6d Main Cabin, and 2/6d Fore Cabin, when she ran three times a week between
Guernsey and Alderney. She was adorned with a figurehead of Queen Victoria.

   Throughout the period of this log, Captain Scott, was the most frequent visitor, making
two or three runs weekly from Guernsey with mails and passengers, and in midwinter
making up about half the total number of entries. She made a trip to Cherbourg and
back most weeks, with the occasional trip to Weymouth or Southampton, sometimes
staying overnight. She was laid up in the harbour under repair from 7-13 April 1870,
and also noted as grounding two or three times for a few minutes on rocks, without any
apparent damage. From May 1869 mails were also brought from Guernsey by Captain
Whales in the seven-ton sailing ship *Ellen*, with between three and six visits a month
for a few months, and less frequently later. Other vessels involved in mail carrying from
Guernsey were *Eclipse*, eight tons, Capt. Corbet; *Liberty*, 42 tons, Capt. Gaudion; *Rover*,
13 tons, Capt. Renier; possibly this same vessel under Captain Renier, is also noted
as Yacht *Rover*, seven tons in July 1870; *Fisherman*, of eight tons, usually skippered
by Capt. Noyan, but recorded in addition, under Capt. Digard, and Capt. Trousseau.
Trousseau also made a single visit most months in his six-ton Boat 'Y', usually arriving
in ballast, and taking a cargo of fish to Jersey or Cherbourg, occasionally bringing salt,
oats or beans from Jersey, either in *Y* or *Fisherman*. Mail was also brought from time to
time by 14-ton *Vermilia*, and from its first appearance in the 'Journal' in July 1868, with
five visits, the Steam Tug *Watt*, 14 tons, Captain Whales, made infrequent runs with
mail and passengers, increasing to three or four times a month, from April 1870, and
was then supported by Capt. Whales' other vessel, the Yacht *Ortach* of 15 tons.

   The Breakwater Superintendent's Journal, No. 9, which gives daily details of the
activity on the breakwater, and in the harbour, from July 1868 to December 1871, also
contains a daily record of all vessels arriving and sailing with their tonnage, port of
lading or destination, Master's name, and brief details of their cargo. An average of one
vessel in and out each day in the winter months, and up to two daily in the summer
are recorded. Maximum activity was in May each year, when cargoes of cement for
the season's work arrived. At times of severe storm, as many as 15-20 sailing vessels,

mostly bound for Cherbourg, with a few to Le Havre and other destinations, are noted as 'windbound' in the harbour, for a day or sometimes two. A notable night was on 9 and 10 March 1870, when 20 vessels took shelter. The large majority of these were of 26-30 tons, with only one larger at 48 tons.

Another regular visitor was the 90-ton government ship *Inkerman*, Captain Oliver, which made a trip most months from Woolwich with military stores and ordnance, and usually went on to Guernsey, a function also carried out on a single occasion each by the similar-sized *Lord Vivian*, Captain Dimond, which brought its cargo from Portsmouth, and *Lord Raglan*, Captain Golding, from Woolwich. HM Paddle-steamer *Dasher*, a frequent and regular visitor, mostly to and from Jersey, either with troops, or on its fishery patrol duties, also made one trip in October 1870 from Chatham with a cargo of field guns.

Other than general cargoes, mostly from Guernsey on the mail boats, few direct imports were recorded. Two cargoes of gunpowder from Southampton and Plymouth, a cargo of drainpipes from Swanage, a shipload of cider and two of oats, from Jersey, a single load of straw from Southampton, pottery from Fareham, and the occasional load of furniture, but whether as personal effects of someone moving to the island, or imported for sale, was never specified. Regular cargoes of cement for the breakwater arrived, a single load in most of the spring and summer months, with usually several loads in May at the start of the repair and maintenance season. The vessels involved in this trade were a small number of sailing ships, all of about 40 tons burthen,, most of them arrived from Cowes, and frequently returned to London with Alderney stone. Those involved were *Enterprise, William and Fanny, The Brothers, The Three Sisters*, and *Phoenix*. Single loads of cement were brought from London by *James, Spirit,* and *Arranah*, and one load from Sittingbourne on *Fairy*.

Regular loads of limestone from Lyme Regis were brought by SS *Freedom*, 105 tons, Captain Callaway, which also brought a single load from Plymouth, and a cargo of iron girders from Sunderland, returning with Alderney 'granite stone'. Coals from Newcastle were also a regular import, mostly in sailing ships of 100-150 tons, with *Admiral Nelson, Shealtiel, Two Friends, Wave, Sarnia, Concordia, Mellona, Emma Eden, Cheval de Troie,* and *Crescent*, in this group, with the larger vessels, *Olive Leaf* 177 tons, *Dublin Lass* at 170 tons, *Albion* at 165 tons, and *Impetuous,* 162 tons. Most of these vessels also took Alderney 'granite stone' back to London as did a number of smaller sailing ships or barges, of around 40-50 tons. *Impetuous* also brought a locomotive for the Alderney Mineral Railway on 23 March 1871.

The early part of 1870 saw loads of Alderney Granite being delivered to Portsmouth, Chatham and Dover, presumably related to defence works being built there, whilst at the same time there was a considerable traffic of dressed granite brought to the island, much of it from Penrhyn in Cornwall, with a few loads coming from Jersey and Guernsey, and probably used, as other records show, for lintels, quoins and steps in the forts. *Freedom, Emma,* and *Fairy* brought the stone from Jersey, whilst *Queen Victoria, Charlotte Anne, Elizabeth Anne, Liberty, Perseverance, Yeoman's Glory* and *Experiment*, all of around 40-60 tons brought it from Cornwall.

Alderney's exports at this time were few; 147-ton *Stapeyrader*, (Capt. de Jersey), took a general cargo in October 1868, and made other visits, a single load of bricks, possibly from the Allées ès Fées brickworks, went to London on *Charlotte Anne* in May 1869, two loads of early potatoes in February to London, and one each to Shoreham, Jersey and Guernsey, with a single load of main-crop in November 1870 to London, empty casks and cement bags were returned to Lyme and Cowes, and surprisingly, in August 1869, 175-ton *Edissa* came in in ballast, and left a week later with a cargo of lead. This was presumably scrap from the flashings and pipes used in constructing the forts. A small cargo of 'old iron' was taken to Jersey in 16-ton *Risk*, and the final 'export' was an unnamed wreck, towed to St Malo in September 1869 by the 13-ton steamer *Gosforth* of Guernsey.

Visits of Naval vessels and private yachts were frequent. THV *Galatea* of 760 tons made regular visits two or three times a year to provision the Casquets Lighthouse, with 207 ton, THV *Vestal*, Captain Traherne, arriving in May 1871 with a cargo of oil for the lights, which took several days to tranship.

The few passenger steamers of these years, listed in the journal are; *Granville*, 50 tons, (Captain Lemeur), *Wonder*, 137 tons, 19-ton *Resane*, (Capt. Lihou), made several day trips, and once stayed overnight, and *Gosforth* mentioned above, to and from Guernsey, *Heather Bell*, 95 tons, to and from Jersey, *Rose*, 30 tons to and from Brixham, with an overnight stay, 123-ton *Fair Rosemary* from Swanage stayed two nights, 137-ton *Aquila*, (Captain Brach), came from Weymouth, stayed overnight and went on to Guernsey. Day-Excursions from Cherbourg were run in July and September by the 119-ton *Notre Dame de Fourrière*.

When the Breakwater works finished, Captain Scott had the 100-ton paddle-steamer *Princess* built to his own specification, to continue operating. Scott died in 1875 and *Princess* was sold for £1,200. She had been under-powered to cope with currents in the Swinge, and was lost off Lundy the following year. He was succeeded by Barbenson and Co., a firm started by Judge Nicholas Barbenson, Captain N. Whales, and Mssrs. Blatchford, Cutler and Willis, (later to become the Alderney Steam Packet Company, registered in February 1897 as a limited company to run the *Couriers*). They bought the first SS *Courier*, specially built for the service by Day and Summers of Southampton, a 136 ton, iron screw-steamer, 99 feet long, launched on 26 February 1876, which then served the islands for many years. She had a speed of 10 knots and burnt three cwt. of coal an hour. A larger (130 foot), 150-ton ship of the same name was also built by Day and Summers, in 1883, at a cost of £7-8,000, and for many years the two ships ran simultaneously, earning them the names of 'Little' and 'Big' *Courier*. She made her first run from Alderney to Guernsey, loaded with cattle, on 5 July under Captain Whales who then commanded her for about 30 years, a fact commemorated on his tombstone in the churchyard.

Both were equipped with sails as well as engines. 'Little' *Courier* was finally sold in 1913 to a Greek company, and renamed *Ahdon*, whilst the other *Courier* continued to serve Alderney for many more years, and was the regular link with Guernsey, four times a week in the summer and twice in the winter, usually under Captain Whales.

17 mars 1905
Georg Hajour...

1526. CHERBOURG
Cliché P. B. Cherbourg
Débarquement des Excursionnistes Anglais sur le Quai Caligny   G. F.

The two SS *Couriers* together in Cherbourg with 'Little' on the left and 'Big' on the right, *c.* 1890.

'Big' *Courier* had quite an eventful career, she rescued 12 men and a woman in August 1897, when the SS *Ville de Malaga* sank off the Casquets, she struck the eastern mole of the New Harbour at Braye in 1905 and was damaged below the waterline and beached. The following year she struck a rock between Herm and Jethou and was beached on Crevichon, the 86 passengers landing on the other two islands, and on Easter Monday, in April 1906 struck another rock off Jethou, and sank in 10 fathoms with some loss of life. It took until 31 July to raise her, and after temporary repairs to the large gash in her side, she was towed back to Southampton to Day and Summers yard, in October, by the tug *Albert Edward*. This vessel was later renamed *Joybell III* and will be referred to again.

From then until the Second World War, her life was busy, but comparatively uneventful, with regular passenger and cargo runs between the islands, and the occasional excursion. The fare between Guernsey and Alderney in 1935 was 9/- return. She was the last free British vessel to visit the island in 1940, and was shelled as she reached Guernsey with her cargo of pigs, evacuated from Alderney. Her Captain beached her, at St Sampson's Harbour, but she was refloated next morning and took the pigs and some passengers to England. She was in service throughout the war in England, and returned to the inter-island run for a short time in 1947, at which time she was probably the oldest steamer still in service in Britain. She remained derelict for a number of years in Weymouth and was finally scrapped in Holland in 1951.

The Stone Trade

From 1895 there was a considerable trade in the export of stone from the island which increased rapidly, although the stone had to be lightered out to the ships. In April that year, SS *Topaz* and *Jersey* took 600 tons each, *Fern* took 180 tons, the Brig *Banshee* 200 tons, SS *Stanley Force* 410 tons, SS *Maggie Bane* and SS *Resolute* took 420 tons each, whilst the SS *Staperayder* took 350 tons. SS *Suna* after loading fouled its propeller and was blown onto the sands in Braye Bay where it sat for five days. Other shipping engaged that year included SS *Iron Duke, Manchester,* and *Cygnus,* the Brig *Algernon,* and the Barge *Mab, or Queen Mab,* which could carry 120 tons in each load. The trade continued to thrive once the 'Stone Jetty' was completed, the first vessel to use which, on Tuesday 31 August 1896, was the ketch *Raleigh,* a 140-ton vessel commanded by Alderneyman Captain John Audoire. This vessel brought a cargo to the island and loaded stone, the new jetty making loading a much simpler task. (*Courier, which usually tied up at the Admiralty slipway or in the New Harbour,* made its first docking at the new jetty on 17 May 1897).

Other vessels engaged in the stone trade once the jetty was complete in 1896 were the SS *Resolute* and *Kennelworth.* In 1897, *Blanche, Fal, Westbury, Vanda* and *Mount Park* were, between them, taking about 2,000 tons a week out. In the last six months of 1897, 21,685 tons of stone were exported, compared with only 100 tons six years previously.

The quarrying and stone trade had become the major employment in the island within a few years, which continued until the island was evacuated in 1940. The picture here, taken in 1936, shows the SS *York Valley* loading stone at the Stone Jetty behind the other vessels, with three Dutch vessels, *Hebe, Albion* and *Argus* waiting, two barges, with the SS *Abbotsford* on the right discharging coal.

SS *York Valley* is behind the other vessels loading stone and SS *Abbotsford* is discharging coal on the right. Three Dutch vessels and two barges are waiting for stone, 1936.

The Railway Steamers

The GWR took over the Weymouth company in 1889, and on Whit Monday 1895 the GWR steamer *Ibex*, Captain Renouf, which had been built for the cross-channel service in 1891, made its first run from Guernsey to Alderney with 460 passengers who all had to be brought ashore in small boats. On August Monday the same year PS *Monarch* brought 210 passengers from Bournemouth on a day trip, and *Courier* took 80 from Alderney to Guernsey. The following week SS *India* brought 60 passengers from Weymouth. The LSWR's cargo boat SS *Alderney* built in 1875 also called at Braye occasionally, until she was sold in 1892.

These vessels were opening the Weymouth route, and a summer service was started to the islands with the screw-steamers *Lynx, Antelope*, and *Gazelle*.

The Southampton route had already developed considerably with a number of ships being brought into service to Jersey, Guernsey and Le Havre, only a few of which would ever have called at Alderney. They were however a link to the island via Guernsey, and their names are worth recording, from an article in the *Southampton Observer* in 1893. The South-western paddle-steamers noted above, were followed by *Havre*, 387 tons, and *Alliance* on the French route, and *Southampton*, 585 tons, *Normandy, Brittany*, each 654 tons, and *Wolf*, 814 tons, coming in that order onto the island route, with *Fanny* and *Alice* helping out in the season.

The next group to be built for the Channel Island run were *South-western II*, 705 tons; *Diana*, 772 tons; *Ella*, 851 tons, and *Hilda*, 849 tons, which were all a success. These were replaced by a new generation of three 1,059-ton 259-foot-long twin-screw steamers, each capable of carrying 735 passengers, with sleeping accommodation for 240 of them. *Frederica*, (Captain Allix), *Lydia*, (Captain Vanderplank), and *Stella*, (Captain Lainson). They made the crossing to Guernsey in just over five hours.

Normandy foundered off the Needles in 1870, with several of her passengers and crew drowning, *Waverley* struck some rocks, and foundered in the Little Russell channel off Guernsey in 1873, and *Havre* foundered in the same spot in 1875, followed in 1880 by *Caledonia* sinking, after hitting a rock off the end of the Jersey breakwater. *Caesarea*, a 262-ton screw-steamer built in 1867, was later rammed and sunk by a potato boat, SS *Strathesk*, in fog 12 miles off Cap de la Hague on 27 June 1884.

Other LSWR ships used on this run at various times, were; the single-screw SS *Guernsey* 572 tons, built 1874 and wrecked off Cap de la Hague on 9 April 1915, when seven people were drowned, *Lynx* which later helped in the rescue from *Stella*, and the triple-screw ships *Caesarea* and *Sarnia*, both of 1,510 tons launched in 1910.

In 1893 in addition to the ships listed above, the South-Western cross-channel fleet contained; *Dora*, 813 tons; *Laura*, 641 tons; *Honfleur*, 429 tons; *Alliance*, 387 tons; *Cherbourg*, 373 tons; *St Malo*, 304 tons; *Griffin* 272 tons, and *Maria*, 261 tons. The fate of *Stella* in 1899 under Captain Reeks, has already been documented in Chapter 12. This tragedy resulted in the services being pooled to avoid the racing which was deemed to be partly the cause of the wreck, and the revenues of the combined routes were shared. The GWR then had *Victoria* introduced in 1896, and *Vera* introduced in 1898, which was also concerned in the rescue from *Stella*, on the route, with *Alberta* expected to be delivered in 1900.

LSWR SS *Roebuck*, delivered with her sister ship *Reindeer* in 1897, was the first cross-channel steamer to be fitted with a wireless telegraphy receiver, in 1908. It was at first fitted amidships, but the engines interfered with reception and it was moved to the forecastle. She went on the rocks off Jersey in 1911 under Capt. Le Feuvre, but was later salvaged and repaired, and no lives were lost.

The Dynamite Trade

At about the same time as the stone trade was increasing, a considerable trade in Dynamite for Australia developed. Several large German Steamships, SS *Chimnitz*, *Sonneberg*, and *Sommerfeld* usually arriving from Antwerp, and SS *Stassfurt*, SS *Meissini*, and SS *Flensburg* from Hamburg, were used on this trade. The dynamite was brought, from Glasgow on the smaller screw-steamers *Alfred Noble, Marmion*, and *Lizzie*, on *Marshall Keith* registered in Hamburg, and on the ketch *Thistle* from Honfleur. The Alderney harbour records, reported weekly in *Le Bailliage*, show the comings and goings in 1897 and 1898. The cargo was transhipped well out in the Bay for safety, as many as 18,000 cases in a shipment, using 50 men and taking several days to transfer it. The large vessels then made the round trip to Port Elizabeth, Sydney, and Melbourne, sometimes calling at Falmouth on the way out, and were back here in about six months. There are no records of any accidents or wrecks caused through this dangerous trade as far as I can ascertain.

The Helcke Explosive Works in Alderney after an explosion caused by lightning on 10 September 1903.

Nevertheless, as a result of this trade a States' Inspector of Explosives was appointed in Alderney, a position which continued until after the Second World War. The German Helcke Brothers, who had had a manufactory at Grande Rocques Chemical Works in Guernsey since 1840, set up an Explosives Works in Ruettes Braye in Guernsey in 1866, with permission from the Royal Court, which was transferred to Alderney in 1885, to a manufactory built at the top of Allées ès Fées. Here fulminate of mercury was made for detonators. 'Cab' Helcke married a Miss Baron in Alderney and lived in Mouriaux House. The Guernsey newspaper *Comet* records in 1885, the presence in St Peter Port Harbour of the SS *Staperayder*, (which had been running from Guernsey to London for Cheeswright and Miskin since about 1868); 'waiting for the fulminate from Alderney for the British Government'. It was used in the warheads of torpedoes, amongst other things, and was highly volatile. All went well for many years, until there was a huge explosion on 10 September 1903, apparently after a bolt of lightning struck, and set fire to, the spirit store, this caused two minor explosions, at 10.10 p.m., followed by an enormous bang, debris rained down on the western end of the town, and the works was badly damaged. Haystacks in the area were set ablaze, and a number of cattle were later affected, probably by eating grass on which poisonous ashes had fallen. The Fire Brigade, and the Military Fire Brigade of the Leicester Regiment, from Fort Albert, arrived on the scene but were unable to do anything, and the flames were reported to have risen to 200 feet. There were no casualties, as the works was closed for the night, and few people were out in the storm, although it was not raining at the time according to the reports.

The States were asked by the Lt Governor to render a report on the affair and one of the Artillery Officers, Major Mosse, made a report which stated that no proper precautions had been made, and there was no earthworks surrounding the powder room as a protection. Great concern was also expressed by States' members about the fortnightly dynamite ships which were still loaded in the bay close to Fort Albert, and the possible effects of an explosion there on both the Breakwater and the Fort.

I can find nothing to suggest that any of the production of the Helcke Works was shipped in conjunction with that trade, but it ceased not long afterwards, and the factory also never reopened.

6. The New Jetty

All of these various increases in traffic in the harbour were suffering greatly from the lack of proper loading facilities, since the larger vessels were unable to tie up at the slipway at the landward end of the Breakwater used by *Courier* and other smaller vessels, or at the Old Pier, and the need to have an alternative to Le Mesurier's Quay was becoming an important issue. *Courier* took 117 passengers on a day trip to Cherbourg in July 1895, leaving at 5 a.m. on the 12th, after being stormbound in Cherbourg they finally returned to Alderney at 3.30 p.m. on the 15th. Two weeks later *Courier* took 160 passengers on a day trip to Jersey, the first time for some years that this run had been made.

SS *Ibex*, Capt. Le Feuvre, came again at Whitsun 1896 with 247 passengers, this time from Jersey. The following year she hit a rock and was beached off south-west Jersey. No lives were lost, and she was repaired and put back into service, together with *Roebuck* starting an extended daytime service. Her Captain later denied that he had been racing with Capt. Allix in *Frederica* at the time of going ashore. In 1900, this time under Captain Baudains, she hit another rock in the Russell channel off Guernsey and sank. Again there was no loss of life and she was eventually salvaged.

On 13 June 1896, not long before the jetty was finally completed there were 10 vessels in the roadsteads at the same time, whilst in July the Paddle-steamer *Monarch* brought over 220 trippers from Bournemouth and Swanage to see the construction.

The Stone Jetty, (now known as the Commercial Quay), was finally built, after 25 years of political wrangling in Alderney which created a division of the island into two factions, the 'Jettyites' led by Count Henry de Faby, and the 'Cockroaches' or supporters of Judge Le Cocq, who were against the scheme. Many Parish Meetings had been held to discuss the scheme, songs and poems had been written and published, there had been a huge amount of comment and letters in the local press, the subject had been debated endlessly at Chief Pleas, Jurats and the Judge had been questioned over Court verdicts, where the person charged had been a member of the other party to those on the bench, or some had been asked to withdraw from the case because of this, and several government agencies had become involved.

The final decision was taken to approve the construction on 13 April 1895, after the Commissioners of Woods and Forests had agreed to pay the £12,000 the jetty was to cost, on condition that Alderney would pay annually thereafter, £100 towards the salaries of the Judge and Crown Officials, out of the Impôt, and in addition 'be responsible for the upkeep of the Court House, Prison, and keep the Jailer's and Greffier's houses in repair'. An order was passed by the Court on 22 June authorising the 'work to start immediately'. It actually began on 25 August, and was completed in almost exactly a year.

A 'Grand Fête' was held to celebrate on 27/28 August. Henry de Faby was President of the Organising Committee. It began with a procession of the island's Benevolent Societies and children lead by the 'Band of Progress' leaving the Butes at 1.30 p.m. for a thanksgiving service in the Parish Church. The congregation then processed to the site of the New Jetty for a blessing by the rector Revd J. E. Le Brun. The procession returned through the main streets of the town for a public tea on Butes, followed by a children's sports programme of 16 races.

At 8.30 p.m. a monster bonfire was lit on York Hill with a 'Grand Pyrotechnic Display' including several set pieces terminating with 'The Brilliant Sun' and 'Grande Feu de Joie'. The band played during the evening and finished with Rule Britannia and God Save the Queen.

The second afternoon started with a sports meeting for the adult islanders, followed in the evening by a public supper at the Victoria Assembly Rooms costing 2s 1d. For the Grand Finale they all sang Auld Lang Syne, Rule Britannia, and Vivat Regina.

The immediate beneficial results from the construction were felt all over the island. Passengers, animals and freight could walk or be carried ashore, ladies no longer had to be exposed to the hazards of climbing down a ladder onto the sands or getting into a dinghy, ships were turned round far more quickly. Passenger trade increased, and in the month the jetty was opened, SS *Ville de Cherbourg* came from Cherbourg with 120 passengers, and SS *Commerce* from Jersey with 160. A firm of London agents, Cheeswright and Miskin had been managing sailing ships since the 1840s, and in 1854 were running two steamers, SS *William Miskin* which started in 1853, and the PS *Foyle* bought in that year, on a route established from London to the islands, with sailings every 10 days. In 1858 the iron Screw-steamer *Metropolis* was specially built for the service and was added to the route to increase the frequency. In 1861 the return fare was £1 2s od She was wrecked off Jersey, and replaced by another, faster Iron Screw-steamer *Esk* the following year, which was itself replaced by SS *Staperayder*, mentioned above, in 1875.

Onesimus Dorey in Guernsey established the Plymouth, Channel Island and Brittany Steamship Co. in 1887 and about 1920 the company became Onesimus Dorey Ltd. They established Condor Shipping Services in the 1960s and ran hydrofoils on a number of routes including those between Weymouth, Jersey, Alderney and St Malo from the 1970s (see below).

Cheeswright and Miskin, which had already become Cheeswright and Cheeswright, became Cheeswright and Ford about 1890, and the company whose ships they were managing changed its name to The London and Channel Island Steam Ship Co. Ltd in 1899, with the 'Queen' boats being brought into service.

In 1900 *Island Queen*, to which was added in 1901 *May Queen*. These boats mainly carried granite from Guernsey and returned with coal. *May Queen* was sold in 1903, and *Ocean Queen* bought. She was wrecked off Guernsey in 1906 and replaced by the smaller *Wave Queen*. Three years later this vessel was also sold and the larger *Foam Queen* replaced her. In 1910 *London Queen* joined the fleet, now of four vessels, and in addition to cargo, could carry 20 passengers.

Sailings were from East London docks every Tuesday and Friday direct to the islands. *Norman Queen* and *Saxon Queen* replaced older vessels, but these were sold in 1913, and *Channel Queen* which could carry 40 passengers as well as cargo replaced them.

Shortly after the start of the First World War, the government took-over all of the GWR steamers except *Ibex*, and business for the L&CI company increased greatly as a result. The old 650-ton *Island Queen* was replaced in 1914 by another, 900-ton vessel, given the same name, and this in its turn was replaced in 1916 by a third *Island Queen*, an 800-ton vessel with accommodation for 60 passengers, and in 1920 by a fourth, of 970 tons. Numerous changes of vessel occurred over the next few years, with successive ships preserving the four main 'Queen' names. The main trade between the wars was the Jersey potato trade. The company was finally sold to Coast Lines Ltd in 1936, and was renamed British Channel Island Shipping Co. in 1937. By the 1950s the 'Queen' names had disappeared, and the vessels were mostly called '... Coast'.

The London route was discontinued in 1968, and in 1969, the local island shipping companies of Coast Lines were sold to The Commodore Shipping Co. Ltd, founded by Jack Norman in 1952.

In February 1897 the Alderney Steam Packet Co. was registered, with Captain Audoire as its principal ship's officer, also managed by Cheeswright and Ford, and in the 1924 edition of Ward Locks Guide to the Channel Islands, offered; 'Regular weekly sailings in fast and commodious steamers from St Peter Port to Alderney, Sark and Cherbourg'. As already noted, it was founded by Judge N. Barbenson, Captain N. Whales, and Mssrs. Blatchford, Cutler and Willis.

The 'fast and commodious steamers' were of course the two *Couriers*, and at this time, from December 1896, they had been offering a service for packages not exceeding 50 lbs in weight brought from England to Guernsey, to be transferred to *Courier* for Alderney for 1*d* each, if brought by the South-Western boats, or 3*d* each package if brought by GWR vessels. Captain Whales was also in command of a third *Courier*, a 37-ton Sail/Steam vessel also owned by the company, and regularly used between Guernsey, Alderney and Cherbourg, until it was wrecked.

Built by Fullerton's, and launched in 1897, the Piprell Lines' SS *Fawn* of 150 tons, was 109 feet long, and carried freight and 59 passengers on the Guernsey and St Malo route, with occasional visits to Alderney, Sark and Jersey. Her maiden run to St Malo was accomplished in five hours. In 1922 she was offering a service between Alderney and Poole, leaving Poole at 9 p.m. on Fridays, and returning from Alderney at 9 p.m. on Sundays. She was replaced in 1923 by the 286-ton SS *New Fawn*, used later in 1940 to evacuate the Machine Gun Unit from the island.

In the early 1900s a thriving export trade in Alderney cattle was beginning, and both *Courier* and the larger LSWR's SS *Guernsey*, were engaged in this trade, the latter after being converted from a passenger vessel. Regular supplies of coal were reaching the island in 1903 aboard the colliers *Clarita* from Hull, and *Nancy* from Goole.

The Guernsey Evening press for Wednesday March 24 1909 advertised an excursion leaving that day from Alderney to Jersey, calling at Guernsey in SS *Courier* under Capt. J. Ingrouille, for the Inter-insular Football Match (Guernsey *v.* Alderney) for the Muratti Vase. The return fare was '6/-Brit', the Franc still being legal tender in the islands then, hence the 'Brit'. The vessel was returning to Guernsey on Friday morning and thence to Alderney on Saturday. For the same match L&SWR and GWR companies were offering return trips from Guernsey to Jersey for 4/-, the GWR vessel leaving at 7 a.m. on Wednesday and the L&SWR at 7 a.m. on the Thursday. Returning either by 'the Mail Steamer' on Friday morning, or for those who were not attending the 'Grand Vaudeville Performance Monster Programme' at the Jersey Opera House on the evening after the match, at which the Cup and Medals were to be presented, SS *Laura* would leave at 7.30 p.m. on Thursday, with a maximum of 354 passengers 'which number cannot be exceeded'.

The Anglo-French Steamship Co. Ltd vessel SS *Devonia*, owned by Onesimus Dorey and Sons, offered a day return leaving Guernsey at 1.15 p.m. and returning at 7.30 p.m. for the same fare. It was to be laid up the following day for its annual survey at Plymouth. The Guernsey Steam Towing and Trading Co. Ltd cancelled their proposed excursion in SS *Alert*, 'Owing to Circumstances'.

In the same edition of the *Press*, the London and Channel Islands Steamship Company Ltd managed by Cheeswright and Ford, advertised their sailings to Guernsey

SS *Guernsey* at the Breakwater slipway. She was frequently used to carry Guernsey cattle to England.

(St Sampson's Harbour) and Jersey from East Dock, London Docks, 'weather and circumstances permitting'. SS *Island Queen* Left every Saturday arriving in Guernsey via Jersey on Monday evening and returning direct that evening. SS *Foam Queen* left every Tuesday evening, reaching Guernsey on Thursday evening via Jersey, and returning direct on Friday. The two vessels carried fruit from Covent Garden, general merchandise and a limited number of passengers.

About 1914 the St Malo and Binic Steamship Company was formed, running between Guernsey, St Malo and Binic, with occasional excursions to Alderney. This was still running in the 1930s, including Cherbourg in it's routes, and calling at Alderney on the return journey.

Many of the local companies were inter linked, and another line in which the Piprell Brothers, Edward and George, grandsons of the founder. were involved in the 1920s and 30s was the Guernsey, Alderney and Sark Steamship Co. Ltd, running *New Fawn* and *Courier* from 1923 to 1940. The Alderney runs were made from Guernsey on Tuesdays at 9 a.m. returning from Alderney at 4 p.m., and between the beginning of July to mid-September on Thursdays as well. The Friday run left Guernsey at 9 a.m., and returned from Alderney at 6 or 6.30 a.m. on the Saturday. In 1933 the fares were 4/6d single or 9/- return with a day-return for 6/6d, reduced by 1938 to 4/6d single or 7/6d return.

The 173-ton PS *Helper,* (built in 1875 as PS *Sir Francis Drake*, the second paddler of that name, and renamed in 1908), was bought by the Alderney Steam Packet Co. in 1920 to use on the Guernsey to Sark run, and made occasional trips to Alderney. Under her first name she

Advert for the St Malo and Binic Steamship Company's boat services in RMS *Courier, c.* 1920.

brought a party of divers from Plymouth in 1900 to assist in the salvage of SS *Ibex* after she sank off Guernsey. *Helper* was badly damaged in Sark in 1926 and scrapped, being replaced by SS *Riduna*, (the former Coastguard Cutter HMS *Argus*), of 350 tons built in 1905.

The single-screw SS *Riduna* was also engaged in the Alderney to Guernsey trade from 1927, when the return fare was 7/6d, and ran a weekly excursion to Cherbourg in summer. In the early 1930s, PS *Monarch* ran Bournemouth to Alderney excursions, and was replaced in 1938 by the former Mail-packet *Canterbury*, renamed *Arpha*, which had been built in 1899. In the late 1930s, SS *Isle of Alderney* formerly the *Devonia* running from Poole to Guernsey was based at St Peter Port on the same run, visiting Alderney from time to time. Also in 1938 MV *Joy Bell III* was in use on the Guernsey to Alderney run. It was used on 17 March that year for the burial at sea of Judge Robert Mellish, and later helped in the evacuation of the Machine Gun unit in 1940.

Kelly's Directory for 1939 lists two companies serving Alderney. Firstly, the Guernsey and Alderney Trading Co. Ltd, operating a service to Guernsey, and to Portsmouth, leaving Alderney on Tuesdays and Fridays, returning on Wednesdays and Saturdays. The Alderney agent was George C. Smith. The second company was Sark Motor Ships Ltd, running to Guernsey daily in the summer except Fridays, and three times weekly in the winter. Their Alderney agent was A. T. Després.

7. Post Second World War Shipping

Immediately after the war, in April 1946, Mssrs. Dashwood and Quick applied to have a monopoly of the Guernsey-Alderney route, and no Alderney vessels would be permitted to operate on the run. This application did not succeed, and in 1948 the franchise was

Riduna carried mail, passengers and cargo between Alderney and Guernsey in the late 1920s.

SS *Arpha*, a former mail-packet steamer ran excursions from 1938 until the island was evacuated.

given to Commodore Cruises Ltd, managed by Island Shipping Co. Ltd, which was itself a subsidiary of Coast Lines Ltd.

Commodore Shipping played a large part in the Alderney trade soon after the island was resettled, for a short time SS *Radford* of about 500 tons used the German Jetty, as did the 200 foot MV *Fallowfield* which could load there with up to 800 tons of Alderney gravel, but these were replaced by the much smaller MV *Island Commodore* in 1948 trading with Guernsey and Poole. She was later renamed *Ile de Serk* and used by the Sark Shipping Company to supply that island. This ship finally went to the Caribbean, where she was wrecked in a hurricane in Dominica in September 1989, still bearing the same name.

SS *Radford*, *Island Commodore* and other vessels used occasionally on the route, *Arrowhead*, *Channel Trader*, and later *Ridunian* were all ex-naval Torpedo Recovery Vessels, either purchased or chartered from HM Government. *Ridunian* was used extensively to carry the cargoes of Alderney Meat Products, and the Cheswick and Wright Silencer Factory, to England.

Commodore Shipping had a terminal, shared with British Rail for container shipping, at Portsmouth from 1971, and in 1977, the fleet consisted of *Commodore Clipper, Island Commodore, Commodore Trader, Commodore Challenger, Commodore Goodwill*, and *Commodore Enterprise*.

The LSWR had become the Southern Railway about 1923, and in 1930 it brought SS *Isle of Guernsey* and SS *Isle of Jersey* onto the route, followed in 1932 by SS *Isle of Sark*, and *Vera* was replaced by SS *Brittany*, introduced in 1933. SS *Autocarrier*, 985 tons, (*above*) built in 1931 to carry vehicles and passengers was also introduced, she played a large part in the evacuation of Jersey in 1940, and brought the islanders back to Alderney in 1945 and 1946. For some months then, she ran a weekly service from Weymouth to Alderney with supplies, building materials, and other necessities, and then returned to her normal work.

At the end of the war, Alderney was blessed with the 500 foot-long German jetty with its hydraulic buffers, and deep water facility. *Isle of Guernsey* was the first steamer back on the route from Southampton, in June 1945, and in June 1946 the Weymouth Mailboat *St Helier*, soon followed by *St Julien*, which had both first been put into service in 1925, ran excursions to Alderney, as did the Southern Railway Steamer *Brittany*, (1,445 tons, 850 passengers), from Southampton. Later Alderney even had excursion and cruise vessels such as *Empress Queen* calling in 1949, and Naval Vessels such as HMS *Grenville* and the submarine HMS *Alderney* docking there from 1947 (next page).

Another SS *Caesarea* and another SS *Sarnia (II)*, both twin screw vessels of 4,174 tons, the last of the all-passenger ships, capable of carrying 1,400 passengers, were introduced to the cross-channel route in 1960. Sailings from Southampton to the islands stopped in 1961, leaving the Weymouth route operating, but by about 1963, when *Brittany* was sold, the cross channel traffic to Alderney had dropped-off markedly, most tourists preferring to come by air, and services stopped. The German jetty fell into disrepair through pure neglect, was left unused for some years, became dangerous, and was eventually demolished between November 1978 and February 1979. The estimated

Soon after the Second World War, SS *Radford*, here tied up at the old jetty, ran a regular service to Alderney.

MV *Island Commodore* ran in the late 1940s.

SS *Autocarrier* brought the main parties of islanders back at Christmas 1945 and early 1946.

cost of demolition was almost the same as that of the alternative proposal to fill it in with concrete to provide a permanent extension to the commercial quay, which would have been of far greater value to the island. In the event it took far longer than was expected, the job was not properly completed, and over the next few years additional demolition work on underwater hazards had to be carried out, all at additional cost to Alderney.

The island thus lost its ability to handle larger vessels, a very great detriment to its facilities for shipping today, and to the ease with which inhabitants and visitors can move goods and vehicles, to and from the island, also adding greatly to the cost of doing so.

With the withdrawal of the direct services to Alderney in the 1960s, travellers using sea routes had to use the British Railways car ferry services from Portsmouth to Guernsey or Jersey. British Rail had been formed by nationalisation of the railways in 1963, and was using *Caesarea* and *Sarnia* on the Channel Island Route. A new type of vessel, known as the 'Ro-Ro' (Roll on, Roll off), was developed, capable of accommodating vehicles driven straight on board via suitable ramps. Terminals were installed for these at Portsmouth and in Jersey, and the service was begun by MV *Falaise* in 1971. Guernsey soon installed the necessary facilities, as did Weymouth later in 1976, when MV *Earl Godwin* was put into service between that port and the islands, and replaced the SS *Caledonia Princess*, a vessel built in 1961. She was of 3,630 tons, could carry 130 cars and 700 passengers at a speed of 19 knots, and had been introduced to the Weymouth-Channel Islands route the previous year. The Portsmouth run was added to by MV *Earl William* in 1977. In 1979 all of the British Rail ferries operating from UK were transferred to a subsidiary company Sea-Link, which continued to operate the service with several sailings a day until 1984, when it was privatised.

To encourage tourism, many cheap package deals for travellers, with or without a motor car had been introduced by Sea-Link, which included a free issue of duty-free wines and

The submarine HMS *Alderney* paid visits in 1947 and later.

spirits from the onboard shop, as well as a choice of several grades of Hotel. One could even bring a small car over on a day trip, arriving at Guernsey around 6 a.m. and returning the same night for £18 return. Although the vessels were frequently packed with vehicles, including a great number of freight lorries, the number of passengers was often quite small, and the service was loosing more than a million pounds a year. The Weymouth connection had already been stopped in 1981, but the Portsmouth route continued, and in the meantime the larger MV *Earl Harold* had joined the run.

The Alderney Tramp Shipping Co. Ltd was established in 1958 running between Portsmouth and Alderney, and in 1961 was offering a cargo service between Jersey, Alderney and Weymouth.

Fred Morton operated MFV *Jolly Gambler* carrying up to 50 tons of cargo, and 12 passengers. In 1959/60, when *Island Commodore* was temporarily out of service she performed the regular Guernsey-Alderney run, then going back on the Portsmouth run.

A proposed thrice-weekly passenger service between Alderney and Cherbourg was inaugurated on 1 April 1969, using MV *Le President Quonian*, 150 tons, with accommodation for up to 150 passengers. The fare was £3, but the service was withdrawn on 5 June the same year for lack of support.

8. More Recent Services

The new private company British Channel Island Ferries, which replaced Sea-Link, carried out extensive refits to upgrade the accommodation, replaced some of the vessels, and in 1990 and 1991, the cross-channel service to Guernsey and Jersey was provided by the Ro-Ro vessels MV *Rozel*, MV *Havelet* and later by MV *Beauport*, with twice daily sailings in each direction from Poole, with a connection being provided from Jersey to St Malo. Special excursion fares are offered, with 20 per cent discounts on ordinary fares for Senior Citizens.

None of these Ro-Ro services called at Alderney, but by means of the local link from Guernsey have provided for many years the principal access for goods, vehicles, and passengers, from England to the island, and today are still the route for most of the cars and cargo to Alderney.

In mid-1969, the States of Alderney negotiated with Sir John Onslow Marine Services Ltd to operate the Guernsey-Alderney run with cargo carried at £7 a ton, compared with the £3.50 charged by Commodore, whose contract would soon terminate. Other tenders from Fred Morton, (who had by then served as a Member of the Alderney States, and had been on the Transport and Harbour Committee for three years), and Jackie Main, were apparently ignored. Morton offered a service five times a week each way, using *Jolly Gambler*, and was prepared to put a refrigeration plant onto a larger vessel, which he already owned in Scotland, and use that on the run to carry fresh meat, and frozen foods as well.

The needs of the island for food, building materials, vehicles etc. have been catered for, almost entirely, for a number of years by the Alderney Shipping Company's cargo vessels, principally running between Guernsey (or Shoreham for sand and cement etc.) and Alderney. Many vessels have been used on this run, mostly on contract hire to the company, *Channel Trader* (1959), *Alderney Courier* sold to the Caribbean after nearly 10 year's service to the island in October 1978, *Alderney Trader,* (formerly *Glen Bride*), 1969-73, *Bandick*, *Sea Trent* (carrying capacity 240 tons), which made her maiden run for the company on 6 September 1973, *Ord*, running from 1978, *La Pia*, (formerly *Pia*), 1979-87, the former *Beta Nord*, bought in February 1981, and renamed *Courier*, *Carrigrennan* (brought onto the run in May 1982 to replace *Sea Trent*, 1982-8), *Mary Coast* (1987-9), *Courtfield* (1989-90), *Port Soif* (1991-93, when she was wrecked off Guernsey), all ran once or twice a week during their periods of service, and others made irregular visits, including MV *Hootact* in 1974.

These coasters are mostly in the 3-600-ton size and, apart from their crew quarters have no accommodation. Their licence however requires them to take up to 12 passengers on the Alderney-Guernsey run if required.

The company was founded on 10 February 1969, by Jackie Main, when MV *Alderney Trader* was purchased, and Link Services Ltd, was registered on 21 June 1969, run by Jackie Main, using the *Alderney Trader* on charter. The following year Jackie and his brother Richard held the controlling interest in the company, and in 1971 Jon Kay-Mouat bought-in to the Link Services company. The Mains sold out in 1973, and after a number of changes of co-directors, Alderney Shipping was controlled by Jon Kay-Mouat, Alderney's President from 1977-93 (and again from 19), his wife Martine, and Link Services. Freight charges are agreed annually between the company and the States'. From 1991 the company carried on with a succession of chartered vessels, still operating a basic once a week service, but rarely carrying passengers although the licence still required it on demand until about 2,000 when the States dropped the requirement.

The company then bought another ship, MV *Isis* (N.R.T. 393, formerly the *Deer Sound)* in 1994. Since the death of Jon Kay-Mouat in 2010 his son Bruno, already MD of the Guernsey company has continued to run the whole enterprise and their contract with Alderney States was renewed in 2011.

Hurd Deep Shipping Company was formed in April 1978 by island resident Ian Waterfall, with the assistance of Tony Forster, in conjunction with Curnow Shipping, and this re-established a direct link with England. Their office was above Dave Peacock's Fish Shop in Les Rocquettes. At first using *Sea Trent*, chartered from Alderney Shipping to operate a monthly freight service between Plymouth and Alderney, starting on 6 October, then going on to Guernsey. Their own vessel, 299 ton, MV *St Anne of Alderney*, bought in Denmark, and registered in Jersey, made her maiden trip from Plymouth with 80 tons of freight on 9 November 1979, and established a fortnightly service. The venture unfortunately lost a considerable amount of money, and after two years the vessel was refused its seaworthiness certificate, and was sold in the Caribbean. The operation was put into co-operation with another freight service from England using MV *Ontic*, and Torbay Seaways began operations in May 1981. MV *Star Libra* also ran freight services, as well as *Ontic* in 1984.

In May 1982, they started a summer service from Torquay, with passengers and freight, including cars. This was at first by the 921 ton, former Scilly Isles vessel MV *Scillonian II*, renamed *Devoniun*, and from 1985 by the former Scottish Mailboat *Clansman*, also renamed *Devoniun*. This vessel has the advantage of a hydraulic lift and ramp which enables vehicles and cargo to be lifted to Quay level and driven on and off. It ran for about nine months of the year, (with a freight-only service continuing through the winter in chartered vessels), and was also used for three-day cruises from Torquay to the islands, for £99. She continued in service until late 1990. Day trips to Alderney from England were possible, leaving at 7.30 in the morning, reaching Alderney at 1.45 p.m., and leaving again at 5.30, returning late at night, arriving at Torquay just before midnight. The return fare in 1989/90 on this trip was a very modest £18, with Pensioners paying only £8 for their day out, and as many as 300 people at a time came to Alderney by this route. For Alderney residents the single fare was £19 in the winter and £26 in the summer, with cars at £40 and £56 respectively, each way.

The service was well patronised from 1985 to 1990, and was providing a much needed route for bringing groceries, and especially fresh vegetables and fruit, to Alderney, on its weekly direct runs. The *Devoniun* was temporarily replaced in February by the freight liner *MV El Taurus*, whilst she was undergoing a refit, but near the end of 1990, Huelin Renouf of Jersey took over Torbay Seaways, and the new company withdrew the vessel, apparently for a large scale refit. They were supposedly to re-establish the passenger service in the spring of 1991. Within a couple of weeks however, they announced that the Alderney run was uneconomic and would not be restarted, and put the vessel up for sale, once again removing the direct link with England.

In 1989 a Hydrofoil service from Torquay was started on a two or three times a week basis, to Alderney only. The nature of the seas that year made most of the journeys slow and uncomfortable, for this design of craft is not intended for rough water, and many of the passengers were ill. The bad conditions caused many sailings to be cancelled, and the service was discontinued. On its inaugural run, bringing the Torquay Bowls Team to Alderney, the woods were all stowed together at the stern of the craft, and the weight distribution was such that it was unable to get up onto the hydrofoils, and had to return to port for the luggage to be restowed, an unfortunate start to what proved to be another disappointing venture, both for the island and the company.

In 1991, in a laudable attempt to preserve the sea link with England, the former Alderney Manager of the Torbay Seaways service, Ian Waterfall, in partnership with Alderney Shipping Ltd, formed Channel Seaways and are continuing the freight link with vessels chartered from Alderney Shipping, which will also take cars in the hold. They tried to find a suitable vessel to carry both passengers and cars, at least for the tourist season, but were unsuccessful, and the service has continued as a freight only carrier on a three-weekly basis.

As already noted, Condor Shipping Services were established in Guernsey in the late 1960s by Peter Dorey, providing inter-island connections, as well as freight from England. It was taken over in 1984 by Commodore. Hydrofoil services from Guernsey were started, the first run to Alderney being by *Condor II* on 2 July 1969. They then ran in the summer several times a week including a Sunday service, taking 40 minutes compared with a conventional vessel's two hours. *Condor III* came onto the service in 1974. Other services from Weymouth to Guernsey and Jersey on a daily basis from March to the end of October, (with a connecting link to St Malo), which called in at Alderney on both outward and return journeys from April to September were run from 1987 to 1989. The six smaller vessels carried about 140 passengers, with *Condor VII* carrying more. The journey to Alderney took just under two hours, and the return trip cost £52 in 1988 and £55 in 1989.

The construction of these Hydrofoils necessitates the insertion of a special pontoon between the ship and the Alderney Quay, each time they arrive, to enable passengers to disembark. In 1990 Condor introduced a newly designed, much larger Hydrofoil, called a Wavecutter to the service, carrying about 450 passengers. It called in at Alderney on its maiden voyage, but was not expected to do so on the scheduled runs, as it was thought to be uneconomic. This voyage was a disaster, the vessel did not perform as expected in choppy seas, it broke down and when it finally reached Guernsey spent many weeks there being made fit for the return journey. Back in Weymouth it was decided to modify the design before trying to reopen the service, and throughout 1990 there was no direct link by this route between Alderney and England. As far as Alderney was concerned the decision had also been made to discontinue the link with Guernsey using the smaller Hydrofoils, and there was no service in 1990 on that route either. The Weymouth service to Guernsey was started again in 1991, but soon ran into further design troubles.

By 1992 most of the problems with *Condor 9* had been overcome and the service was running regularly to Guernsey. (See colour section photo). An even larger catamaran *Condor 10* was built in Tasmania specially for the route and is capable of carrying over 400 passengers and 90 cars using the Ro-Ro ramps. This huge vessel was sailed to Guernsey at the end of the year and, after some minor modifications started a service from Weymouth to Guernsey and Jersey in 1993, taking about two hours for the Channel crossing. Also in 1993, shortly after the French company Emeraude Lines began operating a trimaran service from Guernsey to Alderney three times a week, Condor Shipping put *Condor 9* onto the same route, bringing about 160 passengers on most trips for a return fare of £16. This vessel can tie up at the jetty without any special needs and remains in Alderney from its arrival about 11.30 a.m. until it leaves at 3.30 p.m. Unfortunately a similar day-return service is not available for Alderney residents. An even larger Ro-Ro catamaran *Condor 11* carrying 700 passengers and 170 cars was put onto the Jersey and Guernsey-Weymouth service in 1995.

In 1989, in May, a new service from Weymouth to the islands was started by Weymouth Maritime Services, using a roll-on, roll-off, car ferry the *St Julien*. This vessel was able to carry passengers and cars direct to Jersey and Guernsey, and use the ramps there. A schedule of five runs a week, some by night and some by day was set, calling at Alderney on Wednesday, Saturday and Sunday. By picking suitable combinations, it was at last possible for Alderney residents to take cars direct to and from Jersey, and it also provided an additional service to England for vehicles. At Braye the vehicles were lifted on and off the lowered ramp by crane, but at the other ends they could drive straight on or off. The direct crossing to England took four hours. Special cheap fares of £39 return were available for people starting the return journeys in England, giving them four days in Alderney, no such concessions were available to Alderney residents, and the return fare was £54, with a small car costing £55 each way. Alderney residents were not allowed to take cars to Guernsey by this route, as it competed with the Alderney Shipping Company's service.

In October 1989, the vessel, which had been on Charter from a Norwegian firm, was suddenly repossessed by its owners, and the service ceased overnight, with the firm ceasing trading temporarily. A much larger Car ferry *Smyril* was hired, and made a trial voyage to Alderney in November 1989. When finally docked, it overlapped the length of the quay by about 30 feet, and the service never started. Harbour dues and other debts to the States of Alderney amounting to about £12,000 were owing, and there were other considerable debts to Alderney Shipping Company, when the company went into liquidation at the end of March 1990.

From May 1988 a direct link with France was established for the first time in many years, when H.A.G. Marine Services S.A.R.L., owned by Jon Kay-Mouat and a French colleague, François Peré, opened a service thrice-weekly, from Goury to Alderney, with some services continuing to Guernsey, on the 65-foot Vedette, MV *Sea Fox*. The crossing took 45 minutes, and the vessel could carry 65 passengers. At other times in the week, this vessel operated between Dielette and Guernsey with some trips to Sark. The cost was £14 return from Alderney, with a 10 per cent discount for Alderney electors. The company was liquidated after two years, but the service continued since under entirely French ownership, as Sea Fox S.A. The service ran from April to September, with a small number of sailings in March, October and November as well. A Christmas special shopping trip with coach from Gorey to Cherbourg was run in 1990 and 1991. The service continued throughout 1992, but the need for expensive repairs to the vessel then proved uneconomic and the service was discontinued, the company later going into liquidation and the *Sea Fox* sold.

In 1992 a small group of Alderney residents decided to try to establish a better link with France for freight and vehicles. They set up Island Ferries (C.I.) Ltd and a small Norwegian Ro-Ro vessel, the MV *Trondenes* of about 250 tons was purchased and adapted slightly. This now has a capacity of about 20 cars plus freight containers, and is allowed to carry 12 passengers. A twice-weekly service between Cherbourg and Guernsey was proposed, with a once a week service between Alderney and Cherbourg. When more passengers wish to use the route accompanying their cars, *Sea Fox* acted in conjunction with the ferry boat to take them across. The service started in May 1992, and excellent supplies of cheaper, better quality fresh vegetables and fruit, as well as other goods were welcomed by the islanders. A freight and car transport service to UK via existing cross-channel services from Cherbourg was available. The sudden withdrawal of the UK from the EEC ERM in 1992 unfortunately caused the £ sterling to be devalued by about 20 per cent against the Franc, and this part of the route and the cost of the French produce increased to an unattractive level.

The service was extended to include a route between Weymouth and Alderney in 1993 after the company had been refused a licence to carry passengers or freight between Alderney and Guernsey on the grounds that it would be detrimental to the Alderney Shipping Company route. By late 1993 the company was in financial difficulties and went into receivership with large debts, causing the investors to lose most of their capital.

Regular visits by tankers to supply oil for the electricity station and domestic heating. The National Benzole tanker *Ben Johnson* in the early 1950s, and the *Shell Welder* used the Inner Harbour to unload in the late 1950s, but the pipeline to the power station was extended to the Commercial Quay, and since then Shell tankers have tied up there, including the 217-foot-long *Shell Director* in July 1982 and occasionally since, the largest vessel ever to use the Quay. In September 1992, the *Shell Marketeer* made its first visit and unloaded 531 tons of fuel .

From 1 June 1993 Emeraude Lines established a new Trimaran Service between Alderney and Guernsey and although only three passengers were booked for the inaugural run from Guernsey, on the day, she actually brought 40 passengers to Alderney and brought up to 100 on later occasions. In 1995 *Condor 9* started a Sunday service to Alderney from Guernsey which ran throughout the remainder of the season. Despite promises of a regular run, this service was discontinued soon after the start of the 1996 season.

The author's photographs of a number of the ships mentioned in the next two paragraphs, will be found in the colour section in the middle of this volume.

Frequent visits by sail training vessels, the Brig *Royalist,* belonging to the Sea Cadet Corps, the Sails Training Schooners, *Sir Winston Churchill, Malcolm Miller* and later the *Lord Nelson*, belonging to the Jubilee Sailing Trust and the and visits by various ships of the Royal Navy, including the present HMS *Alderney*, with occasional visits by French Naval vessels, make up the rest of the traffic at Braye. The Royal Yacht *Britannia* has visited on two occasions in the last 20 years, and was always accompanied by a Naval escort which remained outside the harbour. She has now been taken out of service, sold and is moored as a visitor attraction in Edinburgh.

In September 1987, the Smyril Line Cruise-ship MV *Norona* of about 8,000 tons put into Braye for two days with a party of German tourists. This was the largest ship ever to use the roads since the Naval exercises at the turn of the century. A similar large cruise-ship *Aurora II* registered in Nassau made two visits in August/September 1992. Some 160 passengers disembarked from this each time. In 1993 and 1994, several short visits were made by vessels chartered by SAGA Holidays. The 4,000-ton *Caledonian Star* engaged for a bird-watching cruise right round the British Isles came to Braye in thick fog, early on the morning of 20 June 1995 on the first day of her cruise. Whilst being piloted in by Alderney's Harbour Officer, Steve Shaw, she hit the sunken part of the Breakwater and her bottom and propeller were damaged. No-one was hurt and she got into the harbour on her own. The passengers were flown back to England the next day. After surveying she made her return to UK under her own power, was quickly repaired and back in service in about two weeks.

Transatlantic Liners regularly passed quite close to Alderney, within two to three miles. Local pubs had timetables of the *Queen Mary* and *Queen Elizabeth* passages on display, and the bars used to empty whilst the patrons watched them pass. On her last voyage to America after being sold, Cunarder *Queen Mary* came quite close in, at 8.15 p.m. on 13 September 1967, and suddenly switched on all her lights. A bonfire was lit on the Butes to say farewell.

The illustration is of the Queen Mary passing Arch Bay on her way to America.

ARCH BAY, ALDERNEY WITH R.M.S. "QUEEN MARY".

RMS *Queen Mary*, seen passing Alderney before the shipping lanes were changed in 1979.

The shipping visible from Alderney since then, is confined to vessels passing up-Channel, almost on the horizon when seen from the shore level, and lines of Container vessels, cargo ships, tankers, and a few oil-rigs pass by, sometimes as many as seven or eight being visible at the same time. Car ferries regularly pass up and down the Race, to and from Jersey, and through the Ortac passage to and from Guernsey, with a rare trip along the Swinge if the tide is right.

In 2009 another shipper, Huelin-Renouf obtained a licence to collect and deliver freight and carry up to 12 passengers between Alderney, Southampton and Jersey, but is not allowed to carry freight between Guernsey and Alderney. Alderney shipping also agreed to carry a limited number of passengers between Alderney, Guernsey and Poole in addition to its existing freight licence.

Yachting

During the late eighteenth and early nineteenth centuries the Le Mesuriers and their merchant and privateering friends from both Alderney and Guernsey had their own small vessels, variously described as cutters and yachts, used at various times for personal transport, government business, carriage of goods to and from the islands, privateering, and no doubt a bit of smuggling. Some of these have been noted in the Chapter on the Le Mesurier family, in the extracts from Elisha Dobrée's diary, and in Chapter 8. The arrival of Queen Victoria in the Royal Yacht in 1854 and 1857, helped to make Alderney a fashionable stopping point for wealthy owners.

From May to August in the years 1868-71, covered by Breakwater log no. 9, a considerable number of yachts were logged with 'pleasure parties' on board. Many of these originated from Cowes and called in at Alderney overnight en route to or from Guernsey or Cherbourg. Several of the larger ones made a number of visits, and stayed as long as a week or 10 days. Some 45 different vessels were involved, ranging from the 420-ton *Brilliant*, 312-ton *Zara*, and 300-ton *Ceres*, with the 192-ton Steam Yacht *Deerhound* belonging to Sir. E. Sullivan, and the Duke of Marlborough's 146 ton, *Queen Eleanor*, down to the 7-ton *Ranger* owned by Mr Langlois of Guernsey which stayed overnight. The most intriguing entries in this class were on 27 April 1871 when the 15-ton yacht *Ildegonda*, owner Langtry, was logged in for a couple of nights en route from Guernsey to Jersey, and on 3 June the same year when the 148-ton yacht *Red Gauntlet* also logged as 'owner Langtry', arrived from Guernsey, and left for Jersey on the 6th. Was this perhaps the famous actress, Lillie Langtry, the 'Jersey Lillie', visiting Alderney? The yacht was owned by her husband.   A number of others were owned by members of the aristocracy, Lord Louth, Lord Stafford, Lord Colville, Lord Bangor, and Lord Bury, all put in to Braye and stayed a night or two.

At the turn of the century, yacht racing was becoming popular in Guernsey, and annual regattas were held, with Alderney boats taking part. Alderney continued to develop slowly as a tourist centre. After the First World War, and into the 1930s the yachts of the wealthy continued to come to the island, and a number of the wealthier islanders, including several Judges had their own boats in those 40 years. At the time of the evacuation in 1940 Judge French had a small steam-yacht in the island.

After the Second World War, it was a number of years before the island was really fit to receive tourists and offer facilities to visiting yachtsmen, but the tranquility of Alderney, and complete lack of formalities soon attracted them again.

Much has been done since then to encourage visiting yachtsmen, and the facilities are continually being improved. The States built a block of showers and toilets, with washing machines and other facilities, on the quay in 1983. This was privately run by tender from the States until the end of the 1992 season when the States repurchased the lease for £5,000. Mooring fees were then increased slightly to include 'free' use of the showers.

The difficulties of landing from the mooring buoys, by small dinghy, at the commercial quay at certain states of the tide, or the expense of using the water taxi to get ashore, gave rise to many complaints, and resulted in a dinghy pontoon and access ramp being installed, at the landward end of the jetty just below the Yacht Club, in 1989. This was so well used that it had to be extended in 1990 to allow greater numbers of dinghies to moor, whilst their owners were onshore.

From time to time various schemes for a Yacht Marina at one end or the other of Braye Bay have been promoted, but, to date, none has met with approval, either from the States, or the people of Alderney, and an acceptable scheme has yet to be found. It is recognised that tourists arriving in yachts bring a considerable amount of money into the island, in addition to the modest charges for mooring, but at the present time the facilities offered are generally inadequate, particularly for sewage disposal and provision of fresh water. Despite the indirect financial benefit to the island, somewhat optimistically estimated by the Harbour and Tourist Committee in 1990 to be as much as £1 million a year, the actual running costs of the harbour, and its staff and facilities, including pilotage, customs officials, and the cost of installing and maintaining the radio, radar, mooring buoys, and navigation lights, greatly exceeds the direct revenue to the States brought in by all classes of shipping, without taking into account the capital cost of the new facilities provided.

An attempt to redress the balance slightly was made in 1991, by an increase in the berthing, mooring, and landing fees charged, but these still do not cover the costs, and the total loss of passenger services to the island except by MV *Sea Fox*, during 1990, greatly reduced the income from these sources. Landing fees for passengers on commercial vessels were increased and the daily cost of moorings for visiting yachts was also increased. Local boats on seasonal mooring charges, had their fees increased too. Higher fees for docking commercial vessels were set, and pilotage charges, for those few vessels whose masters do not hold an Alderney Harbour certificate, were increased. On average in the last three or four years a pilot has only been requested on about a dozen occasions each year.

Under certain conditions of wind and tide, Braye Bay has a very unpleasant and considerable swell, and there is never enough available accommodation ashore for the yachting families to find beds on land when conditions are bad during the summer season.

Yachtsmen coming ashore, or passengers landing from commercial vessels, when these are running, in the early morning have generally had a very dismal time trying to find breakfast or toilet and washing facilities, or a place to buy bread or milk. Most establishments do not open until 9 a.m., and the Cafés often later. Not surprisingly, the hotels nearest the harbour do not look kindly on large numbers of people using their toilet facilities who are neither guests nor customers, but despite this have not, in general, put themselves out to offer early breakfast meals.

The public toilets at the harbour, which were in need of upgrading, were demolished in 1988 with the intention of rebuilding them. Due to a number of circumstances, after the owner of a restaurant which overlooked them had got up a petition, once they were knocked down, to have them sited elsewhere, and the owner of an hotel near which building of the replacement unit was started by the States, without proper consultation, and in an unsuitable spot, some way from the quay, and not easy of access, had raised a *Clameur de Haro* to stop the work, nothing further was done. As a result of complaints from visitors about the lack of facilities, a Portaloo cabin was placed on the Quay during 1990 at the top of the dinghy ramp. This proved thoroughly unsatisfactory, resulting in many complaints from both visitors and locals, particularly regarding its hygiene and maintenance.

In the following year the new toilets were finally built on the beach between the Douglas Quay and the Sea-View Hotel. In the early 2,000's these were replaced again under the new bar terrace during the large scale alterations after the hotel was sold and became The Braye Beach Hotel.

The site of the old toilets was later, in 2012 turned into a memorial to the crew of HMS *Affray*, a submarine which sank in the Hurd Deep 50 years previously. There is now a large block of Granite bearing a metal plaque bearing the names of the 70 sailors who died in her and two large wooden benches, one either side, overlooking Braye Bay.

In 1990, before the virtual demise of passenger services other than *Sea Fox* was realised, the lease on the Fish and Chip shop and restaurant, standing on the quay, rented from the States, and run by the Jenkins family, which was a boon to the yachtsmen, and much used throughout the year by the islanders, was cancelled, to make way for a new passenger terminal, and Custom's Hall, for people arriving and departing on commercial passenger vessels. The building was converted for this purpose and an extension was built to link it with the Harbour Showers. When it is open to cope with incoming or departing vessels, this now offers extra toilet facilities, including some suitable for the disabled.

In compensation, Peter Jenkins was offered a small piece of States' land behind the Yacht Club at a nominal rent, and built a new shop and restaurant, with an outdoor restaurant terrace, on the site. Recognising the need of the visitors to the island landing at the harbour, in 1991 he opened this for breakfast from 7 a.m., when the boats were running, later changed to 9 a.m., and offered snacks throughout the day, with an extended range of cooked meals in addition to the Fish and Chips. In that first season the premises were often open till midnight or after, and provided a welcome facility for harbour users as well as islanders. It closed for the winters 1991/2 and 1992/3, and the poor tourist seasons in 1992 and 1993 resulted in the premises opening from 5-9 p.m. only. It changed hands in 1995 and during the season was open from 8 a.m. to 11 p.m. In 2012 this is run by a young family one of whom is a trained chef and supplies superb meals with a wide range of alternatives to the excellent fish and chips.

The demand for improved facilities and hotel bathroom accommodation, perhaps combined with the introduction over recent years of automatic dishwashers, and washing machines in both commercial and domestic premises, has resulted in an increasing use of water which in three successive years of drought, 1989 to 1991, placed a considerable strain on the island's limited water resources, and on the sewage disposal system. Part of the problem was found to be leaks in the old mains. These were repaired or replaced and the daily consumption fell by almost half. In 1993, despite a rainfall in the first seven months barely half the annual average **Battery Quarry** remained full.

Now, in 2012 a recent improvement of the collecting system, by picking up a high percentage of the water falling on the NW side of the island and pumping it to Battery Quarry through a high quality cleaning and filtering system, Alderney has almost the purest water supply in the British Isles and the quarry was full for the first time for several years, within two weeks of the system coming into operation and the surplus was being pumped to Corblets quarry which is now also filled most of the time, even in a period of less than average rainfall in 2011 and the first three months of 2012.

Although in the late 1980s and 1990/1 the numbers of tourists visiting the island was considerable, a number of the hotels have changed hands several times recently, with successive owners failing to get an adequate return on both their investment and labour.

In 1992 a general recession in England was greatly reducing the tourist companies' business world-wide. Cross-channel air routes are in no way competitive, on a cost per mile basis, with fares to Spanish, Portuguese, Mediterranean, and Eastern American holiday resorts. With the considerable increase in air fares introduced by Aurigny Airlines, after the demise of Air Sarnia, to try and recoup their reduced profits whilst the other airline had been operating, combined with the present lack of alternative sea-routes, it remains to be seen if Alderney will have a profitable or even a viable tourist trade in the future. Charges for both accommodation and meals in the island have also increased greatly, and compounded the problem.

The world economic situation in 2012, particularly in the EU, has unfortunately not helped with this much needed increase.

Despite this the number of yachts visiting the island each season had increased steadily. By the mid 1980s many hundreds of yachts were coming to Alderney each year, with as many as 250 at one time during *Alderney Week*, the first week in August.

Tables of yachts visiting; and passenger movements through the harbour terminal from commercial passenger carriers.

1. Numbers of visitors and yachts, etc. from 1985-1994

Year	1985	1986	1987	1988	1989	1990	1991	1992	1993	1994
No. yachts	3,718	5,021	6,483	6,004	7,541	6,887	5,845	5,972	6,370	6,525
No. crew	14,872	16,736	21,608	20,016	24,844	22,956	19,588	19,908	25,480	26,100

Average number of crew/passengers per yacht was 3.5

No. of passenger movements from commercial ships through terminal

Year	1985	1986	1987	1988	1989	1990	1991	1992	1993	1994
Number	9484	15,681	8,095	15,314	26,281	11,102	9,570	7,352	7327	6,541
No. ships	54	120	46	282	260	243	222	165	47	66

2. Numbers of visitors and yachts, etc. from 2001-2010

Year	2001	2002	2003	2004	2005	2006	2007	2008	2009	2010
No.yachts	6194	5850	6038	5496	5973	6074	4241	3826	6021	5876
No. crew	24726	24084	22405	21700	23025	22730	15821	14972	30105	29380

Average number of crew/passengers per yacht 2001-2008 was 4.4

Please note that for 2009/10 the States statistics changed from the number of yachts involved to the total number of 'Yacht nights' in the harbour.

No. of passenger movements from commercial ships through terminal

Year	2001	2002	2003	2004	2005	2006	2007	2008	2009	2010
Number	1668	2217	2952	11193	6336	7313	2762	4306	3665	3587
No. ships	132	95	112	112	70	91	22	35	31	23

During the last 10 years as the figures above show and particularly since 2007 the western world economic situation has deteriorated considerably. Wars in the Middle East with European and American involvement, a huge decrease in interest rates especially hitting the more elderly residents and visitors incomes as well as considerable inflation of property, food and fuel prices has left many businesses struggling. Two of the bigger hotels the Chez André and the Sea View were sold and underwent a long period of renovation and modernisation.

The old Sea View Hotel at Braye beach was given an extremely large overhaul amounting almost to a complete rebuild, which has earned it a four-star rating and the name was changed to The Braye Beach Hotel. The Sea View became the Braye Beach Hotel and its ownership was associated with other hotel developments in the Bailiwick and also with Commercial businesses such as Healthspan, and including Rockhopper Airways, which is now the Blue Island Airline. Various routes were set up with flights to Shoreham (Brighton airport), Bournemouth, Guernsey, Jersey and several French locations from Alderney and even more destinations from Guernsey, came and went and in April 2011, the current owner withdrew all services from Alderney after the States had refused him a licence to compete with the long established Aurigny Airlines on the Southampton route. At the same time the four-star Braye Beach which had not done as well as he expected over the previous two years, despite linking many short holiday breaks with the Blue Island Airlines, offering 'free flights', was closed in April 2011 'for four months'. In July 2011 this had not yet occurred, but it reopened again in 2012. It has now withdrawn all services from/to Alderney.

The Chez André was almost ready to open in 2008 after a two to three-year-long high quality refurbishment to what seemed to be a very high standard, when the owners apparently got into a considerable amount of debt with unpaid bills and all work stopped whilst several court cases were pending. For a short time the bar was reopened and served food but that stopped and the premises now appear to be abandoned with no activity over the past two years or so.

The Belle Vue continues to provide its usual excellent accommodation, food and a bar. The unfortunate death of Steve Collins in 2012 has left his family the unenviable task of keeping it running until the business can be sold as a going concern. The Georgian House has had a chequered existence recently and has changed managers and chefs several times and now has new owners for the last few months. It was closed for most of the winter 2011-2012 and reopened in May 2012.

The only other sizeable hotel, The Harbour Lights, is back in business since about 2009 and rapidly securing a good reputation for food, accommodation and service after being almost completely demolished and rebuilt and not 'in business' for about two+ years.

Several of the other restaurants have changed hands in this period, having failed to reach their owners financial expectations or the difficulty of finding a good chef for one reason or another and others are expecting to close for the winter at the end of the 'Tourist Season'.

Part of the problem for the difficulties of these establishments and several of the retail shops has been the large increase in Rates, Taxes and service charges imposed on them by their landlords, the Alderney States, the Guernsey tax authorities, who were left with a huge 'black hole' to fill after changing their business taxation system, a huge increase in the cost of travel to Alderney from anywhere and the electricity and heating oil costs as a result of world price increases. Interference from EU sources in a number of ways, although we are not members, has also had a noticeable effect on both business and private income. The present recession has certainly hit the island hard, it remains to be seen how well our politicians will cope with the struggle to put us back 'in the black'.

16

The Islanders Return, 1945

The first islander to set foot on Alderney after the general surrender of the German forces in the Channel Islands on 9/10 May, was pre-war Pilot Nick Allen who piloted the minesweeper which cleared the channel into Braye Harbour almost a week later, on 15 May, for the unit of Force 135 under Brigadier Alfred Snow, who arrived in an armed trawler, with two landing craft full of the support troops, to accept the surrender of Alderney on 16 May 1945.

The scene which greeted him was one of devastation. The warehouses at Braye had been stripped of their woodwork, roofs, floors, doors and windows were all gone, burnt for fuel, many of those other houses on the island not occupied by the enemy were in a similar state, and a number had been totally destroyed to open up fields of fire for the defences. There were piles of rubble in the streets.

Within a few days a large part of the German garrison was removed to internment in England, a few French women still remained, and about 1,100 Germans were left to clear up the mines and barbed wire, clear the streets and to put some of the houses in order.

Between this date and the time Judge French led the first party of returning islanders ashore from the Lt Governor's launch, MV *Guillemot* at 10.30 a.m. on 2 December, various legal formalities were necessary to re-establish the government of Alderney, but in the intervening seven months much reclamation and rehabilitation work was carried out by both the army and the German prisoners.

Englishman George Pope, and Irishman Peter Doyle, who, with their families, had both been on Alderney throughout the war, working for the Germans, met Brigadier Snow's party, (which included the pre-war Harbourmaster, Fred Baron), and gave him some details about the events of the Occupation. The surrender was signed in a German-built house at the bottom of Braye Road, used as accommodation for German Naval officers, and ever since known as Peacehaven. Lt Col. E. G. Jones RA, accepted the surrender from Col. Schwalm, and the terms were signed at two tables, each of which now bears a brass plate commemorating the fact, which may be found, one in the States Chamber where it is used by the Clerk, and the other in the Museum.

The Germans surrendered their arms, dismantled the booby traps, and had already started clearing the mines. They were confined to the NE part of the island, with the officers at first at Château à L'Étoc. They continued to operate the electricity plant, the cranes at the harbour, and the bakery. The town was placed out of bounds to all troops, British or German, and a temporary British HQ was set up in a ship alongside the jetty with radio communication to Guernsey, to which Brig. Snow returned, leaving Lt Col. Jones in command.

Next day, another former Pilot, Dick Allen, brother of Nick, arrived in the corvette HMS *Leith*. He had been wounded, and spent a few days here looking round and noting the damage and the fortifications.

A few days after, Brigadier Snow returned with Judge French, and Col. Arnold, (later Sir William Arnold, and Bailiff of Guernsey). As well as the wrecked houses and the streets full of rubble, they found the Church locked, with a German caretaker, most of the fittings removed, and in use as a storehouse. The situation so depressed Judge French, that he seriously considered abandoning Alderney for good, and not reuniting the island and its population. In a review of his findings then, written in January 1947, the Judge wrote:

> My return to the island a few days after recapture was a grim experience. My first impression was of damage, destruction and devastation. Houses were broken, and the streets full of indescribable dust and rubble, weeds were everywhere.

A little later still, an Intelligence Officer, Major T. X. H. Pantcheff, whose uncle Dr Ramsbotham had been one of the Island's doctors at the time of the evacuation, arrived from Guernsey in the RASC launch camp, on a four-day visit, during which he interrogated many of the Germans, and the few remaining slave-workers, including a Russian Major. By the time he arrived, most of the rubble had been removed from the streets, and about 15,000 of the 37,000 mines had been cleared.

At the end of May, Major B.E. Arnold, RA, arrived from Guernsey with 130 men of 'A' Battery 614 Rgt RA, and relieved the unit already here. Col. Jones. had set up his HQ in Val des Portes, formerly used by the Germans as an Officer's Mess, and placed Major Arnold in charge of the German prisoners who were still loose at the NE end of the island with some of the Officers in Balmoral and Essex House. He arrested Col. Schwalm, and took him and several other officers to the Alderney Prison to await removal to Guernsey. They found the prison in a filthy state, and the Germans objected strongly, but were told they had made it so and must put up with it. The German troops were rounded up and he organised them into 802 PoW Camp. Most of them were housed in Fort Albert and Fort Tourgis. The British troops were billeted in Borkhum Camp, the only one of the German camps left undamaged, and it was renamed Minerva Camp.

Some Germans were still engaged in clearing the mines, under their own officer Leutenant Beck, others were surveying and repairing the houses in town, whilst yet others were employed in farming activities. Much of the furniture left behind by the departing islanders in 1940 had been looted or destroyed, what remained in the occupied houses, had in many cases been moved to other houses for the convenience of the German garrison. This was all removed to store, principally in the Court House and Balmoral, and locked up pending the return of the islanders.

After some difficulties between Major Arnold and the remaining German Officers and troops in Fort Albert, mainly due to language problems, RSM Willie Schröder was appointed as Lager-Führer to keep discipline. The officers, except for the Doctor, were soon removed from Alderney. The men, now better fed than they had been of late, gave little trouble, and were allowed to organise concerts, bathing at Longis, etc., and a newspaper, Der Tag or the Tourgis Times and Albert Advertiser, was started. A second paper Gun-Fun or Sarnian Salvoes was also started by the sister unit of the Alderney group, 618 Regiment RA in Guernsey, the second issue of which, in June, contained a story, by the Padre of the Alderney unit, of a rough trip to Guernsey in a small launch accompanied by 'The Major'.

Also at the end of May, another former Alderney Pilot, now a Captain, Arthur Jennings, and Bonny Newton in two Tank Landing Craft, were sent to Alderney to help in the disposal at sea of many of the mines, and much of the German ammunition. In August they were joined by two more LCTs, who brought 1,000 tons of engineering stores, two locomotives for the mineral railway, a mechanical digger, and took away scrap metal from the fortifications, to Guernsey.

Sapper George Onions was killed when one of the booby trapped mines he was clearing exploded, and was buried in the Churchyard on 21 June. His grave is still regularly decorated with flowers by the islanders. By the end of August most of the mines, roll bombs from the cliffs, beach tetrad defences and barbed wire had gone. The trenches across the airfield had been filled and levelled, the obstructions cleared, and the three grass runways forming a letter 'A', laid out by the Garrison Engineer, Capt. Tudor, (who also gave his name to part of the road at Newtown where some new houses were erected). This pattern is still retained today, although the main runway has been lengthened, tarmaced, and widened several times since then.

General Sir Phillip Neame was sworn in as Lt Governor of Guernsey on 25 August, and immediately flew himself to Alderney to see how the work was progressing. As a result of his interest, his liaison with the Alderney Rehabilitation Committee, and the work done already under the control of Colonel Power head of the Civil Affairs unit in Guernsey, things were making good progress.

By 23 October the Mignot Memorial Hospital in Victoria Street was again ready for use, 20 shops had been made ready, and repairs to the Breakwater had been started. General Neame paid another visit on 5 November accompanied by two of the W.V.S. ladies, the Misses Bertram and Owen, to make arrangements for the reception of the first group of returning islanders. The arrangements made then, later worked smoothly and to a strict timetable.

Judge French's small advance party, which included Mrs Richards, Brigadier Cosby, Lt & Mrs Vic Carter, Mrs Riou, Mrs P. Forsyth, Miss Martyn, Mr & Mrs Després, Mr & Mrs Osborne, and the two W.V.S. ladies, arrived on 2 December. Two more parties arrived on MV Guillemot on 4 and 6 December, consisting of; Captain Richards, Mr & Mrs Dick Allen, Mr & Mrs George Jennings, Mr & Mrs Tom Herivel, Mr & Mrs John Mignot, Mr & Mrs Archie Rowe, Mr Slade, Mrs Arthur Jennings, (mostly Jurats and Douzaine members and their wives). Mr Gissing, sent by the Home Office to supervise the Communal Farm, and a further W.V.S. detachment. They were fed communally, twice a day at the Convent, by the W.V.S. ladies, and were issued from there with essential equipment, buckets, brooms, bedding etc., whilst the prisoners carried the free, mostly plywood, Government Issue furniture etc. for them from the central store to their own houses, or the places they were occupying until their own homes were fit to use.

A much larger party of 110 islanders arrived on the Southern Railway's SS Autocarrier at 8 a.m. on Saturday, 15 December 1945, and was welcomed by a shower of Verey Lights, an archway bearing the huge sign WELCOME HOME. a Guard of Honour headed by General Neame, and the Guernsey Salvation Army Band which played Home, Sweet Home, as the ship approached with her escort of two naval launches. A speech of welcome was made by the General, the band played the National Anthem as the first passengers stepped ashore to a 21 round salute from the rifles of the soldiers, and Guernseyman Mr C. A. Pritchard, Divisional Marine Manager of the Southern Railway at Southampton read another speech of welcome on behalf of the railway company who had transported them.

40 years later, the anniversary of this event was commemorated by the striking of a bronze lapel badge bearing a representation of the ship, and the date, which is regularly worn, with pride, by those islanders who returned at that time. Two more parties arrived in Autocarrier on 22 and 28 December, making a total of 360 islanders now back in their homeland.

Ten years later, the 50th anniversary was celebrated by the refurbishment of the Memorial Garden in Victoria Street and a special party for all the surviving returnees. The States of Alderney commissioned a special commemorative £2 coin to mark the event. This shows the SS Autocarrier on the reverse and was issued in cupro-nickel (legal tender), piedmont silver and gold versions.

In 1945, the returning islanders were taken to reception centres at the Grand Hotel and the Belle Vue Hotel, run by the W.V.S., where they were housed until they returned to their own homes, carrying the bare necessities issued from the communal store. Meals continued to be provided twice a day at the Convent, as many houses were without a stove. Autocarrier also continued to provide a weekly run from Southampton with baggage, furniture and fresh foodstuffs for some time.

The pre-war civilian administration was liaising closely with the military immediately following their return, whilst trying to set up their own organisation. For the time being, the States Chamber having been stripped of most of its woodwork and fittings by the Germans, and also being full of the impounded furniture, States' Meetings were held in the schoolroom on Saturday afternoons, and the People's Meetings were held in the Cinema. The Judge had leased Val des Portes from the Kay-Mouat family, and set up his administrative offices in the German huts built in the grounds, where he is said to have had the island's only working telephone, with an extension to the Airways office.

At this period the People's Meetings proposed and voted on various matters of common interest, which the Judge then placed before the States, with his own proposals. At the beginning of March 1946, the people, urged on by People's Deputy William

One hundred and ten islanders returned on SS *Autocarrier* at 8 a.m. on Saturday 15 December 1945.

The islanders were welcomed home by the garrison as they disembarked from SS *Autocarrier*.

Above left: This 40th anniversary bronze lapel badge is worn with pride by those islanders who returned in 1945.

Above right: Commemorative £2 coin issued on the 50th anniversary of the islanders' return. This is legal tender.

Herivel, proprietor of the Marais Hall, had proposed, and voted unanimously for, a change in the way the money in the Resettlement Accounts was administered, and the setting up of a committee to supervise it. The only tax currently being levied was the Impôt duty, no property taxes having been assessed, and the Judge also proposed in the Billet for the March States' meeting, either that a committee should be set up to control the finances which, as he said, would have to sit continuously, or that one of several alternatives should be adopted, and that the Douzaine should be asked to assess each item of real property for taxation, to raise revenue. The committee idea was rejected at the States' meeting, and he remained in control of the finances.

A second meeting was held in March, attended by the Lt Governor, at which the disposal of the German huts at 6*d* per square foot for those in good condition, and 2*d* per foot for those in poor condition, was proposed, and also the disposal of the £9,406 18*s* ½*d* remaining from the proceeds of the sale of the cattle and other items officially removed by the Guernsey parties in June 1940 which was then being returned. The Guernsey authorities had deducted some £2,300 for their expenses in relation to the salvage operation, plus their expenses in selling the animals, and had retained the rest in an Alderney Salvage account, without adding any interest, throughout the intervening period. Much to the further discontent of the States members, the Judge decreed that this money was to be placed in the Farm account against the debt to Britain, and not used for the good of the community. Although it really belonged to the individuals whose property had been sold, it was impossible to ascertain who should benefit by what amounts, as no individual records of the sales had been kept.

It was noted in the Billet that the British troops were to be withdrawn on 1 June, and the Judge proposed that the States must prepare a budget for the remainder of 1946 within a month. The April 1946 Billet was concerned with re-establishing communications, running the harbour, and setting up various committees to run the island.

Proposals had been received from Mr Ford of The British Channel Island Shipping Co. in Guernsey to establish a shipping service for goods and passengers, (hitherto provided by the military with the LCT captained by Arthur Jennings), between Guernsey and Alderney, provided they were given a monopoly, and no Alderney boat was so employed, and that if they made a loss in the first year, harbour dues and pilotage would be remitted. A proposal was also received from the Great Western Railway to re-establish a direct link with Weymouth, provided that all harbour dues and pilot's fees were paid by the States for the first year.

Of the cranes which had been left at the harbour by the Germans, two, one German, the other Czech, were handed over to the States, and two of the farm workers were to be trained to replace the German drivers. These cranes would be the responsibility of the Roads Committee, and the drivers would be paid out of States' revenue and not from the farm account.

The more important of the pre-war committees were brought back, at least temporarily, with their original members, and any other people with suitable experience could be co-opted to assist, a Fuel Controller (C. G. Kay-Mouat), was appointed, a Resettlement Stocks Issue Committee, with one States Member, to control the issue of the government furniture, and the redistribution of the items which had remained and been placed in store by the military, to their original owners, and another to control Repatriation and Employment were set up.

The May Billet contained the Budget for the remainder of 1946, and proposals for raising direct taxation on property, which simply amounted to a revival of the Besoin Publique at an increased level to raise an extra £1,000. The Members declined to institute any other taxes despite the Judge's efforts to persuade them. The Budget gave details of the anticipated expenditure of the various committees. These by then included: Education, Roads, Lighting, Building, Sanitation, Plantations, and Publicity. The annual wages of the principal employees were noted: Explosives Inspector £30, Procureur du Roi £50, Treasurer's Clerk £20, HM Sergeant £15, HM Sheriff £1, Police Officer £156, Impôt Receiver £66 10s 0d

A request was also received from Mr H. A. Paine, owner of the Alderney Gravel and Grit Company which he had started in 1936 on Platte Saline beach, to restart operations, despite the fact that the gravel washing machinery he had designed had disappeared, and to lay on a supply of fresh water to wash the gravel, from one of the streams discharging onto Platte Saline, by piping it to the fort. He anticipated giving employment to nine men and a boy. There was also a request for the somewhat belated payment of a bill for £264 19s 2d, from a, by-then deceased, Guernsey Engineer, which was dated 8 August 1938, for work carried out in designing a water and sewage scheme for Alderney. The scheme was to have cost £13,915, but was never carried out.

A Communal food shop had been established in Victoria Street in the premises now occupied by Bell's Estate Agency, potatoes from the crop planted by the Germans were on sale, The Post Office was functioning where Riduna Stores once was, on the corner of

Queen Elizabeth II Street, Capt. Richards had reopened his newsagent and tobacconist shop, the pre-war stock of which he found, surprisingly, where he had hidden it, which still occupies the same premises. There have been several changes of ownership since he retired and it is now also the island Post Office. The airport had been re-opened on 15 February with the first commercial flight, a chartered D.H. Rapide from Liverpool whose passengers were Bert Hammond and his father from the Campania Inn, and the Channel Island Airways office was again open in Victoria Street at what is now Colenso House. The GWR had actually restarted a weekly service from Weymouth with SS *Roebuck* on 25 March, by arrangement with Judge French, before the terms had been agreed in the States.

A new Vicar, Revd E. P. St John from Guernsey, a former RAF Chaplain, had taken up residence in April, and the Campania, the Rose and Crown, Marais Hall, and the Billiard's Inn were all functioning again.

A qualified nurse, Mrs Reg Duplain had started the school again, assisted by Mrs Chris Simon, and 13 year-old Miriam Angel who took the infants, as the children were running wild, and getting into danger in the bunkers. They were paid £1 a week each.

With the withdrawal of the troops due in a week or two's time, the islanders would then become totally dependent on themselves and their own resources to survive. The last of the German prisoners were withdrawn on 1 June, and before they left gave a concert in the Lyceum Cinema to culminate the various concerts and dances provided by their orchestra under the baton of one of the prisoners, a well-known pre-war conductor named Stimmler. The army finally withdrew at the end of the month.

The discontent which was growing, in a population whose activities were primarily limited to the communal farm, had already led to the builders and craftsmen being released from the fields to work at their own trades, at pre-war piecework rates, on the communal building schemes, assisted by German prisoners. This differential in pay of course gave further cause for discontent. In April, the privately owned furniture was still locked up, and Issue Furniture was still in good supply for those returning. French had set up a Resettlement Stocks Issue Committee of four people, with Brigadier Cosby in charge of the War Booty Furniture Stocks. The islanders, not unnaturally, did not agree that their cherished possessions were to be classified as War Booty, and could be issued to people making claims for an article of similar description, and a great deal of discontent arose when some items were found in neighbour's houses.

The extended terms of office of the pre-war members of the legislature were due to expire on 30 September 1946 and elections should have been arranged. As yet there was no electoral roll and no taxes were being paid. The Judge was in favour of elections, (which he presumably hoped would get rid of Billy Herivel who was constantly challenging his actions), but when the States voted against them by a single vote majority, after the Court had tied on their vote, he refused to accept the decision, and made certain threats about the effect on relations with the Home Office. Despite these threats, no elections were held.

General Neame was greatly concerned at the situation in Alderney and came over every two or three weeks in 1946. His concern was shared by the Home Office, and an enquiry was set up which convened in Alderney on 28 September, to which the people were invited.

The Judge called another People's Meeting at the Lyceum Cinema on 22 October, at which, in an eight-point agenda, he proposed to put the current situation before the people with regard to houses and furniture, land ownership, employment prospects, States services including the electricity supply, transport, finances, and the Island administration.

The situation of the people, with food, clothing, fuel and petrol still rationed, bad communications, no outside telephones, and an unreliable electricity supply, was not helped by the unusually harsh winter of 1946-7. There was thick snow, water froze, and the farm horses broke out from their quarters near Essex Castle and came into Town looking for water. The land boundaries had not yet been settled by the Douzaine, the German Huts had not, in many cases, been removed by their purchasers, from the land whose owners did not want them, within the required three months, and other examples of procrastination were lampooned by Ian Glasgow in his revived Island Review. This publication, first printed in 1938 on a duplicator, had been restarted when Glasgow found his pre-war printing machine in Guernsey and brought it back. He operated from the building in Longis Road just beyond the present Telephone Exchange.In March 1947 General Neame told the States of the British Government's decision to disband the Communal Farm at the end of the year, and this was followed by a Home Office letter dated 21 June 1947, and headlined in the Guernsey Press as; *'Great Britain's Ultimatum to Alderney'.*

The ultimate result of all the dissension was the sending of the questionnaire dated 15 August, the setting up of a Home Office Enquiry, and the drafting of the Government of Alderney Law, 1948, which still forms the basis of today's constitution in Alderney.

The States' Meetings were held from July 1947 in the old Militia Arsenal in Ollivier Street, and finally the question of the private furniture still stored in the States' Chamber and at Balmoral, was settled during that summer, when it was laid out at various times on the Butes in fine weather, tables etc. one week, wardrobes and beds another, and so on. People were allowed to examine it and decide which items were theirs. They then lined up at the opposite end of the Butes, and when a whistle was blown ran for the furniture and had to place a hand on the items they claimed. These 'Battles of the Butes' as they came to be called, were the final downfall of the Judge's administration.

His candidates for the two vacancies on the Jurats bench failed to get elected, and when the Commissioners arrived on 15 September, the islanders laid many accusations about his conduct before them.

Judge French, who had almost single-handedly, if somewhat autocratically, guided the affairs of his beloved island since before the war, resigned and retired to the seclusion of his house. He died in 1962, whilst on a visit to South Africa. There is a memorial to him, added to that earlier erected to his wife Anne, in Norwich Cathedral.

GREAT BRITAIN'S ULTIMATUM TO ALDERNEY

PROPOSALS INVITED FOR ALDERNEY STATES REFORM

Home Secretary: " We Cannot Permit Island to Become Derelict "

PRIVY COUNCIL TO HOLD INQUIRY

WHAT AMOUNTS TO AN ULTIMATUM FROM THE BRITISH GOVERNMENT TO ALDERNEY WAS CONVEYED TO THE NORTHERN ISLE BY THE LIEUTENANT-GOVERNOR OF THE BAILIWICK, LT.-GEN. SIR PHILIP NEAME, V.C., K.B.E., C.B., D.S.O., AT AN EMERGENCY MEETING OF THE STATES WHICH WAS CALLED LAST WEEK BY JUDGE F. G. FRENCH, O.B.E.

Sir Philip read a letter from the Home Secretary. It referred to the end of Britain's aid at the close of the year and said that, unless steps are taken to prevent it, Alderney might become derelict — "a result His Majesty's Government could not permit to arise."

One hundred and sixty-six thousand pounds had been advanced towards rehabilitation "to lay the foundations of a prosperous future," but this would not be ensured "unless the administration of the Island can be placed on a sounder and broader basis."

Accordingly, it is proposed that a Committee of the Privy Council shall visit the Island, probably in August or September, to hold an inquiry, "with particular reference to the form of government, financial position and economic prospects."

Alderney States are invited to submit their own proposals, particularly in relation to "reforms or changes in the constitution or laws .... finance and public services .... and better co-operation in the farming of the land and marketing of produce."

After Sir Philip Neame had read the Home Secretary's letter, and told them that they "must make their own proposals or else expect to have proposals and reforms thrust upon you," the States appointed a committee to draw up a reply to the British Government.

H.E.: " ACT OR ACTION WILL BE THRUST UPON YOU "

His Excellency said:

"I have been requested by the Home Secretary to communicate to you the terms of a letter in regard to a proposal for an enquiry into the affairs of Alderney by a Privy Council Committee.

"I will read this letter to you.

Home Office,
Whitehall.
21st June, 1917.

Sir,—I am directed by the Secretary of State to say that since, at the request of the inhabitants of Alderney, the land which has hitherto been requisitioned and farmed on a communal basis is to be restored to its owners by the end of the year, and since the assistance given by H.M.'s Government towards the rehabilitation of the Island will likewise come to an end in December next, consideration will have to be given, as a matter of urgency, to the ways and means by which the public services of the Island are to be provided and administered today and to ensure essential services such as public health and education.

ILL-EQUIPPED

It is apparent that a community with a population of about 800—the size of a medium or small sized parish in England—is ill-equipped to deal with all the problems which arise in the economic and financial field of today and to provide essential services such as public health and education.

The Secretary of State appreciates that the needs of an Island cut off by the sea from its neighbours are in some respects different from the needs of a community which enjoys daily contacts with other communities adjoining it on the mainland, and he is deeply conscious of the very large measure of independence enjoyed from early times by the people of Alderney, but air travel and the improvement of communications have largely diminished and in the future will do more to diminish, the remoteness of the Island, and he considers that the future will in no way diminish in relations with its neighbours must now be reviewed in the light of present day circumstances and requirements,

elsewhere and in the course of time the Island might become derelict—a result which His Majesty's Government could not permit to arise.

Today, the population is less than before the war and very much less than it was before 1911.

In the task of rehabilitation, His Majesty's Government has advanced large sums. It is estimated that the sum so advanced up to the present, on the provision of stores and goods, and on work performed by the military and prisoner-of-war labour, and latterly by the civilian organisation, amounts to no less than £166,000.

FOUNDATIONS

In advancing this money, His Majesty's Government has been anxious that the inhabitants, who incurred serious losses through the evacuation of the Island and its occupation by the enemy, should be provided with the means to rebuild their lives and lay the foundations for a prosperous future.

This expenditure, will not, however, by itself ensure that object, unless at the same time the administration and economy of the Island can be placed on a sounder and broader basis than they are at present.

The Secretary of State accordingly proposes to recommend to His Majesty in Council that a Committee of the Privy Council should be appointed to enquire into the state of Alderney with particular reference to its form of government, and its relationship with the neighbouring Islands, its financial position, and its economic prospects.

QUESTIONS

If such a Committee is appointed, the enquiry will probably take place in August or September, but, in the meanwhile, an opportunity should be given to the States of Alderney to consider whether they have any proposals which they wish to put forward for consideration.

In particular, the Secretary of State would be glad to be informed whether in the view of the States, any reforms or changes in the constitution or laws of the Island are desirable; what arguments the States proposes to make to finance and to administer the public services of the Island

to making the fullest and most economical use of all the available land, and whether they have any suggestions to make to secure better co-operation in the farming of the land and the marketing of its produce.

BY END OF JULY

I am accordingly to request you to communicate the terms of this letter to the States of Alderney and to inform them that if they have any proposals to submit they should submit them through the appropriate channel not later than the end of July.

The terms of this letter should at the same time be communicated to the States of Guernsey for their information.

I am, Sir,
Your obedient Servant,
(Sgd.) A. MAXWELL.

Continuing, Sir Philip Neame said:

"I wish to explain to you briefly what it is necessary for you to do. I know that His Majesty's Government is not happy in regard to the existing state of affairs and the existing conduct of local government by the States of Alderney. So I beg of you not to stand idly by and imagine you have no improvements to make.

"There are many social services and public matters here which you have hitherto neglected or ignored, and which still wait to be revived since the war, or which require to be started on modern lines.

UNLESS . . .

"These are the things on which you must make your own proposals, or else you must expect to have proposals and reforms thrust on you. Guernsey is far ahead of you. Guernsey might help you. This has started already in a small way in education.

"It therefore seems to me necessary that the States of Alderney should presumably by means of a Committee, prepare any proposals which they may wish to get before the Privy Council Committee, in regard to Reforms, Finance, Taxation, Public Health, Relief, Education, Law and Order, Roads, Reforms in Land Tenure or Inheritance, Co-operation in Farming and Marketing.

THE INQUIRY

"These proposals must reach me by the 25th July, four weeks from today. They need not be in the fullest detail — no more than a summary— and can be elaborated later before the Privy Council. If you have no proposals, you should say so.

"The States of Alderney will also be required later to nominate witnesses to give evidence before the Privy Council Committee, witnesses who will be "au fait" with the different subjects under examination. I hope to get a list of subjects and a questionnaire on each subject which the Committee will deal with, just like we had in the Guernsey Privy Council Committee.

"I will try and let you have these in good time before the Committee comes, but you should now consider who will be your official witnesses. In addition I know that the Committee will give opportunity for other individuals to give evidence if they so wish.

COMMITTEE APPOINTED

"I do not propose to prolong the meeting this morning. You will want to consider these grave matters at your leisure. But please remember that the whole future of Alderney is under consideration, and do your best for the community as a whole. I now ask the Judge to proceed with the business of nominating a committee."

After a brief discussion the

Guernsey Press article concerning a Privy Council enquiry about the controversy over Alderney's future.

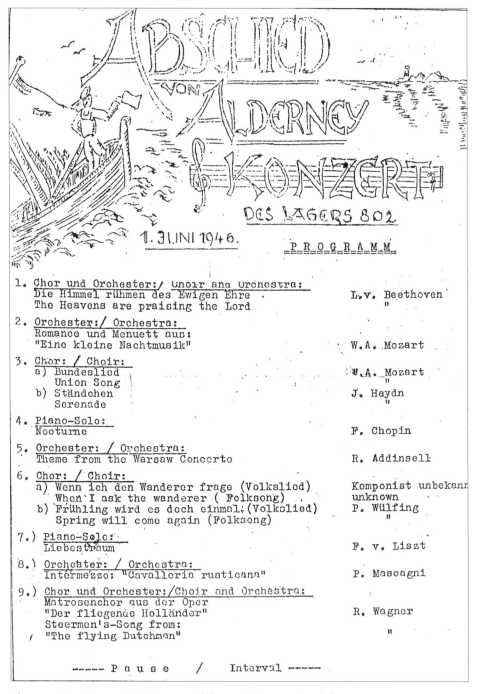

The remaining German PoWs were withdrawn in June 1946 and the musicians gave a concert at the Lyceum Cinema under the baton of a PoW, Herr Stimmler, a well-known pre-war conductor.

Races (Battles) were held on Butes to decide on the allocation of pre-war property to its rightful owners.

Post-war Defences, 1945-90

The withdrawal of the army relieving forces, and all the various units which had helped to refurbish some of the ruined houses in August 1946, left Alderney with a vast chain of defensive positions, and no-one to man them. In the event of any future conflict, the islands would have no strategic defensive value, and could at best serve as a jumping-off ground for a land invasion of Europe, a course of action which is highly unlikely, with modern equipment and techniques.

Effectively then, the forts, which, except for Albert and Tourgis, already belonged to the States of Alderney, or to private individuals, as a result of the sale in 1930, were abandoned, although various Army and Territorial units have spent short periods training here, from time to time, using Forts Albert and Tourgis. A list of the units which have come in this capacity is given below.

By virtue of a Statutory Instrument, the Alderney (Transfer of Property Etc.) Order 1950, dated 24 May, all remaining crown lands and possessions in Alderney, including the seabed for three miles beyond and around the island, except for; the Breakwater, the railway to Mannez, and seven perches of land with the right to draw water from their springs, at Valongis, was handed over to the States of Alderney, for £10,000. In return, Alderney has to offer harbour moorings for naval vessels as needed, stone from the quarries needed to maintain the Breakwater, to maintain all navigation lights and buoys in her waters, provide facilities for Trinity House, pay the Harbour Master and the portion of the Vicar's stipend formerly paid by the Crown, and a few other minor items.

Since 1950 a number of both Territorial and Regular Army units have spent a week or two exercising in Alderney at various times. In the 1960s they were usually housed in Fort Tourgis, but with the deterioration of that building, they now set up a tented encampment on Braye Common or on the Island Camp Site at Saye Bay. The most frequent visitors have belonged to the Royal Corps of Signals.

1969 saw a detachment of Light Infantry under Major Nicholas, in Fort Tourgis for six weeks from 26 June.

The long association which had built up since the war, between the 30th Signals Regiment of the Royal Corps of Signals and Alderney, was recognised on 29 May 1989, when the regiment was presented with the Freedom of Alderney. The island also presented a silver cup for an inter-squadron efficiency competition to the Regiment, and a silver Guernsey Milk-can for the Officer's mess.

There are now occasional visits, usually over a weekend, of assorted units of both the regular and territorial army who exercise with, and help train the Junior Militia.

To recognise the significance of Weymouth's participation in the evacuation in 1940 a ceremony was held at the Harbour on Sunday 24 June 1990, 50 years from that fateful Sunday when almost the whole population left their homes and possessions, and sailed for Weymouth.

Many of the survivors of those who returned to Alderney after the war, in 1945-6, a total of about 160 people, including Mrs Phyllis Forsyth, who was to be 100 years old on 10 July, attended the ceremony at the harbour.

Mrs Forsyth, whose father had been the Vicar of Alderney from 1886 to 1929 had taught in the Alderney School before the war, served on the Alderney Relief Committee throughout the period of exile, and was one of the first group to return to the island when hostilities ceased.

The present Mayor of Weymouth, and the Mayoress, had come from the town where the refugees landed in 1940, to unveil a plaque commemorating the event, at the harbour from which they sailed. A simple commemorative service was held jointly, by the new Vicar, Reverend Stephen Ingham, the Catholic Priest, Father Henry Bradley, the Methodist Minister, Mr Geoffrey Blackmore, and the Salvation Army Leader, Lt Jim Smith. (See photos in the colour section)

At the same time they presented the island with a decorated plate made in their local pottery commemorating the arrival of the evacuees in Weymouth. This may now be seen in the Alderney Museum.

This solemn occasion was supported by a large number of today's Islanders, out of respect for the courage and fortitude shown by the older generation who had either to abandon their homeland, or stay and face oppression, and who steamed off into the unknown, on Sunday 23 June 1940.

During the Gulf War of 1990-1, eight men and women, serving in the various UK services, had close associations with the island, or were members of Island families,

The Mayor of Weymouth presented this plate on the 50th anniversary of the evacuation in 1940.

and one, L/Cpl. Croft, grandson of Maisie Herivel, lost his life there, as the result of an accident. Since the American/UK invasion of Iraq in 2005 and that of Afghanistan, there have been no reports of losses by Alderney people, but one young man Joel Mitton has already done several tours of duty out there.

Although it is unlikely in the future that the island will ever again be garrisoned and sea communications are more or less reduced to the weekly cargo boats from Guernsey and the two or three-weekly service from Weymouth/Poole, by Alderney Shipping with occasional boats from England with building materials and tankers with fuel oil. The addition in 2010 by Huelin Renouf of twice weekly larger cargo boats in each direction between Jersey, Alderney and Southampton has already been mentiond in the previous chapter, reduced in July 2013 to once a week.

Part of the island's income is nevertheless still derived from the sea, with visiting yachts and training ships and occasional Cruise Ships in the summer, and the activities of the small band of commercial fishermen.

The lifeboat, with its volunteer crew, plays an important part in the safety of shipping, especially small craft, in the dangerous waters around our coasts. It also acts as an emergency ambulance to take seriously ill or injured patients to the Guernsey Hospital if the airport is closed due to fog.

17

Alderney's Roll of Honour

There are two War Memorials in Alderney, one on the western wall of the Parish Church and the other in the Memorial Garden in Victoria Street, given to the Island by Judge N.P.Le C. Barbenson in 1921.

The names are given in the order they appear on the memorial.

The 41 names inscribed from the First World War are:

Louis Brochart	S/Sgt F. Quinain	Sgt W. Christie
John Brochart	J. N. Duplain	Désiré Pasquier
Lt J. L. Gamblin	Edward Pippard	William Benwell
Walter Last	James Grier	Harold Squires
C. F. Price DSO	Capt. H.T. Mellish	Arthur Angel
Thomas Lihou RN	Mid. J. Barber RNR	John Bihet
Charles Le Millière RN	Frank Pike	Arsène Garry
Lt Robert McLernon	Arthur Hurst	E. R. Squires
Gustave Riou	Lt M. M. Barney	Reg. Tinniswood RN
Arthur Snaith	Henry Johns	W. O. Harry Bridle
Arthur Hammond	E. R. Underdown	Frank Bideau
C. H. Hammond	Benjamin Walden	Alex Toussaint
Thomas Allen	George Sharpe	Joseph Brady
Sgt W. Bassett	Thomas Butler	

(The 24 names of those who died in the Second World War, 1939-45, are inscribed on a stone placed at the foot of the earlier Memorial.)

Pearce Angel	Harry Duce	David Monteith
Patrick Anson	Ronald Greenway	Leonard Napper
Kenneth Bihet	George Houguez	William Pike
James Bott	Charles Jennings	Edmund Picot
John Catts	Alex McClean	Ronald Redhead

George Caplain	Frank Mackay	Roland Riou
William Clarke	Frank Miller	John Rose
John Cosheril	Bertram Millington	Geoffrey Workman

The British Legion, the Royal Alderney Junior Militia and members of the Lifeboat, Ambulance, Fire and Nursing services, in the island, take part in an annual service in the Church on Remembrance Sunday, followed by a march in procession to the Memorial Gardens for a wreath-laying ceremony.

Ships and Soldiers have indeed played a significant part throughout Alderney's History.

The plaque commemorating these events and the list of casualties in war from our war memorial form a fitting ending to this book.

Index